LOOKING FOR A GREAT VACATION? *A*
CIRCLE NATIONAL PARKS WILL GIVE YO

MW00852230

The seven most amazing national par~~ks within the Southwest United~~
States are covered in full within these pages; from what to do, where to
stay and dining options, both inside the parks and nearby. All surrounding national monuments and state parks are also described in detail. "*A
Complete Guide..*" is packed with maps, pictures, tips, stories, and we dare
say, fun! This book has something for everyone, whether you are traveling
in style or camping, whether you like to hike in the rugged backcountry
or just sightsee.

This is *A COMPLETE GUIDE TO THE GRAND CIRCLE NATIONAL PARKS!*

WHAT OTHERS ARE SAYING:

"A very light fun read. I find a lot of these books can be tedious and can make my
eyes bleed, but this is not only very informative but it is written in a fun, easy to
read format." ~ Rae F.

This is a seriously good guidebook to the Grand Circle! It's well-written -- several
notches above the standard guidebook fare in my experience. Inspiring, helpful
information, and fun to read! Kudos! ~ The Good Gatsby

CAN'T WAIT TO START MY TOUR OF THE CIRCLE! ~ Fermin C.

Family of four use this book extensively during our travel throughout the Grand
Canyon and Utah. Kids really enjoyed reading the family adventures and were able
to map out the trails on their own using this book. Would highly recommend to
anyone taking the Grand Circle trip. ~ Manish J.

"A a fun, easy read and excellent guide for anyone wanting to tour the Southwest
USA, good guide book.." ~ Rich P.

"Loved it! We were planning a trip to three of the parks, but after picking up this
book we added on two others. Really helpful information and definitely helped us
plan out a better vacation.. and the stories were a welcome plus! I want to do this
trip again!" ~ Tanya and Trevor L.

"Made my once in life time vacation a once in a lifetime vacation! Awesome travel
guide, great stories, a great book!" ~ Jenn H.

"Meticulously and exquisitely written, very informative, beautifully illustrated with
photographs." ~ Terry T.

A COMPLETE GUIDE TO THE
GRAND CIRCLE NATIONAL PARKS

COVERING
ZION, BRYCE CANYON, CAPITOL REEF,
ARCHES, CANYONLANDS, MESA VERDE,
AND GRAND CANYON NATIONAL PARKS

Eric Henze

Gone Beyond Guides
Publisher

The Dollhouse - Maze District, Canyonlands National Park

What is the Grand Circle?

So you've been done an Arizona vacation, maybe even Colorado and Utah, but have you done the Grand Circle? You may have heard of the term and likely know it well if you live within it. For those that don't know what the Grand Circle means, you aren't alone. It is, in a nutshell, one of the "must do" vacation destinations in North America.

The Grand Circle encompasses five southwestern states but more importantly, is so named because it contains the highest concentration of national and state parks in the United States. Within this 500-diameter area, there are almost 80 parks and hundreds of other attractions. Simply put, the Grand Circle is a bounty of fun and adventure. This isn't about going to Zion or the Grand Canyon, it's about going on a once in a lifetime vacation, something so incredible that it becomes one of the top things you have ever done.

Within the Grand Circle are attractions found nowhere else in the world. Some of these seem to defy the laws of physics while others defy the boundaries of what you thought was possible. I've taken folks into areas where nobody spoke a word because they simply had never seen land like this before. They were in speechless awe and it's true, the journey can be beyond words, the land can be that striking. Within it are timeless monoliths, thousands of arches, delicately balanced rocks, some of the wildest rapids in the world and the deepest canyons. It contains the darkest nighttime skies in North America and the brightest colors during the day. The land is a symphony, at times thunderous and deafening, at other times a single soft note trailing into the silence of a deep blue sky. Here there are hoodoos, goblins, fins, tall alpine peaks and slot canyons so narrow there is barely room for one person. There are red rock cliffs, sheer vertical walls of rock so high that they are the emotional equal in sandstone what Yosemite is in granite.

This is a place that resets a person. One can't help but slow to the pace of the land. A visit here is a mixture of relaxation and wonder. You will find yourself returning to the pace of nature as you venture farther from the pace of man. It brings with it a connectedness reminding the visitor the things that are truly important in life.

This is a land carved by water and wind over millions of years and the results are astounding natural works of art. It is no wonder that this area contains the largest concentration of national parks and national monuments in the United States. Sure, the circle contains the internationally known Grand Canyon and Zion, but these are just two of its twelve national parks. Add to this list another 30 national monuments, 3 national recreation areas, several tribal parks and 29 more state parks. Moreover, these are just the lands formally set aside.

By the numbers, most of the parks that make up the Grand Circle are within Utah and Arizona, but the full magnitude of the circle encompasses lands within Nevada, New Mexico, and Colorado as well. The imaginary circle is about 500 miles in diameter or roughly 126 million acres of land. As daunting as that sounds, one can comfortably visit the most popular national parks (and several other parks along the way) in 10 days. Of course, the more one is able to slow down and spend here, the more one will see, but the point is, if you are looking for a vacation where every day is different, you can experience a large and varied amount of places in a relatively short amount of time.

Historically, the Grand Circle was a term created when the Southwest National Parks were just beginning. The NPS worked with the Union Pacific Railway and created trips by rail and bus up until the 1970's. Back then, a trip to the Grand Circle was a time of great adventure and romance. There were dance bands at the stops and as your tour bus would drive away from the lodge, employees would line up and "sing away" the visitors. Today, it remains one of the best vacations in North America that one can take. This is a vacation destination of adventure, relaxation, and wonder. It is a land that humbles, inspires, and refreshes the spirit and for those that know of it, they have the Grand Circle as a bucket list place to experience at least once in their lives. The term Grand Circle is a great term to describe this land.

WHEN TO GO

There are really only two factors on when to go, do you like temperate climates or would you prefer less people. Weather plays a hand in both but in different ways.

In general, the Grand Circle is a blisteringly hot place in the summer, starting in mid to late June and going full force through August. That doesn't seem to keep folks away, particularly if you have kids out for the school year. Temperature wise though, the best time to go is during the spring/early summer and fall/early winter. Elevation is another consideration. High elevation parks such as Bryce and Great Basin are typically cooler in the summer than say Canyonlands or Lake Powell.

In terms of going at a time when the crowds have thinned, the best times to go are the dead of winter, followed by the dead of summer. Winter receives a lot fewer crowds for the obvious reasons. It's colder, snowier, and wetter. In fact, it tends to be the antithesis of what folks have in mind when they think of the southwest. That said, these parks in winter are perhaps when they are at their most spectacular. There is something transformative about a dusting of snow across the layered mesas and canyons or topping each hoodoo of Bryce. In fact, for places like Bryce, which receive tons of visitors each summer, the arguably best time to go is winter. I've been out on trails covered in snow on a crisp clear day with the entire park practically to myself.

Winter at any of the parks can be magical, but it does run the risk of being miserable. In fact, you could be snowed in, which isn't the worst thing that could happen to a person, but can be difficult if your boss is expecting you back at work. In addition, some of the parks are simply closed in the winter.

The dead of summer is a good second choice as it is usually too hot for most. That said, given kids are out of school at this time, there are many whose lifestyles gives them nothing else to work with, so it can still be crowded. The parks in summer can be too hot to hike in during the heat of the day, so for those that take this tactic, get in the habit of hitting the trails in the cool of early morning.

WHERE TO GO

If you think about it, there is a fair amount of irony in guidebooks that tell you the best places to go to avoid crowds. They are basically saying, we've learned all these secret cool places that no one goes to and we are now publishing this information in a globally available guidebook for anyone to read. If you see one of these sections, don't believe it, the word is already out on all these "secret places". In fact, places such as Havasu Falls are so impacted, it is nearly impossible to get a permit to hike the trail.

That said, there are some general tips to getting an otherwise crowded national park or monument to yourself. Take the Grand Canyon for example. This park receives some 4.5 million visitors to the South Rim alone. The

vast majority of these folks don't hike any farther than to the overlooks. So simply getting out on any trail cuts the population of the park down by about 90%. Getting out on a trail also helps you connect with the park and really experience it.

There are other tips to share. In general, I've found that the more strenuous the hike is, the harder the trail is to get to, and the longer the trail's length, the greater the chances you will have the trail to yourself. If the trail is a short little paved walkway with interpretive signs, be prepared to share it. If it is one of the routes described in these guides, so rugged there isn't even a trail, be prepared to survive on your own because you are likely the only one out that way.

The same can be said about weather. Heat, rain, snow, and cold tend to filter out a fair amount of people. What's amazing about this is sometimes inclement weather will bring out the most unique views of a trail you will likely ever see. Now keep you in mind that you should add in a large degree of common sense. You don't want to have a slot canyon "all to yourself" in a thunderstorm or hike in the direct heat of a summer's day unless you are fully prepared and acclimated. Don't be stupid in your quest to have the place to yourself. The point here is, in general I've found a rather obvious truth. If a guidebook says it's secret, it isn't. The more remote a place is, the longer the hike, the steeper the inclines, the more extreme the journey, these all act as filters to minimizing the crowd factor.

ENTRANCE FEES

If you are planning on doing the Grand Circle or portions of it, it may make sense to purchase the Annual Pass. This will save you money in the long run, but only if you buy it at the first National Park you visit. For example, the entrance fee at Zion is $35 for a private vehicle. The Annual Pass is $80 and allows you entrance to all National Parks. You will save about $60 for the trip described in this book if using the Annual Pass.

BEING PREPARED

Hiking in the Grand Circle can be highly rewarding. However, don't let the desert fool you. This is an extreme environment, and one shouldn't just venture out without some forethought and preparation. This section seems straightforward, but as the rangers at the Grand Canyon can attest to, there are literally dozens of people that venture out into the wilderness with nothing more than enthusiasm. Since enthusiasm alone can really put a damper on your hike, here are some tips to make your hikes safer and more enjoyable.

WATER

Rule of thumb; bring three quarts per person per day. Some folks prefer two 1.5-liter bottles; some find they can balance their day or backpacks out better with three 1.0-liter bottles. Make sure the bottles do not leak by turning them upside down to see if water comes out. If it's only a drip, it's still a problem.

Water is pretty heavy, but bringing more rather than less keeps you hydrated and allows you to go farther.

If you are traveling with small children, you will likely need to carry their water for them beyond one quart. Keep this in mind as you are packing.

CLOTHING

Bring layers as appropriate for the hike. This means if the temperatures are cooler when you are at rest; bring a layer or two to keep you warm. Windbreakers are great allies in keeping warmth in and cold out and are also lightweight. In really cold temps a good beanie helps as well, as some 15% of your body temperature is lost through your head. If it looks like rain, bring a waterproof version of that windbreaker.

In the heat, most folks go with the t-shirt and shorts, which is fine, but definitely bring a hat. The heat can be oppressing, especially with no shade and that hat will definitely help. I also recommend a full brimmed hat over a baseball cap. This will provide more shade and definitely helps keep the back of your neck from getting sunburned.

In either hot or cold weather, bring another warm layer if you can. This is your emergency backup layer should you find yourself having to spend the night in the wilderness for whatever reason. A windbreaker that can be rolled up or a long sleeve shirt can make a big difference if you find yourself facing the setting sun with nothing but a t-shirt and shorts on a summer trip. I've also found it to be a good thing to have on hand for others that may need some warmth when you don't.

BOOTS, TENNIS AND WATER SHOES

Most people will tend to go for their tennis shoes because they are comfortable and easier to lace up. That said, boots are preferred because they offer a lot more protection, especially around the ankles. Tennis shoes are great for flat surfaces, but boots are made for uneven terrain. It's like taking a sedan tire on a 4WD road instead of an all-terrain tire. You wouldn't do it to your car, don't do it to your feet. Where a good boot and also, be the boot. Wear it in before you start your hiking adventures so you don't get blisters.

If the trail involves some hiking in water, it really helps to have a pair of water shoes. They are lightweight and keep your boots dry. A dry boot makes for a happy hiker, whereas a wet boot can destroy your feet in short order.

DAYPACK

A decent no nonsense day back to hold everything is essential. At the end of the day, you just want something that will last a long time. The more parts the pack has, the more parts that can fail. Zipper quality is number one. Most otherwise solid daypacks fail because of the zipper.

Also, a little tip on the daypack. If you get one that zips like an upside down U, put the zippers on one side or the other, not at the top. I have seen and personally had a branch find its way between the two zippers at top and open the entire contents of the pack onto the trail. In my case, it opened on brushy 30-degree incline I was scrambling up and I watched my lunch and water roll downhill out of sight forever.

OTHER GEAR

At this point, you have three quarts of water, a bunch of layers, some food, and no room for anything else right. Well, it can seem that way. What to bring is a balancing act. On the one hand, you want to be lightweight. The more stuff you have on your back, the more burdensome it will feel. On the other hand, you do want to be prepared. In the excellent book, *Climbing Ice* by Yvon Chouinard, he says something that is about as true a piece of advice I've ever heard in this context.

If you bring it, you will use it.

What this means is if you bring a sleeping bag, you will likely spend the night in it. If you bring rope, you will likely use that rope. So start with packing only what you need for the hike.

ESSENTIALS INCLUDE:

- Water and some food

- A hat

- Extra clothing as appropriate

- Sunscreen

- A map and possibly this trail guide (if you feel you will need it to navigate the trail)

On top of this, I would seriously consider also bringing:

- Some form of fire, a lighter, or fire starter of some kind

- Compass

- Small first aid kit, a whistle, and reflector mirror (for emergencies)

- A sharp knife

- Moleskin (for blisters)

- Ibuprofen (to help if you aren't acclimated to the heat)

- Water purification tablets

- Small flashlight

- Cell phone

- GPS device

It's hard to come up with a list that works under all conditions and the above list is more geared towards summer hiking than winter, so adjust what you bring for cold, rain, or snow. Also, be sure to bring something fun, a little treat goes a long way and is much better appreciated on the trail.

What's Up with the Short Stories?

The first edition of this book came out in 2015 and was then titled "A Family Guide to the Grand Circle National Parks" (There is also a working title out there called "RVing with Monsters", that precedes all editions). At that time, the book focused on a trip to the seven most popular national parks within the Grand Circle, with special focus on the parks themselves. As part of this book, I created several fictional short stories about my family taking this same Grand Circle trip in an RV. The stories were all based on real events and the fact we had never used an RV before helped with the satire.

In 2016, the book was lightly updated with latest prices and I added a few more trails and park overview maps.

In this, the 2017 edition, the book was changed dramatically, becoming the *complete* travel guide I had in mind, hence the title change. Building on the original content, the focus in this edition is on where to stay and eat, plus where to go outside of the seven primary national parks. Plus, I changed the layout to get all this info in and make it easier to use.

My kids have grown older and we loved researching the restaurants and hotels versus staying and eating in an RV, but the stories have remained an enduring part of the book. It's meant to give you something to do while on the longer legs between parks. Most stories are humorous, but some are meant to provoke the reader, in line with the thoughtfullness that the southwest itself brings.

The original edition contained a full bio on my family so you "got to know us" before jumping into the stories. Let me recap here:

I have two boys, Everest, (like the mountain), and Bryce (like the canyon). My wife Angela and I have raised them to their teenage selves at this point. At the time these stories were written, Everest was 14 and Bryce was 9 years old. Everest was and still is a dry-witted, soulful boy, while Bryce is one of the most independent people one will ever meet. The storyline starts with us driving into Vegas, renting an RV and then going from there into stories that are in some way relatable to each park.

I've played with the order, removed a couple of the stories that were more experimental in nature and put them against a colored background so you'll know which are the pieces to look for (or skip depending on your tastes).

I hope you enjoy this book as much as a travel companion as it is a travel guide. It is meant to take some of the hassle out of taking a family vacation to the Grand Circle. I would love to hear your feedback and can be found at www.facebook.com/GBG.GoneBeyond-Guides. Again, Enjoy! ~ Eric Henze

Antelope Canyon

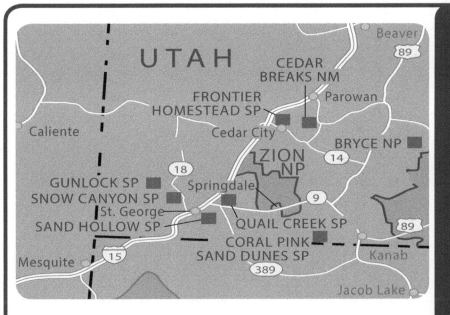

Quick Facts

Official Park Website: www.nps.gov/zion

Visitor Center: (435) 772-3256

Park Size: 146,597 acres

Established: 11/19/1919

Visitors: 3.6 million (2015)

Experience Level:

- Family Friendly to Experienced Hiker

Park Accessibility:

- Okay for 2WD and RVs

- Day and Overnight Use

Nearest Town with Amenities:

- Springdale, Utah is within 1 mi / 2 km of main park entrance

Getting There:

- From St George, UT: Take I-15 North to UT-9 East. Total distance is 41 mi / 66 km to park

Zion National Park

ZION NATIONAL PARK

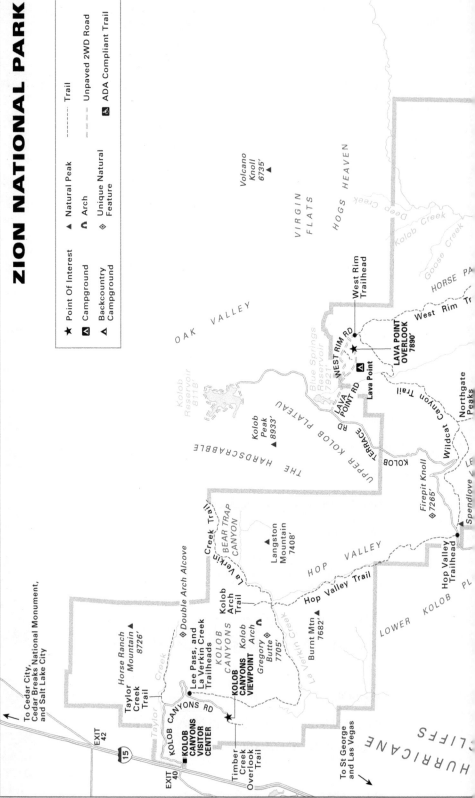

★ Point Of Interest
▲ Campground
▲ Backcountry Campground
▲ Natural Peak
∩ Arch
◈ Unique Natural Feature
------- Trail
= = = Unpaved 2WD Road
♿ ADA Compliant Trail

To Cedar City, Cedar Breaks National Monument, and Salt Lake City

EXIT 42

EXIT 40

15

KOLOB CANYONS RD

KOLOB CANYONS VISITOR CENTER

Timber Creek Overlook Trail

Taylor Creek

Taylor Creek Trail

Horse Ranch Mountain ▲ 8726'

◈ Double Arch Alcove

Lee Pass, and La Verkin Creek Trailheads

KOLOB CANYONS VIEWPOINT ★

KOLOB CANYONS

Kolob Arch ∩

Kolob Arch Trail

Gregory Butte ◈ 7705'

La Verkin Creek

La Verkin Creek Trail

BEAR TRAP CANYON

Langston Mountain 7408' ▲

Burnt Mtn 7682' ▲

HOP VALLEY

Hop Valley Trail

LOWER KOLOB PL

Hop Valley Trailhead

To St George and Las Vegas

HURRICANE CLIFFS

THE HARDSCRABBLE

UPPER KOLOB PLATEAU

Kolob Peak 8933' ▲

Kolob Reservoir 8118'

OAK VALLEY

Blue Springs Reservoir 7921'

LAVA POINT RD

WEST RIM RD

KOLOB TERRACE RD

Lava Point ▲

LAVA POINT OVERLOOK 7890' ♿

West Rim Trailhead

★ ♿

West Rim Trail

Firepit Knoll ◈ 7265'

Wildcat Canyon Trail

Northgate Peaks

Spendlove

LE

VIRGIN FLATS

HOGS HEAVEN

Volcano Knoll 6735' ▲

Deep Creek

Kolob Creek

Goose Creek

HORSE PA

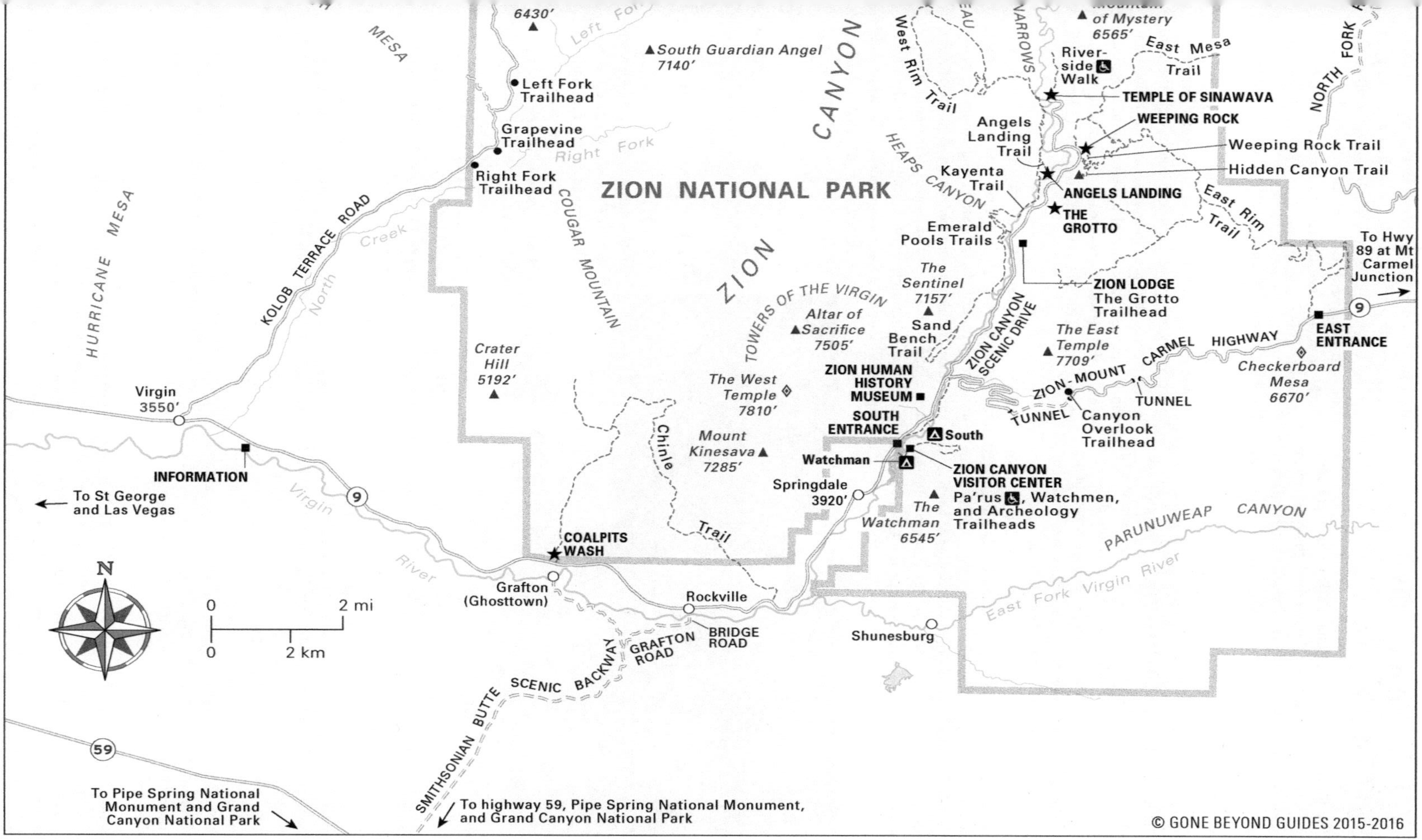

© GONE BEYOND GUIDES 2015-2016

ZION NATIONAL PARK

ZION CANYON

NORTH FORK

To Hwy 89 at Mt Carmel Junction

9

EAST ENTRANCE

Checkerboard Mesa 6670'

PARUNUWEAP CANYON

East Fork Virgin River

Weeping Rock Trail
Hidden Canyon Trail
East Rim Trail

TEMPLE OF SINAWAVA
WEEPING ROCK
ANGELS LANDING
THE GROTTO

ZION LODGE
The Grotto Trailhead

ZION-MOUNT CARMEL HIGHWAY

The East Temple 7709'

Canyon Overlook Trailhead

ZION-MOUNT CARMEL TUNNEL

ZION CANYON VISITOR CENTER
Pa'rus Watchmen, and Archeology Trailheads

Mountain of Mystery 6565'

East Mesa Trail

River-side Walk

NARROWS

PLATEAU

Angels Landing Trail

Kayenta Trail

West Rim Trail

HEAPS CANYON

Emerald Pools Trails

The Sentinel 7157'

Sand Bench Trail

ZION CANYON SCENIC DRIVE

South

The Watchman 6545'

Shunesburg

ZION NATIONAL PARK

Z I O N   CANYON

South Guardian Angel 7140'

TOWERS OF THE VIRGIN

Altar of Sacrifice 7505'

ZION HUMAN HISTORY MUSEUM
SOUTH ENTRANCE

Watchman

Springdale 3920'

The West Temple 7810'

Mount Kinesava 7285'

Chinle

Trail

Rockville

BRIDGE ROAD

GRAFTON ROAD

SMITHSONIAN BUTTE SCENIC BACKWAY

To highway 59, Pipe Spring National Monument, and Grand Canyon National Park

COUGAR MOUNTAIN

Left Fork

Right Fork

6430'

Left Fork Trailhead
Grapevine Trailhead
Right Fork Trailhead

Crater Hill 5192'

COALPITS WASH

Grafton (Ghosttown)

MESA

KOLOB TERRACE ROAD

North Creek

9

Virgin River

2 mi

2 km

0

0

Virgin 3550'

HURRICANE MESA

INFORMATION

To St George and Las Vegas

N

59

To Pipe Spring National Monument and Grand Canyon National Park

WHAT MAKES ZION SPECIAL

The journey to Zion National Park from Vegas starts at St. George, Utah. Before St. George, the land is wide open with an arid barren resonance that borders on melancholy. This is not a bad thing for the first time RVer as it allows you to get comfortable with your new vehicle on straight, distraction-free roads.

The journey starts at St. George because this town is at the foot of the Colorado Plateau, one of the most geologically stable landmasses in the world. This stability has allowed time, wind, water and perhaps divinity a canvas to produce majestic and immense works of natural art. Each presentation spreads itself over thousands of square miles, and each is both wonderfully unique and yet bound to similarity. This collection of natural art is why the Colorado Plateau holds the greatest concentration of National Parks in the United States. Roughly centered among the four corners of Utah, Arizona, Colorado and New Mexico, the Colorado Plateau makes up the overall foundation for the Grand Circle vacation.

like a surgeon into the sandstone layers, creating a thin slot canyon that winds itself slowly higher. During the summer when the river is lower, hikers can walk in the river with steeply cut rock walls on either side of them. The Narrows is a favorite with Zion hikers, both for the adventure of the journey and the ever-changing views.

The lesser-visited Kolob Canyon contains spectacular examples of the soaring red Navajo sandstone cliffs and is a short drive from the main section of the park. There are numerous finger and pocket canyons for hikers and backpackers to explore, including Kolob Arch, the third largest freestanding arch in North America. Kolob Canyon is a peaceful and stunning destination, presenting itself to the viewer more as oasis than desert, whether one explores it on foot or via the five-mile (8 km) scenic drive.

With the protection of the cliff walls and the Virgin River, Zion supports a relatively lush environment. Unlike its drier surroundings, the park is a sanctuary for plants and animals alike. Green vegetation is abundant and deer along with a host of birds are often seen within the park. The lush bounty of life combined with the towering red cliffs makes Zion magnificent. The word Zion itself was introduced by the Latter Day Saints as a reference to a place that is "pure in heart." There is a purity to Zion NP, a sense of peace and calm, but also a sense of adventure.

Ask the Park Ranger About "The Subway"

THE ZION TUNNEL PERMIT

At the same time you buy your Annual Pass or entrance fee, you will be asked if you are planning to go onward through the Zion Mount Carmel Tunnel, which you will need to do if you are going directly to Bryce Canyon National Park next. If you are and you are in an RV of any normal size, you will need to purchase a tunnel permit and be escorted through the tunnel. Specifically, if your RV is 7 feet 10 inches (2.4m) in width and/or 11 feet 4 inches (3.4m) in height or bigger, the NPS will require the permit. The tunnel permit costs $15 and is in addition to the park entrance fee. It will allow you two trips through the tunnel for the same vehicle within seven days of purchase.

If one follows the Grand Circle tour per this book, Zion is the first temple of natural art unveiled to the traveler. It holds massive sandstone cliffs with deep hues and majestic lines, dotted with a green lush canopy of high desert plants. The sheer cliffs of Zion are among the largest sandstone cliffs in the world, reaching heights as high as 2000 feet. They are colossal and proud monoliths, bathed in colors of reds, browns and cream. At the canyon's bottom, the usually quite Virgin River meanders through with as much leisure as the tourists themselves.

Zion Canyon itself is about 15 miles (24 km) long and is considered a box canyon, beginning with a wide mouth at one end and a cul de sac at the other. At the end of the canyon you'll find The Narrows, one of the best gems in the park. Here the Virgin River cuts

The tunnel traffic is controlled by NPS rangers who will verify that you have a valid permit and cue you up for your one-way journey through 1.1 miles (1.8 km) of solid rock in a large moving house. Make sure you know how your lights work prior to going into the tunnel; it is pitch black in sections. Also, the tunnel control has operating hours, it is not a 24/7 service. The operating hours are seasonal and are posted on your permit. You will need the permit before being allowed to pass through, so keep it in a safe and memorable place.

THINGS TO DO IN ZION

HIKING IN THE MAIN PARK

PA'RUS TRAIL

Easy – (3.5 mi / 5.6 km), round trip, allow 2 hours, elev. Δ: 50 ft / 15 m, trailheads at South Campground and Canyon Junction

Pa'rus, which is from the Paiute language, means bubbling, tumbling water. The name describes this trail well as it meanders along the Virgin River. The trail is paved and thus accessible for those with wheelchairs. Pa'rus starts at the visitor center and heads upstream at a very slight incline. The surrounding cliffs and valley open up throughout the journey.

There are several places along the way that provide beach access to the river and it is not uncommon to see families enjoying the heat of the day by cooling off in the water. Pa'rus trail crosses six bridges as it makes its way to trail's end at Canyon Junction. From here you can hike back (downhill all the way) or pick up the shuttle to your next destination. Dogs and bikes are welcome on this trail.

WATCHMAN TRAIL

Moderate – (3.3 mi / 5.3 km), round trip, allow 2 hours, elev. Δ: 368 ft / 112 m, trailhead near visitor center

If you are looking to get higher up for better views but don't want to climb the 2,000 feet or so to the top of the rim, the Watchman Trail is a good alternative. The trail starts at the Zion Canyon Visitor Center and ends at a mesa top that gives some commanding views of Zion NP and even a glimpse of the Towers of the Virgin and the town of Springdale.

The trail begins by following along the banks of the North Fork of the Virgin River and then juts away from the water to connect to a series of moderate switchbacks that wind their way to the top of the mesa. There is a nominal 368 feet elevation gain, but the views are worth every step. Once at the mesa top there is a half-mile loop

Mount Carmel Tunnel

that walks around the edge. Note that the loop mileage isn't listed as part of the distance noted in the NPS hiking guide. This is a popular trail due to both the views and the fact it starts at the visitor center.

ARCHEOLOGY TRAIL

Easy – (0.4 mi / 0.6 km), round trip, allow 0.5 hour, elev. Δ: 80 ft / 24 m, trailhead near visitor center

The Archeology Trail is a great hike if you are looking for an early evening stroll. The trail is short, less than half a mile (0.6 kilometers), but climbs fairly steadily to a 1000-year-old prehistoric storage site. While the site requires a fair amount of imagination to piece together the history, this is not the only reason for going.

The site is close to the Watchman campground and rises to a nice vantage point in a very short distance. One can take in phenomenal views both up and down the canyon. You will notice the green riparian corridor of the Virgin River as it meanders through an ever-widening canyon. In all, this is a short but worthwhile trek you can take if you are looking for something near camp.

SAND BENCH TRAIL

Moderate – (7.6 mi / 12.2 km), round trip, allow 5 hours, elev. Δ: 466 ft / 142 m, trailhead at Zion Lodge or Court of the Patriarchs shuttle stops

This long ambling trail follows along Birch Creek before climbing up to a long and decent sized plateau named Sand Bench. The trail does have a 466-foot elevation gain but for the most part, the gain is felt primarily as you ascend to the plateau.

Start at the Court of the Patriarchs shuttle stop and pick up the Sand Bench Trail as it follows from the Virgin River up Birch Creek. The trail then heads up to and runs the length of the Sand Bench plateau. As the hike unfolds, the Patriarchs, East Temple, Streaked Wall, Sentinel, Mountain of the Sun, and many other peaks can be seen. This trail is shared with horse riders, so be mindful as you take in the views.

LOWER EMERALD POOL TRAIL

Easy – (1.2 mi / 1.9 km), round trip, allow 1 hour,, elev. Δ: 69 ft / 21 m, trailhead at Zion Lodge shuttle stop

There are two trails described in the Zion hiking guide that make up the Emerald Pools, the lower pools and upper pools. Lower Emerald Pools is flat, is paved much of the way, is short in distance and provides incredible views of waterfalls and shallow pools. You do climb a bit on the lower trail, which allows for some nice views of the valley.

The two pools on the lower trail are nice enough, but as is almost always the case, the best pool is at the top. As the canyon is surrounded on both sides by steep cliffs, it will be well into morning before the sun hits the western side of the canyon. By mid-afternoon, the sun will have passed over the other side, providing more shade. In warm weather, plan on hitting the trail either in early morning or late afternoon to stay cool.

Upper Emerald Pool Trail

Moderate – (1.0 mi / 1.6 km), round trip from lower pools, allow 1 hour, elev. Δ: 200 ft / 61 m, trailhead at Zion Lodge shuttle stop

Here the trail continues from the Lower Emerald Pool Trail for the final mile. The paved trail is now dirt and the trail climbs more steeply. If you are doing this trail in the morning, the sun may have passed over the monolith walls and is now part of the climb up. The views do get better as you gain elevation, and the pool at the top is by far the biggest, sitting at the base of the western cliff faces. It is well worth the effort for the views. These pools are not intended for swimming.

Kayenta Trail

Moderate – (2.0 mi / 3.2 km), round trip, allow 2 hours, elev. Δ: 150 ft / 46 m, trailhead at Grotto shuttle stop

Kayenta Trail is often done along with the Grotto Trail and the Emerald Pools Trail to create a loop. The trail is great in its own right, giving some great views deeper into the canyon near the Zion Lodge. The trail has a small 150-foot elevation gain.

The trail can be picked up easily from The Grotto shuttle stop. From the shuttle stop cross the Virgin River via a bridge and follow along its upper banks for a short distance. The trail then enters into Behunin Canyon from the North side before meeting up with the Emerald Pools Trail. To make a loop of it, continue along and down the Emerald Pools Trail until it ends at the Zion Lodge and then pick up the Grotto Trail back to where you started.

The Grotto Trail

Easy – (1.0 mi / 1.6 km), round trip, allow 30 minutes, elev. Δ: 35 ft / 11 m, trailhead at Grotto shuttle stop

The Grotto Trail is a simple little flat jaunt that connects the Zion Lodge with the Grotto Picnic Area. It is used by many to connect the Emerald and Kayenta Trails to make a 2 ½ mile loop. The Grotto area itself contains picnic tables and grates for grilling. It also contains the Grotto Museum, which is the oldest building in Zion. If you are a fan of the historical stonework of the Zion Lodge, be sure to include the Grotto Trail to the mix to see both the museum and the artist in residence house.

Angels Landing via West Rim Trail

Strenuous – (5.4 mi / 8.7 km), round trip, allow 4-5 hours, elev. Δ: 1,488 ft / 453 m, trailhead at Grotto shuttle stop

The views are unparalleled from the unique Angels Landing trail. Built during the wake of the Great Depression by the CCC, it comprises a series of switchbacks cut into solid rock. The final half mile is along a narrow knife-edged ridge that uses chains and carved footholds to assist you to the final destination. It is strenuous, but the end result is well worth it. You will have climbed from the bottom of the canyon to close to the top, giving you a view that will most certainly become a life moment. It is a world famous hike and one of the most popular in Zion.

The trail's name was coined by Frederick Fisher in 1916 when he looked up at the monolith and exclaimed, "only and angel could land on it." With the help of the CCC, (Frederick Fisher) forged a trail to the top.

Climbing up Angels Landing

The trail is composed of six distinct parts. The first follows a paved path along the river before dog legging west from the river toward a cliff wall. If you look carefully at this point in the trail, you will see the second portion of the journey, a series of switchbacks up this cliff wall. Even from a distance, the switchbacks are impressive if not audacious. The trail builders carved a fairly wide paved trail into solid rock and while you are indeed climbing up a cliff face, this portion is merely strenuous and no more dangerous than any well-established trail with exposure.

There is a reprieve at the third portion. At the top of the switchbacks, the trail goes between two massive monolithic columns through what is aptly named Refrigerator Canyon. The monoliths climb high enough to block out the sun and there is a cool breeze that greets visitors as soon as they reach the top of the switchbacks. This lasts for only a short half mile before you arrive at the fourth portion, called Walter's Wiggles. The Wiggles are a series of 21 short but consistently steep switchbacks that wind back and forth until you get to the next respite, called Scout's Lookout.

The lookout is the fifth portion of the journey and a great place to take a rest. The Wiggles are below you and from the lookout, you can see the final half mile pitch ahead of you to Angels Landing. The area offers incredible views. There is also a pit toilet and plenty of places to relax before your final leg. Up to this point you have been on the West Rim Trail, so make sure you follow the signs to the top of Angels Landing, as the West Rim Trail does continue onward.

The final pitch is a bit exciting as it has the adventure of chains that you can grab onto to ensure you get up the last leg. This portion is a razor back ridge. It is fairly narrow with steep drop offs on either side. The trail is well marked by the chains and crosses the back of the ridge several times as you climb. Many hikers have made this journey and in the end, it is not as scary as it sounds. That said, this is not a place to test yourself; a handful of people have fallen to their deaths on this trail. I've seen teenagers on this trail but only two children who were in the single digit age bracket. Use caution, for both yourself and your fellow hikers.

Once at the top, there is a somewhat narrow but flat area to take in the lofty vista. To the north is a grand view of the end of Zion Canyon. You will find yourself gazing at an enormous cul-de-sac of towering rock. As the eye travels from the edge of Angels Landing down the canyon, the citadel of rock stands as one complete sentry extending to the horizon. The red cliff walls meet the green of the desert, culminating in a dense riparian snake of vegetation that surrounds the Virgin River. At times swallows soaring at incredible speeds up to 40 miles per hour (64 km/hour) can be seen. They will soar seemingly straight into the cliff walls only to stop at the last second and land in their nests.

WEEPING ROCK TRAIL

Easy – (0.4 mi / 0.6 km), round trip, allow 30 minutes, elev. Δ: 98 ft / 30 m, trailhead at Weeping Rock shuttle stop

This is a short paved trail that ends at an alcove called Weeping Rock. True to its name, water seeps through the sandstone and then falls gently like a soft rain once it reaches the overhang. It is possible to stand

From the top of Angels Landing

underneath and watch the magic of water and stone, even on a sunny day. The trail is great for kids and casual hikers looking for a great view of the Great White Throne. There is about 100 feet of elevation gain and some trailside exhibits.

HIDDEN CANYON TRAIL

Strenuous – (2.4 mi / 3.9 km), round trip, allow 2-3 hours, elev. Δ: 850 ft / 259 m, trailhead at Weeping Rock shuttle stop

If you don't mind exposure to steep drop offs, this is a really cool hike. Mind you, there are long drops and chains are put in places to assist in some areas, so if you do have a fear of heights, this trail may not be for you. Hidden Canyon starts from the Weeping Rock shuttle

Portion of The Narrows

This is a great backpacking destination due to the numerous spur trails, including Deertrap Mountain and Cable Mountain Trails.

Starting from the East Entrance, views of Checkerboard Mesa and the head of Jolly Gulch can be seen. This initial portion of the trail does have some elevation gain as the trail navigates the contour of the plateau. There are some very dramatic views along this portion. At 6 miles in there is a trail to the left that leads to Cable Mountain and Deertrap Trails as well as a trail junction farther on for Observation Point. The trail then comes to the top of Echo Canyon, where it heads swiftly downwards 1,000 feet (see Observation Point for more details here).

OBSERVATION POINT VIA EAST RIM TRAIL

Strenuous – (8.0 mi / 12.9 km), round trip, allow 6 hours, elev. Δ: 2,148 ft / 655 m, trailhead at Weeping Rock shuttle stop

Okay, if you found yourself wanting to get to the top of Zion Canyon from the moment you arrived, this is one of the trails that will get you there. The trail climbs some 2,148 feet over four miles with some serious drop offs along the way and is all done in full sun. While strenuous, this is a hike to remember.

Start at the Weeping Rock shuttle stop and proceed up the shared trail to Hidden Canyon, East Rim Trail, and Observation Point following a series of well-built switchbacks. At the junction, stay left and continue through Echo Canyon, a narrow and steep canyon with little pools of running water carved into the sandstone. As the climb continues, the trail starts to bring the white Temple Cap formation closer into view. Zion Canyon, Angels Landing, Cathedral Mountain, and Three Patriarchs are in full view. The views from the top as well as the trip through Echo Canyon make this steep hike well worth the effort.

CABLE MOUNTAIN TRAIL

Strenuous – (17.5 mi / 28.2 km from East Entrance), round trip, allow 8-10 hours, elev. Δ: up 1,000 ft, down 2,000 ft

Strenuous (15.5 mi / 25.0 km from Weeping Rock shuttle stop), round trip, allow 7-9 hours, elev. Δ: 2,100 ft / 640 m

Moderate (7.5 mi / 12.1 km from Zion Ponderosa Ranch, round trip, allow 5 hours, elev. Δ: 300 ft / 91 m

There are three ways to get to Cable Mountain Trail. See the trail descriptions for Observation Point and East Rim Trail for additional information on the routes to Cable Mountain Trail. For the Zion Ponderosa Ranch route, head out to the East Entrance and make a left to North Fork Road.

and follows a paved trail steeply upwards along a set of well-constructed switchbacks. At the trail junction for Hidden Canyon, East Rim Trail and Observation Point, keep to the right and head up a series of short and steep switchbacks not unlike Walters Wiggles found over at Angels Landing.

After the switchbacks, the trail clings at various times to the edge of a steeply sloping rock face. In some areas there are chains to assist the hiker, in others, the trail looks a little intimidating but is wide and safe enough. In one part, steps have been carved directly into the sandstone. This whole part of the hike is akin to being Indiana Jones looking for some ancient treasure. This is truly a fun and exhilarating hike. That said, if you aren't a fan of heights, this might not be the best trail.

The hike ends at the mouth of Hidden Canyon. With some basic scrambling, it is possible to continue up the canyon a bit to a small 10-foot arch along a sandy streambed section of the trip. Hidden Canyon throws off a lot of the visitors due to its exposure and while it can be dangerous under wet conditions, is quite fine for those who have figured out how far to trust the grip of sandstone under one's feet. The other plus is the hike is typically in the shade for most of the day, which helps in the heat of the summer. Elevation gain for this trail is 800 feet.

EAST RIM TRAIL

Strenuous – (10.6 mi / 17.1 km), one way, allow 6 – 7 hours, elev. Δ: 1,365 ft / 415 m, two trailheads, described below

Like the West Rim Trail, most hikers start at the upper end with the descent in front of them. For this trail, that is done by starting at the East Rim Trailhead, located at the Zion East Entrance Ranger Station and heading to the Weeping Rock shuttle stop.

Follow the signs to Zion Ponderosa and once at the resort, look for signs to Cable Mountain Trail, making a left at the main entrance, and then going straight past the resort buildings. The trailhead connects with the East Rim Trail and onwards to Cable Mountain Trail.

In 1901, there was a tram that carried lumber from the top of Zion Canyon to the valley floor. This engineering marvel, built by pioneer David Flanigan contained 3,300 feet of cable and could supply lumber to the valley floor in several minutes, which was a massive improvement over the 3-day journey by wagon that it took prior. Many of the original buildings in Zion were built with this lumber. The frameworks were destroyed twice by fire and in 1930; the park service removed the cables. The draw works still sits at the top of Cable Mountain at the end of the trail.

Deertrap Trail

Strenuous – (19.5 mi / 31.4 km from East Entrance), round trip, allow 11-12 hours,, elev. Δ: up 1,000 ft, down 2,000 ft

Strenuous (17.5 mi / 28.2 km from Weeping Rock shuttle stop), round trip, allow 8-10 hours, elev. Δ: 2,100 ft / 640 m

Moderate (9.5 mi / 15.3 km from Zion Ponderosa Ranch, round trip, allow 6 hours, elev. Δ: 300 ft / 91 m

This is certainly a long day hike or as an add on within the East Rim Trail. Use the East Rim, Observation Point and Cable Mountain Trail descriptions to initiate the three routes, as appropriate.

Once on the side trail from East Rim Trail, continue past Cable Mountain Trail for another two miles to a series of overlooks collectively referred to as a sky island. Each view is slightly different, offering expansive views into the north and south portions of Zion Canyon as well as the outer peaks and terrain.

Canyon Overlook Trail

Moderate – (1.0 mi / 1.6 km), round trip, allow 1 hour, elev. Δ: 163 ft / 50 m, trailhead near east Zion Tunnel entrance

This is another in the list of "great views without too much effort" category. The trail starts right before the Zion Tunnel as you head into the park. There are parking lots on either side of the Zion-Mount Carmel Highway. The trail gets a fair amount of "impulse hiking" as folks wait for the directed traffic of the tunnel to open up. After all, hiking in Zion does beat out being stuck in traffic in Zion. The hike has a modest 163-foot elevation gain and climbs some steps cut into the sandstone. At the end of the trail is an overlook with a railing at the cliff's edge giving great views of the lower portions of Zion Canyon and Pine Creek immediately below, as well as an interesting perspective of the Zion Tunnel.

Riverside Walk

Easy – (2.2 mi / 3.5 km), round trip, allow 90 minutes, elev. Δ: 57 ft / 17 m, trailhead at Temple of Sinawava shuttle stop

Riverside Walk starts at roads end of the wide main portion of the Zion box canyon. From here, the canyon begins to narrow but is still wide enough for the paved Riverside Walk trail that meanders until it reaches The Narrows proper. The trail is fairly flat, with several rolling ups and downs as it contours to the land. There are also a few spots with watery grottoes as well as multiple spots for river beach access. The trail ends at a stonework terrace where you can gaze at the mouth of The Narrows and the various hikers beginning or ending their hike of this landmark trek.

The Narrows

Imagine walking up a river flowing clearly and gently around your feet. At times there is no shore, only river and massive sandstone walls that run from the edge of the water and rise swiftly straight up 2000 feet into the sky. There are places where the canyon is wide enough to permit a view of distant sandstone monoliths and other places where the canyon is delightfully slender, only 20-30 feet wide. Each turn gives a different view, all wondrous and grand. For a bit, the river stretches out, allowing a chance to walk on soft sand. You see deer grazing on the banks. Waterfalls come sliding down curved walls from unreachable heights. There is no trail but the river. If you think about it, each step up and down is a step no one has ever taken before in exactly the same way.

Within The Narrows

If You Hike the Narrows

- Have a full understanding of the weather before you go. Flash floods can originate from storms that aren't close to where you are hiking.

- Carry a gallon of water per person and some food, sunscreen and a first aid kit.

- Bring a pullover if the weather is temperate. It is colder in the canyon.

- Bring waterproof bags for cameras and other items that you need to keep dry.

- The only restroom on the hike is at the beginning of the Riverside Walk. There are no other places to go, even if you "have to." This is a popular destination and there are no discreet bushes. Make sure everyone goes prior to beginning the hike.

- Walking sticks are preferred by most folks for added stability, as are sturdy hiking boots. Water shoes and tennis shoes are okay for the casual hike up river. Sandals are not recommended though hiking sandals are okay.

- This is not a great hike for young children. My 9-year-old did fine, but keep in mind it is over two miles of walking just to get to the beginning of The Narrows. While the current is typically fine for adults, it may be too much for smaller ones.

Be warned, it is possible that you won't be able to hike the Narrows. If the Virgin River is running too high, either due to winter/spring runoff or to summer flash floods, you will not be able to go on this hike. That said, if the river is running favorably, then make it a point to add this to your itinerary. The park service actively controls access to the Narrows, which does take the guesswork out of the safety of hiking this trail.

Going Upstream from the Bottom of the Canyon

Easy to Strenuous – (9.4 mi / 15.1 km), round trip, allow up to 8 hours depending on distance traveled, elev. Δ: 334 ft / 102 m, trailhead at Temple of Sinawava shuttle stop

The Narrows is found by taking the shuttle to the very end of the canyon via the Riverside Walk Trail. It will take about 40–45 minutes from the campground to the end of the canyon via the shuttle. It will take another hour to 90 minutes to walk the 2.2 miles (3.5 km) needed to complete the Riverside Walk Trail. Make sure you add in this time when you plan your hike.

The Riverside Walk Trail is flat, easy and paved. The trail follows the Virgin River up along its banks, and there are plenty of places to drop off the trail to explore the river itself. At the end of the trail is a small set of steps down to the river where The Narrows begins and where the hike gets really interesting.

There are a few trails, but for the most part, you walk in the river itself. You will be walking upstream on uneven ground at times, so be prepared to get wet. Depending on how far up you decide to go, you will need to wade and even swim in some stretches. If you feel confident that the trail will be open, it's best to pick up water shoes beforehand and bring them on the trip for this hike. It will make your hike more enjoyable.

Depending on the time of year, the water may be swift and cold. In the summer, usually by June, the river slows down to a steady but not terribly swift pace, and the temperature is more refreshing than cold.

There are restrictions to how far up you are allowed to travel upstream without a permit. There is a tributary creek called Orderville Junction, which is a common destination for most hikers and is the limit of how far up you can travel without a permit. Orderville Junction is about two hours from the trail. That said, it is possible to never make it this far and still have an amazing hike. Each bend offers a different experience and new view with another bend at the end that beckons you farther.

Returning will take slightly less time since you are going downstream with the flow of water. If you are doing the hike in late afternoon, make a note of when you start the hike from the shuttle drop off and how much time you have left before sunset. If you have 3 hours, hike up for 90 minutes and turn around. The Narrows is not an easy hike in the dark especially if you don't have a flashlight.

Going Downstream from the Top of the Canyon

Strenuous – (16 mi / 25.7 km), one way, full day hike, elev. Δ: 1,400 ft / 427 m, trailhead at Zion Narrows parking area

Going downstream can be done with a National Park Service wilderness permit. Allow a full day for this 16-mile hike. You can find private jeep shuttles that regularly go up to the drop off spot. This is a strenuous day's hike. There are ample stories of folks that find themselves having to stick it out for the night because they thought it would be an easier hike. Hiking in streambeds is slow work and is more tiring than walking on even pavement. Underestimating this hike in the wrong conditions can be dangerous as well. Flash floods and exposure from the night's elements are serious matters.

CHINLE TRAIL

Strenuous – (6.8 mi / 10.9 km), round trip to Huber Wash, allow 3 – 5 hours, elev. Δ: 650 ft / 198 m, two trailheads off SR-9

This is a very different hike than most of Zion, showing off the diversity of Lowland Desert Ecology as well as crossing through a petrified forest. The trail is well exposed and will be very hot in the full sun of summer. The trail is more welcoming in spring and fall, with wildflowers present in the spring.

The hike has two trailhead entrances, both from Highway 9. The entrance closest to the town of Springdale requires parking in the designated lot labeled "Trailhead Parking". Parking in the subdivision will get you towed. From the trailhead wind through the local neighborhood to the park's boundary and continue through a forested area with absolutely remarkable views. After 3.2 miles, the trail meets up with Huber Wash. Head back from here.

It is also possible to continue to make this somewhat of a loop trail; however, as some of the loop is Highway 9, it's best to have two cars. Taking the full loop to Coalpits Wash from Chinle Trailhead is a total of 15 miles.

RIGHT FORK TRAILHEAD

Strenuous – (10.6 mi / 17.1 km), round trip from bottom up, allow 8 – 12 hours, elev. Δ: 1,000 ft / 300 m, trailhead on Kolob Terrace Road

Like the Left Fork Trailhead, this is more route than maintained trail. The first couple of miles were hit by a fire in 2006 and the area is in a cycle of recovery. The hike within the streambed is pretty slow going, so allow extra time. That said, while the Right Fork is a bit more rugged to navigate, the scenery is quite peaceful and meandering with the route ending at a set of pretty incredible double waterfalls. Like the Left Fork, this trail can get hot in the summer despite the lure of water.

Start the hike at the Right Fork Trailhead on Kolob Terrace Road. The first quarter mile crosses the fire area to a bluff overlooking North Creek. From here head steeply down and into the creek bed. Do make note of this entrance, as it is easy to miss on the way out. Once at North Creek, start heading upstream passing the confluence of Left Fork. Cross the stream on the left side here and follow the path that crisscrosses the creek multiple times.

At about 2.5 miles into the hike, pass Trail Canyon on the right. A short spur trip up this canyon about one quarter of a mile will lead to a set of cascades. Back in North Creek, at close to 4 miles in, the hiker will encounter a very cool five-foot waterfall pouring through the slickrock into a nice pool. About a half mile further up, the canyon narrows and holds multiple waterfalls, pools, and hanging gardens. Further up another mile is Double Falls, another picturesque set of cascades.

From here, the end of the journey without ropes is Barrier Falls, about a third of a mile further upstream. The going here is tougher, requiring one to scramble up slick rock, bushwhack and otherwise navigate slowly to the falls. There is a set of falls in between, but you will know you are at Barrier Falls, its name holds true.

Unlike the Left Fork Trail, a permit is not required for Right Fork. Coming back, be glad you made note of the trail you came down as getting back up to the rim without the trail can be dangerous.

LEFT FORK TRAILHEAD

Strenuous – (7.0 mi / 11.3 km), round trip, allow 5 - 8 hours, elev. Δ: 1,000 ft / 300 m, trailhead on Kolob Terrace Road

The Left Fork of North Creek is most popular for a stretch labeled The Subway, a short and rather amazing section of the creek that looks more like a worm tunnel than a streambed. This is one of the best hikes in the park and is more route than actual trail. The whole journey is alongside and often in the creek, which makes for slow going. Unlike The Narrows, which can be cooler in the summer heat, this hike is definitely a hot hike when temperatures are high. Start early if it looks to be a hot day.

It is possible to enter from the top and make your way down stream, but this is longer and requires a bit of rappelling and swimming (and carrying your rappelling gear). A permit is required no matter which direction you travel. From bottom to top is described here.

From the bottom, the trail starts by picking ones way down a 400 foot gully starting from the Left Fork Trailhead on Kolob Terrace Road. Once in the creek, head upstream for about two to three hours. The Subway section is a tight section of the creek with several twists and turns right above a cascading set of falls called Red Waterfalls. The Subway itself is spectacular with clear pools and an almost subterranean feel.

It is possible to continue upwards but be mindful of time. Shortly after The Subway you will be met with large black pools that you must swim to get across to continue exploring the slot canyon. Further up is a soothing little waterfall with a secret natural room behind a watery curtain. Journeying from here requires bouldering and rappelling experience. Enjoy and head back down before dark.

Like The Narrows, this slot canyon does experience extreme changes in water volume due to flash floods. The permit process helps provide education along the way for this route, but do enter well informed as to the weather for the day.

Hiking in the Kolob Canyon Section

18 La Verkin Creek Trail (and Kolob Arch)

Strenuous – (14.0 mi / 22.5 km), round trip, allow 8 hours, elev. Δ: 1,037 ft / 316 m, trailhead at Kolob Canyon Road

La Verkin Creek Trail, in the Kolob Canyons section, is a fun trail all around, offering great views including Kolob Arch, one of the largest freestanding arches on earth. The hike itself does have some elevation gain, a little over 1,000 feet; however, the surroundings are amazing enough to help keep your mind off the inclines. Most folks get a permit and camp overnight; however, it is possible to do this as a long day hike to Kolob Arch.

The trail starts at Lee Pass and crosses in front of the southern portion of the Kolob Canyon cliffs. The trail meets up quickly with Timber Creek and follows along its banks, giving some spectacular views in a pinyon juniper forest setting. After about two miles, the trail veers away from the creek into the woods as it heads towards La Verkin Creek. The trail then descends down into the creek's clear waters, with each step putting you into a more immersive Kolob Canyon experience. Cliffs are now towering around you on either side with the sound of water adding to the magic of this hike.

The end of the trail is Kolob Arch viewpoint where the arch can be seen by hiking up about 150 feet to a viewing area. While the official end of the trail listed here is 7 miles, La Verkin Creek Trail does continue up stream for another two miles. There are many side canyons to explore, some of which require canyoneering techniques that lead to triple waterfalls and other delights. If backpacking, it is possible to connect to the Hop Valley Trail, which leads southeast to the Lower Kolob Plateau.

Hop Valley Trail

Strenuous – (15 mi / 24.1 km), round trip, allow 10 hours, elev. Δ: 1,050 ft / 320 m, trailhead off Kolob Terrace Road

The Hop Valley Trail, located in the Kolob Canyons section of Zion is typically done as part of the Trans Zion hike, a 48 mile, 5-day trek that crosses Zion from the Kolobs at Lee Pass to the East Rim. Lacking the fame of the main Zion and Kolob Canyons, the Hop Valley trail is a hidden gem. It is possible to use Hop Valley as a longer and more remote method to Kolob Arch. The route described here is from Kolob Terrace Road to Kolob Arch and back.

From the Hop Valley Trailhead on Kolob Terrace Road pick up the northern trailhead into Hop Valley. The trail starts out in a wide and open valley filled with deep sand and plenty of sagebrush. Walking in deep sand is a consistent trait of this trail. In areas, grazing has left its mark on the vegetation. As you continue, the valley narrows and travel is along a pleasant stream. The trail does have a fair amount of creek crossings; look for NPS trail markers to keep you on the trail. Campsites are about five miles in at an NPS boundary gate. The vegetation is more pristine once you cross into the park. Take a series of switchbacks downhill to connect to La Verkin Creek and follow it downstream to the Kolob Arch Viewpoint.

Overall, this hike has about 1,000 feet elevation gain, mostly felt on the return. That said, the trail is more strenuous due to its length than the elevation.

West Rim Trailhead

Strenuous – (12.9 – 14.4 mi / 20.7 – 23.1 km), one way, allow 10 hours, elev. Δ: 3,600 ft / 1097 m, trailhead at Lava Point

This is a long day hike or a pleasant overnight backpacking trip. The hike is best if started from the West Rim Trailhead at Kolob Terrace Road and heading towards the other end at The Grotto shuttle stop. Since the shuttle doesn't go to both ends of the trail, you will need a means of transportation back to your car.

Kolob Canyon

Starting near Lava Point on Kolob Terrace Road pick up the trail and keep straight to avoid the Wildcat Canyon Trail. The trail heads along the Horse Plateau through sparsely forested ponderosa pines. After 4.5 miles, the trail descends into a happy little meadow named Potato Hollow. Here there is a small pond and a spring that is usually running. This is a good place to relax and fill up canteens, (be sure to treat or filter). There are some great views into Imlay canyon by taking a short side spur to the east.

The trail then climbs about 500 feet out of the hollow and back onto Horse Plateau proper over a distance of 1.5 miles. At this point, the hike offers two routes. There is the primary West Rim Trail, which is 1.5 miles longer, and the Telephone Canyon Trail. The West Rim variation gives great views of Phantom Valley and the southern Zion canyons. The Telephone Canyon variation is named by settlers trying to establish a telephone line into Zion Canyon. The route here is shorter and sticks more to the interior of Horse Plateau.

NORTHGATE PEAKS TRAIL

Easy – (4.5 mi / 7.2 km), round trip, allow 3 hours, elev. Δ: 50 ft / 15 m, trailhead off Wildcat Canyon trail

If you wondered if you could find a hike that wasn't too hard but also wasn't shared with millions of other tourists, this trail is a good bet. Northgate Peaks Trail is off the beaten path and isn't in the popular NPS hiking brochures so it doesn't get as much traffic. The hike also shows a different view of Zion, ambling through large ponderosa pine forests found in the higher elevations. The hike is cooler and walks amongst the white Temple Cap monoliths dotting the landscape.

While the name of this there and back hike makes it sound like it climbs some massive Zion mountain, the elevation gain is only 250 feet. The trail ends at a craggy volcanic knob offering views that are distinctively different from the main portions of Zion and the Kolob Canyons. Access to Northgate Peaks Trail is from the Wildcat Canyon parking lot on Kolob Terrace Road.

Both variations meet up at Cabin Springs, a small seep that collects into a small pool. There are campsites nearby. This water is fine to drink given you filter or treat it and have a strong amount of patience. From Cabin Springs, the real fun begins as the trail heads steeply down into Zion Canyon. There are long drop-offs here, but this is a well-maintained trail. Take the path cut into the slick rock and head downwards until you reach a respite at Lookout Point. From here, the trail is an inverse of what is described for the Angels Landing Trail. Follow down Walters Wiggles, through Refrigerator Canyon and down until you end at The Grotto shuttle stop. It is completely possible and recommended to add the Angels Landing to the journey. If you do, be sure to allow another 45 minutes to the overall duration of the hike.

TIMBER CREEK OVERLOOK TRAIL

Moderate – (1.0 mi / 1.6 km), round trip, allow 30 minutes, elev. Δ: 100 ft / 30 m, trailhead at end of Kolob Canyon Road

This is one of those trails that could labeled as "Easy" without much argument; however, the park lists it as moderate. It does have a 100-foot elevation gain, but is otherwise a straightforward trail. The trail is picked up at the very end of Kolob Canyon Road. From there the

Kolob Arch

trail follows a small ridgeline to an overlook of Kolob Canyon, looking south. On a clear day, it is possible to see all the way to the north rim of the Grand Canyon.

This trail is located within the Kolob Canyon section. Groups are limited to a maximum size of 12 people at a time. Look for wildflowers in season, which can be abundant on this trail.

TAYLOR CREEK TRAIL

Moderate – (5.0 mi / 8.0 km), round trip, allow 4 hours, elev. Δ: 470 ft / 143 m, trailhead at Kolob Canyon Road

This trail lies within the Kolob Canyons Wilderness and ambles up the Middle Fork of Taylor Creek. This entire area gets less visitation than the main Zion Canyon and this trail in particular has strict limits on prohibiting groups larger than 12 people. Taylor Creek Trail heads into a narrow box canyon of red Navajo Sandstone along a normally gently flowing creek. There is a welcome interplay of the green vegetation and the red hue of the rocks here and the hike overall is one of delight and wonder. Before the trail begins to fade as it nears the end of the box canyon, look for Double Arch Alcove, an impressive set of alcoves, one on top of the other.

OTHER THINGS TO DO

SPRINGDALE

Springdale was once a Mormon settlement at the mouth of Zion Canyon and is now a quaint little tourist town. The town has everything for a visitor, including gift shops, art galleries, restaurants, ice cream and gifts. The spunky little town of just 529 inhabitants even has a movie theater. It's a nice alternative to hiking if your family is just not the hiking type or has had enough of the outdoors for now. It is also where you can pick up alternative journeys via jeep tours and mountain biking. The NPS runs shuttle service to Springdale, which can be picked up near the visitors center. Check the visitors center for a schedule.

VISITOR CENTER

The visitors center is located within walking distance of the Watchman Campground and is a great place to start your Zion journey. Here you can get a lay of the land, talk to rangers and, if your kids are interested, pick up a Junior Ranger Program. This is also the hub for finding a shuttle both into the park and out to Springdale.

If the center is closed or overly busy, the NPS has set up some very nice kiosks that allow you to get the information you need. The kiosks list out things to do based on how much time you have in the park and are definitely a great way to get started.

The visitor center is open every day except for Christmas Day. Hours are seasonal. Spring: 8:00 a.m. to 6:00 p.m., Summer: 8:00 a.m. to 7:00 p.m., Fall: 8:00 a.m. to 6:00 p.m. and Winter: 8:00 a.m. to 5:00 p.m.

A quick note on the Junior Ranger Programs. If you have younger kids, you likely know about this program. Almost every national and state park offers its own version of the Junior Ranger Program. The program allows children to explore and learn more about the park they are visiting. Each child receives an activity book that asks questions about the animals, plants, geography and history of the park. The booklets do take some time to fill out and parents can work with the younger ones to help. Upon completion, kids get a badge or patch and sometimes a park pin. The Junior Ranger Program is a great way to engage your family in the national parks, conservation and ecology. Depending on the ranger who reviews the completed activity book, the receiving of the official park junior ranger badge can be quite ceremonial with the entire visitor center applauding as the child receives public accolades for his/her accomplishment on becoming a Junior Ranger.

ZION HUMAN HISTORY MUSEUM

The Zion Human History Museum opens one to two hours later than the visitors center and requires taking a short trip on the shuttle. The museum itself is nicely laid out albeit fairly broad and basic in its offerings. The best part of the museum is its grand view located on the backside of the building. The museum was built with the view of the Court of the Patriarchs in mind—three immense and stately monoliths named after the biblical figures Abraham, Isaac, and Jacob. Whether the museum is open or closed, the trip is worth the journey for the view alone.

TOOLING AROUND ON THE SHUTTLE

If you read this and find yourself not really wanting to hike a whole lot, take the shuttle and enjoy the view. The shuttle is a wonderful way to explore the park at your leisure. Shuttles are abundant, so it's easy to get off at the various stops, take in the view, explore a bit and then catch the next shuttle. The shuttles are designed to offer clear views of the canyon. The shuttles can get crowded, especially on a summer morning when everyone is trying to head to his/her chosen trailhead while the air temperatures are cooler.

The magic of color at Zion

Zion Lodge

ZION LODGING

STAYING INSIDE THE PARK

ZION LODGE

1 Zion Canyon Scenic Dr, Springdale, UT 84767, (888) 297-2757, www.zionlodge.com/lodging/reservations

Zion Lodge was originally designed by Architect Stanley Gilbert Underwood in 1924 and carries much of the great Southwest character that went into many of his national park lodge designs. The original lodge burned down in 1966 and was rebuilt in 100 days with expedience in mind. In 1990 the lodge was renovated to return the grounds to the look and feel of Underwood's original designs. Today, despite the many visitors, Zion Lodge exudes a feeling of serenity and calm. The grounds are spacious and the interior is warm and inviting. The lodge is within walking distance of the Emerald Pools Trail, which is an excellent family friendly trail.

Zion Lodge offers twenty eight cabins with two double beds and twelve cabins with one queen bed. For most families, the cabin offers more privacy and containment than staying inside the hotel itself, thus they go quickly. All cabins have a private porch, full bath and a nice gas fireplace and scattered close to the lodge itself.

If double beds aren't cutting it, the lodge rooms may be a better option. Most of the rooms within the lodge have two queen-size beds and a television plus a full bath and private porch or balcony. The rooms are clean but as this lodge is well frequented, expect a little use. There are also second floor suites and accessible rooms available.

WATCHMAN CAMPGROUND

There are two campgrounds in Zion NP. Of the two, the Watchman Campground has the most amenities for RV travelers. What sets this campground apart is the ability to make reservations during the peak season. For many of the sites, electricity hookups are available.

If you are following the route spelled out in this book and you are a first time RVer, this will be your first (and one of the few) times that you will hook up your RV to an electrical outlet. More on that in a bit.

The Watchman Campground is located just ¼ mile (0.4 km) from the South Entrance. There are 162 sites, two that are wheel chair accessible and seven group sites. Of these, 95 have electrical outlets. The remainders are tent and walk-in sites. The group sites are tent only as well. Campsites can be reserved at the Watchman from March through December six months prior to your date of arrival. Go to www.recreation.gov or call 877-444-6777. Camping is seasonal at Watchman, so check the Zion National Park Service for the latest information.

Before going into the other features of Watchman, if this is your first time in an RV and this is your first campground, here are a few tips that may help. Reserve the Zion campground beforehand and make sure your campsite has electricity. If you can't find availability for the dates you are looking for, keep checking, and check often. People do cancel, but those sites go quickly. Also, be flexible. We stayed in a different campsite each night in Zion, which is a minor hassle since you have to move each day but far easier than leaving the campground entirely.

The reason you want to reserve your site and get electrical is simply because this is your first time behind the wheel of a large motor home. Reduce the stress by knowing a site will be there to meet you. Make sure it has electricity so that the gang is comfortable on their inaugural night in the RV. You can run the AC if you have electricity. Since you are not allowed to run generators in the campground, the AC will help take the edge off of a hot summer's day. This little secret will help make your first night a pleasant one and hold the RV experience in the warm light of creature comforts-meets-the outdoors that you were hoping for.

The third tip for first timers is to allow enough time to get to the park before dark. You will be backing in your RV into the campsite. Doing this in the daytime is much easier than doing it at night, especially if you've never done it before.

Some of the sites are shaded but will only accommodate motor homes that are a maximum of 13 feet (3.69m). Electric campsites in loops A and B run $30 per night. Tent sites in loops C, D, and E are $20 per night. The campground does have relatively clean flush toilet restrooms as well as a slop sink to do dishes in and water stations. Watchman is within walking distance to the visitor center and the shuttle.

SOUTH CAMPGROUND

South Campground has 127 campsites. All sites are first come, first served, and there are no electrical hookups. There are a good number of RV-friendly sites, though, and generators are allowed from 8:00 a.m. to 10:00 a.m. and from 6:00 p.m. to 8:00 p.m. Campsites here are a little less than at Watchman at $20 per night.

South Campground is otherwise the equal of Watchman with one exception, the walk in campsites. There are eight walk-in campgrounds that are situated along the banks of the Virgin River. For these, find your designated parking spot, hoof your gear a short distance down to the river and then bask in the glory that you have secured one of the best campsites in the park. Please note that some of these sites do have red ants. There is certainly some consternation in seeing your site's best tent location surrounded by foraging biting fiery red ants. The fact is, these little guys will bed down for the night back at their home far away from your tent and are typically not a problem. Still, if you have small children, these river side sites might not be your best option.

Lava Point Campground

This is a first come first serve primitive campground with just six sites. There is no water and no fee to stay at these sites. Getting to this campground is an 80 minute drive from the main section of Zion so check at the Visitor Center to see if they have any update on availability before making the drive. The campground's primitive exclusiveness is a plus for many and offers trailhead entry points that are less frequented. Vehicles over 19 feet are not allowed.

Lodging Near Zion

The town of Springdale is very close to Zion National Park and offers a lot to the traveler. **As with all of the lodging AND dining sections in this book, options are listed in order of proximity to the main entrance to the park, from closest to farthest. Also, most establishments vary hours by season. Please check locally for hours of operation. Lastly, menu item prices vary, the prices are a guideline only.**

Cable Mountain Lodge

147 Zion Park Blvd, Springdale, UT 84767, (435) 772-3366, cablemountainlodge.com

Cable Mountain Lodge's motto is "Steps to Zion" and as the closest accommodation to the park, this is a true statement. What's great about this hotel is that it doesn't hang on its laurels, the rooms, the lodge itself, the staff, the views, everything is done with a high level of service. They offer rooms, villas, and suites, filled with just about every amenity, including a full size fridge in the villas, and large HDTV's in every room. The villas sleep up to 10 people and can be one of the best options in Springdale if you have a large group.

Cliffrose Lodge & Gardens

281 Zion Park Blvd, Springdale, UT 84767, (800) 243-8824, cliffroselodge.com

One of the lucky hotels that are a stone's throw from Zion National Park, Cliffrose Lodge doesn't disappoint. The rooms are decorated in what could be described as contemporary southwest. The hotel itself is a little dated architecturally, but its proximity to Zion and the heart of Springdale can't be beat.

Flanigan's Inn

450 Zion Park Blvd, Springdale, UT 84767, (435) 772-3244, flanigans.com

Flanigan's Inn is so close to Zion, you can walk directly into the park from your room. This 3 star hotel offers one of the best options overall for Zion lodging. The inn has exceptional views, an outdoor pool, and The Spotted Dog Café. All rooms are comfortable, airy, and well appointed. A great choice.

West Temple and Altar of Sacrifice

Zion Canyon Bed and Breakfast

101 Kokopelli Cir, Springdale, UT 84767, (435) 772-9466, zioncanyonbnb.com

From the outside, Zion Canyon B&B gives an impression of entering into a sprawling but modern hacienda. The interior continues to delight the senses with southwest style reminiscent of old Mexico. This place is truly a delight to stay in. The rooms are spacious and well-appointed with easy access to the Virgin River to cool off. One can also opt to stay inside and play their pinball machines or simply enjoy the view from your patio.

Harvest House Bed and Breakfast

29 Canyon View Dr, Box 125, Springdale, UT 84767, (435) 772-3880, harvesthouse.net

Don't be put off by Harvest's House modern architecture. On the outside this B&B looks like a typical suburban home, but there is much warmth and hospitality once you cross the threshold. The rooms are spacious with private bathrooms and free Wi-Fi. The breakfasts are hearty and delicious.

Desert Pearl Inn

707 Zion Park Blvd, Springdale, UT 84767, (435) 772-8888, www.desertpearl.com/

Desert Pearl Inn is a 3.5 start hotel that offers a warm and modern atmosphere as a backdrop to your vacation. The hotel surrounds a large outdoor pool and cabana area. The rooms are spacious and each has a kitchenette, complete with dining table, desk and a sofa that converts to a bed. Each room also has a terrace with relaxing views complete with Adirondack chairs to sit in. It's a perfect place for families who are looking to treat themselves while on vacation.

Bumbleberry Inn

97 Bumbleberry Lane, Springdale, UT 84767, (800) 828-1534, bumbleberry.com

A 3 star hotel within a mile of Zion National Park. The Zion park shuttle system stops at the Inn, making this a convenient base camp. They offer Wi-Fi, air conditioning, fitness room and outdoor pool. The exterior is dated but this typically the best deal in town. Close to shops and restaurants.

Under The Eaves Inn

980 Zion Park Blvd, Box 29, Springdale, UT 84767, (435) 772-3457, www.undertheeaves.com

A very cute B&B on the main drag in Springdale, Utah. Every room is a little different, but overall the decorations are open and warm to the eye. This is a small cottage style house with well-manicured grounds and within walking distance of much of the southern portion of the town. There are no TV in the rooms and they offer vouchers for breakfast at local eateries.

Red Rock Inn Bed and Breakfast Cottages

998 Zion Park Blvd, Springdale, UT 84767, (435) 772-3139, redrockinn.com

Red Rock Inn is listed as a bed and breakfast, but it is unique. Sure, they serve an incredible breakfast, but it is delivered to your own little cottage. They offer four cottages and 2 suites. All offer a private entrance, patio, Wi-Fi, air conditioning, TV and DVD player. As expected the suites offer more room and a kitchenette for their newest suite. The Red Rock Inn is located in the southern end of Springdale.

Hampton Inn & Suites Springdale Zion National Park

1127 Zion Park Boulevard, Springdale, UT 84767, (435) 627-9191, hamptoninn3.hilton.com

A mid-range hotel with free breakfast, Wi-Fi and outdoor pool. Stopping point for the Zion park shuttle. Basic rooms but fairly up to date overall.

Holiday Inn Express Springdale

1215 Zion Park Blvd, Springdale, UT 84767, (435) 772-3200, ihg.com

3 star hotel with easy access to much of Springdale. Overall, modern and up to date accommodations inside and out with a large pool and free breakfast. The hotel is very nice and will likely meet or exceed expectations you might have for a mid-range hotel. Zion park shuttle stops right in front of the hotel.

Driftwood Lodge

1515 Zion Park Blvd, Springdale, UT 84767, (435) 772-3262, driftwoodlodge.net

Driftwood Lodge is a 2.5 star hotel offering many of the same views and comfort of higher end hotels, but at a lessor cost. The grounds offer expansive views into Zion Canyon, giving the feeling that it's just you and the park. The rooms are clean and fresh, yet a little basic. Overall though, this is a good value for a visit to Zion.

Majestic View Lodge

2400 Zion Park Boulevard, Springdale, UT 84767, (435) 772-0665, majesticviewlodge.com

Located "downstream" in the southern section of Springdale, Majestic View Lodge offers quaint rooms and its own restaurant, Arkansas Al's Steakhouse. While the restaurant can be hit or miss, the lodge itself does a better job of providing a good experience. The overall atmosphere is cozy with touches of the Great West.

ZION DINING

DINING INSIDE THE PARK

RED ROCK GRILL

AMERICAN, meals for under $30, At Zion Lodge, (435) 772-3213, http://www.zionlodge.com, open daily, 6:30am - 10:30am, 11:30am - 3pm, and 5pm - 10pm

The food is good, views are great. The ambiance is classy, yet accommodating to all. A solid choice if you are in the park and want a sit down meal. Open year round. Dinner reservations are advised

CASTLE DOME CAFE

AMERICAN, meals for under $10, At Zion Lodge, (435) 772-3213, http://www.zionlodge.com, open daily in season, 6:30am - 5pm

Castle Dome Cafe offers pizza, burgers and fries, and grilled sandwiches along with coffee, sodas, soft serve ice cream and beer. While the food is standard quality, the beers are distinctive and refreshing. They offer a selection of local microbrews which can be enjoyed outside on the patio with canyon views in every direction.

DINING NEAR ZION

THE SPOTTED DOG CAFE

AMERICAN, meals for under $30, 428 Zion Park Blvd, Springdale, UT 84767, (435) 772-0700, flanigans.com/dining, open daily, 7am - 11am, 5pm - 9pm, closed in winter

The Spotted Dog Café is located within Flanigan's Inn. The restaurant does breakfast and dinner service. This is a causal yet upscale farm to table bistro, offering locally sourced produce, sustainably harvested seafood and hormone-free meats. The cafe is a delight to the senses without being a sink hole for the pocket book. The wine puts the experience over the top, with one of the best selections in town. This doesn't go unnoticed either. Wine Spectator has given them an Award of Excellence for the last 7 years. In 2016, only 19 restaurants were honored with this award in Utah. This is a contender for the best restaurant in Springdale. Reservations are recommended.

WHIPTAIL GRILL

MEXICAN, meals for under $30, 445 Zion Park Blvd, Springdale, UT 84767, (435) 772-0283, www.whiptailgrillzion.com, open daily, 11:30am - 9:30pm

Small and with a fair amount of invented personality to cover up its low key location, don't let these first appearances fool you. Whiptail Grill offers a nice menu of mostly Fresh Mex fare. This is a great place for lunch if you just got off a hike and want to satisfy your hunger and settle into a lazy afternoon by the Virgin River.

9 EAST RESTAURANT

ITALIAN, meals for under $40, 709 Zion Park Blvd, Springdale, UT 84767, (435) 619-8200, open daily, 11am - 10:30pm

The first thing you notice about 9 East is its hip, modern and airy atmosphere. As you sit down you'll notice beautifully plated dishes and the occasional smoked duck pizza along with an artsy beet salad. This is a place where you can see the vanilla bean in the ice cream and taste the crème brûlée before your spoon digs into it. The full experience of 9 East is to order a lot of different small plates and share. If going this route isn't in the cards, try one of their pizzas, which are also amazing. Service can be on the slow side, even when there are few tables.

Waterfall at Emerald Pools

WILDCAT WILLIES

AMERICAN/STEAKHOUSE, meals for under $30, 897 Zion Park Blvd, Springdale, UT 84767, (435) 772-0115, wildcatwillies.com, open daily, 7am - 10pm

Wildcat Willies offers pastas, salads, burgers, pizzas, fish and chips, and of course, steaks and chops. This is that restaurant in your vacation where everyone got what they wanted and you all left full and satisfied.

OSCAR'S CAFÉ

MEXICAN, meals for under $30, 948 Zion Park Blvd, Springdale, UT 84767, (435) 772-3232, cafeoscars.com, open daily, 7am - 10pm

The location is prime real estate, which tends to drive the "something for everybody" menu, despite being touted as a Mexican restaurant. For the breakfast crowd, Oscar's offers a mix of the expected selection of breakfast burritos along with the great selection of omelets, pancakes and French toast. One nice feature their non-egg offerings. If you are looking for lunch or dinner, Oscar's lightly covers a handful of Mexican dishes, but more than 2/3 of their menu offers the standard array of sandwiches, salads, and burgers. So while not a true Mexican cuisine only restaurant, the place makes up for it with quick service and tasty food, making it one of the most popular food haunts in Springdale. Oscar's is vegan, gluten free, and vegetarian friendly.

MEME'S CAFE

AMERICAN, meals for under $30, 975 Zion Park Blvd, Springdale, UT 84767, (435) 772-0114, memescafezion.com, open daily, 7am -10pm

Located in downtown Springdale, MeMe's Café does a great job of quenching the desire to indulge in something a little bit naughty while on vacation. They serve up a nice assortment of comfort food dishes, such as slow roasted pork, grilled cheese and crepes. The ever changing menu is fresh and delightful, maintaining in that comfort food zone whether you are coming for breakfast, lunch or dinner. Service is friendly and quick in a relaxing atmosphere.

SWITCHBACK GRILLE STEAK AND FISH

STEAKS AND SEAFOOD, meals for under $60, 1149 Zion Park Blvd, Springdale, UT 84767, (435) 772-3700, switchbackgrille.com, open daily, 7am - 10pm

This is one of those restaurants where you get the menu and then can't decide what to have because EVERYTHING on it sounds really good. Whatever you choose, it's hard to go wrong. Choices of starters and salads, followed by steaks and sides, a robust seafood selection, special entrees and desserts. They have a decent wine selection and take reservations. Be sure to ask for a window table for best views. In the same complex is Jacks Sports Grille, which offers more casual fare of wings, burgers, brats and beer. Both places offer hearty breakfasts as well.

BIT & SPUR RESTAURANT & SALOON

TEX MEX, meals for under $30, 1212 Zion Park Blvd, Springdale, UT 84767, (435) 772-3498, bitandspur.com, open daily, 5pm - midnight

Tex-Mex style Mexican is typically heavier on the cheese and includes such dishes as the fajita, nachos and the always fun to pronounce chili con carne, (using a Texas accent of course). Bit & Spur does a fine job with the Tex-Mex name, aiming a little more towards the American side, which allows them to offer a unique variety of dishes. Notables include pollo relleno and carne asada, but they also offer glazed salmon and a solid rib eye. The restaurant has a great location, which is more of a warning during the dinner hour, as it is often busy. Their full bar allows one to find ways to fill the time while waiting for their table.

KING'S LANDING BISTRO

AMERICAN, meals for under $30, 1515 Zion Park Blvd, Springdale, UT 84767, (435) 772-7422, kingslandingbistro.com, open daily, 5pm - 10pm

Open exclusively for dinner, King's Landing provides a relaxed yet elegant atmosphere to set the mood with amazing views from the patio. Each dish, from the salads to the deserts, are well prepared and delightfully plated. The menu isn't terribly huge, which can be a downside if you don't see the dish you were craving. Overall, King's Landing is a nice place to relax with drinks and friends, with good food and great views.

PARK HOUSE CAFE

AMERICAN, meals for under $30, 1880 Zion Park Blvd, Springdale, UT 84737, (435) 772-0100, parkhousecafezion.com, open daily, 8am - 2pm

The Park House Café offers a healthy and fresh menu for breakfast, making it a good pit stop before hitting the trails. One of the best values for breakfast is The Standard, consisting of two eggs, home fries, and toast for 3 bucks. Lunch however, is where the place really shines, offering a great variety of American fare that is fresh and tasty. They offer a good selection of sandwiches as well as tacos, kabobs and even a buffalo burger. You can finish things off with a banana split or a root beer float.

ARKANSAS AL'S STEAKHOUSE

STEAKHOUSE, meals for under $60, 2400 Zion Park Blvd, Springdale, UT 84767, (435) 772-0665, majesticviewlodge.com, open daily, 8am - 8pm

There is definitely a correlation with menu prices and value. The higher the price, the higher the expectation. Unfortunately for Arkansas Al's Steakhouse, the quality is inconsistent. Sometimes it's really good, other times not so much. The food is on or slightly below par with other restaurants in the area, but with higher prices.

☕COFFEES AND SWEETS!☕

PERKS AT ZION

COFFEE, SMOOTHIES, 147 Zion Park Blvd, Springdale, UT 84767, (435) 772-0529, open daily, 7am - 6pm

The baristas here make espresso coffees worthy of praise or at least a decent tip. Quality beans, good micro foam, latte art, and super friendly service. Perks is within a short walking distance to Zion National Park.

CAFE SOLEIL

COFFEE, FULL MEALS, 205 Zion Park Blvd, Springdale, UT 84767, (435) 772-0505, cafesoleilzion-park.com, open daily, 6:30am - 9pm

Best place in town for espresso drinks which is why Cafe Soleil is in this section, but they also offer great food as well. Breakfast menu is fresh and varied with quick service. For lunch, they offer great paninis, sandwiches, salads, wraps and pizzas. They also offer a nice selection of fruit smoothies and milkshakes. Café Soleil does a great job of offering healthy fare with great atmosphere. They support local artists, whose work can be seen on the cafe's walls. This is a great spot to fill the belly after a long hike without feeling too weighed down afterwards.

HOODOOS GENERAL STORE & ICE CREAM PARLOR

ICE CREAM, 35 Lion Blvd, Springdale, UT 84767, (435) 772-3101, open daily, 8am - 10pm

The rich maple syrup aroma of Hoodoos is amazing. Large scoops of Blue Bunny ice cream housed nicely into homemade waffle cones. A straight shooter in the world of great ice cream shops.

SPRINGDALE CANDY COMPANY

ICE CREAM, CANDY STORE, 855A Zion Park Blvd, Springdale, UT 84767, (435) 772-0485, springdalecandycompany.com, open daily, 11am - 9:30pm, Wed from 3pm - 9:30

Time for something sweet? Springdale Candy Company will have what you are looking for, no matter what that might be. They offer chocolates, caramels, brittles, English toffee and peppermint bark along with a wide assortment of ice cream flavors and other fun treats. Huckleberry is their signature flavor.

ZION PARK GIFT & DELI

ICE CREAM, 866 Zion Park Blvd, Springdale, UT 84767, (435) 772-3843,

Ice cream, fudge, toffees, plus deli sandwiches on fresh home baked breads. This is a typical tourist oriented shop, but does a good job of delivering treats, souvenirs, and sandwiches.

DEEP CREEK COFFEE

COFFEE, 932 Zion Park Blvd, Springdale, UT 84767, (435) 767-0272, deepcreekcoffee.com, open daily, 6am - 3pm

Great little coffee shop and local haunt. They offer truly excellent espresso drinks, with rich flavor, fantastic micro foam and with a touch of latte art. The atmosphere is laid back and seemingly distanced from the usual tourist bustle. Deep Creek also offers some awesome breakfast and lunch items. One signature item is the "bro-ito", a gourmet breakfast burrito.

PARK HISTORY

FIRST INHABITANTS

While it is not known exactly when people began occupying North America, the most suggested time frame is around 11,000 years ago. These people, known as the Paleo-Indian, were primarily nomadic hunter-gatherers. Early on, they hunted woolly mammoths, camels, and armadillo-like creatures that were as large as cars and known as glyptodonts. While there is no evidence of the Paleo-Indian culture in Zion, they are important to note as the forebearers of those who were.

The Paleo-Indian culture would evolve and advance into what is referred to people from the Archaic period. There is evidence that people occupied Zion from about 7,000 to 2,500 years ago. These people were still fairly mobile hunter-gatherers, but some groups settled and developed an ability to harvest from their location. They gained knowledge of all plants in the area, they understood what worked as food, what worked as medicine and what caused bodily harm. They learned the habits of the animals they hunted and of those that could hunt them. They formed an understanding of the resources around them, what rocks worked well for cutting and what worked as aids in processing and harvesting. The people of the Archaic period were likely the first visitors to Zion.

Fast forward to about 2,000 years ago, the sophistication of the people took on elements of a complex culture and even political systems, similar to some degree to what modern people have today. This culture, referred to as the Anasazi, was now deeply rooted to the land. They had history that was tied to the land, and they developed their own languages and subcultures, but at the same time they shared their inventions and revelations through the process of trade. They learned how to farm the land, growing corn, squash and beans. Farming allowed for permanent structures to be built. They built homes, spiritual centers, and granaries.

Zion Lodge circa 1929

They were no longer limited to the possessions they could carry with them. This allowed not only for more utilitarian items such as pottery and basketry, but also for art and spiritual objects that had become a part of their everyday lives. They lived in a society with rules, customs, social classes and all the drama, love and heartache that we face in our own modern world. Don't let the fact that they didn't have smart phones fool you; these were a remarkably sophisticated people.

What is interesting to note is that Zion occupied the extreme west-northwestern boundaries of the Anasazi territory. Being on the edge cut them off from the major trade and cultural centers; however, the flip side was that this made the Anasazi of Zion a culturally unique group. Despite the lack of absence of large community structures and kivas, evidence of living structures, rock art, clothing, pottery, baskets and food granaries point to a smaller scale but significant society that inhabited the canyon.

At about 1200 CE, the Anasazi left the Four Corners region altogether. There are many theories as to why, but none can be irrefutably proven. The area was repopulated fairly soon after the Anasazi left by the Southern Paiutes. Like the Anasazi, the Paiutes were a highly sophisticated culture. The Paiutes were seminomadic, following the animals as they migrated with the changing seasons and resources. Winters were at lower elevations, summers at higher elevations where the pinyon pine nut was a plentiful and a staple part of their diet.

Even when European settlers began to expand west, the geographic isolation of Zion Canyon allowed the Paiutes to live in relative peace. In 1849, the Gold Rush and the theme of Manifest Destiny started an occupation explosion of the western territories. California became ground zero for this westward surge. The state grew from a population of 15,000 to 300,000 in just three years after gold was discovered. However, the "spaces between" the east and west were not immune to occupation. Settlers traveled perhaps with the goal of California in mind, only to find a lovely spot in which to settle down on the way. By the 1860s, about a dozen settlers found their way to Zion mainly under the leadership of Brigham Young.

The influx of settlers caused a near extinction of most Native Americans. The Paiutes were no exception. With little knowledge of the land, the settlers overgrazed, overhunted and brought a cloud of disease that together irrevocably changed the culture of the Paiutes. Some communities lost 75 percent of their population, and with such a blow came a retreat toward survival at the expense of old ways. Many who survived became ranch hands for the European settlers.

Pioneers

The modern history of Zion and all of Utah comprises two major historical events. One was the Gold Rush that created a general movement westward. The other, in Utah in particular, was the Church of Jesus Christ of Latter-day Saints, (LDS or Mormons for short). At the time of early migration, the territory of Utah was owned by Mexico. Between 1847 and 1890, some 70,000 pioneers made their way on foot or by wagon to Utah under the direction of their Mormon leader Brigham Young, creating settlements in what they called the Kingdom of Deseret, now known as Utah.

Mormon Nephi Johnson was the first pioneer to visit Zion Canyon in November 1858, using a Southern Paiute as a scout. Nephi settled farther down the Virgin River and with his settlement group founded the town of Virgin. Others came and built their own towns nearby, Rockville and Shunesberg around 1861 and Springdale in the fall of 1862. By 1864 there were 765 pioneers settled into the Upper Virgin Valley region.

The Crawford Ranch Near the Mouth of Zion

One of the new Mormon settlers, named Joseph Black, explored the upper reaches of Zion Canyon and returned with marvelous tales of its beauty. Joseph's words of the wondrous canyon caught the interest of Isaac Behunin, who built the first cabin in the canyon, near the present day Zion Lodge. He dug a ditch from the river allowing irrigation to several acres of land, growing various fruit trees, corn, vegetables and tobacco.

The tranquility of the canyon drew a few other settlers, among them the families of William Heap and John Rolf. Isaac Behunin and most of his neighbors had two cabins. They summered in Zion and move in winter to the lower elevations of Springdale. Isaac had originally been asked by church elders to help settle the town of Springdale and had worked with the church on helping establish other settlements. He is cited, though not proven, as the person who named the canyon Zion.

Park Poster circa 1938

He even compared the impressive LDS Church in Salt Lake City to Zion stating, "These are the Temples of God, built without the use of human hands. A man can worship God among these great cathedrals as well as in any man-made church. This is Zion."

While the first years of settlement in Zion were peaceful ones, this was about to change. Increasing numbers of settlers created tensions among the Paiutes and Navajo, which ultimately led to bloodshed. The pioneers fortified themselves within Springdale and then Virgin, creating armed parties as lookouts. Additionally, Zion Canyon itself produced its own discord. During the summer monsoons the Virgin River flooded, wiping out the pioneer's crops. Poor soils didn't help matters. Isaac Behunin left Zion in 1874 to help found the town of Orderville, where he died in 1881.

The Birth of a Park

Word spread about the scenic and often unworldly sites of southern Utah. Much of the west had been tamed enough to allow thoughts of tourism to become the next chapter in Zion's story. In 1909, President William Howard Taft gave the canyon itself National Monument protection under the name of Mukuntuweap National Monument. By 1918, Mukuntuweap was expanded from the canyon floor of 5,840 acres to 76,800 acres and renamed Zion National Monument through the executive order of President Wilson. The next year Congress upgraded Zion to a National Park, making it the first in Utah.

Still, access to Zion was rough going. A road had been built into the canyon, even a railroad up to Cedar City, but getting to Zion via an easterly route proved to be a tremendous challenge.

In 1927, the Zion-Mount Carmel Highway was started to create a reliable throughway. The road opened in 1930 and, as a result, park visitation increased. The most famous part of this highway is the Zion Tunnel, a 1.1-mile (1,711 m) testament to engineering. The tunnel features side openings, called galleries, that provide light and ventilation. The galleries were also used to make it easier to dump the rock generated through the construction of the tunnel.

In the early days, the galleries held parking spaces to tourists to get out and look at the neighboring monoliths. As car frame sizes increased over the decades, however, parking and even walking in the tunnel were halted due to safety concerns. Today, with the advent of RVs, the tunnel is now a managed resource. RVs must be checked out prior to being allowed in the tunnel and for the duration of the motor home's journey, the tunnel is open in only one direction.

In 1937, the Kolob Canyon area was declared Zion National Monument and sits adjacent to Zion National Park. It was then added to Zion National Park in 1956. Another addition was the Zion Lodge, which was originally designed by the famous architect Gilbert Stanley Underwood. Gilbert designed a vast number of "rustic style" yet grand park lodges, including the Ahwahnee at Yosemite, Old Faithful Lodge at those at Yellowstone, Zion, Bryce, Cedar Breaks and the North Rim of the Grand Canyon. While the original Zion Lodge Underwood designed burned down in 1966, it was restored to look much like the original during a remodel in 1990.

The Contribution of the CCC

The Great Depression had few silver linings, the Civilian Conservation Corps (CCC) being one of them. As part of President Franklin D. Roosevelt's New Deal, an unemployed unmarried man aged 18–25 could get a job. The jobs required unskilled manual labor and their purpose was that of conservation development of natural resources. In the nine years the CCC was incorporated, 3 million young men found work. They received shelter, food and clothes plus $30 a month in wages. A full $25 of that wage had to be sent home as part of their terms of employment.

The CCC was applauded by Americans at the time both in its contributions to the nation and to the employees themselves. For the nation, the CCC planted nearly 3 billion trees, helping reforest much of America. They helped in the construction of 800 parks nationally and in building remote public roadways and service buildings. With this focus came attention to conservation and overall awareness of our national and state park systems. The CCC employee left more physically fit with a strong sense of working as a team and was thus seen as a good candidate with future potential employers.

Some of the work done by the CCC in Zion has yet to be repeated. This was a period of engineering ingenuity combined with sheer audacity. Tunneling through solid rock, building trails up cliff faces, bolting in chains and carving steps directly into the rock were all signatures of the CCC era. They developed trails that delight the visitor and become part of the adventure as you walk them. When on a CCC-built trail, there is wonder not only in the surrounding nature but often in the creation of the trail itself.

At Zion, the CCC made additional improvements by removing invasive plants, creating campgrounds and building a measure of flood control along the Virgin River. It was all backbreaking work; however, from the journals of the workers, the time spent was one of joy rather than hardship.

The onset of World War II brought an end to the CCC, though it does make one wonder how much more they would have done on behalf of America's natural resource conservation if the program had continued to exist through the twenty-first century.

Modern Zion

By 1990 Zion National Park was reaching visitor capacity with each year receiving more than 2 million visitors. With the canyon roads congested with cars, the Park Service began a shuttle system in 2000. Today, the only way to visit the canyon floor past Zion Lodge is by shuttle. While the shuttle system may seem limiting, it is designed rather well. The shuttles are timely and offer the visitor the opportunity to slow down and take in the view. They do increase travel times significantly, especially if you are going deep within the canyon, say to the Narrows. However, the shuttle system offers something you came for in the first place—an opportunity to relax and slow down.

Today Zion receives more than 2.7 million visitors annually. While the shuttle has contained much of the congestion of years past, the struggle to offer up Zion as a national treasure for all to enjoy while preserving that treasure remains a challenge.

PARK GEOLOGY

The geology section presented here and in other sections is not meant to provide detailed descriptions of all the different geological periods and layers of rock. While the study of geology itself is a fascinating one, it is also one of great depth, filled with foreign terms, a fair amount of complexity and an equal amount of debate. There is no textbook geology here.

Instead, these sections attempt to capture more of the wonder of geology by explaining the geological story using everyday terms. For a deeper study into the geology of Zion or any of the parks listed in this book, strike up a conversation with your park ranger or even just check out the visitor center. The fact is, most of the parks in the Grand Circle owe their uniqueness to geology, so to that end, these sections tease out the most amazing and salient geological aspects of the park.

What's amazing about Zion's geology is the journey it took to get here. Starting some 300 million years ago, all of Utah and Wyoming were situated near the equator on the western edge of the then massive super continent called Pangaea. At this time the area of Zion was covered by a shallow body of water referred to as the Kaibab Sea.

At around 200 million years ago, the supercontinent began to break up and the area of Zion continued in its journey northward towards its present location. Seas came and retreated over long, mind-boggling stretches of time, depositing sediments and plant and animal life. Sometimes tropical, other times arid, the area within the Colorado Plateau continued to change, each time adding a slightly different context to the layers.

One of the most notable layers for Zion anyway is the Navajo Formation. They make up the sky-high Navajo red monoliths that tower above you. At one time, for about 10 million years, these monoliths were sand. An area seemingly as vast as the Sahara Desert, some 150,000 square miles (338,500 km2) of sand dunes occupied this area around 176 million years ago. For 10 million years, much of the Colorado Plateau was nothing but a sea of sand and the thickest deposits of this sand landed where Zion is today.

Trail up Angels Landing

How did all this sand become sandstone? Another sea covered the dunes about 150 million years ago. This sea flattened the dunes and slowly deposited more sediment on top of them. Through pressure, simple chemistry and a lot of time, the particles of sand cemented together to form sandstone. The red color is due simply to the presence of iron oxide, or rust. The deposit from this shallow sea became the cap of rock called the Temple Cap and Carmel Formations. The most significant example of this formation can be seen as the top of the Altar of Sacrifice, the monolithic cap that can be seen from a great distance as you climb up to the park's entrance.

The present chapter of Zion started 13 million years ago when tectonic forces uplifted the whole of the Colorado Plateau. What makes the Colorado Plateau so unusual is that it was primarily lifted straight up rather than at an angle. This has allowed water to carve out deep gorges into the layers of rock. As the land rose up, water carved down into the layers, the battle resulting in what you see today. Water, wind and the patience of nature are what carved out the current version of Zion that lies before you.

The Virgin River was at some points aided by the end of the glacial period of the Pleistocene Era. As the glaciers melted, water levels increased, carving into the layers at a faster pace. Most of what is seen today was not even visible 1 million years ago and the relatively recent slot canyons of The Narrows had not yet been formed.

It is hard to imagine such vast sand dunes, or Utah existing at the equator, or vast tropical oceans as the roots of Zion. It's even harder to imagine the amount of time involved that led up to the creation of this wonder. Even more amazing, the visual results that you see before you are relatively recent work. Perhaps harder still is to realize that even these monoliths are transient in nature, slowly eroding and evolving into something that may be completely different from what you see today. Think about if you could install a web cam that took a picture a day for a million years and then somehow could look at it in fast motion. While that sounds like an immense amount of time and amazing in its own right, it's a drop in the bucket for geology! The whole science really puts your life into perspective; we are viewers for such a short amount of time that it all looks like it is static and unchangeable. Pretty humbling this geology stuff.

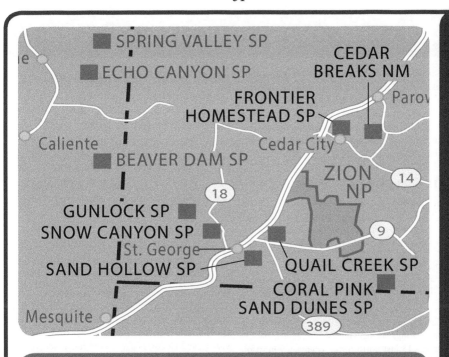

SPRING VALLEY SP

ECHO CANYON SP

CEDAR BREAKS NM

FRONTIER HOMESTEAD SP

Parow

Caliente

Cedar City

BEAVER DAM SP

ZION NP

14

18

GUNLOCK SP
SNOW CANYON SP

St. George

9

SAND HOLLOW SP

QUAIL CREEK SP

CORAL PINK SAND DUNES SP

Mesquite

389

Parks Near Zion

Cedar Breaks National Monument

QUAIL CREEK AND SAND HOLLOW STATE PARKS

Quail Creek and Sand Hollow State Parks offer camping, relaxation and water filled recreation for those traveling to and from Zion National Park. Both parks are located between St. George, UT and Zion NP on State Route 9. Quail Creek is a bit more on the mellow laid back side, whereas Sand Hollow is all about water filled fun in the middle of the desert.

QUAIL CREEK STATE PARK

Camping in Park:
- Quail Creek Campground: 22 T/RV, drinking water, restrooms, showers, no hookup, reservable at www.reserveamerica.com/

Getting There:
- From St George, UT: Take I-15 North to State Hwy 9 East. Total distance is 17 mi / 27 km to park

Quail Creek State Park manages a deep reservoir for camping, boating, fishing, and swimming. The park is off Interstate 15 just north of the Highway 9 junction to Zion. Peaceful sweeping views of red rocks with the Pine Valley Mountains in the distance. A good place to stop for the night if you are heading to Zion NP.

SAND HOLLOW STATE PARK

Camping in Park:
2 campgrounds in park, all sites reservable at http://utahstateparks.reserveamerica.com
- Westside Campground: 40 + 3 ADA T/RV, drinking water, showers, restrooms, hookups, some pull thru sites, dump station
- Sand Pit Campground: 29 T/RV, drinking water, showers, restrooms, hookups, some pull thru sites, dump station

Getting There:
- From St George, UT: Take I-15 North to State Hwy 9 East to Sand Hollow Road. Total distance is 18 mi / 29 km to park

Although Sand Hollow is very close to Quail Creek State Park and despite both being water themed recreational parks, Sand Hollow is very different. Whereas Quail Creek is peaceful and serene, with wandering vistas, Sand Hollow is playful and fun amidst red rock formations. There are sand dunes to dig your ATV into as well as slick rock to jump off into the waters below. Besides boating, fishing, and swimming, there are two campgrounds.

CORAL PINK SAND DUNES STATE PARK

Camping in Park:
- Coral Pink Sand Dunes Campground: 16 T/RV plus 1 group site, drinking water, showers, restrooms, no hookups, many pull thru sites, reservable at www.reserveamerica.com/

Getting There:
- From St George, UT: Take I-15 North to State Hwy 9 East/State St to UT-59 South to AZ-389 East to Co Hwy 237 to Co Rd 43. Note that final 4 miles is a dirt road. Typically, passable by 2WD and smaller RV's. Total distance is 62 mi / 100 km to park.
- From Page, AZ: Take US-89 West to Hancock Road to Coral Pink Sand Dunes Road. Note that final leg from Hancock Road to park is on an unpaved gravel road, suitable for all vehicles.

Coral Pink Sand Dunes After a Rain Shower

Parks Near Zion

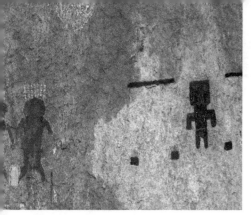

Pictographs at South Fork Indian Canyon

The first thing to note about this park is while the color is distinctly different from other sand dunes; it may not be the pink color you envisioned when you first pull up. The color is more of a sandstone red much of the time and requires the right soft and low but direct lighting to bring out the picture perfect coral color.

The elusive pink color aside, the park is a great stay over spot within the typical route of the Grand Circle. Here there are nice campgrounds, good restroom facilities and a playground of sand nearby. Perhaps the only downside if you aren't riding an ATV is all the ATV's in the dunes area. One definitely needs to be mindful of these high-speed vehicles in this multiuse area. That said, if you do have an ATV, the area allows exploration into canyons that are very much like Zion NP, but without all the people. For many locals, this is how they see Zion, by riding into the wilderness surrounding it.

There is one other minor but very cool feature of this park. It has an extensive collection of sand from all over the world. Each little jar is labeled with the sand's location. The collection, which takes up an entire wall in the visitor center, started as a ranger's hobby, but has grown considerably as tourists have sent in their local samples. It is quite possibly the largest collection of sand in the world and is worth checking out.

HIKING IN CORAL PINK SAND DUNES STATE PARK

CORAL PINK SAND DUNES ARCH

Easy – (0.2 mi / 0.3 km), round trip, allow 15 minutes elev. Δ: 50 ft / 15 m, trailhead on Hancock Road

This is by no means the grandest arch you will see, but is a welcome surprise for a park whose primary feature is a set of sand dunes. Getting to this arch is easy. At the turnoff from Hancock Road from Highway 89, mark your trip meter and drive 0.8 miles. Drive off the road on your right for about 150 yards, heading towards the sole obvious hoodoo. From here, get out and walk past this hoodoo using the ATV trail on the left and look for two rock outcroppings. Here you will find a small but definite arch.

CORAL PINK SAND DUNES

Easy – (1.0 mi / 1.6 km), round trip, allow 1 - 2 hours, elev. Δ: a00 ft / 30 m, trailhead at campground

The dunes are in easy sight as you pull up and the trailhead is easy enough to find, however it is recommended to keep along the established route so as not to disturb the fragile flora. Like all dunes, walking in sand can be more tiring than the same distance on hard ground. Also, hiking to the tallest dune, at a 300 feet elevation gain from its base, will add to the time. Look for insect and animal tracks, as well as areas of "plant art", where tall grasses have left their marks in the sand by the prevailing winds.

The one caution with the dunes is that the area is shared with ATV's. Keep an eye out for fast moving visitors. The ATV's can be a bit loud, but they are also fun to watch from the tall dunes.

SOUTH FORK INDIAN CANYON

Easy – (1.0 mi / 1.6 km), round trip, allow 30 minutes, elev. Δ: 150 ft / 46 m, trailhead at end of South Fork Indian Canyon Road off Sand Spring Road

This trail leads to some truly amazing pictographs. Formed around 1200 BCE, this rock art was created using natural pigments versus a petroglyph, which are formed by actually carving into the rock. The pictographs are quite rare and sit behind a protective fence. Bring a zoom lens if you want great pictures. This trail requires a 4WD vehicle that can handle the aptly named Sand Spring Road.

Take Sand Spring Road from Hancock for about a mile through the edge of the dunes and then a little less than two miles up South Fork Indian Canyon to the obvious parking lot for the pictographs. In many ways, this is the gem of the park and not the only one of its kind (See Hell Dive Canyon below)

HELL DIVE CANYON

Moderate – (6.6 mi / 10.6 km), round trip, allow 4 – 5 hours, elev. Δ: 580 ft / 177 m, trailhead on 4WD road west of Water Canyon

This is another set of pictographs that are farther to get to and not protected. Please do not touch these very fragile pieces of history. Any contact with them can do permanent harm. To get here, head to the South Fork Indian Canyon road on Sand Spring Road and upon reaching it, stay right for about 0.8 miles, continuing on Sand Spring Road. At a fork in the road, head left and continue another 0.75 miles stopping when the road gets too rough for vehicles.

After parking, continue hiking down this road. The road becomes more trail and winds down to the bottom of Water Canyon and then climbs up a ridge to another intersection. Turn left here and continue in a southerly direction. Don't fret, as the trail veers to the northeast for a couple of miles, just make sure you don't take any right turns and you'll end up at Hell Dive Canyon. Continue into the alcove, where the pictographs can be found. Again, please be respectful in this area and don't touch the art.

Camping in Park:
- Point Supreme Campground: 25 T/RV, drinking water, showers, restrooms, no hookups

Getting There:
- From St. George, UT: Take I-15 North to UT-14 East to UT-148. Total distance is 75 mi / 121 km to park entrance.

Cedar Breaks is a natural amphitheater, similar to what you would expect to see at Bryce Canyon, but with colors that are darker and richer. The tones are deeper and more subdued at Cedar Breaks, something akin to Bryce Canyon's older, but wiser, fun-sized brother.

At 6,150 acres, the park is easily covered. There are only a handful of trails but most folks just come to lean up against the overlook and gaze out at "the breaks". For those that do stay at the campground and hike around, the reward is an intimate experience in the park coupled with a satisfying feeling you were able to "see it all".

Hiking in Cedar Breaks National Monument

The one constant for all of these hikes is the altitude. The elevation here is 10,000 plus feet, which can cause shortness of breath and will make an easy hike feel more strenuous. Also, there is less sun protection at this altitude, so make sure you lather up with sunscreen, and wear a hat and sunglasses. This is high enough in the mountains where odd parts get burned, such as the tips of your ears or the top of one's head for the hair challenged. Be prepared and as always, bring plenty of water and some clothing layers.

Campground Trail

Easy – (1.0 mi / 1.6 km), round trip, allow 30 minutes

This is a partially ADA compliant one mile walk that provide views of the amphitheater. The trail starts at the campground and ends at the visitor center. A great walk for kids wanting to get their junior badge programs or just to stretch the legs. The trail is dog friendly, as long as there is a leash involved.

Spectra Point & Ramparts Overlook Trail

Moderate – (4.0 mi / 6.4 km), round trip, allow 2 hours

This is the best hike to take for views of the Cedar Breaks amphitheater. The hike to Spectra Point Overlook is just one mile, which gives a more face on view of the amphitheater. If you do continue on the second mile of this there and back hike, you'll be treated to upclose views of ancient bristlecone pines.

Alpine Pond Nature Trail

Easy – (2.0 mi / 3.2 km), round trip, allow 1 hour

This is a great double loop through the high alpine woodlands of the Dixie National Forest. There are great views of the Cedar Breaks amphitheater, but often, sprays of native wildflowers will do a good job of trying to steal the show. There is also a small strand of ancient bristlecone pines to be seen along the way. The trail passes by the small Alpine Pond and is picked up from Chessman Ridge Overlook. To cut the hiking time in half, simply do not take the upper loop.

Panoramic View of Cedar Breaks National Monument

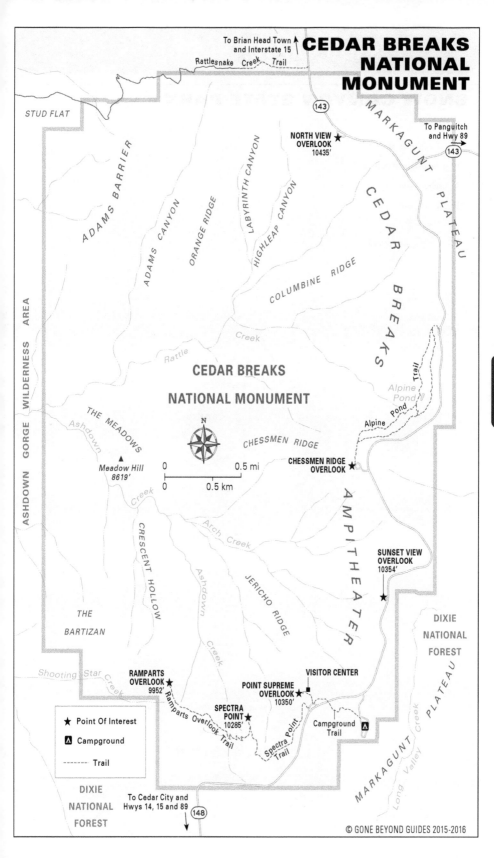

CEDAR BREAKS NATIONAL MONUMENT

To Brian Head Town and Interstate 15

Rattlesnake Creek Trail

143

To Panguitch and Hwy 89

143

MARKAGUNT PLATEAU

STUD FLAT

ADAMS BARRIER

ADAMS CANYON

ORANGE RIDGE

LABYRINTH CANYON

HIGHLEAP CANYON

COLUMBINE RIDGE

CEDAR BREAKS

NORTH VIEW OVERLOOK
10435'

ASHDOWN GORGE WILDERNESS AREA

Rattle Creek

CEDAR BREAKS

NATIONAL MONUMENT

Alpine Pond

Alpine Pond Trail

THE MEADOWS

Ashdown

Meadow Hill
8619'

N

0   0.5 mi

0   0.5 km

CHESSMEN RIDGE

CHESSMEN RIDGE OVERLOOK

AMPITHEATER

Creek

CRESCENT HOLLOW

Arch Creek

Ashdown

JERICHO RIDGE

SUNSET VIEW OVERLOOK
10354'

THE

BARTIZAN

Creek

DIXIE

NATIONAL

FOREST

Shooting Star Creek

RAMPARTS OVERLOOK
9952'

Ramparts Overlook Trail

SPECTRA POINT
10285'

POINT SUPREME OVERLOOK
10350'

VISITOR CENTER

Spectra Point Trail

Campground Trail

MARKAGUNT PLATEAU

Long Valley Creek

★ Point Of Interest

🅐 Campground

- - - Trail

DIXIE

NATIONAL

FOREST

To Cedar City and
Hwys 14, 15 and 89

148

© GONE BEYOND GUIDES 2015-2016

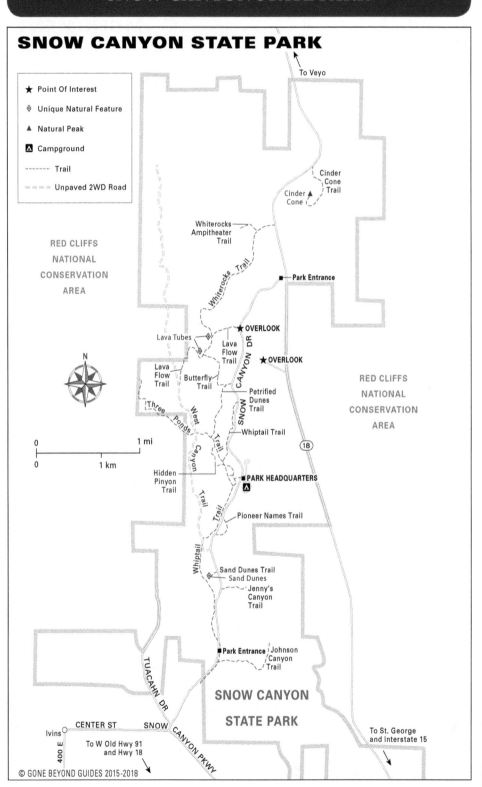

SNOW CANYON STATE PARK

Legend:
- ★ Point Of Interest
- ◇ Unique Natural Feature
- ▲ Natural Peak
- ⌂ Campground
- ------- Trail
- = = = Unpaved 2WD Road

To Veyo

Cinder Cone Trail

Cinder Cone ▲

Whiterocks Ampitheater Trail

Whiterocks Trail

RED CLIFFS NATIONAL CONSERVATION AREA

■ Park Entrance

Lava Tubes ◇

★ OVERLOOK

Lava Flow Trail

★ OVERLOOK

Lava Flow Trail

Butterfly Trail

Petrified Dunes Trail

RED CLIFFS NATIONAL CONSERVATION AREA

SNOW CANYON DR

West Canyon Trail

Three Ponds

Whiptail Trail

18

N

0   1 mi
0   1 km

Hidden Pinyon Trail

■ PARK HEADQUARTERS ⌂

Whiptail Trail

Pioneer Names Trail

Sand Dunes Trail
Sand Dunes ◇

Jenny's Canyon Trail

■ Park Entrance   Johnson Canyon Trail

SNOW CANYON

STATE PARK

TUACAHN DR

CENTER ST   SNOW CANYON PKWY

Ivins

400 E

To W Old Hwy 91 and Hwy 18

To St. George and Interstate 15

© GONE BEYOND GUIDES 2015-2018

Camping in Park:

- Snow Canyon Campground: 31 T/RV, drinking water, flush toilets, showers, hookups, dump station, some pull thru sites, call visitor center for reservations

Getting There:

- From St George, UT: Take UT-18 North to Snow Canyon Drive. Total distance is 13 mi / 21 km to park

Snow Canyon State Park has some amazing views, even as you pull up. From a distance, the broad panorama of red and white sandstone, with a hint of lava-capped adventure in the background, is simply breathtaking. One's eye can gaze merrily for hours, sweeping back and forth along the lines of white to red sandstone. It is a place of sandstone as art.

This natural display is only intensified as one draws in and onto the trail. There are sand dunes, hoodoos, fins, razor thin labyrinths, and canyons that beckon with their twists and turns to hike around just one more bend. The rock is bright with color and the possibilities for hiking seem endless. There are petroglyphs and other evidence of use prior to modern times as well.

Snow Canyon is a place of slickrock magic to be sure, but there is more to the park than just carved sandstone. There is also a section where lava has covered the land, creating a different exploration. Within this area are lava tubes, caves, and lava flows with some cool features to discover. In fact, the park's tallest feature is a cinder cone.

Snow Canyon offers camping and a lot of established trails. Given that it's close to St. George and Ivins, Utah makes this a great day hiking spot for travelers that don't want to camp.

HIKING SNOW CANYON STATE PARK

JOHNSON CANYON

Easy – (2.0 mi / 3.2 km), round trip, allow 1 hour

This trail is closed from March 15 to October 31 to protect nesting bird populations. When open, this is considered one of the top hikes in the park. Easy and level, the trail passes by a natural spring and ends at a monster thick arch spanning 200 feet.

WHIPTAIL TRAIL

Easy – (6.0 mi / 9.7 km), round trip, allow 3 hours

Whiptail is a paved there and back route popular with the locals. There are plenty of bikers, joggers, and walkers on this trail. The trail sits at the base of Snow Canyon's red (and white) rocks, giving a nice backdrop for all users. There is a small elevation gain but the trail is wheelchair accessible. This is a popular hike, especially on weekends.

PIONEER NAMES TRAIL

Easy – (0.5 mi / 0.8 km), round trip, allow 30 minutes

Pioneer Names Trail takes a somewhat sandy but otherwise ambling and quick path to a red rock alcove. Within it are the names of several Mormon pioneers from 1881. Getting to the alcove and up close to the pioneer graffiti requires a short but steep climb up slick rock at the end. The surroundings are a pleasing mix of red sandstone and the green of the desert pinyon juniper woodlands.

WEST CANYON TRAIL

Moderate – (8.0 mi / 12.9 km), round trip, allow 4 hours

This trail is an old dirt road that leads up into the main canyon in the park. The hike itself is level for the most part and offers great views into all of the side washes, sand stone hills, and cliff faces. This is a great place to go on an adventure, with plenty of slickrock to explore. The canyon is wide and inviting, traveling much of the time through grasslands. Stay on the trail whenever possible and avoid walking on undisturbed soil.

WHITEROCKS AMPHITHEATER

Moderate – (4.0 mi / 6.4 km), round trip, allow 2 hours

This is a straightforward trail into the main white sandstone area of Snow Canyon. The trail starts out in moderately deep sand, but quickly hits the slickrock for an ascent of about 100 feet. The trail officially ends at a bowl of white rock, surrounding the hiker in amphitheater fashion, on three sides. It is possible to continue on in scramble mode to the top for better views. Some parts require Class 3 level scrambling. At the top, the hiker is rewarded with some fantastic views of the park.

There is a shorter trail of about one mile in length located north of the junction of Snow Canyon Drive and SR18 (north of the junction 0.5 miles).

Snow Canyon

FRONTIER HOMESTEAD STATE PARK MUSEUM

Nearest Town with Amenities:

- The park is located in the town of Cedar City, UT

Getting There:

- From St George, UT: Take I-15 North. Total distance is 54 mi / 87 km to park

One of the best places to see Mormon pioneering history and artifacts, plus, some iron mining history, all in a clean mid-sized American town.

Frontier Homestead State Park Museum

Frontier Homestead State Park Museum is located on Main Street in the pleasant town of Cedar, Utah. Cedar is one of those towns that started out through a defined purpose, in this case mining for iron. When the primary reason to be there ran dry, enough people stuck around anyway and figured out how to keep the town thriving. Today, Cedar is one of the larger towns in Utah and home to Southern Utah University and the Utah Shakespeare Festival.

Within the clean and well-organized society of Cedar is a museum holding a healthy amount of Mormon pioneer artifacts. The museum doesn't just hold little stuff; this place is large enough to showcase stagecoaches and horse buggies as well as the expected assortment of pioneer and ancestral inhabitant artifacts. The museum also tells the story of iron mining in the area under the direction of Brigham Young. Occasionally, the park holds frontier days, where folks dress up in period costumes and take part in pioneer tasks such as washing clothes by hand and roping cattle.

GUNLOCK STATE PARK

The Picturesque Waterfalls at Gunlock State Park

Camping in Park:

- Gunlock Campground: 5 T/RV, no water, vault toilets, first come-first served

Getting There:

- From St George, UT: Take Old US Hwy 91 East. Total distance is 20 mi / 32 km to park

Gunlock is a small 266-acre park that protects a reservoir of the same name. The park is mainly a day use area for boating and fishing, though there is a campground for overnighters.

One of the nicest part of Gunlock Park is a beautiful set of waterfalls at the south end of the park. Referred to as the Gunlock Falls and Pools, this area of cascading waterfalls over angled and red slickrock is a favorite amongst locals.

The Triple H

Whenever it came to asking my friends to go on a hike with me, most went once. Getting them to go a second time was a tall order. You see, as a kid I sucked at baseball, football, basketball—pretty much any sport that involved a ball, but there was one thing at which I excelled. That one thing was hiking. My friends nicknamed me "Billy Goat Henze" and referred to the hikes I took them on as "Triple Hs," which stood for "Henze Hike from Hell." A typical scenario went like this and usually started several miles into a trail.

new ground to reach a destination or some grand view that would be worth whatever suffering we would have to endure in order to get there. I was delighted to be able to take my friend on this journey with me as we climbed a steep and long hill to some praiseworthy destination. My comrade, my wonderful buddy! We would surely become closer friends as a result, having shared this painful but highly rewarding journey together.

39

While I passionately forged ahead at a steady pace, my friend just glared at me, knowing that he was in the middle of a horrific trip that after near heatstroke and a possible sprained ankle would lead him to a rock. A big freaking rock. A rock you could easily Google and see from a hundred different angles. It wouldn't look any cooler in real life, despite the enthusiastic ramblings of the madman who was carrying the food and water and was the only person who knew how to get him back. He was forced to follow me. As he climbed up the hot dusty line I called a trail, he plotted my death, if only to keep his mind off the burning pain in his legs.

Back during the prime of the Triple Hs, only the hikes marked "strenuous" were worthy. On a trip to Zion National Park, there was one such hike, a hike that not only was strenuous, but also whose trail was forged into the sides of the cliff walls of Zion itself. The trail climbed from the shores of the Virgin River to the very top of the massive sandstone walls of the park. The last leg of the hike involved climbing the back of a knife edged ridge that went steeply down on either side. Chains were installed to hold onto. Footholds were cut into the rock.

"Hey, let's check out this trail!" I'd say.

"What trail? There is no trail where you are pointing."

"There's a deer track right there we can follow. See it?"

"Nope, I only see vast amounts of dense shrubbery."

I would divert off the main trail and take us on what was for me a wonderful bushwhacking adventure. I felt like a pioneer frontiersman, invigorated, forging

The trail was pure adventure and not for those who were afraid of heights. If you had it in you to make it to the top, your reward was a view from the heavens. You would be standing on a mesa that jutted out into the valley of Zion, right in the middle of the valley, offering a full 360-degree view of magnificent and unparalleled beauty. The spot was so breathtaking it was called Angels Landing, reserved only for Heaven's most virtuous and hallowed in spirit. Anyone who has been to the top of Angels Landing knows they were on sacred ground.

It was twenty years ago almost to the day that I did that hike. Back then I was hiking with a buddy from England who had just finished a 30-day stint of tramping in New Zealand. He was a great hiking companion. We challenged ourselves to a speed climb to see how fast we could ascend to the top of Angels Landing. We made good time—great time. Today I wanted to challenge myself to beat that record. Sure, I was 20 years older and mainly sat in front of a computer all day, but I still had the passion, the fire to outperform my younger self. I was wiser, more confident. The fact we pulled into Zion during a heat wave didn't deter me; it emboldened me. Bring it. The harder the better. My wife, of course, thought I was nuts, even more so than normal. Then there was Everest. He wanted to go with me.

"What do you mean, you want to come along"? I said to Ev.

"I don't know, you've been talking about this hike for so long. I think it would be fun."

How could I explain this to him? We had done our family hike to the Emerald Pools earlier that morning, which meant the only time left for Angels Landing was during the heat of the afternoon. It would be unbearably hot. For a lack of gloves, I brought socks to put over my hands for the chains. A ranger had warned me that they were getting too hot to touch with bare hands.

"But it's 106, son! It's going to be a grueling hot hike. Straight up pretty much. I don't know…"

"Dad, come on! I want to do a hike with you. I think I'm ready for a Triple H."

I wanted to say no because I knew what this meant, there would be no ascending Angels Landing today. Everest would poop out half way up, and like a stubborn burro would turn on me until I agreed to turn back. Plus, how long would it be before I made it back out to Zion? This was likely my last chance at ever climbing Angels Landing again.

My son stood his ground. "I'll carry my own water, Dad. Please, I'm bored here. I don't want to sit in the RV with Bryce all afternoon. Please!" I looked at my young boy and realized I couldn't say no.

On the ride up the canyon, Everest read me the following passage from the park brochure:

"Caution: The route to Angels Landing involves travel along a steep, narrow ridge with support chains anchored intermittently along the route. Footing can be slippery even when the rock is dry. Unevenly surfaced steps are cut into the rock with major cliff drop-offs adjacent. Keep off when it is wet, icy or thunderstorms are in the area. Plan to be off before dark. Younger children should skip this trail; older children must be closely supervised."

"Are you worried, son?"

"Nope! This should be fun. Hey, can I see your hat?" I warily handed him the hat that had been on every hike I had taken for the last 30 years. It was a Peruvian wool hat and while unconventional, kept me cool in the heat of the sun and warm on colder hikes.

He took it and smelled it. "Wow!" he said looking up at me. "It smells like adventure! Can I wear it?"

I shook my head and smiled. "Sorry, this hat's been with me around the world and over many years." I took it back and smelled it. It did smell like adventure.

As we pulled up to the Grotto shuttle stop for Angels Landing, I saw a couple lying on their backs on picnic tables. They looked completely spent in every way and didn't move an inch as the bus pulled up. We were the only two that got off the shuttle at the Angels Landing trailhead. It was 3 pm and now an oppressive 107 degrees. I was beginning to have doubts that this was a good idea.

One of the prone hikers moved his head a bit. "How was the hike?" I asked.

"Good… good." Long pause. "Intense," said the man.

The woman opened one eye and glared at me. Her fevered stare said everything. She had to see who the really stupid person was who was stupid enough to go on a stupid hike in the middle of a heat wave.

"Bring water," she mumbled.

We made good pace, my son and I, traveling along the banks of the Virgin River. It was hot; no doubt about it, but the tall walls of Zion provided good shade in the late afternoon. The smell of cool waters flowing in the near distance invigorated me. My son was keeping up and I was glad to have him with me.

As we left the river, the trail steepened a bit and went from dirt to pavement. I quickened my step, and Ev followed immediately behind me. Up ahead was the first real challenge, a series of long switchbacks that went straight up the canyon's cliff face. These switchbacks were carved into the rock face itself. They were built in 1926 as a symbol of both the conquest and harmony of man's interactions with nature. The solid sandstone has held firm in support of this effort for almost ninety years, bearing the weight of man's inconvenience to its natural face gracefully and without much fuss.

As we literally walked up the canyon's wall, a sense of throbbing came over me. I had been drinking enough water, but my head would not be appeased no matter how much I quaffed. The pulse of my blood came to a high volume within my temple, and the air seemed to get unnaturally thinner as we climbed upward. The heat felt like a repressive weight upon me. I put myself into four-wheel drive mode, which is slower but ever so steady. All thoughts were put to keeping one foot moving in front of the other one, a repetitious and controlled meter up the steep incline. I thought the pavement would make the hike a cakewalk and at first condemned it for not being a true dirt trail. I now blessed the trailblazers who built this damned thing for making the trail a little bit easier. They were wise. We were going straight up a cliff face and needed every bit of help we could get.

"Do you mind if I lead, Dad?" Everest said cheerfully. "It's amazing how quickly you obtain elevation, right? Look at that view!" I stopped my slumped over sad oxen posture and turned around. I noticed through my heavy breaths that Ev was barely out of breath at all.

"You all right, Dad?"

"Yeah, yeah. Let's keep going. You lead but don't get too far ahead of me. Keep me in sight."

The switchbacks were a seemingly relentless hell. The trail never stopped chasing me upwards, never getting nearer, never getting farther, grinning in the heat of that hot afternoon sun like some dingo chasing a kangaroo. My son, however, was glowing, smiling, almost springy in his step. I was losing him. He would soon find me collapsed from the heat. He would be forced to stuff me into a crevice in the rocks for safety while he went to get help.

We reached a reprieve, an upper canyon within the main Zion canyon. The air was cooler and even better, this portion of the trip was flat. We sat and gathered ourselves, drank water, ate a granola bar. The combined effect rejuvenated me, filled me with renewal. The majority of Angels Landing was the West Rim Trail. Only the final half mile was the steep pitch with chained handrails to the top. I was almost there, I thought, one more final pitch, less than a half a mile, easy peasy. We can do this.

Then we got to Walter's Wiggles. I'd forgotten about that part. Walter's Wiggles are best viewed by taking your head and looking straight up, where you'll see a steep series of switchbacks, each climbing as sharply as the next. There are 21 "wiggles" in all, and before you can make it to the final ascent of Angels Landing, you must pass through the Wiggles of Walter.

"Wow, Dad! Check these out! Isn't it amazing that they built this up the side of the rock face?"

I looked at Everest like a beaten donkey being asked to carry the load of another recently deceased donkey.

"Oh, shit," I mumbled. "I forgot about these."

"Did you just curse, Dad?"

"Yeah. Ah no, no, come on! Let's do this!" The flat part had invigorated me enough to lie a little. I really didn't want to do this at all. The heat, these steep switchbacks. Shit.

"Hey dad, you want to do a speed climb like you told me you did the last time? Come on. Let's see how fast we can get up this part!"

"No speed climbing, too hot. We don't want to get heat stroke." The kid was obviously nuts.

"Oh, yeah, okay dad. I can stay with you, that's fine." Ev sounded defeated. He kept up with my glacial rapidity for about two Wiggles before we mutually agreed it was best if he went ahead. Within thirty seconds, he was out of range of sight and sound.

Alone, my pace upwards slowed to that of an intravenous drip feed. I figured I would soon pass out prone and stiffened on the side of the trail, feet in the air like road kill. Somebody would tie a "Get Well Soon" balloon to my boot and give word to the rangers when they got back down, perhaps cover me with leaves. That sounded like a fine plan; at least then I wouldn't have to continue walking. I looked up. The top of those infernal switchbacks continued to look the same distance away. I was convinced they were building a new Wiggle for every one I completed. Somebody needed to stop this Walter guy.

I could see people below gaining on me and, out of delirious pride, I stopped and took pictures of the rocks as they passed. Of course they caught up to me in the least photographic section of the entire hike, but I stood there and clicked away as if these rocks were the most interesting things I had ever seen. "I could have easily beaten them," I thought. "Of course I wanted to take pictures of gravel."

At about Wiggle 16 Everest came running back down the hill.

"Dad! Oh my god! That was amazing! Can you give me the GoPro camera? I want to go back up."

"Go back up? Where? To the saddle?" I tried to not seem completely out of breath.

"No! I went to the top dad! The view was AMAZING! I love this! I told them I would run back down and get the GoPro."

"Them? Wait, what? How did you get to the top? I told you to stay at the saddle at the top of this…never-ending Wiggles thing. And who is 'them'?"

"Oh! I met a bunch of boys my age at the rest thingy. They belong to a club or something. We got to talking and we even waited around for you a bit and finally the scout leader asked if you would mind if he took me up."

"And you said yes…"

"Dad, he's taking the second group up in five minutes. Can I please take the camera and go with him? Please Dad!"

While I myself had given up hope of ever finding my second wind, my son stood in front of me with an overwhelming sense of boundless energy. He couldn't wait to run back up and join his new friends. I pursed my lips and said, "Son. Give me your hat."

"What?" Ev didn't understand.

"Just give me your hat, Everest."

Puzzled, he handed his baseball cap to me.

I removed my wool sombrero and put it on him. "Here, take it. It looks better on you anyway."

"Wow. Thanks, Dad!" He took the hat off, smelled it and then put it back on.

I cinched up the drawstring. "Don't lose it, okay?"

"No way! Thanks again, Dad. Can I have the GoPro too?"

"Oh yeah, sorry! Here, go. Take it. Do what the lead guy says and be careful. It's still dangerous up there".

"Sure! Will do, Dad." Ev started bolting back up the Wiggles as if they were level. One switchback up, he stopped and looked down at me.

"Hey, Dad! Thanks again for the hat!" he shouted.

I gave an ear-to-ear grin. "No problem son! You earned it."

"Oh and Dad, what did you say your time was that one time you did this?"

"70 minutes from the shuttle to the top." I shouted.

"Did it in 60."

"In this heat! That's just freakish."

"Sorry, Dad! See you at the top!"

At the top with my son, I never felt older or prouder. We were two people drenched in copious amounts of sweat, sitting on the top of one of the most transcendent and spectacular views in North America. We watched the slow migration of shadow against tremendous rock. We witnessed light play of a thousand hues, dance inside subtlety, delight and strike deep inside. As grimy as he was, I put my arm around my son. I had finally found a friend who got this as much as I did.

My son took a drink of water. "So. Freakish, huh?"

"Yeah, that's right. It's 107 degrees outside. You were practically levitating up the trail. And that smile, you are actually enjoying this heat!"

"You realize it's your DNA, right?"

I paused, then said, "True enough, I started insisting on DNA testing after little Fatima was born."

"The brother with the afro that came before me?"

"That's him."

"How is little Fatima these days?"

"I'm not sure. We lost contact with him after we sold him. He paid for this trip, though."

Everest looked at me and started laughing. He gave me a solid hug and then raised his water bottle to Zion Canyon. "To Fatima!" he shouted.

"To Fatima!" I exclaimed. "Wherever you are!"

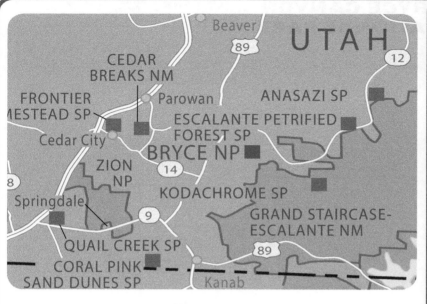

Quick Facts

Official Park Website: www.nps.gov/brca

Visitor Center: (435) 834-5322

Park Size: 35,835 acres

Established: 02/25/1928

Visitors: 1.4 million (2014)

Experience Level:

- Family Friendly to Experienced Hiker

Park Accessibility:

- Okay for 2WD and RVs
- Day and Overnight Use

Nearest Town with Amenities:

- Bryce, UT is 1.5 mi / 2.4 km from park

Getting There:

- From Zion NP South Entrance: Take UT-9 East, US-89 North and UT-12 East to UT-63 South, 84 mi / 135 km to park entrance

Bryce Canyon National Park

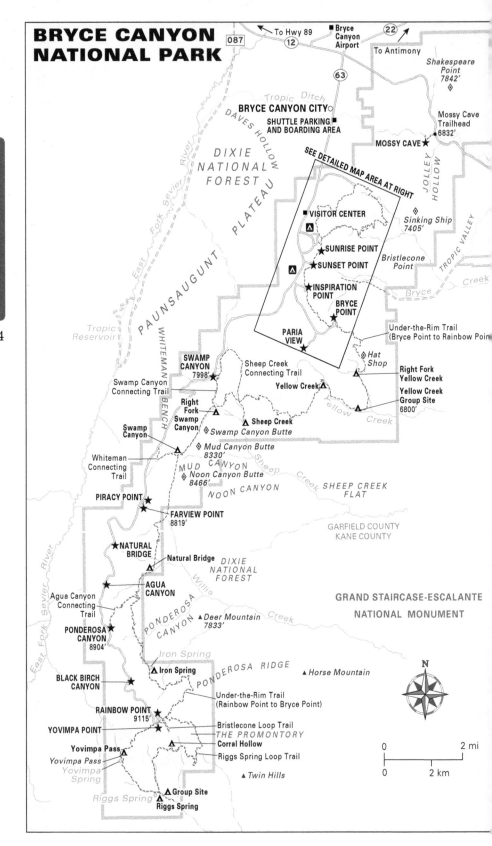

BRYCE CANYON NATIONAL PARK

To Hwy 89
Bryce Canyon Airport
087
12
22
To Antimony

63

Shakespeare Point 7842'

Tropic Ditch

BRYCE CANYON CITY
SHUTTLE PARKING AND BOARDING AREA

Mossy Cave Trailhead 6832'
MOSSY CAVE

DAVES HOLLOW

DIXIE NATIONAL FOREST

SEE DETAILED MAP AREA AT RIGHT

PLATEAU

VISITOR CENTER

SUNRISE POINT
SUNSET POINT

INSPIRATION POINT

BRYCE POINT

PARIA VIEW

Sinking Ship 7405'

Bristlecone Point

Bryce

Creek

TROPIC VALLEY

JOLLEY HOLLOW

East Fork Sevier River

PAUNSAUGUNT

Tropic Reservoir

Under-the-Rim Trail (Bryce Point to Rainbow Point)

SWAMP CANYON 7998'

Swamp Canyon Connecting Trail

Sheep Creek Connecting Trail

Yellow Creek

Hat Shop

Right Fork Yellow Creek
Yellow Creek Group Site 6800'

WHITEMAN BENCH

Right Fork Swamp Canyon

Swamp Canyon

Swamp Canyon Butte

Sheep Creek

Mud Canyon Butte 8330'

MUD CANYON

Noon Canyon Butte 8466'

NOON CANYON

Sheep Creek

Yellow Creek

SHEEP CREEK FLAT

Whiteman Connecting Trail

PIRACY POINT

FARVIEW POINT 8819'

GARFIELD COUNTY
KANE COUNTY

NATURAL BRIDGE

Natural Bridge

DIXIE NATIONAL FOREST

GRAND STAIRCASE-ESCALANTE

NATIONAL MONUMENT

Agua Canyon Connecting Trail

AGUA CANYON

PONDEROSA CANYON

Willis Creek

Deer Mountain 7833'

PONDEROSA CANYON 8904'

East Fork Sevier River

Iron Spring

Iron Spring

PONDEROSA RIDGE

Horse Mountain

N

BLACK BIRCH CANYON

Under-the-Rim Trail (Rainbow Point to Bryce Point)

RAINBOW POINT 9115'

YOVIMPA POINT

Bristlecone Loop Trail
THE PROMONTORY
Corral Hollow
Riggs Spring Loop Trail

Yovimpa Pass

Yovimpa Pass

Yovimpa Spring

Twin Hills

0   2 mi

0   2 km

Riggs Spring

Group Site

Riggs Spring

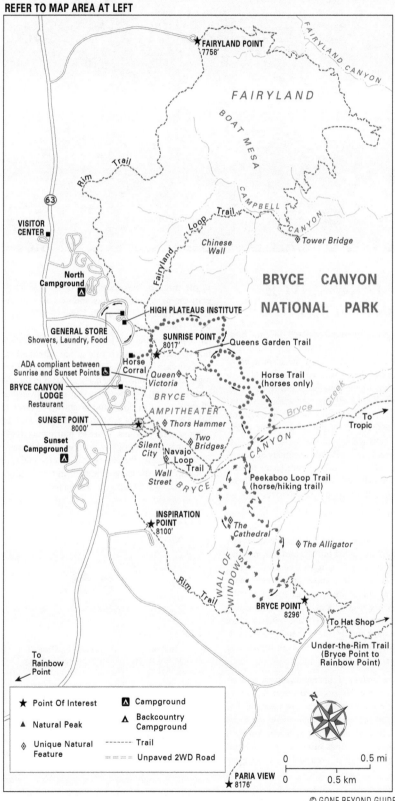

★ FAIRYLAND POINT
7758'

FAIRLAND CANYON

FAIRYLAND

BOAT MESA

Rim Trail

63

VISITOR
CENTER ■

CAMPBELL CANYON

Loop Trail

Chinese Wall

◇ *Tower Bridge*

North
Campground ⚑

GENERAL STORE
Showers, Laundry, Food

HIGH PLATEAUS INSTITUTE

SUNRISE POINT
8017'

Queens Garden Trail

ADA compliant between
Sunset and Sunset Points ♿

Horse
Corral

Horse Trail
(horses only)

*Queen ◇
Victoria*

BRYCE CANYON
LODGE
Restaurant

*BRYCE
AMPITHEATER*

◇ Thors Hammer

Bryce Creek

To
Tropic

SUNSET POINT
8000'

*Silent
City*

Two
◇ Bridges

Navajo
◇ Loop
Trail

Sunset
Campground ⚑

Wall
Street

BRYCE

CANYON

Peekaboo Loop Trail
(horse/hiking trail)

INSPIRATION
★ POINT
8100'

◇ *The
Cathedral*

◇ *The Alligator*

WALL OF WINDOWS

Rim Trail

BRYCE POINT
8296'

To Hat Shop

Under-the-Rim Trail
(Bryce Point to
Rainbow Point)

To
Rainbow
Point

Legend:
- ★ Point Of Interest
- ▲ Natural Peak
- ◇ Unique Natural Feature
- ⚑ Campground
- ⚑ Backcountry Campground
- ----- Trail
- ==== Unpaved 2WD Road

BRYCE CANYON NATIONAL PARK

0   0.5 mi
0   0.5 km

★ PARIA VIEW
8176'

© GONE BEYOND GUIDES 2015-2016

BRYCE CANYON

45

Bryce Canyon

WHAT MAKES BRYCE CANYON SPECIAL

Bryce Canyon is a wonderland of fluted rock and hoo-doo pinnacles, hoodoos being thin tall spires of rock common in this park. It has been the inspiration of movies, desert rides, desert-themed musicals and art to the point of being the template for Southwest scenery. It is grandness and color all wrapped within a succession of massive natural amphitheaters. Bryce Canyon holds the entire spectrum of the colors of the desert in one place. From the top of the mesa, the view is breathtaking, grand, and colorful in so many hundreds of tones that it defies description. Light seems to emit from the canyon walls rather than reflect off of them, radiating to a glow at the tips of each hoodoo.

Hiking down inside Bryce amphitheater is like going on an amusement park ride. All journeys wind steadily downward followed by a delightful tramp up and down knolls, through man-carved tunnels and past massive hoodoos that form fragile spires. Once down below, the canyon floor is more whimsy and wonder with pines growing as tall as the spires, each turn worthy of another amazing shot. Hiking or horseback riding within Bryce is simply a fun experience. When you are done, you are a short shuttle ride back to Bryce Canyon Lodge, where they serve hearty meals in an atmosphere fashioned after the mid-1920s.

The other special quality of this national park is its elevation. Bryce Canyon NP sits at 9000 feet (2743 meters). From the mesa tops, one can see clear out 150 miles (241 km) to the horizon, an amazing view and one of the farthest horizons visible in North America. The high elevation also brings snow in the winter and spring, capping the fruity-colored rocks with a sugary coating.

In the summer, Bryce Canyon NP is typically cooler than the neighboring parks and acts as a wonderful reprieve from the heat of the lower Utah deserts. The water tastes wonderful and is always cold. You can listen to pine needles sing in the wind, and while you may find yourself catching a breath due to the elevation, rest assured each one is delightfully crisp and clean. At night, the sky is one of the darkest places in the contiguous United States. The Milky Way is clearly visible and all the stars seem closer and brighter. For this reason, Bryce is a favorite of astronomers looking for a better glimpse of the heavens. Whether touring overlooks via the shuttle bus, hiking into the hoodoos themselves or stepping out into the vastness of a starry night, Bryce will help reset the traveler and affirm that the decision to tour the Grand Circle was a great one.

HIKING IN BRYCE CANYON

MOSSY CAVE

Easy – (0.8 mi / 1.3 km), round trip, allow 30 minutes, elev. Δ: 300 ft / 91 m, trailhead on Highway 12, 4 mi east of SR 63

A short hike that follows along a stream created by a man made diversion during the late 1800's by Mormon Pioneers. There are two spurs to this hike. The left spur ends at Mossy Cave, a large rocky overhang with a small waterfall that creates a nice mossy environment for plants. During the winter, look for icicle sheets created by the dripping waters, which are very cool and unusual. The right spur leads to a good-sized waterfall that also has been known to freeze completely during the winter.

RIM TRAIL

Easy – (0.9 mi / 1.5 km), one way, allow 1 hour, elev. Δ: 1,235 ft / 376 m, multiple trailheads along rim of Bryce Canyon

The Rim Trail from Sunrise Point to Sunset Point is flat and offers a leisurely way to take in the park. Pick up the trail from either point and follow the well-marked path. The Rim Trail does continue south from Sunset Point for a total of 5.5 miles (9.2km) one-way, but the trail from here has a lot of ups and downs and is considered strenuous.

FAIRYLAND LOOP

Strenuous – (8.0 mi /12.9 km), round trip, allow 5 hours, elev. Δ: 2,309 ft / 704 m, trailheads at Sunrise and Fairyland Points

Fairyland Loop is similar to Peekaboo but as it is a little longer, offers even more to the hiker. There is plenty to see on the trail, including China Wall, an impressively long wall of rock. You can also see a double arch with unique monolithic sentinels called Tower Bridge. Fairyland Loop is the least crowded trail of the popular trails at Bryce Canyon and is well worth it if you want to do a longer hike. Pick up the trail at Fairyland Point. The trail uses the Rim Trail to create a full loop.

TOWER BRIDGE

Moderate – (3.0 mi / 4.8 km), round trip, allow 2 – 3 hours, elev. Δ: 950 ft / 290 m, trailhead at Sunrise Point

See Fairyland Loop for additional details. The trail starts at Sunrise Point and follows Fairyland Loop partially down until a juncture to a short spur trail to view Tower Bridge. Tower Bridge is a formation of two colorful hoodoos connected by a fragile layer of rock mid-way down the "towers". There is another natural bridge that can be seen in the same view. Head back up the same way you came down or continue onwards on the longer Fairyland Loop.

QUEEN'S GARDEN TRAIL

Easy – (1.8 mi / 2.9 km), round trip, allow 2 hours, elev. Δ: 320 ft / 98 m, trailhead at Sunrise Point

Queen's Garden is 0.9 miles (1.4 km) down and the same distance back up. The trail is the least strenuous in terms of steepness compared to the other trails that head into the canyon, but it is by no means a flat trail.

Picking up the Queen's Garden trail from Sunrise Point, hike down and wind your way through tunnels to the hoodoo called Queen Victoria and the surrounding rock formations that make up her garden. You can follow the trail back to the top, though many folks opt to combine this trail with the Navajo Trail to create a loop.

PEEKABOO TRAIL

Strenuous – (5.5 mi / 8.8 km), round trip, allow 3 – 4 hours, elev. Δ: 1,555 ft / 473 m, trailhead at Bryce Point

Peekaboo is one of the best trails in Bryce Canyon. The loop is picked up from either Bryce Point or Sunset via the Navajo Trail. The trail gives the hiker a sense of remoteness and a personal experience as you walk up and down gullies and past goblins, fins and rows of hoodoos. Every bend rewards the hiker with a different view of often-unimaginable rock shapes. You will find yourself a ways from the rim, in the heart of the amphitheater, which gives a better sense of grandness of Bryce Canyon. The loop can be done on its own or combined with Navajo or Queen's Garden Trails. Peekaboo is not terribly crowded, though it does get a fair amount of horse traffic.

HAT SHOP TRAIL

Moderate – (4.0 mi /6.4 km), round trip, allow 2 - 3 hours, elev. Δ: 1,436 ft / 438 m, trailhead at Bryce Point

From the trailhead, descend via the Under the Rim Trail for 2 miles to a set of thin spired hoodoos with delicately balanced capstones defying gravity. The hike is a down and up, there and back hike. There are ample other Bryce Canyon type features along the way to the final destination.

SWAMP CANYON

Moderate – (4.3 mi / 7.2 km), round trip, allow 2 - 3 hours, elev. Δ: 800 ft / 244 m, trailhead at Swamp Canyon Overlook

Swamp Canyon Trail starts at about the mid-point in the park, further south of the main amphitheaters. This loop trail offers a mixture of denser forest and the famous hoodoos. Unlike the endless stream of hikers coming down Navajo Trail, Swamp Canyon is definitely more intimate and may be a better option on crowded days.

Panorama of Bryce Canyon

Wall Street Section of Navajo Trail

BRISTLECONE LOOP

Easy – (1.0 mi / 1.6 km), round trip, allow 30 minutes, elev. Δ: 195 ft / 59 m, trailhead at Rainbow Point, southern end of park

While most of the attention in Bryce is near the entrance of the park, the southern section of the park receives lets attention. Here the area contains more of a pleasant evergreen forest offering. Bristlecone Loop is a short hike in the southern section, displaying expansive views from 9,100 feet across a forested and green part of the state. As the trail name suggests, there are examples of the bristlecone pine, a gnarled and aged tree that can grow to 1,800 years here. The hike is pleasant and as the highest trail in the park, can be a little breathtaking for many reasons.

RIGGS SPRING LOOP

Strenuous – (8.5 mi / 13.7 km), round trip, allow 4 – 5 hours, elev. Δ: 2,248 ft / 685 m, trailhead at Yovimpa Point

A very different side of Bryce, Riggs Spring is an ambling pleasant hike through fir, spruce, quaking aspens, and even ancient bristlecone pines. The hike is the southernmost trail in the park. As the trail's title suggests, there is a little spring in a shady setting. Do treat the water before using. This is a popular trail for overnight campers.

BRYCE LODGING

STAYING INSIDE THE PARK

LODGE AT BRYCE CANYON

Bryce Canyon National Park, Bryce, UT 84764, (435) 834-8700, www.brycecanyonforever.com

The Bryce Canyon Lodge is the only original lodge designed by Architect Stanley Gilbert Underwood that remains standing within the Grand Circle. To be fair, many of the lodges have been rebuilt with Underwood's design and intentions in mind. That said, Bryce Canyon Lodge is an original. Located inside the park, the Bryce Canyon Lodge is everything you would imagine it to be. It is filled with character and nearly 100 years of history. Simple yet artistic, non-demanding yet graceful, a great example of the Arts and Craft period of architecture done only as Underwood could have done it.

The lodge contains rooms, suites and cabins, 114 in all. The cabins are one of the better bets for a family, containing two queen beds and a little more privacy. The cabins come with a full bath and semi-private porch plus a heater. Many of the lodge rooms come with two queen beds plus have a refrigerator, the one thing the cabins do not have. None of the rooms have a TV or air-conditioning. Both the cabins and the rooms fill up pretty quickly, so definitely plan ahead to get a reservation. The other thing to note is the lodge is not open year round, closing in winter and reopening in early spring.

NORTH CAMPGROUND

North Campground is right inside the entrance to the park (as well as its exit, there is only one-way in and out of Bryce Canyon NP). It sits across from the visitor center and is within walking distance of both the center and the shuttle. There are 99 sites, 52 of which are designated for RVs, found in Loops A and B. Of these, 13 sites can be reserved during the summer months in Loop A, but they go very quickly, so count yourself either lucky or a very good planner if you get one.

Bryce Canyon Lodge

Bryce Point in Winter

To reserve, call (877) 444-6777 or click www.recreation.gov. All sites for both campgrounds are $30 for RV's and $20 for tents.

There is a central dump station but it isn't always open, especially early in the season and in the winter. There is also potable water available and a slop sink near the flush toilets. Beyond that, there are no hookups for water or electricity, though each site does come with a picnic table and fire ring.

The sites are all within a tidy, fresh smelling pine forest. Nearby is a walking trail to the visitor center. The campgrounds are not guaranteed to be open during the winter months due to snow. Laundry and showers can be had at nearby Ruby's Inn.

SUNSET CAMPGROUND

Like North Campground, the campsites at Sunset Campground are nestled among the pines and are fairly well laid out. Sunset is about 1.5 miles (2.41 km) farther down from the visitor center and is closer to some of the more popular hiking trails. There are 100 sites total, 48 of them designed for RVs, all in Loop A. While there are 20 tent sites that can be reserved, all RV sites at this campground are first come first served. Sunset Campground is at a similar elevation as North and may be closed due to snow. A dump station is available during the summer months for a $5 use fee.

If you are wondering which campground is better, they both have tradeoffs. Sunset is closer to the general store, laundry and showers as well as closer to the canyon itself and all of its trails. North is probably slightly better suited for families with small children who like to take in a deeper exploration of the visitor center and gift shop. That said, these are small tradeoffs.

LODGING NEAR BRYCE CANYON

There are two towns near Bryce Canyon National Park. The first is aptly named Bryce, Utah and sits close to the park's entrance. This town gets a lot of the visitor traffic and as a result can take on a touristy feel during peak season. The other option is Tropic, Utah. Tropic is just east of the park and looks up into Bryce Canyon proper. It is about 11 miles from the park's entrance but presents a smaller and less traveled option for visitors.

All lodging and food destinations are listed in order of distance to Bryce Canyon National Park, starting with those closest to the entrance.

BEST WESTERN PLUS RUBY'S INN

26 South Main Street, Bryce Canyon City, UT 84764-8002, (435) 834-5341, rubysinn.com

Ruby's Best Western is pretty basic, but otherwise fits the bill for cleanliness and good value. What really makes Ruby's stand out are the folks that run it. The staff are super friendly and have done a great job at making this a fun place to stay, especially for families. Small rooms come with two queen beds with larger suites also available. There are small touches that fill out the experience, such as cribs, rollaway beds and adjoining rooms. Ruby's is a great hotel.

If you are looking for more of an upscale approach to RVing and need full hookups, Ruby's is your best bet. It is so close to Bryce Canyon NP that the shuttle stops there as part of its regular route. Ruby's does a great job of being able to accommodate just about any need, including larger RVs and folks who are looking for optional hookups (water, electrical and wastewater). Nearby is a fairly decent selection of restaurants, including a steak house and a pizza place. Hot showers, laundry, cable, a heated swimming pool and clean restrooms round out the offering.

Ruby's also has cabins, an inn and even a set of teepees for the adventurous at heart. While you may think this could be a full-blown cheesy tourist trap, Ruby's staff really does a fantastic job of creating a fun experience. For many, it is a highlight of their trip within the Grand Circle.

BEST WESTERN PLUS BRYCE CANYON GRAND HOTEL

30 N 100 E, Bryce Canyon, UT 84764, (435) 834-5700, brycecanyongrand.com

The Best Western Grand Hotel is arguably the overall best bet in the area. It's tucked off the main drag, yet close to Bryce Canyon National Park. The grand room is very spacious and welcoming. Their pool is large and architecturally pleasing and the rooms are clean and comfy. The hotel went through a robust renovation in 2016 and the rate includes a free breakfast. Definitely look here first. As you will see in the other reviews, decent lodging in Bryce can be a challenge.

50

BRYCE VIEW LODGE

105 Center St, Bryce Canyon, UT 84764, (888) 279-2304, bryceviewlodge.com

The overall bar for hotel quality is low in Bryce, Utah. Unfortunately, the advantage of proximity is used as an excuse for offering a lessor experience. Within the grouping of accommodations in this area, Bryce View Lodge hits the median on quality and does an adequate job of meeting the needs hotels are supposed to offer. The rooms are decent, though the fixtures are outdated. Overall, the service is on par with expectations.

BRYCE CANYON RESORT

13500 E Hwy 12, Bryce, UT 84764, (435) 834-5351, brycecanyonresort.com

Bryce Canyon Resort is no resort. Each room is more analogous to an old and beaten pack mule, bearing the load of guest after guest through the decades. The rooms are musty and worn, yet still command a hefty price, all because this hotel is near Bryce Canyon National Park. Keep looking if you are trying to find a resort or even a clean room.

FOSTER'S MOTEL

1150 UT-12, Bryce, UT 84764, (435) 834-5227, fostersmotel.com

A relatively budget friendly place to sleep. Not a first choice for most folks but can be the right option for some.

BRYCE CANYON PINES

Highway 12, Mile post 10, Bryce, UT 84764, (435) 503-9521, www.brycecanyonmotel.com

One of the breaths of fresh air in the circle of Bryce Canyon accommodations. This 2 star budget hotel offers clean rooms and comfy beds and is 12 minutes from the park's visitor center. The other nice feature of this hotel is that it is outside the craziness of the main part of town and closer to some of the better dining options in the area (see restaurants).

AMERICAS BEST VALUE INN & SUITES-BRYCE VALLEY

181 North Main Street, Tropic, UT 84776, (435) 679-8811, vantagehotels.com

Americas Best Value Inn and Suites is a 2 star hotel about 16 minutes from Bryce Canyon National Park. Clean rooms, free breakfast.

BRYCE PIONEER VILLAGE

80 South Main Hwy 12, Tropic, UT 84776, (435) 679-8546, brycepioneervillage.com

Located about 16 minutes from Bryce Canyon National Park, the Pioneer Village is more of a roadside attraction than a place to stay, though lodging is offered. This hotel will do if you are looking for a budget friendly place, but overall expect too few employees and lack of pride in the services provided.

STONE CANYON INN

1380 W. Stone Canyon Lane, Tropic, UT 84776, (866) 489-4680, stonecanyoninn.com

Stone Canyon Inn offers comfortable cabins in the town of Tropic, about 20 minutes away from Bryce Canyon NP. Private bungalows and cabins are available, each built in 2000 and 2014 on an 80 acre lot. The inn houses the well received Stone Hearth Grille and is overall a pleasant and relaxing choice for those visiting Bryce Canyon.

Bryce Canyon in early spring

BRYCE DINING

DINING INSIDE THE PARK

LODGE AT BRYCE CANYON RESTAURANT

AMERICAN, meals for under $30, At the Lodge in Bryce Canyon National Park, (435) 834-8700, www.brycecanyonforever.com/dining, open daily, 7am - 10am, 11:30am - 3pm, and 5pm - 10pm

This place is truly one of the reasons you come to Bryce Canyon National Park and it is recommended that you eat here at least once. Dining here is truly like stepping back through time to the early 1920's when the lodge and restaurant where built. They offer a full breakfast, lunch, and dinner menu, all of which are robust in both choice and flavor. The staff is attentive and offers a consistently high quality. It is a fun and satisfying place to eat, knowing that just by sitting in its grand dining hall, you are a part of history.

VALHALLA PIZZERIA AND COFFEE SHOP

PIZZA, COFFEE, meals for under $30, Hwy 63, Bryce Canyon, UT 84764, (435) 834-8709, open daily, 6am - 10pm

For breakfast, Valhalla's offers espresso drinks and baked goods. The place is more known for its pizzas for the lunch and dinner crowds. The pizzas, calzones and subs are worth coming in for.

DINING NEAR BRYCE CANYON

RUBY'S INN RESTAURANT

AMERICAN/BUFFET, meals for under $30, 26 S Main St, Bryce Canyon City, UT 84764, (866) 866-6616, rubysinn.com, open daily, 6:30am - 9:30pm

Full menu and buffet serving breakfast, lunch and dinners. Ruby's gets a lot of traffic, being one of the few places to eat in Bryce Canyon and the most famous. Expect wait times that can extend to over an hour, so get there early. The staff are friendly though may be slammed. The food itself is best if you stay away from the buffet and instead order off the menu.

EBENEZER'S BARN & GRILL

AMERICAN DINNER THEATER, meals for under $40, 110 E Center St, Bryce Canyon City, UT 84764, (435) 834-5341, ebenezersbarnandgrill.com, open April - October, doors open at 7pm, music starts at 8:30pm

Located across from and owned by the Ruby's Inn folks, Ebenezer's offers live music and dinner theater combined with American style menu items. The food is not worth writing home about but the live entertainment makes for a nice diversion from sitting in your hotel room, RV, or tent. The whole thing is a bit touristy, but is good fun. They seat you family style so you may get a chance to meet folks from other countries or areas in the US.

Canyon Diner

AMERICAN, meals for under $10 25 N Main St, Bryce Canyon, UT 84764, (435) 834-8030, rubysinn. com, 11:30am - 8pm

Canyon Diner is part of Ruby's Inn which has been the center point of Bryce Canyon's lodging and dining for as long as Bryce Canyon has been a park. Go here if you are looking for fast and cheap food. This is a no frills venue and the food is not much different than that served at amusement parks, so set expectations accordingly.

Cowboy Ranch House

AMERICAN, meals for under $20, 13700 E State Hwy 12, Bryce, UT 84764, (435) 834-5100, brycecanyonresort.com, open daily, 7 - 9:30am, 5 - 11pm

The Cowboy Ranch House is part of the Bryce Canyon Resort, with "just okay" food and hit or miss service. You will get fed and leave full, but unfortunately, this place isn't a bright spot for the area's dining options.

Foster's Family Steak House

STEAKHOUSE/AMERICAN, meals for under $30, 1152 Hwy 12, Bryce, UT 84764, (435) 834-5227, fostersmotel.com, open daily, 7am - 10pm

Foster's is a notch above the other offerings and is just 3.5 miles outside the main strip of town. Breakfasts are delightful and filling, the steaks are in line with expectations and the service is friendly. Prime rib cuts are huge, and their trout and fried chicken are also awesome.

Bryce Canyon Pines

Restaurant

AMERICAN, meals for under $30, Hwy 12 Mile Marker 10, Bryce, UT 84764, (435) 834-5441, brycecanyonrestaurant.com, open daily, 7am - 9pm

Most people drive by this place on their way into Bryce Canyon from Zion. Many wonder if they should eat there. Then they drive the final five miles and somehow get sucked into the offerings within the main town of Bryce. This is unfortunate because Bryce Canyon Pines Restaurant is a great place to eat. Quaint cowboy themed decor and a robust set of menu choices. Open for breakfast, lunch and dinner.

Rustlers Restaurant

AMERICAN, meals for under $20, 141 N Main St, Tropic, UT 84776, (435) 679-8383, brycevalleyinn. com, open daily, 7am - 10pm

Rustlers is a rustic and warm diner that offers a wide variety of breakfast, lunch and dinner options. If you have been wanting a nice place to eat that isn't too touristy, this is a good bet. They are family owned and operated by nice folks.

Douglas firs within the hoodoos

Pizza Place

PIZZA, meals for under $20, 21 N Main St, Tropic, UT 84776, (435) 679-8888, www.brycecanyon. com/bryce-canyon-pizza, open daily, 4pm - 8:30pm

Though this is a bit out of the way in the town of Tropic, if you are in the mood for pizza, this is the best bet in the area. They do a good job on both the food and the service.

Stone Hearth Grille

AMERICAN/STEAKHOUSE, meals for under $60, 1380 W Stone Canyon Ln, Tropic, UT 84776, (435) 679-8923, stonehearthgrille.com, open seasonally March - Oct, Daily 5pm - 10pm

Stone Hearth Grille is located about 20 minutes from the Bryce Canyon Visitor Center. It is by far the best fine dining experience in the vicinity of the park. They have their seafood flown in daily and serve locally grown beef. While they are known for their steaks, all of the dishes are consistently excellent. Beyond the food, what also makes this restaurant stand out are its views looking up into Bryce Canyon. This is a great all around fine dining experience.

☕ Coffees and Sweets! ☕

Bryce Canyon Coffee Co

COFFEE, 21 N Main St Hwy 12, Tropic, UT 84776. (435) 616-2693, brycecanyoncoffeeco.com, open daily, 8am - 7pm

Drip and espresso coffee, teas, and smoothies in a natural atmosphere reminiscent of a knotty pine lodge. They also offer a selection of pastries, bagels, and other snacks.

BRYCE CANYON HISTORY

EARLY INHABITANTS

There is a fair amount of evidence to suggest that the Ancestral Puebloan Indians hunted in Bryce Canyon and lived in the nearby vicinity 2000 years ago. The Fremont Indians and then the Paiute Indians were the next sets of inhabitants.

The Paiutes tell of the real reason for the existence of Bryce Canyon. There was an ancient people known as the To-when-an-ung-wa. They were a greedy selfish lot who did not care about sharing their environment. They ate all the food and drank all the water, leaving little for the animals that lived with them. The animals took their complaints to Coyote, who is a powerful trickster god. They explained the rude behavior of the To-when-an-ung-wa, and Coyote agreed he would do something about it.

Coyote invited the entire tribe of the To-when-an-ung-wa to a huge feast, a feast that had all manner of food and drink and lasted all day. The To-when-an-ung-wa were very excited for such a feast and came to the location Coyote specified. They dressed in their best outfits and painted their faces and bodies with the colorful red, orange and yellow war paints for the occasion. Before they could take one bite, however, Coyote cast a spell on each of them, turning them to rock. The people of the To-when-an-ung-wa can be seen climbing on top of each other to get to the top of the plateau.

Some of the Paiutes could identify the past personages of the hoodoos they saw and named off many of them to Wesley Powell when he came through the area. They felt the place was haunted and indeed, even the current definition of hoodoo means both a rock formation and a spell cast on others. Perhaps the cracking of the rocks at night are the sounds of the To-when-an-ung-wa trying in desperation to free themselves from the spell that binds them to the edge of the Paunsaugunt Plateau.

Bryce Cabin circa 1881

MORMON LIFE AND PARK CREATION

Bryce Canyon was not a preferred spot for Mormon settlement and was left alone during the initial years. By 1875, Ebenezer Bryce saw the area both as land suitable for raising cattle and as a climate more suitable for his wife's fragile health. He moved down from Salt Lake City with a handful of other families to form a life in the valley near the current town of Cannonville, Utah. He built a seven-mile (11.2 km) irrigation ditch from the Paria River to provide water for his livestock and crops.

The amazing scenery near his settlement was soon referred to as Bryce's Canyon. Ebenezer once remarked the area was "a hell of a place to lose a cow." Looking for lost cattle was for the most part the only way Ebenezer Bryce could explore his canyon as most of his days were spent scratching out a life in this remote area.

There was a small amount of surveying in the canyon, but for the most part, Bryce Canyon was virtually unknown to most of America. While other major destinations of scenic wonder had nearby towns and railroad access, Bryce had only a roughly hewn wagon road to the rim of the Paunsaugunt Plateau. This changed in 1915 when J. W. Humphrey became the Forest Supervisor for the Sevier National Forest. Upon visiting Bryce Canyon, Humphrey knew he had to promote it to others. He built the first trail and the first real road to the rim, and he organized the distribution of the first promotion through articles in the Union Pacific Railroad publication.

By 1919, the unique qualities of Bryce Canyon enabled Utah State to enact legislation for its preservation. The canyon was then established as a National Monument in June 1923 by President Warren G. Harding and finally became Bryce Canyon National Park in 1927. At the time, Bryce Canyon received 24,000 visitors. Today it receives more than 1.5 million visitors each year and has become an icon of the west.

BRYCE CANYON GEOLOGY

When looking at Bryce Canyon from a geologic point of view, the first problem to overcome is its name. Bryce Canyon is not a canyon; it's the edge of a mesa. The various campgrounds, visitor center and overlooks are located at the top of the Paunsaugunt Plateau (pronounced "PAWN-suh-gant"). At the plateau's rim, water runoff has eroded away the edge of the Paunsaugunt creating the fins and hoodoos that make up Bryce Canyon.

The Paunsaugunt Plateau is the earliest member of the Grand Staircase, an enormous dissection of rock layers starting from the Grand Canyon to Bryce Canyon. The Grand Canyon holds the oldest layers while Bryce Canyon is made up of the youngest layers. The Paunsaugunt Plateau is cut by the East Fork Sevier River to the west.

The Grand Staircase

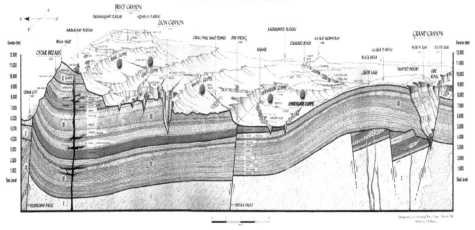

While both Zion and Bryce Canyon were formed by water erosion, Zion was carved primarily by the Virgin River, whereas Bryce Canyon was carved by rainfall and snowmelt eroding away at the edge of a plateau. Much of the hoodoos and fins you see before you were formed 60 million years ago. Water runs off the rim finding the path of least resistance, which is typically the softest portion of the plateau's edge. These paths become gullies for the water runoff, which enlarge over time from the scouring of softer rock by any debris as it flows downhill. Gullies slowly widen to become canyons and, at the same time, continue to eat away the rim's western edge.

The canyon walls that are formed are not frozen in time but are themselves subjects of erosion. The park has about 200 days each year that temperature is below freezing. As you know, water expands when it freezes. This simple law of nature does an amazing amount of the carving of Bryce Canyon. Water fills the vertical cracks within the canyon walls and then freezes overnight.

The pressures on the rock are enough to peel off layers, which over time create the hoodoos and narrow the canyon walls to fins. In the wintertime, it is actually possible to hear the walls crack under the might of water.

As mentioned, the erosion of the plateau's rim continues every day, pushing the creation of gullies, fins and hoodoos in a westward direction. The plateau including Bryce Canyon is eroding at a fairly rapid rate of 2–4 feet (0.6–1.3 m) every 100 years, primarily due to the softness of the rock layer itself. What this means is the canyon's creation will continue westward and one day erode into the campgrounds, lodge and visitor center. Eventually, Bryce Canyon will erode all the way to the East Fork Sevier River itself. When this happens, the river will become the dominant erosional factor, which will likely wash away the hoodoos and fins. Not to worry, though, you still have plenty of time to enjoy the scenery. The estimated time for Bryce to meet with the Sevier River is a very long 3 million years from now. Still, it is interesting to note that what you look down upon from the overlooks is not at all a constant. Each day brings change to Bryce Canyon.

Rush Hour

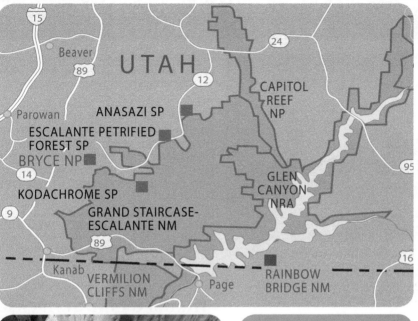

Little Death Hollow Slot Canyon

Wahweap Hoodoo

Parks Near Bryce Canyon

Paria Rimrocks - Toadstool Trail

Camping in Park:
- No developed campground, backcountry camping okay with permit

Getting There:
- From St. George, UT: Take UT-59 South and AZ-389 East 81 mi / 130 km to park entrance
- From Page, AZ: Take US-89 North 17 mi / 27 km to park entrance

A connection can be made with Glen Canyon National Recreation Area and the Grand Staircase-Escalante National Monument. The most obvious is that they are two very large parks siting right next to each other. Glen Canyon NRA protects a substantial portion of the Escalante River and its watershed, so they both share the last river to be named in the continental US. They both cover land that has been little disturbed, primarily because it is so rugged a country as to make it hard for the toils of man to penetrate. This is in fact why nearby Glen Canyon was filled with water, because there were no roads or towns to move. From the lens of the Bureau of Reclamation, there was nothing there.

It was only after the deed was done that folks realized there was something there after all, that this was a land worth protecting. Perhaps then, this is the deepest connection between the two parks. Within the profound disappointment by many of burying Glen Canyon with water, there was an acknowledgment that more must be done for those lands around it that are similar in spirit. To that, using the Antiquities Act, President Bill Clinton created Grand Staircase-Escalante National Monument in 1996. It is the largest land area of all the US National Monuments.

While this act was applauded by environmentalists and can be seen as a sentiment in the right direction over what was done with Glen Canyon, it was not seen as positive by many of the residents of Utah.

Clinton barely gave 24-hour notice to the Utah governor and state congress, giving them no time to react. The designation was attacked from many different angles and remains a sore subject with Utah residents.

Politics aside, Grand Staircase-Escalante is a massive, rugged, and pristine world. Entering it requires preparation, topo maps, and backcountry skills and for all of this preparation, its rewards are many. It is in many ways, the last frontier within the contiguous United States, where the meter of a person is on equal ground with the land.

As of December 4, 2017, the Grand Staircase-Escalante National Monument was reduced by 46% to just over 1M acres and is now three separate parks. A lawsuit has been filed against this action. Until the dust settles, this section continues to describe the pre-Dec 2017 version of the park.

HIKING GRAND STAIRCASE-ESCALANTE NATIONAL MONUMENT

All of these hikes have dozens of variants. The routes described below are the most commonly traveled routes.

LOWER CALF CREEK FALLS

Moderate – (5.9 mi / 9.5 km), round trip, allow 3 hours, elev. Δ: 250 ft / 76 m, trailhead at Calf Creek Campground

The trail starts by acknowledging the soft sand underneath your feet on a trail that seems nearly surreal in its beauty. The trail cuts into a tree-lined oasis as the canyon floor meets with massive blocks of darkly streaked walls of Navajo Sandstone that tower above on each side. The hike up has to be seen to be believed. Look for numerous cliff dwelling ruins tucked into alcoves as well as alien looking humanoid petroglyphs.

The trail leads to one of two falls on Calf Creek. The lower set of falls is spectacular and in fact is the higher of the two at 130 feet. There is a nice swimming hole to relax in as you take in the grotto like setting of the falls, greenery, and colored layers of rock. This is one of the best-known trails in the park.

UPPER CALF CREEK FALLS

Strenuous – (2.2 mi / 3.5 km), round trip, allow 1 – 2 hours, elev. Δ: 505 ft / 154 m, trailhead on SR 12, east of milepost 81

More strenuous but no less beautiful, the Upper Calf Creek Falls may be the better choice during peak season. The trail starts on the west side UT 12 further up from the more popular parking area for the lower falls. The trailhead, near milepost 81, does not have a signpost.

Start by heading downslope steeply on slickrock, using cairns as guides. The route descends 600 feet to the rim overlooking the falls. From there, follow the route down to the base of the falls.

The falls are more of a free fall of water and are shorter at 88 feet in height. There is a nice and deep swimming hole here and typically less people. As far as the hike quality goes, both the upper and lower falls are worth seeing.

DEATH HOLLOW

Strenuous – (14.0 mi / 22.5 km), round trip, full day trip or overnight backpacking trip, elev. Δ: 600 ft / 183 m, trailhead 24 mi from Escalante on Hell's Backbone Road north

Death Hollow is one of the largest tributaries into the Escalante River. This hike description takes the Boulder Mail Trail route. The hike is an excellent way to see the park and doesn't require more than minimal scrambling. Best done as a shuttle with two cars at each trailhead.

Start by driving about 3.8 miles south on UT 12 from Anasazi State Park to the Boulder Landing Strip on McGath Bench Road, which is your very first left after turning right onto Hells Backbone Road. Begin the hike at the junction on the northeast side of the McGath Point Bench along the Boulder Mail Trail. Travel along McGrath Bench, Sand Creek, and then Slickrock Saddle Bench for about 3.5 miles until you meet up with Death Hollow. Access here is straightforward, with a couple of places where you'll need some Class 3 type scrambling.

Once in, the water flows pretty well, but is never too strong to be a problem. The hike down involves a mixture of walking in the stream coupled with multiple crossings to paths on either bank.

Lower Calf Creek Falls

Death Hollow becomes more overgrown as you hit the confluence to the Escalante River. There are lots of little side canyons to explore and some deep pools to swim in. Hike out to the Overlook for Death Hollow Parking Area.

UPPER ESCALANTE RIVER

Moderate to Strenuous – (13.0 mi / 20.9 km), one-way, elev. Δ: 500 ft / 152 m, trailhead along river at Escalante, UT

There aren't many hikes in the world where you can literally close the door to your hotel room and just take a long walk down a river canyon and when you are done, get picked up with ease right from the highway. This hike exists and it is one of the gems of the Southwest in terms of beauty. It meanders gently downstream and passes arches and natural bridges, thick wonderful canyon walls, and even some swimming holes.

First off, for hikers, this description can be followed during the dry season when the river is low enough to wade down. During the wet season, the route is more suitable for river rafting, inner tubing, and kayaking.

The hike starts just about anywhere within the town of Escalante where you can access the river. If you want to reduce the amount of river wading whilst in town, find your way to the Pine Creek Escalante River Confluence at the northeast end of town. Not much in the way of parking here, but you'll soon be in the thick of the riparian desert wilderness from here.

Once inside the canyon, the river meanders almost as a rule, snaking along one bend after the other, giving to the curious the wonder of what could be around the next bend. The meanders allow for constantly changing views as well. One of the first notable formations to see is the Escalante Natural Arch, which sits high up on the south wall and is super easy to miss. Look for it after the confluence with Sand Creek. Less than 0.5 miles further on is Escalante Natural Bridge, a humbling and beautiful sight as well as the largest formation in the park. The bridge also marks the home stretch of the hike. Look for the UT 12 Bridge and your ride to home base back in Escalante. Your ride will pass by the Kiva Koffeehouse, which serves espressos seasonally from April to October in a very nice rustic building with great views.

ESCALANTE NATURAL BRIDGE

Easy – (3.5 mi / 5.6 km), round trip, allow 2 hours, elev. Δ: 100 ft / 30 m, trailhead at Highway 12 bridge over Escalante River

For those that don't have the time to hike downstream from the town of Escalante, it is possible to see the Escalante Natural Bridge and do a bit of river trail hiking coming from the UT 12 Bridge that crosses over the Escalante River. Look for signs that indicate Escalante River trailhead access about 14 miles from the town of Escalante, heading south. The Escalante Natural Arch is about 0.5 miles further upstream (add 1.0 mile to your round trip distance).

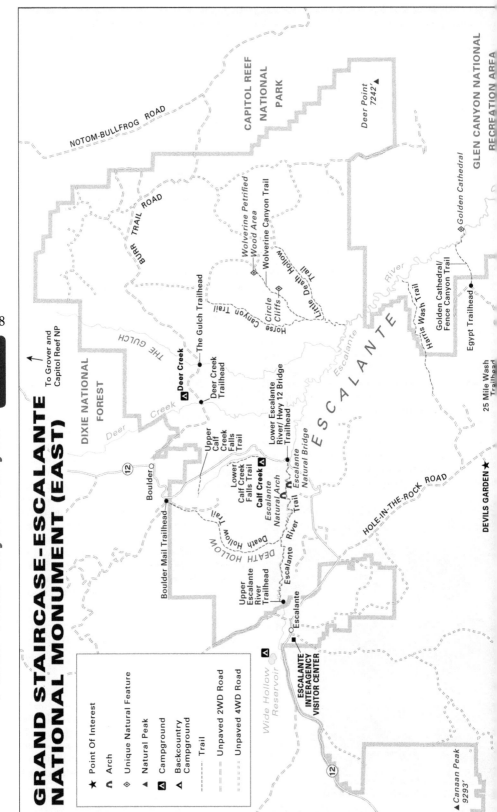

GRAND STAIRCASE-ESCALANTE
NATIONAL MONUMENT (EAST)

★ Point Of Interest

∩ Arch

◇ Unique Natural Feature

▲ Natural Peak

🅰 Campground

△ Backcountry Campground

- - - - - - - Trail

= = = = = Unpaved 2WD Road

= = = = = Unpaved 4WD Road

CAPITOL REEF

NATIONAL

PARK

GLEN CANYON NATIONAL

RECREATION AREA

NOTOM-BULLFROG ROAD

*Deer Point
7242'* ▲

BURR TRAIL ROAD

◇ *Golden Cathedral*

Wolverine Petrified
Wood Area

Wolverine Canyon Trail

*Little Death Hollow
Trail*

Horse Canyon Trail

*Circle
Cliffs*

Golden Cathedral/
Fence Canyon Trail

River

Harris Wash Trail

Egypt Trailhead ●

The Gulch Trailhead

To Grover and
Capitol Reef NP

DIXIE NATIONAL

FOREST

THE GULCH

Escalante

E S C A L A N T E

△ *Deer Creek*

Deer Creek
Trailhead

Deer   *Creek*

Upper
Calf
Creek
Falls
Trail

Lower Escalante
River/ Hwy 12 Bridge
Trailhead

25 Mile Wash
Trailhead

12

Boulder ○

Lower
Calf Creek
Falls Trail

🅰 **Calf Creek**

*Escalante
Natural Arch*

Escalante Natural Bridge

Boulder Mail Trailhead ●

Death Hollow Trail

DEATH HOLLOW

Escalante River Trail

HOLE-IN-THE-ROCK ROAD

DEVILS GARDEN ★

Upper
Escalante
River
Trailhead

Escalante

Escalante ○

ESCALANTE
INTERAGENCY
VISITOR CENTER

🅰

*Wide Hollow
Reservoir*

12

▲ *Canaan Peak
9293'*

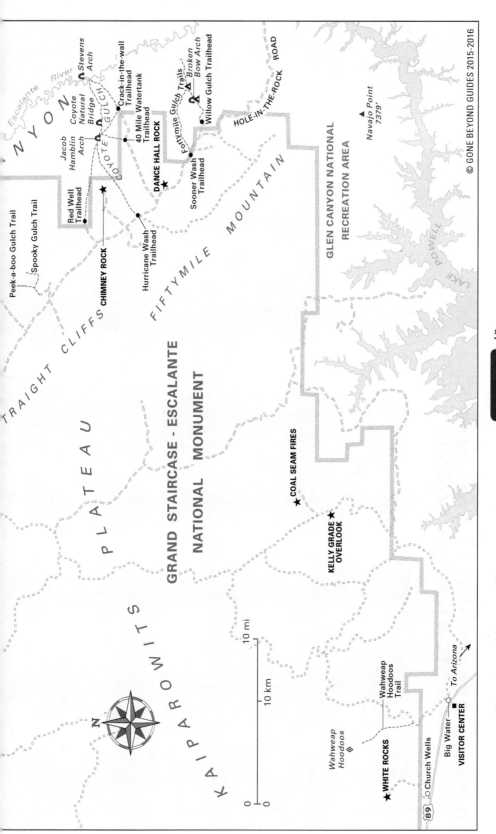

© GONE BEYOND GUIDES 2015-2016

Parks Near Bryce Canyon

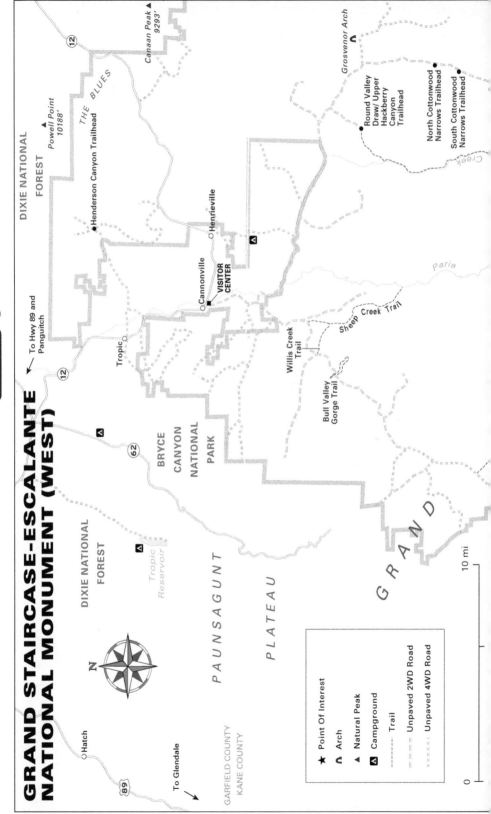

GRAND STAIRCASE-ESCALANTE
NATIONAL MONUMENT (WEST)

To Hwy 89 and
Panguitch

DIXIE NATIONAL
FOREST

THE BLUES

Canaan Peak ▲
9293'

Powell Point ▲
10188'

Henderson Canyon Trailhead

Grosvenor Arch ⌒

Round Valley
Draw/ Upper
Hackberry
Canyon
Trailhead

North Cottonwood
Narrows Trailhead

South Cottonwood
Narrows Trailhead

Creek

Henrieville

Cannonville

VISITOR
CENTER

Paria

Tropic

Sheep Creek Trail

Willis Creek
Trail

Bull Valley
Gorge Trail

12

To Glendale

To Hwy 89 and
Panguitch

Hatch

89

62

DIXIE NATIONAL
FOREST

Tropic
Reservoir

BRYCE
CANYON
NATIONAL
PARK

PAUNSAGUNT

PLATEAU

GRAND

GARFIELD COUNTY
KANE COUNTY

N

★ Point Of Interest
⌒ Arch
▲ Natural Peak
◮ Campground
------ Trail
= = = Unpaved 2WD Road
= = = Unpaved 4WD Road

0   10 mi

© GONE BEYOND GUIDES 2015-2016

Parks Near Bryce Canyon

FORTYMILE AND WILLOW GULCH LOOP

Moderate – (11.0 mi / 17.7 km), round trip, allow 6 hours, elev. Δ: 540 ft / 165 m, trailhead at Sooner Wash Trailhead off Hole in the Rock Road

Narrow canyons, bold rock faces, and a maze of seemingly endless hiking possibilities, this is Fortymile and Willow Gulch. There are many ways to explore this area, but in this description, the route starts at Sooner Wash Trailhead. Folks can start out at the adjacent Dance Hall Rock Campsite and check out the cool looking Sooner Rocks. The trailhead and the campsite are off Hole in the Rock Road. Note that this hike has spots where you will need to wade through waterholes and depending on water levels, may even require some swimming to get past the water obstacles.

Devils Garden at night

From Sooner Wash Trailhead hike for 1.5 miles into the confluence of Sooner Wash and Fortymile Gulch. This portion will have some areas that require wading through canyon water pockets. Continue for several miles to the Willow Gulch confluence. Here you can keep going down Fortymile Gulch as it meets up with Lake Powell, however the going is muddier. This description heads up Willow Gulch, which avoids the mucky bits and takes the hiker to Broken Bow Arch, which is about 0.5 miles up Willow Gulch from the confluence.

Willow Gulch is definitely the more pristine of the two choices at the juncture. To exit, hike up any of the three main streams that feed the tributary. The northernmost stream is the most convenient of the three as it passes by a parking area near Hole in the Rock Road. Either hike back to your car from here or be thankful you brought two cars and parked one at the exit site. If you do have a second car, the total trip is 8.2 miles.

HOLE IN THE ROCK TRAIL

Strenuous – (1.0 mi / 1.6 km), round trip, allow 1 hour, elev. Δ: 600 ft / 182 m, trailhead on Highway 12, just southeast of Escalante

Early Mormon pioneers used this steep but marginally passable draw as the route down to the Colorado River. The first thing one thinks when coming to the rim of the steep and narrow gully is something along the lines of, "They took their wagons and animals down that??" The pioneers blasted the crevice to make it wide enough for wagons.

Today, this old supply route can be hiked down to what is now Lake Powell. It's very steep and very rocky, but fortunately only about a half mile. The trail has a plaque at the bottom commemorating the tenacity of these early settlers.

DEVILS GARDEN

Easy – (0.5 mi / 0.8 km), round trip, allow 30 – 60 minutes, elev. Δ: 10 ft / 3 m, trailhead on Hole in the Rock Road

This is a great family trail just off the Hole in the Rock Road. Here there be hoodoos and arches, of all manner of shapes and sizes, oddly misshapen things, every last one of them. To get to this garden of the devil himself, simply head east five miles on UT 12 from Escalante to the unpaved Hole in the Rock Road, which is suitable for 2WD vehicles in dry weather. Another 13 miles on Hole in the Rock takes you to a signed turnoff to Devils Garden. Park and roam around. There are picnic tables, BBQ grills and a pit toilet here, making this a nice lunch spot. This is a great place to make a deal..

GOLDEN CATHEDRAL

Moderate – (9.5 mi / 15.3 km), round trip, allow 5 - 6 hours, elev. Δ: 1,260 ft / 384 m, trailhead in Egypt area off Hole in the Rock Road

Golden Cathedral is a strikingly beautiful and unworldly set of three arches. Together they form a line of holes that resemble a massive rock spine. There is great light play here, that helps give the formation its name. The hike requires some decent navigational skill, winding down Fence Canyon into the confluence of Neon Canyon and the Escalante River.

Take Hole in the Rock Road to Egypt Bench Road and follow it for 9.9 miles. High clearance vehicles recommended here, as there are several washes to cross. At 2.9 miles, you will pass the trailhead for Twentyfive Mile Wash. At 6.4 miles, the road will turn sharply right into a wash and one mile later, you will need to navigate up a short but rocky and steep incline. Take the fork at 9.3 miles and turn right, parking the car at the Egypt trailhead after 9.9 miles.

From here, while there isn't much in the way of official trail, there are plenty of cairns to follow. You are at the highest point in the hike and will now drop down into Fence Canyon. Keep to the left of Fence Canyon as you come to it in order to head down into the wash and the confluence of the Escalante River and Fence Canyon.

In Coyote Gulch

From here, pull out your water shoes and follow the Escalante River downstream one-mile south from the confluence with Fence Canyon to Neon Canyon, which is the first side canyon on your left.

Head up Neon Canyon for another 0.9 miles to Golden Cathedral. This last stretch and the triptych of arches is serene and majestic and worth the trek to get there. Heading further up Neon Canyon requires ropes and technical skills.

PEEK-A-BOO GULCH

Moderate – (2.0 mi / 3.2 km), round trip, allow 1 – 2 hours, elev. Δ: 100 ft / 30 m, trailhead at Dry Fork area off Hole in the Rock Road

Peek-a-Boo is a really fun little slot canyon. The trailhead is 26 miles northeast on Hole in the Rock Road and then take Dry Fork Turnoff, staying left. Take the short hike from Dry Fork Overlook to the bottom of Dry Fork. Peek-a-Boo is just ahead to the north. Dry Fork Road is barely passable by 2WD vehicles, but is better for high clearance rigs.

What makes this slot canyon fun is all of the little scramble puzzles that need to be figured out with lots of little dry falls and chockstones. Finding the right route up the dry fall or figuring out whether to go under the big rock in the way or climb over it makes this a fun canyon to solve. A great hike for kids as none of the scrambling is that technical, though smaller children may need the occasional boost up.

The slot canyon is very narrow, though Spooky Gulch, which is typically combined with a hike through Peek-a-Boo, makes this gulch seem wide and spacious by comparison. Most folks scramble up Peek-a-Boo and then cross over and head into Spooky Gulch.

To combine the two slot canyons and make it a loop hike, scramble up Peek-a-Boo and then head overland through sandy red open terrain to the wide dry wash of Spooky Gulch. From there, head through Spooky back to Dry Fork and your car. This loop is 3.5 miles total.

SPOOKY GULCH

Moderate – (3.2 mi / 5.1 km), round trip, allow 2 -3 hours, elev. Δ: 100 ft / 30 m, trailhead at Dry Fork area off Hole in the Rock Road

Spooky Gulch is another short slot canyon that can be done alone or by combining with Peek-a-Boo Gulch. To get to Spooky Gulch, take the same route as to Peek-a-Boo from the Dry Fork Road.

Spooky Gulch is very different from Peek-a-Boo, though they are right next to each other. Whereas Peek-a-Boo is essentially a fun series of scramble puzzles to solve, Spooky is an extremely thin and deep slot canyon. It is so narrow that in some places there is only room for one person at time to pass. The canyon can make it feel like you are being compressed by the walls and some folks hit the narrow section at first thinking that it is too narrow to enter. You can and it does go all the way through, but it is definitely more of a spooky slot canyon than a soulful one. Those that are claustrophobic might want to take a pass on this one.

COYOTE GULCH

Strenuous – (11.5 mi / 18.5 km), round trip, allow 5 - 6 hours or two-night backpacking trip, elev. Δ: 970 ft / 296 m, trailhead, see below

Coyote Gulch offers incredible scenery and some unique formations along the way. The trek is strenuous and it is recommended to make this a two-day jaunt. There is one section, Crack-in-the-Wall, that makes an argument for the day hike option if you don't have two days to spare, simply because it such an amazing and cool way to get down a cliff face.

The hike starts at some water tanks located 4.4 miles up Fortymile Ridge Road after coming from Hole-in-the-Rock Road in Escalante. The trail climbs up to Crack-in-the-Wall (or Crack-in-the-Rock), which is the first obstacle to surmount. The crack in question is a massive section of sandstone cliff that has broken off from the main section and moved outwards just enough for a grown person to shimmy in between. For the uninitiated, this may sound terrifying but it is easier than it may sound. Start by following the cairns to the very edge of the cliff and head right and down to what looks like the end of the cliff. Here you will find a crack that you shimmy in between to work to the canyon floor. There are two areas of exposure, but for the most part, the crack is safe and is an exhilarating means of getting down to the river and upstream from there. If you are backpacking, it is recommended to lower your packs down by rope.

The scenery is amazing throughout and Coyote Gulch itself does not disappoint. Here one can fine one of the largest arches in the United States, Stevens Arch, standing 160 feet tall and spanning 225 feet. This is a hulk of an arch, simply massive. Then there is Coyote Bridge, a very picturesque natural bridge with water flowing underneath it year round.

Cottonwood Canyon Road

Finally, there is Jacob Hamblin Arch, which marks the exit point for the hike. This is for some the hardest part of the hike. Hikers must be able to navigate up a 100-foot section of very steep slickrock to exit onto Fortymile Ridge. If you have anyone in the group that has doubts about this section, have the leader ascend and drop a rope down to aid in the climb up. This section is very exposed and at 45 degrees, is very steep. Once at the top of the ridge, head back to the water tanks and your vehicle.

LITTLE DEATH HOLLOW

Easy – (16.0 mi / 25.7 km), round trip, full day or backpacking trip, elev. Δ: 600 ft / 183 m, trailhead: see description below

Grand Staircase has not one but two areas named Death Hollow. This hike refers to the beautiful slot canyon of Little Death Hollow. No one is sure what the relationship is between the Hollows, father and son perhaps? Whatever the connection, you can discuss this as you travel through this remote canyon. Little Death Hollow is popular for its long and narrow slot canyon, which is for the most part, obstacle free. The hike heads into the canyon and slot canyon further up with a turnaround point at the confluence with Horse Canyon. As with all hikes that involve narrow slot canyons, be well aware of the weather to avoid being caught in a flash flood.

Little Death Hollow is in a more remote and generally less accessible part of the park, east of UT 12. To get there drive 19 miles east from Boulder, UT along Burr Trail Road and then turn right and head south on the unpaved Wolverine Loop Road. From this junction you will see a signpost indicating that the trailhead for Little

Death Hollow is 12 miles on. This road is recommended for high clearance vehicles and even then, is impassable when wet. The main problem areas are at the two streambed crossings, Horse Canyon and Wolverine Creek. It will look level and inviting at the junction, but the road has some steep and sandy parts that are designed by nature to get 2WD cars stuck.

Once the turnoff for Wolverine Loop Road is found, take the right junction, heading counter-clockwise around the loop. This will allow for checking out the Wolverine Petrified Wood Natural Area, which is as amazing as Petrified Forest National Park, but without the crowds. Be courteous to all of the generations ahead of you and refrain from picking up any pieces. From the petrified wood area, continue on the loop. It will cut east and then south into a valley before the entrance to Little Death Hollow. As remote as this is, there is a trail register and official trailhead. If you gotten this far, "Woot!" Let the hiking begin.

The canyon of Little Death Hollow starts out wide at first with cattle tracks paralleling the trail at first. The canyon continues to narrow and at some point, you realize you are in the slot canyon. In some sections, the canyon is just two feet wide and the water cut sandstone produces multiple lines horizontal to the ground. Depending on the season, there are pools of standing water that need to be crossed. These can be more like quicksand at times, especially after a rainstorm, so be careful.

The route ends at the confluence with Horse Canyon. From here, you can continue downstream to the Escalante River (about 3 miles further on) or head upstream to Wolverine Creek. If you take the upstream route, you can head up Wolverine Creek and hike the length of it to the head of the canyon, which sits just below the Wolverine Petrified Wood Natural Area. This adds another 1.5 miles to the hike, but gives a completely different view on the way back. Wolverine Creek is the first canyon on the right as you head up Horse Canyon. There is one junction as you head up Wolverine, stay to the right to exit closer to the Little Death Hollow Trailhead.

COTTONWOOD CANYON ROAD

Easy to Strenuous – Distance Varies

Cottonwood Road loosely follows the Paria River through Grand Staircase-Escalante NM from Highway 89 to Cannonville 46 miles to the north. The road offers incredible scenery, with views of river canyons, fins, and barren alien lands that look as if not of this planet. The road is impassable when wet, but is otherwise a great way to see a decent cross section of the park. Along the stretch are seemingly endless hiking opportunities. Sites to explore include Hackberry Canyon, Yellow Mountain, Cottonwood Canyon Narrows, the Cockscomb, and Grosvenor Arch.

The road also leads to Kodachrome State Park. Cottonwood Canyon Road can be picked up near milepost 18 on Highway 89 or from Kodachrome State Park Road.

ROUND VALLEY DRAW

Moderate – (4.3 mi / 6.9 km), round trip, allow 2 -3 hours, elev. Δ: 400 ft / 122 m, trailhead is 1.5 miles on Rush Beds Road

Off Cottonwood Canyon Road and close to Grosvenor Arch is another slot canyon called Round Valley Draw. This slot canyon has some beautiful striations and in some areas is covered by suspended rock fall held in place above by the canyon walls.

From the north end of Cottonwood Canyon Road, drive

south, then east for 14 miles. There is a signed spur road that heads south and winds up the Round Valley Wash to the mouth of the slot canyon. Off roaders can take the creek bed right up to the mouth, use good judgment on when to get out and start hiking otherwise.

From here, descend into the slot from the mesa top. There is a tree stump at the initial descent point to help navigate down into the slot. The total elevation down is about 15 feet. When the canyon opens up again, climb out back onto the mesa and hike out the way you came. For a longer journey, continue down the draw to Hackberry Creek. Round trip from Hackberry Creek is 5.5 miles.

Note that this slot canyon has contained obstacles that are best navigated with canyoneering skill and equipment (a good length of rope). There is one boulder that can sometimes be navigated by going under while at other times, the 15-foot obstacle requires a rope or good free climbing skills.

PARIA RIMROCKS TRAIL

Moderate – (1.5 mi / 2.4 km), round trip, allow 30 minutes, elev. Δ: 100 ft / 30 m, trailhead: see description below

Some of the coolest rock features in the area; Paria Rimrocks has to be seen to be believed. The trail follows a wash and then cairns to a goblin and hoodoo garden. The area is laden with hoodoos and toadstools, including one known as ET (aka Red Toadstool). Bring your camera; this is one of the more amazing hikes in the area.

Paria Rimrocks are near Highway 89 near mile marker 19. If driving north from Glen Canyon Dam, there will be a dirt parking area on the right just past the marker. There are maps available at the Grand Staircase-Escalante NM Visitor Center.

Harris Wash

HARRIS WASH

Moderate – (21.2 mi / 34.1 km), round trip, full day or backpacking trip, elev. Δ: 700 ft / 213 m, trailhead is 4.5 mi south of Escalante on Hole-in-the-Rock Road

Harris Wash is one of the more accessible areas of Grand Staircase-Escalante NM and is also one of the most rewarding. It is the longest tributary of the Escalante River and can be done in full to the river as an overnight backpacking trip or as a day hike, going as far one's spirit of adventure takes them. There are many tributaries to explore, including Zebra and Tunnel Slot canyons, making this one of those hikes where there is seemingly something new around every bend.

Upper Harris Wash offers little in terms of scenery. The beginning of the route is as a small child, shy at first and not showing its true self until deeper into the draw. Big Horn Canyon joins from the north about 1.8 miles in and holds many interesting branches and narrow sections to explore.

At 4.3 miles one reaches Zebra Slot canyon, known for its orange sandstone layers striped with thin bands of white. This tributary is well worth exploring. There are some dryfall obstacles to overcome as well as water filled pools, especially in wet weather.

Going downstream in Harris Wash another mile from Zebra Slot canyon leads to Tunnel Slot canyon. This is a short and cave like section, that follows for about 50 yards with high cliff walls surrounding a narrow passage. One typically will need to wade or even swim through a deep pool at start. The canyon then opens up to a scene of riparian brush and trees. The tunnel is just a few minutes from the main canyon.

There is another tributary about a half mile further downstream, containing serene vistas, several small springs and a simply pleasant vibe all around. Further down is Red Breaks, a seldom explored side canyon with deep passages and some shallow slot canyons. Opposite Red Breaks is the Harris Wash trailhead, used as a short cut to Escalante River from Halfway Hollow. It is possible to take Halfway Hollow back to Hole-in-the-Rock Road and north 3.5 miles to your car.

66

ESCALANTE PETRIFIED FOREST STATE PARK

Camping in Park:
- Lake View and Wide Hollow Campgrounds: 22 T/RV, 1 group site, drinking water, showers, restrooms, partial hookups

Getting There:
- From Escalante, UT: Take West Main Street (UT 12) to N 300 W to Pine Creek Lane

Located just outside the town of Escalante, this park protects 1,350 acres of petrified logs and fossilized dinosaur bones. The agate logs are full of color and one log on display is 50 feet in length.

Besides the campground and the stocked Wide Hollow Reservoir, there are three trails for visitors. The Petrified Forest Trail winds from the campground to the top of a ridge. This one-mile round trip loop takes about 45-60 minutes. The steeper Sleeping Rainbows Trail comes off the Petrified Forest Trail and is 0.75 miles. Sleeping Rainbows Trail contains some excellent examples of petrified logs but is steep and requires some scrambling. Finally, the short (0.1 mi) and wheelchair accessible Petrified Wood Cove Trail offers quick access to specimens and flora near the Wide Hollow Reservoir.

KODACHROME BASIN STATE PARK

Camping in Park:

For reservations, call the visitor center

- Basin Campgrounds: 37 T/RV, mix of reservable and first come-first served, some sites allow generators, flush toilets, showers, restrooms

- Bryce View Campground: 11 T/RV, all reservable, vault toilets, drinking water, no hookups

Getting There:
- From St George, UT: Take I-15 North to UT-20 East to US-89 South to UT-12 East to Kodachrome Road in Cannonville, UT. Total distance is 151 mi / 243 km to park.

Kodachrome Basin State Park holds one of the most unique features in all of the Grand Circle, the sand pipe or chimney. The sand pipes are similar in shape to sandstone towers but the process of formation is radically different. In fact, they are so different that geologists don't exactly know how these things were created.

Sand pipe at Kodachrome Basin State Park

There are 67 recorded sand pipes in the park, ranging from six feet to 170 feet high. They stand as vertical round chimneys of rock. There are two theories on how they were formed. One is that there were once geysers here and the vents eventually filled up with sediment and solidified. The strata around these sediment pipes then eroded, leaving the sand pipes. The other theory is that there was a tectonic force that essentially liquefied the strata and forced the "liquid rock" into the surrounding strata, essentially an extrusion into rock. All of this occurred beneath the surface and again, the surrounding strata eroded away, leaving the spires.

Beyond the spires, the park itself is worth seeing in its own right. Located within the Grand Staircase-Escalante NM, the area is full of great views. There are plenty of trails in this small park as well, making this one of the top places to visit for its uniqueness and beauty.

HIKING IN KODACHROME BASIN STATE PARK

SHAKESPEARE ARCH TRAIL

Easy – (0.5 mi / 0.8 km), round trip, allow 15 minutes

To hike or not to hike this trail, that is the question. Pick up a guide pamphlet at the trailhead and follow this trail to a small arch named after Shakespeare (or "Willy the Shake" to his hip hop friends).

SENTINEL TRAIL

Easy – (1.0 mi / 1.6 km), round trip, allow 30 -45 minutes

This trail starts near the Shakespeare Arch Trail to create an extension that takes one to an overlook about 100 feet above. Sweeping panoramic views.

GRAND PARADE TRAIL

Easy – (1.5 mi / 2.4 km), round trip, allow 45 minutes

Good family friendly loop hike that passes by a handful of the famous Kodachrome sand pipes and into and out of two box canyons. The box canyons are picturesque, making this a great hike for all.

EAGLE'S VIEW TRAIL

Moderate to Strenuous – (0.5 mi / 0.8 km), round trip, allow 30 minutes

Eagle's View is a short but steep climb to a viewpoint that allows for exceptional views of the park and surrounding area.

NATURE TRAIL

Easy – (0.5 mi / 0.8 km), round trip, allow 15 minutes

This is a kid friendly paved interpretative trail that showcases a sand pipe and the pinyon juniper forest setting of the park.

PANORAMA TRAIL

Moderate – (5.3 mi / 8.5 km), round trip, allow 3- 4 hours

The best bang for the buck trail in the park. The hike covers a number of different sand pipes, as well as incredible panoramic views. It is possible to see to Bryce Canyon and overall is an absolutely breathtaking hike. Along the way is Cool Cave, a cove with a slot canyon look. There are many side trips that one can take to see all of the different sand pipes.

ANGELS PALACE TRAIL

Easy – (1.3 mi / 2.1 km), round trip, allow 30 minutes

Angel's Palace Trail offers unique rock formations along a trail up a small canyon. Great views of the surrounding area and an excellent location for late afternoon photography.

ANASAZI STATE PARK MUSEUM

Nearest Town with Amenities
- The park is located in the town of Boulder, UT

Getting There:
- From St George, UT: Take UT-12 West to Boulder, UT. Total distance is 37 mi / 60 km to park

Anasazi State Park Museum is a small 6-acre park within the town of Boulder, Utah. The park holds a visitor center, museum, and a guided tour of the Coombs Village Site, a reconstruction of ruins of the Ancestral Puebloan. Visitors can walk through the ruins and piece together the past using interpretive signs along the way.

For reference, Anasazi is an outdated term. The word is from the Navajo language and means "ancestors of the enemies". The term Ancestral Puebloan is the more commonly used term for the people of this period. The term Anasazi was put into use in 1927 by archaeologist Linda Cordell and the name stuck. Anasazi was widely used through the park's creation in 1960 and began to fall out of favor in the late 1990's to early 2000's.

Since we are here, the term "American Indian" is right out baffling to most who are referred to by this term. It's easy to see why, seeing as the term defines a people that are neither from India or ever called themselves American prior to the Europeans coming over. Most just prefer to be referred to by their nation's name, such as Navajo, Hopi, Ute, etc.

Parks Near Bryce Canyon

[Everest]: *You love my brother more than me.*

[Me]: *What! Why do you say that?*

[Everest]: *You got him a bumper sticker that says Bryce National Park.*

[Me]: *You realize that it's a three-week trek just to get to the base of Everest and that it's a full day's plane ride to fly over there and that they don't have a gift shop at the base camp and that what you are asking for likely doesn't even exist, right?*

[Everest]: *Still.*

Where's Bryce?

68

I felt the RV rumble enough to wake me from my dead slumber. Opening one eye, I noticed the slide-out of our RV was mysteriously pulling itself back in. This getting my other eye's attention, I looked up to discover that Bryce, in only his tighty whiteys, was stretched with one skinny leg on the bunk ladder and the other on the kitchen counter. His head was scraping the ceiling. He had figured out how to gain access to the normally inaccessible RV control panel and was operating the slide-out, but why I thought? Before I could give it too much thought, my attention was diverted to the sound of a plastic water bottle being mangled under the moving dining room table. The bottle pleaded to be released from its torment before being crushed fully into silence.

With all sounds stopped, I closed my eyes again. No harm, I thought. I'm sure that water bottle won't destroy any chance of getting our deposit back. Besides, what could I do now at six in the morning? From the sound of things, that bottle wasn't going anywhere. So I again let myself fall into the dreamlands of slumber, but right before I dropped completely, I sensed a presence and reopened an eye. It was Bryce, now inches away, looking at me in casual observation. I wondered how long he had been standing there and how it was I hadn't heard him get down from his acrobatic perch. I then began to wonder if I should be concerned about this ninja-like quality down the road when he was older and could get into more trouble.

With drowsy eye contact made, my youngest decided it was okay to engage in conversation. "So, Dad, you know how you said we could leave early for Bryce?"

I sat up on one elbow and blinked a bunch of times to get a little more focus. "Well, yeah, we did talk about heading out early to make sure we get a campsite. We don't have a reservation at Bryce Canyon."

"Well, umm, I have everything packed up," Bryce said. "We can leave now if you want."

"What do you mean 'everything'?"

"Well, I kinda snuck out, you know, and packed up all the chairs. Then I got water and made sure the fire was fully out. Oh and I unplugged the electrical outlet and plugged it back into the RV and locked up all the storage cabinets and then I pulled in the RV thing."

"Wow!" I said nodding in affirmation. He was obviously proud and I was amazed how quickly he had figured everything out. "Yeah, I heard you pulling it in!"

"Yeah, Dad! It was kind of hard to get to the switch so I kinda, you know, had to stretch across the bed to the counter and well, then I could hit the pull-in switch. At first it didn't work and then I remembered you had to start the engine, so I kinda did that first. Then I got the slide-out pulled in."

I just then realized the RV engine was running and leapt out of bed. I ducked under the stairs to the driver's seat and turned it off. Bryce was beaming with pride over his accomplishments; I had to find a positive way to handle this.

I got down to his height and looked him in the eye. "Bryce, that's awesome you did all that, but next time, don't ever start the RV without my permission okay?"

"Yeah, sure. Sorry, Dad, I just, you know, wanted to get everything ready for you. So can we go, you know to Bryce Cannon? I kinda want to see it."

Bryce was excited to see his namesake and yes, he does, despite being nine years old and having been corrected countless times, pronounces "canyon" as "cannon."

I was on board. Why not? Let's get a move on to our next national park, I thought! Ang rolled over in bed and groaned on seeing my enthusiasm. I did a quick survey of Bryce's handiwork and then sped off at the crack of dawn to the Zion Tunnel.

To get to Bryce you need to go through the Zion Tunnel. To get through the Zion Tunnel in an RV, you need to buy a permit and have the park ranger help you get through the tunnel. This is for one simple reason; the tunnel was built before big fat RVs. The tunnel is very narrow.

As we drove up to this burrow of rock, I learned the hard way that it is always helpful to read the directions with regards to tunnels that may be obstacles to your passage. I had failed to pay attention to the operating hours on the tunnel permit, which meant that we had woken up far earlier than we needed to. We got to the tunnel in record time only to wait for it to open. It was not a terribly long wait, a mere two hours, but two hours my family reminded me were hours they could have slept in had I simply read the permit. I made coffee and eggs as penance.

When the tunnel finally opened and we were allowed to go through it, I set off with much enthusiasm. We were all anxious to get to Bryce. What I failed to figure out is how to engage the headlamps prior to setting out. As your RV slips into a cave-like darkness, you immediately realize this is crucial knowledge to have to avoid crashing into the tunnel. There were no cars in front of me, but as there was a line of cars behind me, I didn't want to be the guy that held up the entire caravan. I scrambled to maintain speed while frantically trying to figure out where the lights were. Just before we lost the remaining slivers of sun, I managed to find the lever that flashes the high beams. This prevented the crashing into the tunnel part, except now I had to steer with one hand and hold the lever with the other all while driving through a tunnel that seems about a quarter inch higher than the RV itself. It was all very dignified and a defining moment for this authoritative figure on how to operate an RV.

"Honk the horn!" Bryce said. I ignored him. With one hand on the light switch and the other on the steering wheel, both hands were occupied.

"Honk the horn, Dad!" Everest commanded.

I'm thinking, "Come on kids, I only have two hands here and the slightest deviation will scrape off the roof. Let's not honk the horn."

Everyone, including my wife now chanted in a chorused mantra, "Honk-the-horn! Honk-the-horn! Honk-the-horn!"

With pressures mounting, I managed to find a way to honk the horn by quickly letting go of the steering wheel. I honked it a few times all the while without my wife ever knowing how close we came to careening through one of the gallery windows to our fiery deaths as I lost control of the RV. It would have been spectacular. People would have pulled over and looked down on us. We would have exploded when we hit the bottom, and I'm pretty sure Bryce would have jumped out at the last minute, barely clenching to the edge of the cliff. He's good like that.

As we drove the 84 miles to Bryce Canyon National Park, our son Bryce read out loud the 14-page collection of facts he had pulled from the Internet. We asked both kids to help us choose what to do in the various National Parks and sites along the way. Everest did zero research while Bryce spent several days copying and pasting a volume of work all around one subject: Bryce Canyon. He then printed it out and performed mandatory book readings, usually in captive audience situations. We were certainly well informed going into this park.

After about two hours or, as I timed it, four readings, we pulled into Bryce Canyon and found a few campsites available. Finding a good campsite is a bit like finding good parking. If parking is tough, you can take the first one you see way out in the boonies, but you don't know if there is a better one unless you drive around more. Of course, in looking for the better spot, you are giving up the one you just found. Picking an RV spot is the same thing, only you are finding a place to park your home for the night. After looping around the campground several times, we found a level one suitable to everyone's liking and immediately set off to see the views.

We walked to the shuttle stop and waited. I listened to this couple discuss the shuttle route, which went in one continuous circle to Bryce Point and back. It seemed easy enough. On discovering we had about ten minutes to wait, Ang took the boys in to get Junior Ranger activity books.

When she came back she asked, "How long did you say we were in Bryce again?"

"Just today."

"We need to stay longer," she said.

"Why is that?"

"The Junior Ranger activity book requires seeing a ranger program. At the minimum we need to get to Inspiration Point for the next one at 11:30am."

I looked at the clock. It was 10:50.

"Let's see if we can make it. If not we can figure something out."

"We need to make this ranger talk. I want Bryce to get his junior ranger pin. This is his park after all."

"Okay okay. Look, there's the shuttle now." We got on the shuttle. Bryce looked around and immediately became stoic and quiet. All around him his name was plastered in large letters throughout the bus. Back at the visitor center it was on pamphlets, T-shirts, letter openers and refrigerator magnets. Plus he had heard what his mom said. This was his park. He filled out the Junior Ranger activity book as if it held lost treasure. He only looked up when someone used the word Bryce in a sentence.

Our first stop was Bryce Point, and we all walked to our first viewing of the canyon. Bryce folded his hands

on the rail and looked deep into the colored hoodoos and spires below. It was a thoughtful repose as if he was looking at a puzzle, a question without an answer. I've never seen my son look at something so deeply.

We lost some time at the first stop, but it was well worth it. It was "Bryce's Point," after all; this was the spot he requested to go to first. The next stop was Inspiration Point where the ranger's talk would be held.

With now just 15 minutes to get to the talk, the shuttle seemed to slow through time. My wife kept twisting my wrist to see what time it was on my watch. Three minutes to talk time. Angela does not like to be late to anything and while technically we could have taken our time in an enjoyable manner and strolled up for the last five minutes of the talk, she would have none of that. We had to be there on time.

"When is this blasted shuttle going to get to the next stop?" she asked. I had been married long enough to know not to answer rhetorical questions as they only encouraged additional questions of an unanswerable nature.

"We're going to miss it. We are going to miss the talk," she said, looking ahead of the bus for anything that would indicate Inspiration Point was close.

"I'm sure we will catch most of it, if not all of it," I said calmly. She was only being Type A out of love for her son.

"What if they run out of seating and we miss the whole thing?"

"We won't miss it dear, don't worry." I saw a sign. "Look, we're here."

As the shuttle pulled to the stop, everyone stood up in preparation to disembark. Ang helped lobby the kids for a quick exit. She clapped her hands to rally their attention and said, "Okay kids, get your water bottles back in your packs. Let's get ready to go. We don't want to miss the ranger talk."

The kids gathered their stuff as the bus pulled up. We all got off the shuttle in a manner of hurried patience as we melded with the crowd around us. Everyone seemed to be getting off the shuttle at this stop. I watched the kids get off and then ran to catch up with Ang, who was speed walking to the edge of the canyon.

"Come on! We are going to miss it!" she said loudly to the people in front of her. No time to turn around for this woman. She was going to make this talk.

"Okay, okay! Kids, come on." I motioned for Ev to take the lead in front of me. "Come on, Ev."

"Sure, Dad", and then with a slight pause Everest added, "Dad, where's Bryce?" I turned around to see the shuttle bus driving away and then turned my attention to the crowd, quickly surveying it. Bryce was not with us. Then as the shuttle was pulling out of reach I saw him, on the bus.

"Ang! We left Bryce on the bus!"

"No we didn't, he got off with me."

"He's not here, dear. He must have gotten back on the bus."

Ang stopped dead in her tracks so fast everyone behind her had to quickly adjust to avoid running into her. "What?!" she exclaimed.

71

"He's not here." I tried to sound calming, as if that would help.

"Eric! BB! Oh my God! BB's lost! We need to find him!"

"I'll go see when the next shuttle's coming! See if you can find someone." I ran over to a kiosk that showed the shuttle times. Another shuttle would come in less than 10 minutes.

Ang saw the ranger who was going to give the geology talk. She stopped him in his tracks and said in a panicked flurry of words, "Excuse me! You have to help me please! We've lost Bryce! We've lost our Bryce!"

The ranger looked at her confused and took a step back. "I'm sorry, ma'am. You've lost Bryce?"

"Yes! Where's Bryce? Where's Bryce? We've lost Bryce!" she said in a frantic Southern undertone.

The ranger maintained composure. "Not to worry, ma'am, lots of people get disoriented up here. Bryce is right over there." The ranger pointed to Bryce Canyon. "I'm pretty sure it's not lost."

Ang looked briefly at where he pointed and then turned right back to the ranger. "What! No! You don't understand! Listen! Bryce is gone!"

"Ma'am, I ah..." the ranger looked confused and now a little concerned at my wife's odd behavior. A couple of tourists gathered to help calm Angela down by repeatedly pointing to the rim of Bryce Canyon and saying, "Bryce is right there! Bryce is right there!"

"I'm not looking for the stupid canyon, I'm looking for Bryce! My Bryce!" she exclaimed.

Everest quickly stepped in. "My brother's name is Bryce and he got back on the shuttle," he said, trying to help.

"Please! He's only nine years old!" she cried.

"Oh! You have a son named Bryce!"

"That's what I've been saying! Bryce David! He's lost on the shuttle!"

By this time a small crowd had gathered around my wife to either help or try to make sense of the lost crazy woman. I ran back from the kiosk with a plan to get on the next shuttle and have Ang stay put with Ev. If Bryce got off, I would find him. If he stayed on the shuttle, it would eventually return to Inspiration Point.

This proved unnecessary thanks to the ranger's walkie-talkie. Once the ranger understood that we were indeed looking for our son Bryce, he called the shuttle drivers. After a short back and forth between the drivers and the ranger, there was a sigh of relief. They found him.

I returned as the ranger said into his walkie-talkie, "Put him at Table 3."

"Table 3?" I asked.

"You'll find him at Bryce Lodge. Take the next shuttle and get off at the lodge and find the hostess. Her name is Phyllis. Don't worry, we have a system.   You aren't the first parents to lose your child in Bryce Canyon, but I have to say you are the first to lose one named after Bryce Canyon."

My wife was profoundly grateful. "Thank you! Thank you so much. I'm so glad you found him! I'm sorry I got so excited. Bryce is a Celtic name, you know."

"I'm just glad we found him ma'am. Sorry for not understanding you at first," he chuckled. We were still a little too shaken up to laugh at that point, though it was the topic well into the evening of how we lost Bryce in Bryce and how only Bryce could pull that off.

We found our B Bear at Bryce Canyon Lodge enjoying a hot fudge sundae. He was nonplussed at the situation. "Hey, Mom" he said calmly, giving a short wave.

"We normally just give them a scoop of ice cream," the hostess said. She was a kind maternal woman. "But he was so cute; I gave him a full hot fudge sundae. I hope you don't mind. I couldn't help but spoil him a little. Unless a child is closer to the visitor center, they drop him off here at the lodge. He said he forgot his junior ranger book and that he was named after the park and didn't want to not miss getting his junior ranger badge. You had quite an adventure today, didn't you Bryce?" She patted him on the head.

Bryce took another bite of hot fudge. "Ummmm. I guess so. I'm sorry, Mom! I just wanted to get my badge!"

"BB! We were worried sick about you!" Ang exclaimed, hugging him and then petting his hair.

"Sorry Bro Bro, were you scared?" Everest asked.

"No, not really. They just asked if there was a Bryce Henze on the bus and I said yes and they put me here and gave me ice cream. I figure it's because I'm, well, you know, we're in Bryce Cannon and I'm named Bryce, just like the cannon." He then pointed at the hostess. "She told me I was lost and should be happy that they found me, but come on, guys! I would have just taken the shuttle in a circle back to where you were. It's not like I'm 4!"

Ang chuckled and hugged her little man. "Bryce, what am I going to do with you? You are going to be the death of me."

"Me too!" Everest stated. "I was freaking out!" He let out a big sigh and piled onto mom's hug.

I joined in on the group hug. I was so glad we had found our little guy.

"B Bear," I thought. "Our skinny little bundle of chaos, what are we going to do with you indeed."

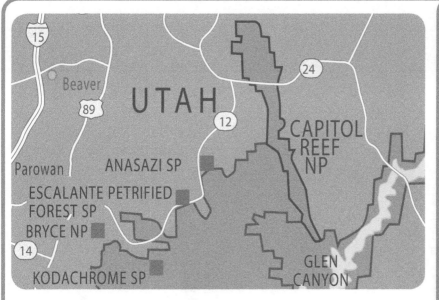

Quick Facts

Official Park Website: www.nps.gov/care

Visitor Center: (435) 425-3791

Park Size: 241,904 acres

Established: 12/18/1971

Visitors: 0.8 million (2014)

Experience Level:

- Family Friendly to Backcountry Hiker

Park Accessibility:

- Okay for 2WD and RVs
- 4WD recommended in some areas
- Day and Overnight Use

Nearest Town with Amenities:

- Torrey, UT is 11 mi / 18 km from park

Getting There:

- From Bryce Canyon National Park: Take UT-22 North, UT-62 North and UT-24 East 119 mi / 192 km to park entrance
- From Moab, UT: Take US-191 North, I-70 West-and UT-24 West 146 mi / 235 km to park entrance

Capitol Reef National Park

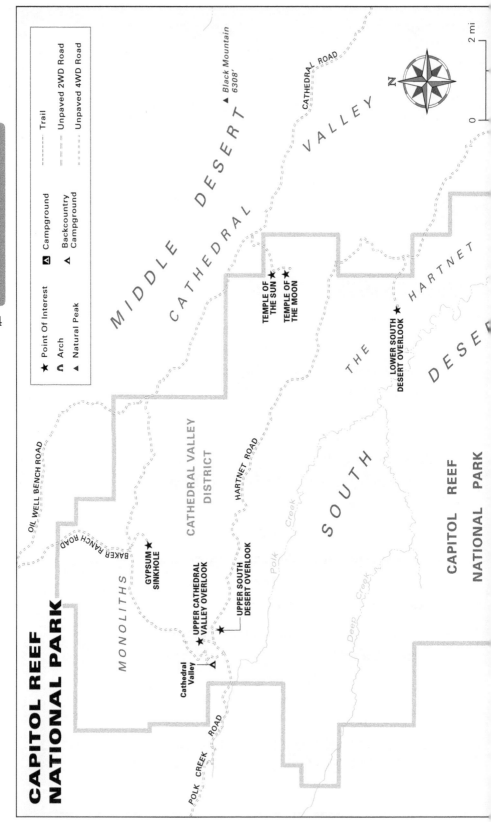

CAPITOL REEF
NATIONAL PARK

Legend:
★ Point Of Interest
∩ Arch
▲ Natural Peak
🅐 Campground
▲ Backcountry Campground
------- Trail
===== Unpaved 2WD Road
===== Unpaved 4WD Road

MIDDLE DESERT

CATHEDRAL VALLEY

▲ Black Mountain 6308'

CATHEDRAL ROAD

HARTNET

★ TEMPLE OF THE SUN
★ TEMPLE OF THE MOON

THE SOUTH DESERT

★ LOWER SOUTH DESERT OVERLOOK

OIL WELL BENCH ROAD

BAKER RANCH ROAD

MONOLITHS

★ GYPSUM SINKHOLE

CATHEDRAL VALLEY DISTRICT

HARTNET ROAD

★ UPPER CATHEDRAL VALLEY OVERLOOK

★ UPPER SOUTH DESERT OVERLOOK

▲ Cathedral Valley

Polk Creek

Deep Creek

POLK CREEK ROAD

CAPITOL REEF NATIONAL PARK

N

0   2 mi

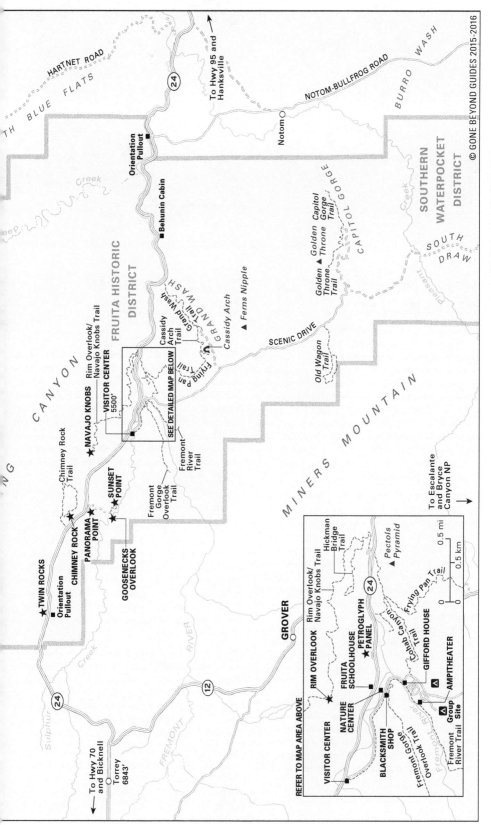

HARTNET ROAD

BLUE FLATS

24

To Hwy 95 and
Hanksville

NOTOM-BULLFROG ROAD

BURRO WASH

Notom

Orientation
Pullout

Behunin Cabin

FRUITA HISTORIC
DISTRICT

SOUTHERN
WATERPOCKET
DISTRICT

SOUTH
DRAW

CAPITOL GORGE

Golden
Throne
Trail

Golden
Throne

Capitol
Gorge
Trail

Ferns Nipple

Cassidy Arch

Cassidy
Arch
Trail

GRAND WASH

Grand Wash
Trail

Frying Pan Trail

SCENIC DRIVE

Old Wagon
Trail

CANYON

Rim Overlook/
Navajo Knobs Trail

NAVAJO KNOBS

VISITOR CENTER
5500'

SEE DETAILED MAP BELOW

★ Chimney Rock

Chimney Rock
Trail

★ SUNSET
POINT

Fremont
Gorge Overlook
Trail

Fremont River
Trail

MINERS MOUNTAIN

To Escalante
and Bryce
Canyon NP

★ TWIN ROCKS

Orientation
Pullout

★ CHIMNEY ROCK
★ PANORAMA
POINT

GOOSENECKS
OVERLOOK

Creek

RIVER

GROVER

12

Sulphur Creek

24

To Hwy 70
and Bicknell

Torrey
6843'

FREMONT RIVER

REFER TO MAP AREA ABOVE

Rim Overlook/
Navajo Knobs Trail

RIM OVERLOOK ★

FRUITA
SCHOOLHOUSE

★ PETROGLYPH
PANEL

VISITOR CENTER

NATURE
CENTER

BLACKSMITH
SHOP

Fremont Gorge
Overlook Trail

Group
Trail Site

Fremont
River Trail

GIFFORD HOUSE

AMPITHEATER

Cohab Canyon Trail

Hickman
Bridge
Trail

Pectols
Pyramid

24

Frying Pan Trail

0.5 mi

0.5 km

0

Pendleton Barn in Fruita

WHAT MAKES CAPITOL REEF SPECIAL

At this point, you will have driven through the Colorado Plateau for several days. Much of it is various compositions of nature's handiwork in stone; slow sculpting, sanding, and weathering of red rock that was born from millions of winters and as many summers. Each national park represents some of the best works for our enjoyment, and Capitol Reef is no different. Here there are temples of stone, magnificent cliffs and monoliths that are able to fill the eye with awe. As much as Capitol Reef is filled with such wonders of rock and canyon, there is something a bit more manmade that makes the park so special. It is a place called Fruita.

Fruita (pronounced "fruit-ahh") is a lush oasis within the hot dry desert. It is green, cool, and wonderfully sleepy. All day somewhere a sprinkler is casting sprays of water wrapped within a quiet "swoosh-swoosh-swoosh" lullaby. Visitors can pick their own fruit (when in season) from the park's orchards, view the nearby rambling waters of the Fremont River or visit historic buildings. In the spring, the tidy little valley is awash with the sight and smell of cherry, peach, apple and apricot blossoms. The rest of the year, the air smells fresh and green, which is a welcome reprieve from the desert. They sell homemade pies and your campsite is flat and surrounded by freshly mown grass. Large tree trunks lift up a canopy of leaves to shade you. Fruita is a paradise.

After all the hiking in Zion and Bryce, Capitol Reef offers a chance to relax. It is a place to rediscover the reason you took time off work, a place to reconnect with what in life has importance. Here you feel okay allowing time to stop while you simply do nothing but gaze at the surrounding cliffs and take another bite of pie. All this for $20 a night.

THINGS TO DO IN CAPITOL REEF

GIFFORD HOUSE (PIE SHOP)

The Gifford House is listed here first because it contains one very important thing: fresh pies for sale. This is not to diminish the self-guided historical tour of the Gifford Home, but let's get our bearings straight. You are on vacation. You have been traveling together for several days at this point, roughing it to some extent and burning off a lot of calories exploring Zion and Bryce canyons NPs. Its likely hot outside, at least one of your family snores too much and while that RV shower does get the job done, it is hardly resort pressure.

Plus, let's not forget one simple fact. You are out in the middle of nowhere, literally.

Yet here, in the middle of the desert, is pie. Not only pie, which in and of itself is flaky and wonderful yet not too sweet, but ice cream as well, in multiple flavors. The point here is that there has never been a time in your life since your childhood when the stars have aligned to quite this extent that you can sit down and eat a big piece of pie with ice cream without feeling one weensy iota of guilt. It's one of those more straightforward "you deserve it" decisions.

The pies are made locally in Torrey, Utah. The offering varies, but typically you can choose from apple, cherry, berry, peach, blueberry, and strawberry rhubarb. Each comes in its own individual-sized tin. There are covered picnic tables and even recycle bins specifically made for the pie tins. The gift shop also has locally made salsas, breads, scones, jams and other assorted goodies.

The Gifford House itself has been well restored to represent the mid 20s and earlier and, as stated, has many historical artifacts and a self-guided tour. The Gifford House is within walking distance from the Fruita campground. If you head toward the Fremont River, there is a quick back entrance trail to the home.

SCENIC DRIVE

(8.2 mi / 13.2 km), one way, allow 1 – 2 hours

There is an entrance fee of $10 per vehicle, which is covered if you have the Annual Pass. The drive provides a nice view into the initial heartlands of Capitol Reef. It is paved for the 8.2 miles and is thus accessible for an RV. Keep in mind that this is not a loop, but there is an obvious turnaround at the end of the paved road. Also, RV's over 27 feet are not recommended on any of the spur roads of Scenic Drive.

HIKING IN THE FRUITA HISTORIC DISTRICT

CHIMNEY ROCK LOOP

Strenuous – (3.6 mi / 5.8 km), round trip, allow 2 -3 hours, elev. Δ: 800 ft / 244 m, trailhead on Highway 24, 3 mi west of visitor center

Chimney Rock Loop, located near the park's western boarder along Highway 24, offers some great views of Chimney Rock and the surrounding landscape. For many traveling from Bryce Canyon NP to Capitol Reef, this area represents the first of many "Wow" moments as you drive into the park. Regardless of which direction you entered, this is one of the best trails in Capitol Reef and is well worth the time. This trail is great for sunsets, but bring good headlamps just in case you enjoy the scenery too long.

From the parking lot, the trail starts off wide and gentle, then climbs to meet with a junction to a longer hike to Chimney Rock Canyon and beyond. Stay to the right to catch the loop trail. The loop is slightly less strenuous if taken counterclockwise. Excellent views of Chimney Rock can be seen as the trail rises above the formation, especially in the afternoon once it is out the shadows. From here, the best description of the hike is panoramic, with views from Mummy Cliff, the high point of the hike, to Boulder and Miners Mountains, the Goosenecks of Sulphur Creek and Panorama Point. As you circle to the east, there are views of the Navajo Knobs and The Castle with the Henry Mountains towering in the distance. The route then descends down to the mouth of Chimney Rock Canyon. Stay left at the junction and return to the trailhead or if backpacking, take the right into Chimney Rock Canyon and on to Spring Canyon.

GOOSENECKS OVERLOOK

4 mi / 6.4 km drive from Fruita Campground

Goosenecks Overlook is an easy drive and subsequent walk from the campground and gives nice views of the goosenecks of Sulphur Creek. Goosenecks are relatively rare geologic formations. They are formed when the underlying rock is thrust upward where a creek is running.

With the creek running over soft sandstone, it is allowed to cut deeper into the rock, imprinting the initial meanderings of the creek or river into a deep impression as a gooseneck.

SUNSET POINT

Easy – (0.7 mi / 1.1 km), round trip, allow 30 minutes, elev. Δ: negligible, trailhead at Goosenecks parking area

The Fruita campground is situated low in a canyon near the Fremont River. While it is pleasant enough to watch the sun light fall off the distant surrounding rock walls from camp, for those looking for a more expansive vantage point can head to Sunset Point. This is a short little trail that spurs from the Goosenecks, allowing a decent view of the broader Waterpocket Fold. Along with a great sunset behind the Aquarius Plateau, there are different views down into Sulphur Creek Gorge, some 600 feet below. If going for the sunset, start out about an hour before the sun sets.

COHAB CANYON TRAIL

Moderate– (1.7 mi / 2.7 km), one way, allow 90 minutes, elev. Δ: 402 ft / 123 m, trailhead just across Fruita Campground

When Federal law officials were looking for polygamists in the late 1800's, the men folk of Fruita would hide all but one wife in nearby Cohab (short for cohabitation) Canyon. It's not hard to imagine that the phrase, "all those other beds are for guests", was a common one when the law came around.

Of course this is pure legend and would have many a park ranger rolling their eyes when asked about the provenance of the canyon's name, but it does make for an interesting story. The trail itself, being close to Fruita campground, is one of the most popular hikes in the park. The hike climbs 22 switchbacks for 400 feet elevation gain to give some great views of Fruita and the Fremont River.

Because you can't eat the pie tin

After completing the switchbacks, the trail become flat to the mouth of Cohab Canyon. Inside the canyon, one is surrounded by Wingate Sandstone. In many places you can see "tafoni" formations, which look like Swiss Cheese like holes in the rock walls. Tafoni are formed when the calcium carbonate holding the sand together into sandstone dissolves, leaving a sponge like system of holes.

Inside Cohab Canyon are several side canyons worth exploring, locally referred to as the "Wives". In the main canyon, look for the Cohab Arch and some solitary hoodoos. If you want to add a little more to the hike, take the spur trail from the Cohab Arch to the Fruita Overlooks. This side trip is well worth taking, providing some excellent views of the Fremont River Canyon and Walker Peak. There are two overlooks, named North and South respectively. The spur trails add an additional 1.2 miles and an hour to the hike.

Back on the main trail, continue heading up Cohab Canyon. Along the way, the trail passes Frying Pan Trail and onwards to Highway 24 a little more than a half mile further on. This final leg gives some great views of the Fremont River Canyon and Capitol Dome off in the distance. Hikers can opt to get picked up from here, head on to Hickman Bridge or turn around and head back.

Hickman Bridge

Moderate – (0.9 mi / 1.4 km), round trip, allow 1 – 2 hours, elev. Δ: 379 ft / 116 m, trailhead on Highway 24, 2 mi east of visitor center

This is a great little hike and a comfortable add on to the Cohab Canyon trail. It is one of the most hiked trails in the park and for good reason, as it offers great views along the way to a 133-foot natural bridge. The trail starts at Highway 24 or from Fruita Campground via Cohab Canyon. The lighting in this hike can be exceptional in the morning, plus getting an early start will also ensure a parking space during peak season. The trail starts along the Fremont River for a small stretch before climbing a series of switchbacks. Elevation gain here is about 100 feet, coming out onto a small grassy shelf. At this point, look for an informal looking spur trail that quickly ends at the remains of a pit house built by the Fremont people somewhere between 600-1300 AD.

After a very short distance, the trail meets with the junction to the Rim Overlook and Navajo Knobs. Stick to the left and climb again, passing the cone shaped Navajo Dome to the north. Capitol Dome is to the east and is where the park gets half of its name. The trail then descends through pinyon juniper forests, giving a good feel of immersion into the wilds of the park. After a short distance, the trail passes a small bridge in a wash, known as Nels Johnson Bridge. The trail ends at a 1/3-mile loop that passes under and around Hickman Bridge.

A couple of things about Hickman Bridge, it is pretty tough to photograph since it is surrounded by cliff walls. It is 125 feet high and 133 feet long. Arches and bridges both have water as one of the erosional elements that help create them. Bridges are distinguished from arches in that they are created from the direct result of free flowing water. Arches on the other hand are caused by the indirect effects of water, wind, and time on sandstone fins.

Rim Overlook / Navajo Knobs Trail

Strenuous – (4.6 mi / 7.4 km), round trip for Rim Overlook, (9.4 mi / 15.2 km), round trip for Navajo Knobs), elev. Δ: 540 ft / 165 m to Rim Overlook, trailhead at Hickman Bridge trailhead

The Rim Overlook starts from the Hickman Bridge trail. The full hike is strenuous due to elevation gains. The Rim Overlook is 4.5 miles (7.2 km) round trip,

The Waterpocket Fold from Strike Valley Overlook

climbs 1,110 feet and gives great views of Fruita and the surrounding valley. The Navajo Knobs trail extends from the Rim Overlook trail. The Knobs are a collection of Navajo sandstone hills that are uniquely formed. The trail leads to one of the smaller knobs, though it is possible for a skilled scrambler to scale the other formations as well. The Navajo Knobs give 360-degree views as the reward for climbing an additional 500 feet over 2.5 miles (4.0 km).

FRYING PAN

Strenuous – (2.9 mi / 4.7 km), one way, allow 1 – 2 hours, elev. Δ: 810 ft / 247 m, trailhead at Grand Wash Trailhead

Frying Pan Trail is a connector trail linking Cohab Canyon and Cassidy Arch Trails and beyond to the Grand Wash Trail. The trail travels along high and scenic ridgetops offering great and expansive views. There is a spur trail into Frying Pan Canyon, which starts about 2.2 miles in from Cassidy Arch Trail junction. This little canyon is fun to explore, with water pockets and high walls at the end of the canyon. Add another mile to the trip if going into the Frying Pan (Canyon, that is).

FREMONT GORGE OVERLOOK

Strenuous – (4.6 mi / 7.4 km), round trip, allow 3 - 4 hours, elev. Δ: 1,090 ft / 332 m, trailhead on Scenic Drive

This is a great hike. There is a short ascent of about 1/3 of a mile that puts the hiker on a wonderful mesa trail. If you enjoy being on a lone single track within a mesa top of desert brush, high up with the blue sky yet above you, the grassy shrubs below and thick red rock cliffs looming grand in the front, this is the hike for you. Look for rounded and varnished volcanic black boulders along the way.

After the gentle stroll across the mesa, the trail ascends steeply to Fremont Gorge Overlook. This last stretch is strenuous at times leading to a solitary formation of Moenkopi rock. Once past this formation, the trail juts left to the rim of Fremont Gorge. The overlook gives spectacular views down into the deep gorge. From here, enjoy a snack and head on back the way you came.

FREMONT RIVER

Easy to Moderate – (2.6 mi / 4.2 km), round trip, allow 1.5 – 2 hours, elev. Δ: 400 ft / 122 m, trailhead near Fruita Campground, loop B

As the name of this trail suggests, this little path follows along the Fremont River. The first stretch is flat and open to dogs and bikes and is ADA accessible. After about 0.4 miles, the trail switches into more of a rugged single track, with a gated passage that asks that all but hikers turn back. From here, the trail climbs steadily, ending at absolutely stunning views of the Fremont Gorge and river as well as the Waterpocket Fold. At trails end, it is possible to wander around the area. Look for Fern's Nipple, a cone shaped formation that stands out in the southeast.

CASSIDY ARCH

Strenuous – (3.4 mi / 5.5 km), round trip, allow 2 -3 hours, elev. Δ: 670 ft / 204 m, trailhead at Grand Wash trailhead

The arch is named after none other than Butch Cassidy, the leader of an infamous band of thieves known as the "Wild Bunch" in the 1890's. It is reputed that Butch had dinner at the cabin of area pioneer Elijah Cutler Behunin along the Fremont River and that the group frequented the area. For a hike through land good enough for outlaws to an arch worthy of Butch Cassidy himself, look no further than Cassidy Arch trail.

The hike begins at the end of Grand Wash Road and immediately starts into a 600-foot ascent. Along the climb, the ledges of Kayenta sandstone are quite evident. As elevation is gained, the ecology of the trail changes to more densely packed pinyon juniper forest with stunning views of the surrounding sandstone. At the juncture to Frying Pan Trail, Cassidy Arch Trail juts to the left, down a gradual grade of slickrock to the canyon's rim and Cassidy Arch.

Once at your destination, look for the western themed Starbucks served by the great-great grandson of Butch Cassidy himself at the apex of the arch. As one hiker put it, "It was a delightful end to the hike", while another hiker has been quoted as saying, "The apex of the arch? Seriously? The author has clearly been out in the desert too long." Anyway, you get back to me with *your* experience.

GRAND WASH

Easy – (4.8 mi / 7.7 km), round trip, allow 2 hours, elev. Δ: 200 ft / 61 m, trailhead on Scenic Drive, 4.7 mi from visitor center

This there and back trail is one of the flattest hikes in the park. It's a great walk for children (even small kids part way) and can be accessed from either the Scenic Drive or Highway 24. One of the highlights is the Narrows, which is found about 0.7 miles in from the Highway 24 trailhead. This half-mile narrow stretch is banded by sheer walls of Navajo red sandstone, towering 500 feet on either side, with dark stains of desert varnish running down the cliffs. Farther into the hike, the canyon widens, allowing the hiker to take in the views at a leisurely pace. This section also contains more plant life than the regularly scoured sections of the Narrows.

OLD WAGON TRAIL

Strenuous – (3.8 mi / 6.1 km), round trip, allow 2 -3 hours, elev. Δ: 1,080 ft / 329 m, trailhead on Scenic Drive, 6.5 mi from visitor center

Perhaps the best part of this hike is its closeness to the Fruita Campground yet relatively unused aspect of the trail. While most of the trails along Scenic Drive take the hiker into the canyons and washes, Old Wagon Trail heads west away from them. This dishes up a hike that is more pinyon juniper in terrain. The trail is as persistent as it is straight as it climbs the 1,000 feet upwards, but does reward with some great views once

Hickman Bridge

elevation is reached. The Old Wagon Trail is not Capitol Reef's darling, sometimes the views are obscured by forest and the elevation gain can feel more like a dull march up alluvium, but it does offer unique views and hikers will likely have the entire journey to themselves.

GOLDEN THRONE TRAIL

Strenuous – (4.0 mi / 6.4 km), round trip, allow 2 - 3 hours, elev. Δ: 1,100 ft / 335 m, trailhead at Capitol Gorge parking area off Scenic Drive

Golden Throne trail is a short but steep trail that winds through the backcountry of the Waterpocket Fold. It takes the viewer to the base of a large monolith known as the Golden Throne. This up-then-down hike gets the hiker up in elevation quickly, climbing 800 feet and following a series of well-marked switchbacks. This is a great hike to climb up into the higher realms of the backcountry in short order and still leave time to take in the amazing views.

CAPITOL GORGE

Easy – (2.0 mi / 3.2 km), round trip, allow 1 hour, elev. Δ: 100 ft / 30 m, trailhead at Capitol Gorge parking area off Scenic Drive

Until 1962, this was the only road that passed through the Waterpocket Fold. The road passes through a high cliff-walled gorge that displays pleasant shadows in the late afternoon. For those up for a short hike, continue to the Pioneer Register, which contains the names of early Mormon pioneers etched into the side of the canyon. Across the wall where the pioneers "signed in," and all over, one can find petroglyphs as well. Also visible are the remains of old telephone lines. The trail officially ends at "The Tanks", a set of water pockets set in a row above the canyon floor. The natural curvature of these pools makes for a great resting spot. Those with more time can continue through Capitol Gorge to the eastern boundary of the park.

HIKING IN CATHEDRAL VALLEY DISTRICT

Getting to all of the hikes in the Cathedral Valley area requires traveling on the unpaved 28 mile Hartnet Road as part of a 59-mile loop. Much of the road is okay for most cars; however, there are a couple of spots, including a river crossing, which bumps up the need for a high clearance vehicle. This northern section of the park is very different than the rest of the park, being cooler, more densely forested in pinyon juniper and with the fluted monolithic spires collectively referred to as the Cathedrals.

UPPER SOUTH DESERT OVERLOOK

Easy – (0.4 mi / 0.6 km), round trip, allow 15 minutes, elev. Δ: 80 ft / 24 m, trailhead is 39 mi NW of visitor center on Hartnet Road to South Desert trailhead

This overlook provides wide expansive views of the Upper South Desert, a region dominated by a wide expansive valley of grasslands banded by sloping sandstone and some volcanic intrusion. Off in the distance, the Henry Mountains, the last mountain range in the contiguous United States to be mapped, lie as a centerpiece to this natural diorama. To the northwest lie the Thousand Lake Mountains, a wholly different world of Aspen trees, rambling creeks and even a bit of snow.

Take the obvious trail from the parking area and take the short hike to the overlook. The last portion does have a very short but steep ascent to the final viewing area.

CATHEDRAL VALLEY OVERLOOK

Easy – (0.2 mi / 0.3 km), round trip, allow 15 minutes, elev. Δ: 50 ft / 15 m, trailhead on Hartnet Road

The Cathedral Valley is special. Within it are 400-foot sheets of monolithic rock, distinctly orange in color, standing vertical right to their pointed tips. They look like curtains of rock, being a juxtaposition of fluidity and motion standing against an impression of eternal stillness. The Cathedral Valley Overlook is a little hike that gives one of the best views of this valley. Standing at the end of a rock peninsula, as high as the monoliths themselves, the overlook gives one of the most majestic views in the entire park.

There are picnic tables with some shade at the start of the trail. From the picnic area, follow the obvious trail through some trees down to the end of the peninsula. Note that the trail becomes a narrower route towards the end, with very steep drop-offs on either side. Use caution here.

Upper Cathedral Valley

CATHEDRALS TRAIL

Moderate – (2.2 mi / 3.5 km), round trip, allow 90 minutes, elev. Δ: 375 ft / 114 m, trailhead on Hartnet Road

Given the amount of time needed to undertake the 59-mile loop through Cathedral Valley, this trail often is overlooked. That said, what a wonderful little hike this is, hiking through arguably the heart of the Cathedrals, with some elevation gain to help give proper perspective to these unique and magical spires of Entrada Sandstone.

The trail starts in the Upper Cathedral Valley a couple miles prior to making the climb up to the primitive Cathedral Valley Campground (or down from the campground, depending). As the road climbs a small hill look for a sign that says, "Cathedral Trail Trails End 1.1". Park near the sign and head out on the trail, which starts to climb at a descent rate. As you round a corner past some trees, look for Needle Mountain and other Cathedrals. It will be easy to spot Cathedral Mountain, the largest of the monoliths. The trail levels out from here, giving up pleasant hiking and great views, and then climbs steeply to the final viewpoint at the end. If one looks closely, the Morrell Cabin can be seen along the trail.

MORRELL CABIN TRAIL

Easy – (0.4 mi / 0.6 km), round trip, allow 30 minutes, elev. Δ: negligible, trailhead on Hartnet Road

This little cabin still contains a few artifacts just laying around to examine. They are still around because folks leave them be, so please keep with the sentiment of past hikers. The cabin is part of a ranch owned by a cattle rancher by the name of Lesley Morrell in the 1930's. For many, it became a way station for ranchers looking for a place to bed down for the night until the 70's, when it was placed into a preservation mode by the park. The little one room cabin is now listed on National Register of Historic Places

For those that make it out to Cathedral Valley, this becomes one of the must do hikes along the way as it hard to justify coming all this way and NOT seeing the cabin. The hike itself is straightforward with no real elevation gain and is accessed along a very well maintained path. It is possible to go inside the cabin, where there are tons of old relics found around the area. The views along the way are impressive and peaceful to the eye. Wildlife is often spotted along the trail.

HIKING IN THE SOUTHERN WATERPOCKET DISTRICT

This is the least visited section of the park and as such, the trails are often more rugged and unmaintained. For most that make it out here, the Waterpocket District offers a more immersive experience, where the route taken is defined only by one's skill. The section below outlines the various trails in this region of the park. Consult with a ranger at the visitor center for more detail on any of these hikes.

BURRO WASH

Strenuous – (3.4 mi / 5.5 km), round trip, allow 3 -4 hours, elev. Δ: 350 ft / 107 m, trailhead is 9 mi south on Notom-Bullfrog Road

The "stubbornest" of the three slot canyons in this area. Expect many chockstone obstacles and two sets of narrows that confine the hiker to shoulder width. It is not unheard of in some places to climb out of the slot canyon briefly to reengage it at wider spot or to navigate a chockstone.

COTTONWOOD WASH

Strenuous – (3.3 mi / 5.3 km), round trip, allow 3 -5 hours, elev. Δ: 350 ft / 107 m, trailhead is 9 mi south on Notom-Bullfrog Road

This is the most obstacle laden and wettest of the slot canyons in this area. Start by scrambling up and over or around a set of large chockstones as the canyon narrows. Continue to a thin lens of water that must be waded through to continue. If you decide to continue (first off congrats, most folks turn around here), you will be rewarded with yet more chockstones that need to negotiated often and even more pools of water. Finally, gaze upon an impassable 35-foot dry fall and either turn around or get out the ropes and continue deeper into the canyon for more. After all this hard work, just think how good dinner will taste when you get back to your camp!

SHEETS GULCH

Strenuous – (6.7 mi / 10.8 km), round trip, allow 5-7 hours, elev. Δ: 500 ft / 152 m, trailhead is 13 mi south on Notom-Bullfrog Road

A rough around the edges slot canyon in three sections. Plenty of chockstone and waterpocket pool obstacles to navigate, making this a nice scramble puzzle, and potentially wet fun.

RED CANYON TRAIL

Moderate – (4.5 mi / 7.2 km), round trip, allow 2 - 3 hours, elev. Δ: 400 ft / 122 m, trailhead is 21 mi south on Notom-Bullfrog Road

This hike offers wide-open expanses to slot canyons; Red Canyon Trail showcases the varied aspects of Capitol Reef National Park.

UPPER MULEY TWIST CANYON

Strenuous – (9.0 mi / 14.5 km), round trip, hard day hike or 2-3 day backpacking trip, elev. Δ: 800 ft / 244 m, trailhead is 2.9 mi south on Strike Valley Road

Freedom, surprise, and possibly even a little wonder combine in this multi-faceted citadel of red rock, white rock, arches, double arches, and even narrows. Some of the best views of the Waterpocket Fold to be seen are on this trail.

STRIKE VALLEY OVERLOOK

Moderate – (0.8 mi / 1.3 km), round trip, allow 30 minutes, elev. Δ: 100 ft / 30 m, trailhead is 2.9 mi south on Strike Valley Road

A great hike for those looking for that picture perfect view of the Waterpocket Fold. This is a short hike but gives views of the classic picture of the monocline that is seen in brochures.

LOWER MULEY TWIST CANYON

Easy – (8.0 mi / 12.9 km), round trip, allow 4 -5 hours, elev. Δ: 600 ft / 183 m, trailhead at Burr Trail, 2 mi west of Notom-Bullfrog Road junction

For this description, the trail starts at the Lower Muley Twist Canyon and ends at the Post Cut Off Junction. A great canyon hike, more wonder and scenic charm than slotted narrows, but well worth the effort. Lots of red rock in all its varieties to be seen along the way.

SURPRISE CANYON

Easy – (2.0 mi / 3.2 km), round trip, allow 90 minutes, elev. Δ: 240 ft / 73 m, trailhead is 34 mi south on Notom-Bullfrog Road

Surprise Canyon is the next-door neighbor to Headquarters Canyon. The biggest difference between the two canyons is Surprise opens up wide at the end versus Headquarters, which remains narrow throughout.

HEADQUARTERS CANYON

Easy – (3.4 mi / 5.5 km), round trip, allow 2 hours, elev. Δ: 400 ft / 122 m, trailhead is 35 mi south on Notom-Bullfrog Road

Headquarters Canyon is a narrow slot canyon with a sandy floor and tan water carved walls. This is a good hike for families, though be sure to check the weather before entering.

Oak Creek Canyon Trail

Moderate – (5.0 mi / 8.0 km), round trip, allow 2 -3 hours, elev. Δ: 200 ft / 61 m, trailhead is 4 mi east on Oak Creek access road

Waterfalls, diversions, dams, and scenic expanses can all be found on this hike with only 200 feet in elevation gain. Pleasant and peaceful, with a little alcove at the end to stop and have a snack while peering out into the canyon. A very worthwhile hike.

Lower Muley Twist Canyon and Hamburger Rocks

Strenuous – (17.0 mi / 27.4 km), round trip, hard day hike or 2-3 day backpacking trip, elev. Δ: 900 ft / 274 m, trailhead at Post Corral off Notom-Bullfrog Road

A dreamland of rock with unreal curvatures, heights, colors, and form. Akin to hiking in a museum of art for the day, where even the corridors to the next gallery are impressive. One highlight is the Hamburger Rocks, a study in erosion creating a series of logic defying toadstool like formations that just have to be seen to be believed. Allow another 3 hours to take the spur trail to these rocks.

Halls Creek Narrows

Strenuous – (22.4 mi / 36.0 km), round trip, hard day hike or 2-3 day backpacking trip, elev. Δ: 1,000 ft / 304 m, trailhead is 3.6 mi south of Halls Creek Overlook on airport road

The hike is like combining the Narrows of Zion with the purity of Capitol Reef. Towering rock walls bend and turn on the whims of the watercourse that created this slot canyon, all coming together to create one of the best-kept secrets in the entire park.

CAPITOL REEF LODGING

Staying in the Park

While Zion has a plethora of lodging and Bryce has a fair assortment, the weary traveler realizes that the variety has narrowed by the time you get to Capitol Reef NP. For those traveling by RV or tent, it can be said that you have chosen wisely as Fruita is one of the nicest campgrounds in Utah. For those looking for a motel

or something nicer, there are several in Torrey, UT and they do the job nicely. However, unlike Zion and Bryce, the town is about 10 miles from the park's entrance.

Also unlike Zion and Bryce, Capitol Reef doesn't have a lodge. Putting this all together in a good light, the lack of lodging is part of what makes Capitol Reef special. It is one of the over looked national parks, but is indeed as great a national park as any that garner the title. For this reason it is a hidden gem amongst the Grand Circle and I hasten to even write about it, lest I spill the secret out and the area becomes laden with all manner of hotels and inns. Capitol Reef contains areas that you can have all to yourself at times and those that stay a night or two within it are indeed the lucky few. This too is one of the main reasons why this book pushes the RV mode of traveling, it gives the family vacationer increased choice and consistency in the more remote areas along the Grand Circle journey.

Fruita

As mentioned, the campsites of Fruita are the best option available. Fruita is nestled in a small canyon near the Fremont River. The entire area is encapsulated by massive red rock cliffs that are spectacular in the late afternoon light. There are 71 sites, all available on a first come, first served basis. There are three loops that all offer great sites. Loops A and B are open year round, loop C and the group site closes from late fall to early spring. The campground is within a short walk of the Gifford house and the orchards. Across from the barn is a colony of marmots living in the nearby hills. Please watch from a distance so as not to disturb their community.

Fruita was listed in Sunset Magazine's 2013 Camping Guide as one of the best places in the nation to camp. While the official thumbs up are welcome in some ways, it means the word is out on this campground. Plan to arrive early; typically the place fills up by 10am in spring and fall.

There is a campground host and a self-service kiosk for the easy payment of $20. The campground also has two dumping stations, which is included in the camping fee. Generator hours are strictly enforced. You can only run your generator for two hours in the morning and two hours in the evening (8-10 am and 6-8 pm). The limited generator hours does add to the overall peace and harmony of the place, but it makes it hard to charge electronic devices.

STAYING OUTSIDE THE PARK

As a reminder, all lodging and dining is stated in order of distance from the park's Fruita entrance, from closest to farthest.

CAPITOL REEF RESORT

2600 East Highway 24, Torrey, UT 84775, (435) 425-3761, capitolreefresort.com

Any lodging located in the vast nothingness of the Southwest that has the word "resort" in its name should offer more than just a room. Thank goodness then that Capitol Reef Resort offers just that! Starting with the heated outdoor pool, it is large and inviting, with a stunning red rock view that is the southwest equivalent of beachfront property. The lodging itself is where the resort really shines. The rooms are some of the best in the Grand Circle, from the standard offerings to the studio king suites. On their 59 acre property, one can stay in a spacious cabin, with choices of king or two queen beds. The cabins are nicely decorated in a southwest style and are just plain relaxing to the eye and soul. They also offer surprisingly well appointed teepees (I mean, let's face it, one doesn't expect much from a teepee. These teepees will become the standard from which you will judge all other teepees).

It doesn't end there, they also offer cuddly Conestoga Wagons. Here they have taken an old school pioneer wagon and up leveled it to the point of singular luxury, singular because each wagon pretty much holds one king bed and two twin bunk beds, leaving little room for anything else. Still, this will be one of the few sleeping arrangements that will get lots of family photos. Private bathrooms for the wagons and the teepees are nearby. The resort also offers horseback riding, hiking and off road tours seasonally.

NOOR HOTEL OF CAPITOL REEF

877 UT-24, Torrey, UT 84775, (435) 425-2525, https://thenoorhotel.com/

This is a 2 star budget hotel under new management and still in need of renovation. Not at the top of the places to stay in Torrey, but the price is reflective of the quality and is good for those on a budget.

SkyRidge Inn Bed & Breakfast

1092 E Hwy 24, Torrey, UT 84775, (435) 425-3222, skyridgeinn.com

Another great lodging choice for those looking for a full immersion into the truly peaceful lands of Capitol Reef. The rooms are nicely appointed and the hosts are very welcoming. This B&B is just off the beaten path of the small town of Torrey.

DAYS INN TORREY CAPITAL REEF

825 E SR 24 , Torrey, UT 84775 US, (435) 425-3111, wyndhamhotels.com

Other than not knowing how to spell the park they represent, this is a fine place to stay, giving a lot of value for the price, including a pool and free breakfast. This might just allow one to save some "capital" while vacationing in Capitol Reef National Park. (Hey, trying to make lemonade here folks).

BROKEN SPUR INN

955 East SR24, Torrey, UT 84775, (435) 425-3775, brokenspurinn.com

2.5 star budget hotel with large indoor pool and pleasant accommodations. You'll have a nice quite room and are close to their steakhouse. The rooms are on the edge of needing a renovation.

TORREY PINES BED AND BREAKFAST INN

250 S Pine drive, Torrey, UT 84775, (435) 425-2405,

Cozy home set on 20 acres, Torrey Pines B&B is a good choice if you want to experience the great open southwest of Capitol Reef. The inn itself is quiet with great breakfasts, but the real value of this place is the location, which allows one to step outside day or at night and feel as if you have the entire state of Utah to yourself.

RED SANDS HOTEL

670 UT-24, Torrey, UT 84775, (435) 425-3688, redsandshotel.com

2.5 star mid-range hotel, offering clean rooms and a free breakfast. This is a solid choice from a value perspective. The hotel has an indoor pool and hot tub, free Wi-Fi, HBO, and on site guest laundry.

AUSTIN'S CHUCKWAGON LODGE AND GENERAL STORE

12 W Main St, Torrey, UT 84775, (435) 425-3335, austinschuckwagonmotel.com

What sets Austin's Chuckwagon Lodge apart is that it offers clean standalone cabins and suites and has a freshly stocked deli and grocery store. This is a 3 star hotel with 4 star service.

Golden Throne

Torrey Schoolhouse B&B Inn

150 N. Center St, Torrey, UT 84775, (435) 633-0230, torreyschoolhouse.com

This is a very unique B&B by any standard and certainly a one of its kind in Torrey. As the name implies, this is the old 1914 Torrey schoolhouse, now completely renovated with hardwood floors and an open floor plan. From the outside, the inn's brick exterior acts as a landmark for the town. On the inside, the grand room is as much as beacon, welcoming guests with its inviting approach and large space. The rooms are also bright and friendly and the breakfasts use organic ingredients served family style.

CAPITOL REEF DINING

The Rim Rock Restaurant

AMERICAN/STEAKHOUSE, meals for under $30, 2523 E Hwy 24, Torrey, UT 84775, (435) 425-3388, therimrock.net, daily for breakfast from 7am - 10am and dinner from 5pm - 9pm, (Seasonal hours, check locally for hours in off season)

Rim Rock Restaurant is found within the Inn of the same name. The dinners are well prepared with nice portions, offering fowl, fish, and beef dishes. The best part of Rim Rock Restaurant are the views. From the comfort of southwestern interiors, large pane windows look out into distant red rock mesas. The inn also offers a more informal dining option at their Patio, where one can purchase pizza and barbecue sandwiches.

La Cueva Restaurante Mexicano

MEXICAN, meals for under $20, 875 N SR 24, Torrey, UT 84775, (435) 425-2000, open daily, 12pm - 3pm, 5pm 9pm

As far as Mexican food goes, La Cueva is pretty decent. The cuisine is fresh and not greasy. The service is small town hit or miss. You may at times be pulled into the restaurant's drama and idiosyncrasies, which vacillates between entertaining and annoying.

Broken Spur Inn & Steakhouse

STEAKHOUSE, meals for under $30, 955 E SR 24, Torrey, UT 84775, (435) 425-3775, brokenspurinn. com, breakfasts from 7am - 10am and dinner from 5pm - 9pm, open from March 15th - November 15

The Broken Spur Steakhouse will not disappoint if you are looking for a good steak. This is one of those go to places after a long day of hiking to tank up and relax.

Slacker's Burger Joint

BURGERS, meals items for under $10 165 E Main St, Torrey, UT 84773, (435) 425-3710, open daily, 11am - 8:30pm, (Seasonal hours, check locally first)

The patties come from the freezer, which drops Slacker's down a notch on the quality scale. That said, the burgers do hit the spot after a day of hiking and the shakes and fries don't disappoint either, so all in all, this is a worthy spot if you are in the mood for a burger.

Red Cliff Restaurant

AMERICAN AND ITALIAN, 156 E Main St, Torrey, UT 84775, (435) 425-3797, redcliffrestaurant.com, meals for under $10, open daily, 11:30am - 9pm, Sundays till 8pm

Red Cliff Restaurant is a nice go to place if you are having trouble finding something everyone can agree on. They offer a selection of pizza, hot sandwiches and burgers along with a small Italian entrée menu and salads. They also offer ice cream cones, sundaes and even banana splits! Straightforward service, selection, and prices.

The Saddlery Cowboy Bar and Steakhouse

AMERICAN/STEAKHOUSE, meals for under $30, 422 W Hwy 24, Torrey, UT 84775, (435) 425-2424, saddlerycowboybar.com, open daily, 5pm - 1am, closed Monday and Tuesday

Capitol Reef National Park has been good to the town of Torrey, allowing for two steakhouses to do a good business. The steaks are worth a nod of approval but what really makes this place stand out is the ambiance and the fact it doesn't close until 1am. Imagine a spacious bar with rows of bison heads lording over pool tables and saddles for bar seats. Fun drink menu, dart boards, live music, deep fried pickles, bison meatloaf and... well, you get the picture. This place is cool.

Cafe Diablo

AMERICAN, meals for under $60, 599 W Main St, Torrey, UT 84775, (435) 425-3070, cafediablo.net, open daily, 11:30am - 10pm

Café Diablo offers fine dining within a short distance from Capitol Reef. The menu is labeled as "Southwest Fusion" and overall the experience is a good one. That said, the dishes are missing a boldness. Flavors remain comfortably within their boundaries, occasionally hinting that the chef could deliver much more. Perhaps the restaurant suffers from the fate of having to dial in the menu to cater to the largest possible tourist crowd. It's hard to pinpoint what's going on here, but it seems the spirit of the food gets removed somewhere between the menu listing and the dish itself.

COFFEES AND SWEETS!

Castlerock Coffee & Candy

COFFEE, CHOCOLATES, 875 E UT-24, Torrey, UT 84775, (435) 425-2100, castlerockcoffee.com, open daily, 7am - 4pm

Small cafe offering coffee drinks, along with breakfast and lunch menu items. They also make their own chocolates which come in different flavors and are fresh and delicious.

CAPITOL REEF HISTORY

Native Inhabitants

The earliest recorded evidence of habitation in Utah dates back 12,000 years. These were among the first North Americans, traveling over land bridges of ice created during the last Ice Age. Evidence is hard to find, but research suggests a people who lived in caves and natural rock shelters. They hunted mammoth and smaller game with sharpened chert arrowheads. There is no evidence that these early people lived in the Capitol Reef area, but there is enough to piece together the plausibility that they at least migrated through the Waterpocket Fold.

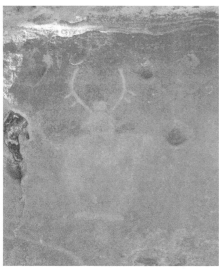

Petroglyph in Capitol Gorge

As the climate changed, so did the ecosystem. The native inhabitants changed with their environment and are characterized as people known as the Desert Archaic Indians. Living some 8,000 to 1,600 years ago, there is more evidence on these peoples that allow archaeologists to piece together their life. They were fairly nomadic, following the migration patterns of the animals they hunted. They had extensive knowledge of the plant life around them and from this wove baskets and clothing. They relied on plants for food, harvesting and grinding nuts and seeds into a flour.

They hunted game with throwing spears called atlatls. An atlatl is pretty ingenious. It comes in two parts and is similar in principle to a modern day tennis ball throwing stick for dogs. There is the dart, or spear, which has a sharpened point. The other piece is the atlatl which is a straight handle-like stick. One end has a buttress for the spear to rest against. The other end is where the hunter holds the device. A hunter holds the atlatl and the spear in one hand and casts the spear in a similar motion you would use to throw a ball or stick. The lever-like

action of the atlatl creates a fast-moving extension of the throwing arm. This extra length increases the force of the dart and the distance it can travel.

Evidence suggests that the native inhabitants began to incorporate farming into their lifestyle around 2,000 years ago. These inhabitants are referred to as the Fremont culture, named after the nearby Fremont River.

The Fremont culture expanded on their ancestral knowledge. They continued to hunt and live off of gathered plants and to follow the migrations of animals and seasonal patterns. There is evidence they used rock shelters as before. They also began to build their own shelters by digging pit houses, which are areas dug into the ground and then covered with brush. There is evidence that they lived within a social structure consisting of several families. Living by the Fremont River, they grew squash varieties, beans and corn to augment their diets.

There are four traits that distinguish the Fremont from other native cultures. They utilized willow, yucca and other natural fibers to create a unique style of basketry referred to as one-rod-and-bundle. This style of construction wraps fibers around willow or other naturally bendable rods in the form of a circle. They created moccasins from the hock of a deer or mountain sheep leg. Other tribes also made moccasins but in a very different method, using woven yucca. The third trait can be seen in their petroglyphs, examples of which can be seen right off of Utah Highway 24. The panels represent figures in trapezoidal shapes, which are unique to the Fremont. Lastly, their gray coil pottery is constructed in a fashion similar to that of other cultures but with unique patterns.

Evidence of the Fremont culture ceases to exist around CE 1300. There is no one archaeological study that has managed to explain why the Fremont ended their lifeway. It will likely continue to remain a mystery to both researchers and casual observers for generations to come.

Explorers, Surveyors and Pioneers

The historic period of early exploration of the Southwest was an exciting time. There were formal expeditions to find routes for man and rail. There were other less formal expeditions carried out by true frontiersman who took several years to cross from the East Coast to the west, hunting and trapping along the way, always a rifle in hand. They found a warm protected valley during the winter and built their only shelter for the season to protect them from the cold. While the tales of these informal expeditions are captured only in journals, they tell of a country that was truly grand and untamed, pure.

Of the formal expeditions, there are two of note. One was led by a couple of Franciscan Priests sent to find a route from Santa Fe to the second California Mission San Carlos Borromeo de Carmelo in 1770. Francisco

Atanasio Domínguez and Silvestre Vélez de Escalante set out with a handful of men in 1776, and while they neither went through the Waterpocket Fold per se nor made it to Carmel, California, they did cross through what is now Utah. Their detailed records added greatly to the relatively scant knowledge of Utah, which comprised the last territories to be charted in the lower 48 states.

Explorer John C. Fremont set out in the winter of 1853 to find a passable winter route for the railroad. This was Fremont's fifth expedition within the western territories and the second attempt at finding a decent railway route to California from Saint Louis, and he was well prepared for the challenge. However, the Waterpocket Fold with its repeated impassibility of rock and a particularly harsh winter made the journey difficult to the point that they lost one of their men and were forced to eat their horses. They did get out of the Capitol Reef area and were befriended by the inhabitants of a small Mormon settlement in nearby Parowan.

The Church of the Latter-day Saints in Salt Lake City sent pioneers to settle the Capitol Reef area. They established several settlements, including that of Junction, which was later renamed Fruita. Major Wesley Powell and several geologists and geographers also mapped out the area during this same period in the 1870s. These settlements did well along the Fremont River, including those of Loa, Bicknell, Torrey and Fremont. By 1880, Nels Johnson moved into Junction and leveraged the nearby river to plant apples, plums, pears, peaches, walnuts and almond trees. The settlement was renamed Fruita at the turn of the century and was nicknamed The Eden of Wayne County.

In 1892, a wagon trail was cleared by a group of pioneers led by Elijah Cutler Behunin, finally allowing passage through the Waterpocket Fold. The Fruita Schoolhouse was completed in 1896 from land donated by Behunin. His twelve-year-old daughter Nettie became the school's first teacher. The land was farmed successfully. No more than ten families worked and lived in the settlement at any given time. Life was good, work was hard and the area remained remote, fostering a tight community. The 1920s and the onset of the automobile brought Fruita a little closer to the rest of the world, but by 1941, the Fruita Schoolhouse closed and students were consolidated to Torrey schools.

The Gifford house was built by Dewey Gifford, one of the last settlers to farm in Fruita. He and his wife Nell built the two-story house and raised four children. Dewey later ran a small motel for visitors when the area was known as the Capitol Reef National Monument. They were the last settlers to leave Fruita, moving to nearby Torrey in 1969.

CREATION OF CAPITOL REEF NATIONAL PARK

In 1921, Ephraim Portman Pectol and his brother-in-law, Joseph S. Hickman, lived in nearby Torrey, Utah, and began to promote Capitol Reef in periodicals and newspapers. They created a local promotion booster, collected $150 to hire a photographer and called their club the Wayne Wonderland Club. Pectol was a Mormon Bishop at the time, but in 1928, he was elected to the Utah State legislature. He continued to attract interest to the area by going straight to President Roosevelt, asking for the creation of the Wayne Wonderland National Monument. President Roosevelt was convinced and on August 2, 1937 set aside 37,711 acres (15,261 ha) for the creation of the Capitol Reef National Monument.

The park was put under the control of Zion National Park. In 1943, Charles Kelly was appointed "custodian without pay" of Capitol Reef National Monument. Charles was passionate about the area, studying the area's history and archaeology. He finally became the park's first superintendent in 1950 at the age of 62. In the 1950s, the U.S. Atomic Energy Commission successfully lobbied to open up the area in and around Capitol Reef to uranium mining, which deeply troubled Kelly. This was a time of national security taking the front row given the demands of the Cold War. To the fortune of the park, there was not enough mineable uranium in Capitol Reef, and by the 1960s, the park's future was brightened by Mission 66.

The National Park Service was seeing demand increase at all of their parks and created Mission 66 to help meet this demand. The Fruita campground was built along with a new visitor center and staff housing to accommodate the increase in park personnel. This along with a paved road through the Fremont River canyon saw the park's visitation climb to nearly 150,000 in 1967. Along the way, the NPS began purchasing private land parcels at Fruita and Pleasant Creek.

Capitol Gorge Road

The Ancient Fold

Waterpocket Fold Today

In 1970, two bills were introduced into Congress to protect the entirety of the Waterpocket Fold by creation of a National Park. On December 18, 1971, President Nixon signed the act to establish 254,000 acres to be set aside as Capitol Reef National Park.

Today, the awe of Capitol Reef is in the fact that it has been relatively left alone since the Franciscan priests ventured through Utah in 1776. Much of its wonder must be discovered on foot. Much of its treasure comes only by getting out of one's car and, even then, the amount of land that is protected is enough for a lifetime of adventure. Yet even if you never stray from the campground, the presence of "Eden" is undeniable. There is a soft, enduring timelessness about Capitol Reef. Its future in the chronicles of history is represented by its visitors and what they do or, more importantly, don't do.

CAPITOL REEF GEOLOGY

It's interesting to write about Capitol Reef National Park from a geologic standpoint because this national park was created primarily to protect a very special form of geology. In fact, it's the largest form of this type of geology in North America. What is this amazing geological feature you ask? Why, it's a monocline! I know, fascinating right?! Okay, if you are like 99 percent of the population and saying to yourself, "What the heck is a monocline?" keep reading.

To best describe a monocline, look no further than Capitol Reef's very own Ripple Rock Nature Center. Designed for kids, they have a big layered piece of colored foam to help folks understand the definition of a monocline. If you simply set the foam down on a table, you can visualize layer after layer of sediment placed one on top of each other over the eons. If you push one end of the foam off the table, it bends. That bend is described as a monocline when it happens on a geologic scale.

There are other types of "clines" which are equally easy to explain. If you took the foam and bent it upward into a hill shape, you would have an anticline. If you bent it the other way to look like the letter "U," you would have a syncline. You are quickly becoming an expert in geology; you now know all the major clines!

Let's get back to Capitol Reef. Capitol Reef National Park protects a monocline called the Waterpocket Fold. If you think the foam version that you created in your head was cool, imagine it being comprised of a whopping 7,000 feet worth of different sedimentary deposits. These strata were then eroded along the bend exposing each of the layers. Going back to the foam example, it is as if a big chunk of the foam was removed, revealing all of the different layers at the surface. The oldest strata exposed are on the western side of the monocline with the youngest on the eastern side. The Waterpocket Fold is exposed north to south stretching for 100 miles (160 km).

The Waterpocket Fold is one of many monoclines that developed during the creation of the Rocky Mountains. As one tectonic plate pushed under the other, the Rocky Mountains rose as a result. While the brunt of the action was at the point of impact between the two plates, there were also gentle upward folds of rock layers that occurred downstream from the major action, folding the rock layers like waves.

The Waterpocket Fold was then eroded over time to expose the angled rock strata that you see today at Capitol Reef NP. These massive layers of rock, thrust up at acute angles, presented a huge challenge to pioneers who were driving westward. The Waterpocket Fold, with its length of 100 miles (160 km) was a barrier that could take days to get around. They saw this great land barrier as similar to the oceanic reefs around which some of the settlers had sailed previously. To the pioneers, the Waterpocket Fold was a land reef and thus the meaning of the second part of the park's name. By the way, the first part of Capitol Reef's name is also geologic in nature. The Navajo Sandstone layers at the tops of Capitol Reef NP have eroded away into soft white domes, resembling the United States Capitol.

While the Waterpocket Fold is the major geologic feature and is completely encompassed by Capitol Reef National Park, each individual layer is fascinating in its own right. For the geologic enthusiast, the best place to start understanding these layers is the Capitol Reef Visitor Center. The rangers hold a wealth of information and are happy to share what they know. For the casual observer, the biggest thing to keep in mind is that the oldest rock layers are on the western side of the park and the youngest on the east. If you are coming from Bryce and heading to Canyonlands, keep this in mind as you drive in and out of the park. The oldest rock layers in Capitol Reef date back some 270 million years. By the time you leave the park, the layers are merely 80 million years old.

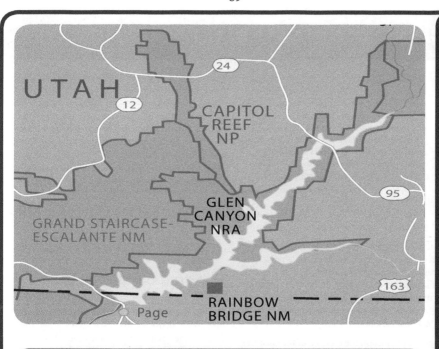

Horseshoe Bend

Parks Near Capitol Reef

Camping in Park:

- There are several campgrounds within the Glen Canyon NRA. Some are operated by the National Park Service, while others are operated by private concessionaires. There is also primitive camping allowed on the Lake Powell shoreline. Go here for a full list of camping opportunities within the park: http://www.nps.gov/glca/planyourvisit/camping.htm

Getting There:

- From Flagstaff, AZ: Take US-89A North 135 miles / 217 km to park entrance

While public sentiment is more positive these days, the creation of Glen Canyon NRA has been a point of intense frustration amongst the many who saw it as it was before the waters came. To have the land under the protection of the National Park Service is ironic in a sense because underneath Lake Powell lies an area worthy of being a national park in its own right.

In another twist of irony, the creation of the Glen Canyon Dam has its originations with the Sierra Club. Paved with good intentions, David Brower, the first Executive Director of the Sierra Club, fought to keep a dam from being built in Echo Park, Colorado, in Dinosaur National Monument. This site was under consideration by the U.S. Bureau of Reclamation from the 1940's into the 1950's.

David Brower and the Sierra Club did a great job of defeating the Bureau's bid to build a dam in Colorado. David published a picture book of Echo Park raising awareness of the unique beauty of the area. The Sierra Club ended up defeating the Bureau, but with the consolation that the Sierra Club would not get in the way of the Bureau's Plan B of putting the dam further south, in Glen Canyon. Brower had never seen the area, but when he did, he realized his mistake. This was a world of red rock, with over 125 side canyons, incredible amphitheaters of rock, arches, and lands sacred to some and home to the flora and fauna that lived there.

By 1957, construction had begun and while Brower tried to stop the Bureau Commissioner Floyd Dominy from changing "the environment for the benefit of man", the fate of Glen Canyon had been cast. Archaeologists took on a five-year salvage expedition to catalogue, photograph, and remove artifacts from over 250 sites. To get a full sense of the importance of what Glen Canyon was, the following video provides an excellent perspective. http://video.nationalgeographic.com/video/short-film-showcase/damnation-desert-goddess-remembers-arizonas-glen-canyon (Note: the video shows some B&W artistic nude photos and may not be appropriate for all audiences).

Today, most folks accept Lake Powell and Glen Canyon NRA on its own terms. What was will never be again, but what is, can still be enjoyed. The park has a large abundance of hikes and plenty of off trail trekking for those with a solid sense of adventure. There is also of course, camping, mountain biking, boating, fishing, and other water sports. The park is a mecca for the weekend road warrior, the family looking for some outdoor fun and the retired couple finding some warmth and solitude near the shores of this park that is at the same time a man made wonder and an atrocity to the even greater wonders of nature.

HIKING GLEN CANYON NRA

PAGE/WAHWEAP AREA

HANGING GARDEN TRAIL

Easy – (1.0 mi / 1.6 km), round trip, allow 30 minutes

Pick up the trail guide and take this short interpretive hike to an alcove created by a seep spring. The seep feeds a large amount of ferns and other plants as well as animals that frequent the moist oasis. Great panoramic views along the way.

HORSESHOE BEND TRAIL

Easy – (1.5 mi / 2.4 km), round trip, allow 30 minutes

If you are looking for the most iconic and picture perfect gooseneck ever to grace a southwest themed calendar, this is the hike you want to take. This is a short and straightforward hike to the overlook of Horseshoe Bend. Once you get to the overlook and gaze over, the image should be immediately recognizable. Watching the rafters float into sight, around the bend and out of sight is a peaceful thing to watch, akin to leaves floating down a stream.

ANTELOPE POINT

Easy to Moderate – Distance Varies

Antelope Point Marina is a good launching point for a walk along the red rock shores of Lake Powell. There are no trails here, but easy enough to just park and walk around. Hiking here is a pleasant activity after a lunch at the marina. Great scenery with excellent spots for a swim in the lake, plus an added bonus of watching the boats come and go.

THE CHAINS

Easy to Moderate – Distance Varies

The Chains is the name of a popular lakeshore access spot. The lake is calm and deep with some steep sections getting down to it. This spot is a favorite and is well known. This place can be a bit of a party spot, mind the broken glass, and boom boxes if you go here.

HWY 89 NORTH

BUCKTANK DRAW AND BIRTHDAY ARCH

Moderate – (6.0 mi / 9.7 km), round trip, allow 4 hours

Located just west of Big Water on Highway 89 is a trail to Birthday Arch and a small slot canyon. Drive towards Big Water from Carl Hayden Visitor Center to mile marker 9, hit your trip meter and drive another 0.75 miles to a pull off big enough for 3-4 cars and the trailhead.

The trail follows up a sandy wash with two small dry-falls to navigate. At about 1.8 miles look for the trail that breaks out of the wash towards the arch. There are typically some cairns to mark this exit point, but nothing official from the BLM. The arch is not easy to see and there are a lot of false trails created by those that have come before. Head west uphill over a sandy incline. The arch is not seen until you are nearly right under it. It is possible to stand directly underneath the arch, though doing so will require Class 3 scrambling and a good eye for the correct route.

From the arch, if you look across the valley you will see a very narrow short slot canyon. Heading back to the wash and up it will get you to this canyon or you can scramble down in more of a straight line to the same destination. Look for cairns to lead you out of the wash to the slot canyon. There is a petroglyph and some apparently ancient notches that looked like handholds to climb up the chute. The mouth of this slot canyon is overgrown, but not impassable.

WIREGRASS CANYON ROUTE

Moderate – (6.0 mi / 9.7 km), round trip, allow

This trail uses a wash as the route to a natural bridge with other small arches, side canyons, and balanced rocks to be seen along the way. This is a fun and easy "off trail" hike that doesn't require a huge amount of experience but allows for the feeling you are heading into the wilderness. There are a few dry falls to navigate, but all can be detoured by walking briefly out of the wash and around them. This trail is very exposed in the summer.

PAHREAH TOWNSITE

Easy – (1.0 mi / 1.6 km), round trip, allow 30 minutes

This is the movie location for Clint Eastwood's Outlaw of Josie Wales and many others. Take Paria River Valley Road five miles from milepost 31 on Highway 89. Panoramic views along the way via this dirt road that also passes the Paria Cemetery and Pahreah Townsite across the Paria River from the cemetery. Most of the area has been returned to the area's natural state due to natural flooding that has occurred. There is not much left of the Client Eastwood movie site but the area is still very recognizable if you are fan. See Starlight Canyon below for a hike that starts from the Pahreah Townsite.

STARLIGHT CANYON

Easy – (5.8 mi / 9.3 km), round trip, allow 3 – 4 hours

Starlight Canyon is a fun little slot canyon that is a tributary of the Paria River. Continue from the Pahreah Townsite another six miles (when dry, impassable when wet) to the canyon. The hike in the canyon is short but deep and narrow. There are lots of side canyons and camping spots available at the end the road.

LEES FERRY AREA

LONELY DELL

Easy – (1.0 mi / 1.6 km), round trip, allow 30 minutes

This hike is a flat and easy walk to the Lonely Dell Ranch site. The ranch was built by John D. Lee (of Lees Ferry fame). Poor John D. Lee was convicted of the Mountains Meadow Massacre and sentenced to death for this crime in 1877, the only Mormon to be convicted. Two years later, the LDS Church purchased the rights to Lee's Ferry from his widowed wife Emma. Brigham Young married John and Emma back in 1858 and the church was well aware of the importance of this river crossing as a link between settlements in Utah and Arizona.

It is possible to continue up the canyon as a day hike extension or a multi-day backpacking trip. The Paria Canyon continues for another 45 miles one way. A permit is required for overnight trips.

RIVER TRAIL/LEES FORT

Easy – (2.0 mi / 3.2 km), round trip, allow 1 hour

This sandy but otherwise easy trail follows the shores of the Colorado to Lees Fort. Construction for this fort began in 1874 due to mounting tensions between the Navajo and the Mormons.

SPENCER TRAIL

Strenuous – (2.2 mi / 3.5 km), round trip, allow 1 -2 hours

This trail starts from the end of River Trail (see above) near Lees Ferry. Spencer trail climbs steadily to the top of the Vermilion Cliffs for an absolutely stunning panoramic view of the Colorado River, Lake Powell, and surrounding area. Be advised of numerous switchbacks and steep inclines going up on this there and back trail, but the top of the world views are worth the ascent.

BULLFROG

PEDESTAL ALLEY

Easy – (3.0 mi / 4.8 km), round trip, allow 2 – 3 hours

One of the best hikes in the Bullfrog area. Starts up a sandy wash for about one mile then travels across slick rock via well-established cairns for another half mile to an area of eroded hoodoos balanced precariously for the time being.

GLEN CANYON NATIONAL RECREATION AREA

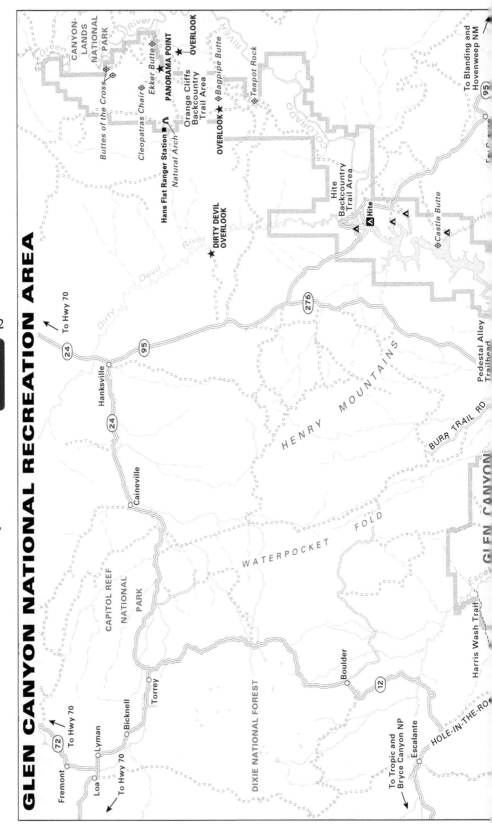

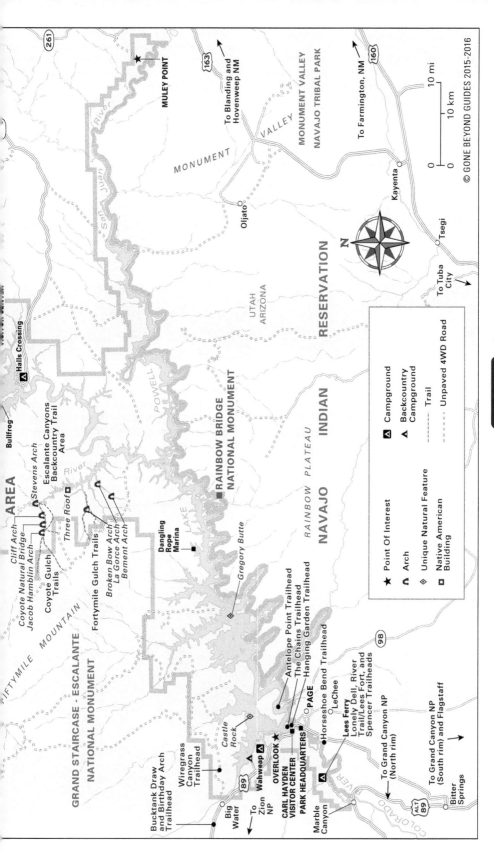

Parts Near Capitol Reef

Map labels:

MULEY POINT

261
163
160

To Blanding and
Hovenweep NM

To Farmington, NM

MONUMENT VALLEY
NAVAJO TRIBAL PARK

10 mi
10 km
0

Kayenta

Tsegi

Oljato

MONUMENT VALLEY

UTAH
ARIZONA

RESERVATION

To Tuba
City

N

POWELL

Halls Crossing

Bullfrog

FIFTYMILE MOUNTAIN

AREA

GRAND STAIRCASE - ESCALANTE
NATIONAL MONUMENT

Cliff Arch
Coyote Natural Bridge
Jacob Hamblin Arch

Coyote Gulch
Trails

Three Roof

Stevens Arch

Escalante Canyons
Backcountry Trail
Area

River

Fortymile Gulch Trails

Broken Bow Arch
La Gorce Arch
Bement Arch

Dangling
Rope
Marina

LAKE

Gregory Butte

RAINBOW BRIDGE
NATIONAL MONUMENT

RAINBOW PLATEAU

NAVAJO   INDIAN

San Juan River

Bucktank Draw
and Birthday Arch
Trailhead

Wiregrass
Canyon
Trailhead

Castle
Rock

Big
Water

To Zion
NP

89

Wahweap

OVERLOOK

CARL HAYDEN
VISITOR CENTER
PARK HEADQUARTERS

PAGE

Antelope Point Trailhead
The Chains Trailhead
Hanging Garden Trailhead

Horseshoe Bend Trailhead

LeChee

Lees Ferry
Lonely Dell, River
Trail/Lees Fort, and
Spencer Trailheads

98

To Grand Canyon NP
(North rim)

To Grand Canyon NP
(South rim) and Flagstaff

Marble
Canyon

Bitter
Springs

ALT
89

COLORADO RIVER

Legend:

★ Point Of Interest

⌒ Arch

◈ Unique Natural Feature

▢ Native American
Building

▲ Campground

▲ Backcountry
Campground

------ Trail

===== Unpaved 4WD Road

ESCALANTE CANYON

A good portion of Glen Canyon NRA protects the watershed of the Escalante River. Here, not only is the river itself within the park's boundaries, but also a very large portion of land surrounding the river. In fact, this area is so large as to make up nearly half of the park. Factoring in that this already large segment of the Colorado Plateau is surrounding by the even larger Grand Staircase-Escalante NM means one thing; a vast area that is remote, rugged and pristine.

The Escalante River was the last river to be named in the continuous United States. There was little development prior to its protection meaning much of this land is as it was 10,000 years ago. A trip to this area of the Southwest is to see what few have seen and large enough that return trips can be to and new area with each visit.

This area is jointly managed by the National Park Service, Bureau of Land Management, and the Dixie National Forest Service. All travel into the Escalante Canyons section requires a backcountry permit. These can be picked up at the Escalante Visitor Center within the Grand Staircase-Escalante NM. The hikes below are backcountry trips and are more routes than trails. This is an area where desert-backpacking experience is a must. This includes knowing how to read topo maps and a compass. Most of these trips are done after a lot of planning and typically done as multiday trips. This is some of the most remote land in the United States, venture into it with this in mind.

There is an excellent 32-page brochure on many of the hikes in this area. The brochure describes everything needed to have an enjoyable trip in the Escalante Canyon area. http://www.nps.gov/glca/planyourvisit/upload/Canyons%20of%20the%20Escalante.pdf

RAINBOW BRIDGE NATIONAL MONUMENT

Park Accessibility:

- Park can be accessed primarily by boat and on foot via permit. Boating tour information can be found here: http://www.lakepowell.com/

Rainbow Bridge is a bit of an oddity. To some it is an incredible feat of nature, protected by President Taft in 1910 with the words that this is an "extraordinary natural bridge". For others, the area has long been held sacred to the original inhabitants and their descendants, to a point of reverence such that even walking on and under the bridge is seen as disrespectful. For others still, it is something to do while boating on Lake Powell, a cool must see for those that are able.

The oddity here is that the bridge tries to be many things to many people. On the one hand, it truly is a place held sacred, to the point of lawsuits and continual mediation between the NPS and the five tribes that hold it as such. Yet it is also a tourist destination, amazing all the same, but often for very different reasons. The reason this is pointed out is if you do go, visit with respect. If there is one thing requested by the five tribes that hold Rainbow Bridge as deeply sacred is simply enjoy it from the viewing area, don't walk underneath it and don't try to climb it.

The bridge itself is 290 feet high and spans 275 feet across the river. What truly makes this natural bridge impressive is in its girth and rounded rainbow like shape. The top of the arch is an impressive 42 feet thick and 33 feet wide.

Most everyone gets to the bridge via a tour boat or private boat. There is a courtesy dock for temporary boat parking. From the dock, it is a 2-mile hike to the viewing area. In the summer, temperatures can get to an excess of 100 degrees, so plan accordingly with water and sun protection.

It is possible to backpack to the bridge; however, a permit is needed directly from the Navajo Nation. Write to Navajo Nation, Parks and Recreation Department, Box 9000, Window Rock, Arizona 86515.

Rainbow Bridge within Glen Canyon

[Mom]: *Son, why did you take so long to come back from the restroom? Your food is getting cold.*

[Bryce]: *Well, I had to go, you know, to the bathroom.*

[Mom]: *Bryce, I just worry about you when you go to the bathroom.*

[Bryce]: *Why mom? I don't worry about you when you go the bathroom.*

Oh Blackwater

The Vegas that most people know, the Vegas that exists along the banks of the river known as "The Strip," is like nothing else in the world. It is so unique an entity as to be foreign, as unworldly as going to another country. You come to be a different person, to be larger than life and, for a brief moment, this world allows you to achieve that goal. If then the "on strip" Vegas is like a foreign city, going outside the thin veneer of Las Vegas Boulevard is like venturing into a border town. The rest of Las Vegas exists as a transition zone, a manmade area of great turbulence where the overindulgent worlds of Vegas and normal society combine, leaving in its path the worst of both. Off strip Vegas is where you can still get $2.99 steak dinners and $8 buffets, but also where seediness mixes with shoe repair and you can buy lettuce at the supermarket while playing the slots. As you leave the strip, the rest of Vegas seems dodgy, run down, as if it is weary of trying to keep up with its more glorious self. You see people who are just trying to live a normal life in a normal town, but for whatever reason, they chose Vegas. For us, leaving our hotel and heading off the strip was a bitter realization that the world called Las Vegas was an illusion and that the ordinary day-to-day task we were driving into to pick up our RV was the reality.

RV rental places all seem to have one common rule that they live by: they are (for the most part) only open on weekdays. They do have a small window between 9am and noon on Saturday only, but as it takes about 90 minutes to complete the checkout process, it's a tight window. For us, we were on vacation and thus could have planned an RV pick up on a weekday, but let's face it, hotels in Vegas are cheap during the week. Conversely, they are expensive on the weekends so we opted to drive to the RV place on a Saturday, walk through the checkout process and somehow drive the darn thing off the lot in the three hours the rental company was open.

As we drew nearer, Ang said, "Now kids, I don't want any discussions about blowing each other up or

bombing your dad or shooting anyone. I don't want any violent talk of any kind when we are at this place, do you understand? Sparkle ponies! I want you to think sparkle ponies!"

A quick note on "sparkle ponies." First off, our boys are not overly violent future mass murderers, they are simply boys. If they cannot wrestle to get the wiggles out, they will turn to verbal onslaughts, slinging at each other ever-increasing tales of doom, usually through means that are physically impossible, such as gathering up an army of alligators to attack the other's army of trained fire ants. At some point, one of them will cross a line, that line typically having something to do with the aforementioned alligators and the other brother's genitals.

Angela will then stop this unworldly war and try to reset their boyish brains with simple, pleasant terms. "Think sparkle ponies" was the current term in use. This phrase is actually a derivation from her previously used term, "Think rainbows and unicorns," which did at one time work to reorient their minds toward peaceful thoughts. For whatever reason, Ang wanted a new phrase and sparkle ponies was chosen. It was the mantra that somehow returned our children to the precious adorable cherubs that we thought we were getting when we first decided to conceive.

"This RV checkout process is bound to take a while, and I don't want you to get rambunctious while we are at the rental agency" she said.

"Your mom's right, you two are representing the Henze family." I felt like I was really adding value here.

"So no shooting my brodder?" Bryce grinned.

"Face palm," said Everest. "Bryce, did you not hear what Mom just said? Mom, Bryce is shooting me. You should punish him."

"I'm aiming right at your giggly puffs!" Bryce grinned, pointing his finger directly at Ev's nether regions.

"Mom! Now he's using bad language and pointing guns. Please punish him!"

"What? Giggly puffs isn't a bad word!" Bryce said, still grinning and quickly holstering his finger.

"Yea, but we know what it represents and that is an inappropriate area. No giggly puffs." I commanded.

"How about asphalt? Can we say ASPHALT?" Bryce asked.

"What? No! I think you know the answer to that. Look buddy, you need to reel it in and real quick," I said with some impatience. Bryce was acting like a true nine year old.

"Sure, Dad. Can I sing, you know, a song until we get to the RV place?" he asked.

"Depends." I said with a tone of distrust.

Bryce started to sing. "Giggly! Giggly! Giggly! Everest is one big Giggly Puff!"

"Bryce, that's enough!"

Both boys laughed heartily.

"What! I'm just singing a happy tune!"

"You're going to be singing the blues if you don't stop. Now reel it in, buddy. You know what happened to Fatima after all, right?"

"Okay, Dad. Sorry," Bryce said.

Fatima was my weapon. While Ang had sparkle ponies, I had a fictitious third son named Fatima. It didn't really matter that Fatima was a girl's name or that the whole premise was completely inappropriate, this simple story had a fantastic effect on calming the boys down. Pronounced "Fat – ee –ma", he was the son we had in myth and legend prior to Everest but because he was such a bad child, we decided to let him go. The story becomes incredibly vague from there for

obvious reasons but in a slightly humorous off-color manner, it did put a seed of doubt in my boys and they cleaned up real quick so as to be spared the fate of this nonexistent fifth Henze. They knew he wasn't real but were only 99 percent sure. It was that 1 percent of doubt that I could be telling the truth that mattered.

Apollo RV is about 30 minutes outside of town, a tremendous distance for a family excited to get started on their first RV trip. We pulled in and parked among a sea of RVs, all of which looked exactly the same. Not knowing what to do next, we went inside the office and met Sue, a pleasant down-home redhead who seemed to be the brains of the operation. She answered phones, cued up other renters that came in, loaded up the RV with miscellaneous items, suffered through the mounds of paperwork and ran our credit card all the while keeping a smile on her face.

"Hi there!" I said with an exuberance found only by someone not currently at work. "We are here to pick up our RV!" Sue gets our name and does some lookup magic on the computer. After a tense 45 seconds, she finds us in the system.

"So, you excited about renting an RV?" she asked.

"Yes ma'am!" I said.

"Have you ever driven an RV before?"

"No ma'am, I have not," I stated as enthusiastically.

"Oh, you're fired then," she said. She was kidding.

Renting an RV is a process, especially the first time. There is the bit about going over the contract, the proof of insurance, the realization you're going to need to buy the toilet treatment, the discussion around anticipated miles and finally the review of all manner of possible additional side items you can rent. These include linens and towels, tables, iPad docking stations, solar bun ovens and about 100 other items. The list is seemingly endless but finally you get to the big moment, your first encounter with one of the actual RV units. You saw a bevy of them as you pulled in but up until now you didn't know which one was going to be yours. Finally, you get to meet your home for the next ten days. I was like a kid at Christmas.

Sue walked us past all the other less suitable RVs to ours, the shining pride of the rental company. It was certainly the finest RV on the lot, and I secretly felt sorry for all those poor tourists inside who would have to suffer with the lesser quality RVs they would certainly be given. Yes sir, though our RV looked exactly like every other one on the lot, I was confident without a doubt we were getting the best one.

We immediately asked if we could go inside. The door was open, after all. This beautiful home on wheels was practically inviting us to come inside, so I headed for the RV door. Sue stopped in her tracks and paused. She had seen this doe-eyed look before. We were a couple of noobs excited as heck to just get in and drive off on our amazing vacation, and unless she reeled us in quick, she knew we would likely only get about a mile down the road before we hit something. So she paused and, with a deep breath, changed her sweet behind-the-counter persona to the cold personality of a focused drill sergeant.

"No. We can't go inside until we've finished the exterior walk-through. This is your first time, right?" She walked us through the features of each side of the RV, opening every panel and explaining what each was for in careful detail. There were so many hookups, I thought. There were cable hookups, water tank hookups, city water hookups, electrical hookups. I struggled to memorize all of them.

Any time our attention strayed in the slightest, say to wipe the sweat forming on our brows in the 105-degree heat, she slowed down until she had our complete attention. "Now, this is important," she kept saying. So many things we had to keep track of. It was mind-boggling.

In the end, we found if we nodded as if we completely understood her, Sue moved on to the next thing. My wife and I quickly became trained to stand, listen, say nothing and nod every time Sue wanted our assurance. After a short time, my brain filled up to capacity and all I could say to myself were things like "City water hook up. Check. Must figure that out tonight. Electrical hookup with generator bypass. Doesn't seem too hard, so check, another thing to fiddle with until I figure it out."

Then Sue came around to the gray and black water plumbing. She explained that the black water held the poo. Got it. I'm not a big fan of poo, so I'd better get this right. Perhaps if I listened carefully enough, I may not have to see, smell or god forbid touch poo. I could live comfortably not having any of these interactions, so I had better pay attention here. I somehow managed to carve out a bit more capacity to absorb what Sue was saying.

"Now this is the nasty part of the tour. This is where your gray water and black water are disposed of. The black water comes out first. The black water is the big pipe, and it connects to your toilet. The gray water is the smaller pipe and it contains your shower and sink water. Both the gray and black water pipes connect to one big outlet pipe where everything comes out." Sue pointed at the pipes.

"There is normally a cap on the bottom, but it seems to be missing. First time I've seen this." She paused to write down the missing item on her checkout list. "Not to worry, though, the RV has been emptied, so nothing's going to come out. Okay, you would normally remove the cap, clamp on and turn the hose I showed you on this end, put the other end of the hose into the dumping station inlet and use this valve to release the black water. Let the black water drain first and then run the gray water with this valve, which will help flush the black water. Get a bucket, which we provide, and fill it with some water and flush that down the toilet. This will ensure you flushed everything out. Any questions?" I liked Sue, she was all business.

I really didn't want to ask any questions. I wanted to get in and drive off. However, there was one thing she did that didn't make sense. As she went through the instructions, Sue kept pulling on the valve handle instead of turning the valve. Most valves I had worked with were turned to open them, not pulled. I needed clarification. This was, after all, an important task.

"So do you pull on the valve or turn it?" I asked sheepishly.

With full command of the situation, Sue stated, "No. You don't turn it. You pull on it."

To clarify further, she reached down to the black water valve and gave the handle a hearty tug. Without any warning, gallons of poo, toilet treatment fluid and well, all matter of hell flowed out of this valve, right in front of us, immediately hitting the hot pavement and burning into our nostrils.

We all stepped back quickly with eyes opened wide with horror.

"Oh! Oh! Nasty!" my wife exclaimed, reeling back from the stench until she bumped into the RV parked next to us. She was beginning to dry heave a little. It was certainly bad. Unworldly bad. It was poop in 105-degree weather bad. Demons could have flown out from that pipe and it would not have been worse.

Sue closed the valve as quickly as she could and, to her credit, calmly stood up and said, "Excuse me for a moment" and rapidly headed off to get help. I really admired Sue at that point; she was remaining composed against overwhelming odds. I pulled my shirt over my nose and looked at my wife with deep concern as to how she was taking all this. Her first impression of an RV was poop. Not a good start.

She looked me sternly in the eye and paused for a moment before speaking. "Well, honey," Ang said in what I call her "soft but firm" voice, "I'm just glad you're doing this because there is no way in hell I'm ever going near those pipes. That is just plain disgusting! It smells like, well I don't know... it smells like a beached whale covered in toilet bowl cleaner, that's what it smells like. For all that is green and golden I'm just disgusted." As she spoke, the wind changed direction, throwing a blow to our senses. We were forced to dry heave together back to the office while Sue made it go away.

The kids saw the look on their mom's face. "Mom, what happened?" Everest asked.

"Ask your father," she grumbled as she headed toward the air conditioning vent.

"Dad! What happened?"

"Well son. We learned that daddy's doing all of the dumping station duties on this trip," I said glumly.

Everest said, "Yeah, we knew that already, Dad. What the heck is that smell?"

"Son, we had an accident. The RV, umm, took a dump in the parking lot."

"It what?"

"The RV pinched a loaf. It dropped the kids off at the pool, laid a brick, made a deposit. I cannot make this clearer and I am more than a little traumatized, so let's not talk about it. You know how I am around poo."

"Yea, we know dad. Mom changed all the diapers."

"And god blesses her for it. I'm going to join your mom over there by the AC. I can still smell it. Ugh!"

"Take it easy, Dad. We're here if you need us."

"What happened to Dad?" Bryce asked.

"The RV couldn't hold it in or something and did a number two outside." Everest answered.

"Oh god! I thought I smelled something. I hope the RV can hold it in while we are on the trip!"

Sue cleaned up the mess, and we all pretended it never happened, as is the standard protocol of adults when bodily functions are concerned. For some reason the staff put up with our kids wrestling in their waiting lounge as she completed the tour. We drove off and since I had recorded the RV walkthrough so as to not forget anything, the kids watched the poo scene over and over, laughing each time as if it was the first time seeing it. We quickly put this little incident behind us, but one thing is for sure, I will forever know that one does not turn the black water valve on an RV. One pulls on it.

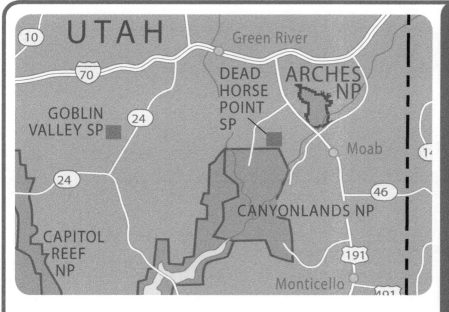

QUICK FACTS

Official Park Website: www.nps.gov/arch

Visitor Center: (435) 719-2299

Park Size: 76,679 acres

Established: 04/12/1929

Visitors: 1.4 million (2015)

Experience Level:

- Family Friendly to Backcountry Hiker

Park Accessibility:

- Okay for 2WD and RVs

- Day and Overnight Use

Nearest Town with Amenities:

- Moab, UT is 5 mi / 8 km from park

Getting There:

- From Capitol Reef NP: Take UT-24 East, I-70 East, and US-191 South 141 mi / 226 km to park entrance

- From Moab, UT: Take US-191 North 5 mi / 8 km to park entrance

Arches National Park

ARCHES NATIONAL PARK

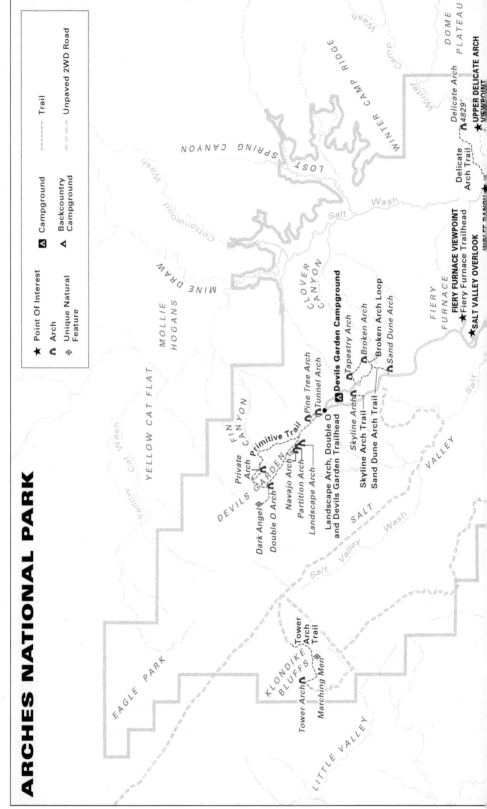

Point Of Interest ★

Arch ∩

Unique Natural ◇
Feature

Campground ◢

Backcountry ▲
Campground

Trail - - - - -

Unpaved 2WD Road = = =

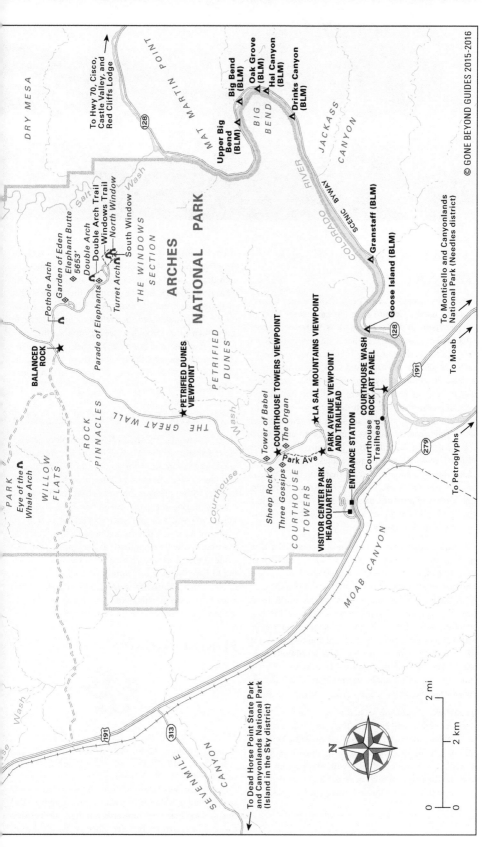

ARCHES

WHAT MAKES ARCHES SPECIAL

I'm always surprised when people tell me they did everything on the Grand Circle but have never been to Arches National Park. This park is truly special, but what makes it so special is that it isn't pretentious. It's simply a fun park to explore. There are more than 2000 arches of all sorts of shapes and sizes, and a new one is around just about every turn. Many of the arches are visible from the road and there are dozens that are accessible via short hikes. Even the entrance is fun. The road climbs up a tall cliff face from the visitor center like a roller coaster gaining some height before starting the thrill of the ride. Once in the park proper, the visitor is met with a seemingly endless combination of rock rainbows. There are arches that look like a parade of elephants, keyholes to doors and the eye of a needle. There are double arches, balanced rock towers standing on top of arches and even arches that look like the eye of some massive creature.

The park contains some of the most recognized arches in the world. At the top of the list is Delicate Arch. Most everyone who visits takes this hike, even though it does have a fairly strenuous climb at the front end of the trail. Even the hike to Delicate Arch is fun. It's a little hard, has amazing views along the way and just at the moment the weary hiker feels they really don't want to go any further, you turn around a bend and there it is, big as life with the often-snowcapped La Sal Mountains in the background adding a surreal context to the view. You can even stand under nearby Frame Arch to capture a very unique picture of the famous Delicate Arch.

Then there's Landscape Arch, the longest arch in North America and second largest in the world, with a span of 306 feet base to base. It is an easy 1.6-mile (2.4 km) hike and baffles the imagination with its threadlike frailty. It has in fact lost a bit of itself with three decent stone slabs falling from the arch in recent years. In 1991, the trail to walking under the arch was closed as a result.

There is something wonderful and even magical about stepping through an arch. For everyone who comes, the arch draws them in, invites them to stand underneath these bows of rock and step through them to see what they look like from the other side. Watch your fellow visitor. They walk up to the arch, look up underneath it and then carry through to see it from the other side. Arches fascinate, and at Arches NP, there is a lot of fascination. Nowhere in the world is there a place quite like this park. The arches are an invitation, every one of them.

THINGS TO DO IN ARCHES

Unlike Canyonlands, Arches NP is both more accessible and smaller in size. Many of the popular formations are short hikes from the parking lot and consolidated so that you can see a number of different arches and other features within one stop. This does have its drawbacks. Parking during the peak season can be a challenge. Oftentimes you will find yourself parking your RV a good five minutes from the trailhead by foot. Once on the trail, you will find yourself among many who have come to see the same arches and views. If you are looking to have the park to yourself, remember that many of your fellow tourists are staying in nearby Moab. This means that early mornings and dinnertime are typically gentler and more peaceful times to explore.

HIKING ARCHES

PARK AVENUE

Easy – (2.0 mi / 3.2 km), round trip, allow 1 – 2 hours, elev. Δ: 330 ft / 101 m, trailheads at Park Avenue or North Park Avenue parking areas

Park Avenue has a small elevation change as it descends steeply into a wide canyon with amazing thin-walled fins of rock that sheer upwards hundreds of feet into the air. The scenery is best described as epic southwest,

Landscape Arch

as grand as anything the Colorado Plateau has to offer. Once in the canyon, the walk is easy enough, allowing one to take in the view of the Courthouse Towers, including The Organ, a massive sandstone fin tower. Other notables are Sheep Rock, which looks like a lamb on a rock, and the Three Gossips, which resemble three figures standing around. If you are of the paranoid type, the Three Gossips are definitely talking about you! If you look to your left of Sheep Rock, you can see a newly forming arch that some have nicknamed "Baby Arch." Sheep Rock itself is thought to have once been part of a double arch. See if you can make out the remnant towers that have sparked this theory.

The area is well marked and is one of the first pull-offs as you enter the park. To get back to your car, either return the way you came or arrange for a shuttle car to pick you up at the end of the trail. The Park Service discourages hikers from walking on the park road.

COURTHOUSE WASH ROCK ART

Moderate to Strenuous – (5.5 mi / 8.9 km), round trip, allow 6 – 8 hours, elev. Δ: 210 ft / 64 m, trailhead on Highway 191, 0.5 mi north of the Colorado River

The Courthouse Wash Panel is one of the more colorful and intriguing petroglyphs in the area. It shows humanoid figures with trapezoidal forms representative of Barrier Canyon Style rock art. The anthropomorphic figures are ordained with abstract, almost alien, heads. While still full of color, the panel was vandalized in 1980 when someone splashed bleach on it. As disappointing as this is, the National Park Service was able to perform some restoration, although not to its original grandeur.

The panel sits just inside the outlet of Courthouse Wash into the Colorado River. There is parking off Highway 191 and the panel sits less than a quarter mile (1.2 km) upstream from this lower trailhead. The route described here is from the upper Courthouse Wash Trailhead accessed from the main park road. Come into the park and look for the Courthouse Wash parking area on your right, just across the obvious bridge. The hike is a delight, winding gently down the Courthouse Wash either alongside it or by walking in the creek itself. It can be a sandy walk, and there are pockets of non-life-threatening quicksand as you cut through tall canyon walls to the lower trailhead. The route is one way and is best pre-planned with a shuttle car waiting at the lower trailhead. Otherwise, admire the panel and return by walking back upstream. There are several side canyons to explore along this hike, the first encountered that cuts in a northerly fashion is a favorite.

BALANCED ROCK

Easy – (0.3 mi / 0.5 km), round trip, allow 30 minutes, elev. Δ: negligible, trailhead at Balanced Rock parking area

Balanced Rock is one of the more iconic landforms in Arches NP and the Southwest. It has been photographed and copied in movie sets so many times; it will likely be a familiar form when you first see it. The landform itself is a 128-foot tower of different layers of sandstone that are eroding at different rates. The capstone is eroding slower, which makes for the look of a large rock balancing on a smaller pedestal. Balanced Rock can be accessed just before turning right into the Windows Section.

Courthouse Wash Rock Art

WINDOWS

Easy – (1.0 mi / 1.6 km), round trip, allow 30 – 60 minutes, elev. Δ: 115 ft / 35 m, trailhead at end of Windows Road

The Windows Trail, starting at the Windows parking area, is an easy climb up a well-graded path that leads to three huge arches, the North and South Windows and Turret Arch. A slightly longer and often pleasant primitive loop can be used to get to these arches as well. The primitive loop trail starts at the South Window viewpoint.

DOUBLE ARCH

Easy – (0.5 mi / 0.8 km), round trip, allow 30 minutes, elev. Δ: 62 ft / 19 m, trailhead at north end of circle for Windows arches

Double Arch is one of the more magical landforms within Arches NP. Not only is it a true double arch, but also both arches are massive and seem to interconnect with each other from certain angles. It is tough to make out the nature of this landform from the road, and it is easily overlooked by folks who just got back in their vehicle from the Windows trailhead. That said, this is not a formation you want to miss; it is one of the highlights of the park. The trail from the parking lot is sandy and flat. It is possible to scramble up into the bases of both arches.

Double Arch

DELICATE ARCH

Strenuous – (3.0 mi / 4.8 km), round trip, allow 2 – 3 hours, elev. Δ: 500 ft / 152 m, trailhead at Wolfe Ranch parking area

The hike up to Delicate Arch is not as strenuous as some will tell you. Granted, there is no shade, so bring plenty of water and wear a hat and sunscreen. There is a decent 500-foot ascent on slick rock after a half mile (0.8 km) of easy hiking. Once you summit the ascent, the trail levels out for the most part and is fairly straightforward. There is a rock ledge about 200 yards long that is navigable for two-way traffic. The nice thing about this hike is that the arch is hidden from you until you are right on it. You turn a corner and bam, there it is, Delicate Arch.

The arch is a juxtaposition of themes for the viewer, with the often-snowcapped La Sal Mountains in the distance framing the fiery and dry sandstone in the foreground. Front and center it all is the showpiece, the most famous arch in the world. The lighting can be nothing less than spiritual at sunset, though be prepared to share your life moment with your fellow hikers during peak season.

DEVILS GARDEN (FULL LOOP)

Strenuous – (7.2 mi / 11.6 km), round trip, allow 30 minutes, elev. Δ: 355 ft / 108 m, trailhead at Devils Garden trailhead

This is the longest maintained trail in the park and covers many of the north canyon fins and arches of Salt Valley. Expect a fair amount of scrambling and generally rugged terrain as you span farther into the canyon. The hike is worth doing, weaning out many of the visitors looking for shorter hikes and providing views of eight arches total, including the solemn Navajo Arch and the remote Private Arch.

SAND DUNE ARCH

Easy – (0.3 mi / 0.5 km), round trip, allow 30 minutes, elev. Δ: negligible, trailhead at Sand Dune Arch parking area

Sand Dune Arch is a secluded arch that is an easy hike along an orange red sand path. The arch is between two large fins, giving a sense of isolation within a very short hike. During windy days, be prepared to get a little sandblasting exfoliation, especially around the shins.

BROKEN ARCH LOOP

Easy – (2.0 mi / 3.2 km), round trip, allow 60 minutes, elev. Δ: negligible, trailhead at Sand Dune Arch parking area

Broken Arch is an easy loop that makes for a nice walk from Devils Garden Campground, especially in the cooler times of morning or evening. The trail ambles across a large meadow to an arch with a visible crack in the middle of it, hence the name. Clear views of the La Sal Mountains can be seen in the distance. There is also a short spur trail to the triple arch feature called Tapestry Arch as well as a connection to Sand Dune Arch.

SKYLINE ARCH

Easy – (0.4 mi / 0.6 km), round trip, allow 30 minutes, elev. Δ: negligible, trailhead at Skyline Arch parking area

This trail is straightforward and very short, crossing a small meadow area to Skyline Arch, which is one of the characteristically visible arches from the road. A large boulder fell out of the arch in 1940, doubling the size of the opening. This is a nice trail to take in the twilight hours for a chance to see wildlife. There are many spur trails at the end to entice the hiker for more adventure within the rock garden surroundings.

Delicate Arch

LANDSCAPE ARCH

Easy – (1.6 mi / 2.6 km), round trip, allow 60 minutes, elev. Δ: 60 ft / 18 m, trailhead at Devils Garden trailhead

What makes Landscape Arch so popular is that it defies logic. It is fragile, seemingly ribbon thin in spots, yet it is the longest arch in the park and the second largest in the world. Landscape Arch is so fragile it prompted the Secretary of the Air Force to put a stop to supersonic jet flight over or even near national parks in 1972 after an outcry from local citizens. The arch measures 306 feet from base to base and can be accessed via a fairly flat gravel trail.

This trail can be a destination in itself or the beginning of the longer hikes to Double O Arch and the Devils Garden Loop. There are nice spur trails down to the Tunnel Arch and quaint Pine Tree Arch.

DOUBLE O ARCH

Strenuous – (4.0 mi / 6.4 km), round trip, allow 2 – 3 hours, elev. Δ: 277 ft / 84 m, trailhead at Devils Garden trailhead

Double O Arch is listed in case you don't want to do the more primitive loop portion of the Devils Garden Loop or some of the other spur trails to other arches. Double O is an arch on top of an arch, hence the name. It is one of the cooler landforms in the park, looking like a fin of sandstone Swiss cheese. Dark Angel, a monolithic tower of darker sandstone, is off a spur trail another 0.5 mi (0.8 km) further on.

FIERY FURNACE

Strenuous – (2.0 mi / 3.2 km), round trip, allow 2 – 3 hours, elev. Δ: 250 ft / 76 m, trailhead at Fiery Furnace Viewpoint

Fiery Furnace is a special section of Arches. The area itself is a labyrinth of rock, containing no trails, and lots of scrambling, wedging, and the need for equal helpings of agility and endurance. It is best seen through the park's ranger-led programs, as this minimizes the damage that has been caused of late through too much hiker love. You can access the area on your own, but only if you obtain a permit at the visitor center and watch a minimum impact video. The fee for a permit is $6 for each adult and $3 for children 5 through 12 and can be purchased at the visitor center. For both the permit and the ranger-led programs, children under five are not permitted.

The ranger-led tour is a tremendous amount of fun for an active family but isn't for everyone. Once you start on the hike, you are committed to completing it. The hike includes squeezing through narrow gaps, scrambling up at times, jumping over small gaps, and navigating through a maze of rock containing the usual assortment of narrow ledges, loose sandstone, and broken rocks.

This ranger-led program contains a fair number of historical and geographical descriptions from likely one of the most passionate advocates of the park you will meet. Bring good hiking shoes, plenty of water and a backpack to store everything because you will be using your hands from time to time to make your way through the terrain.

Tickets for the ranger-led program are by reservation during the peak season. They can be purchased up to six months in advance through www.recreation.gov. Like the campground in Arches, this program is quite popular and requires a bit of planning, tenacity, and patience to get the spot you want. Tickets during November and early spring can be obtained at the visitor center. Costs are $16 for adults and $8 for children 5 through 12.

TOWER ARCH

Strenuous – (3.4 mi / 5.5 km), round trip, allow 2 – 3 hours, elev. Δ: 450 ft / 137 m, trailhead at Devils Garden trailhead

Fins, hoodoos, and arches, oh my! This trail is off the beaten track in the northwestern Klondike Bluffs. This is a fun little area, with a bit of elevation gain to keep you in shape, but providing one sandstone oddity after the other along the way. Even the end point, Tower Arch, is unusual, giving clear sight to an arch, but with what looks like a big submarine, complete with an observation control tower on top. The "submarine" clearly overshadows the poor arch. The whole place has an M. C. Escher meets Salvador Dali element to it with fins tilted to the winds and hoodoos standing like kids getting in trouble or others that resemble little Buddhas having tea. If you are good at finding patterns in clouds, this is the place for you.

From the park map, the trail shows unpaved roads on either end. Take the Salt Valley Road and turn at the second left into the Klondike Bluffs. It is possible to enter the trail from the other end, but this is a seldom-traveled high clearance 4WD road.

ARCHES LODGING

STAYING INSIDE THE PARK

There is one campground in Arches, eighteen miles (29 km) from the park entrance. The Devils Garden Campground contains 50 sites, all of which can be reserved in advance between March 1 and October 31. You can reserve sites online at www.recreation.gov or by phone at (877) 444-6677.

The sites do book up early during peak times and can be booked up to six months in advance. One tip if you aren't seeing availability is to keep checking. In fact, check as if you have OCD. Folks do cancel, but the sites will be gobbled up within ten minutes. If you really want to stay in Devils Garden during peak times, bring equal measures of tenacity and resilience. There is a good reason to stay in the park—accessibility. Hiking trails are right off the campground, leading to more than a dozen arches within a relatively short distance.

Devils Garden Campground does have potable water plus the usual round of amenities, including a picnic table, grill and both pit and flush toilets. Some of the sites accommodate longer RVs up to 30 feet. There are no showers or RV dump station in Arches. Sites are $25 per night. During the winter months, (November 1 to February 28) sites 1 –24 are available on a self-serve basis. NOTE: this campground will be closed from March 1 - October 31, 2017 due to construction.

LODGING IN MOAB

Though there is but a small campground within the park, there are plenty of campgrounds and lodging accommodations near Arches National Park. Note that since Canyonland's Island in the Sky District is literally next door to Arches NP, accommodations listed here are for both park areas.

CANYONLANDS LODGING

6198 S Hwy 191, PO Box 203, Monticello, UT 84535, (435) 220-1050, www.canyonlandslodging.com

Canyonlands Lodging is a vacation rental property management broker offering dozens of cabins throughout the Canyonlands and Arches area. They rent 1 bedroom to 19 bedroom cabins sleeping from 2 to 60 people. Their offerings are top notch and worthy of exploration if you are looking for a personal base camp in this area. There are too many homes to describe here. This is a delightful alternative to the usual hotel or B&B. Renting a vacation home can be a cost effective way to vacation because you are not eating out as much, though make sure everyone helps out with the cooking!

FAIRFIELD INN & SUITES MOAB

1863 N Highway 191, Moab, UT 84532-9623, (435) 259-5350, marriott.com

Fairfield Inn Moab is so close to Arches, it is within walking distance from the Courthouse Wash rock art panel (described earlier). This Marriott owned property offers consistent quality within every element of the stay. The inn sits near the top of what one would expect for a 3 star hotel. They offer free breakfast and an outdoor pool.

AARCHWAY INN

1551 N Highway 191, Moab, UT 84532-2096, (435) 259-2599, aarchwayinn.com

Aarchway is one of a few hotels located on the north side of town. It is close to the Colorado River and close to both Arches National Park and Canyonlands's Island in the Sky District. The rooms are nicely decorated, with warm wood furnishings and southwest style decor. The grounds themselves are laid out nicely as well. They offer an outdoor pool, full kitchen suites, and free breakfast. All in all, Aarchway offers one of the best values in Moab.

INCA INN

570 N Main St, Moab, UT 84532-2129, (435) 259-7261, www.incainn.com

Inca Inn is your best bet within the budget motels. While they get top marks for their rooms and do offer a pool and free breakfast, it is the hospitality that makes this place special. The employees are thoughtful and go out of their way to be helpful and make you feel like home.

COMFORT SUITES

400 North Main, Moab, UT 84532-2127, (435) 259-5455, choicehotels.com

Comfort Suites does a nice job in Moab, offering within expectations for a 3 star hotel and then some. The rooms are updated and look sharp. They offer an outdoor pool, fitness center, laundry, a small snack shop, and free breakfast.

BOWEN MOTEL

169 N Main St, Moab, UT 84532-2394, (800) 874-5439, bowenmotel.com

The Bowen is on the lower end of mid-range priced hotels in terms of value. The hotel is clean overall with no real negatives other than being in need of some updating. They do offer an outdoor pool and laundry facilities.

HOMEWOOD SUITES BY HILTON MOAB

132 N Main St, Moab, UT 84532-2341, (435) 259-7000, homewoodsuites3.hilton.com

3 star hotel with a "southwest modern" architectural theme. Interiors are done with muted earth tones that lean towards the gray side of the color palate, which comes off as either Zen-like or stark, depending on your interpretation. They do offer a free breakfast and a small indoor pool.

BEST WESTERN PLUS CANYONLANDS INN

16 S Main St, Moab, UT 84532-2503, (435) 259-2300, bestwestern.com

Located in the center of Moab, the Best Western Plus is almost a destination in its own right. The exterior is grand and welcoming which extends into its spacious lobby. The rooms vary in size and family suites (complete with kitchen and small living area) are available. They have several pools designed for every age adorned with lots of rich masonry. The Best Western get top marks for bringing a little luxury to their property but still remaining an affordable option.

KOKOPELLI LODGINGS

72 S 100 E, Moab, UT 84532-2638, (800) 505-5343, kokopellilodge.com

Kokopelli Lodgings is a property management broker offering everything from offbeat rooms to larger guest houses complete with a private pool and hot tub. Check out their website to learn more.

QUALITY SUITES

800 S Main St, Moab, UT 84532-2961, (435) 259-5252, www.choicehotels.com

A solid 3 star hotel, with pool, hot tub, free breakfast, fitness center, and laundry facilities. The beds are big and comfortable and the rooms are clean and updated.

THE GONZO INN

100 W 200 S, Moab, UT 84532-2535, (435) 259-2515, gonzoinn.com

The Gonzo Inn prides itself on being a one-of-a-kind hotel and if you are into eclectic furnishes and touches, this may be the right place. It's fun, quirky and doesn't take itself too seriously as a hotel. There is an outdoor pool and a free continental breakfast is offered. If you need a break from the typical hotel, you'll go gonzo for Gonzo Inn.

RED CLIFFS LODGE

Mile Post 14 Hwy 128, Moab, UT 84532, (435) 259-2002, redcliffslodge.com

Red Cliffs Lodge is about 30 minutes from the town of Moab off of UT-128 which follows the Colorado River upstream. Once on the property, there is much to do, including wine tasting, horseback riding and exploring the richest movie museum in southern Utah. The rooms are all nicely done, with pastel colors mimicking sunset hues. Red Cliffs offers standard rooms and cabin suites. They have a restaurant and gift shop on the property as well as an outdoor pool. The place is an all-inclusive stop and its surroundings of red rock and the Colorado River make for a relaxing respite from the towns and park crowds.

SORREL RIVER RANCH RESORT AND SPA

Mile 17 Highway 128, Moab, UT 84532, (435) 259-4642, sorrelriver.com

Sorrel River Ranch Resort is about 30 minutes away from the town of Moab, following the Colorado River up UT-128. The ranch is all inclusive, offering multiple day excursions as well as a high end restaurant open for all meals. There is a pool and day spa, but perhaps the best part are the grounds themselves. One can sit along the banks of the Colorado River and take in the views. Sorrel River Ranch Resort offers luxury and elegance within a backdrop of stunning scenery.

CAMPING OPTIONS

DEAD HORSE POINT STATE PARK – KAYENTA CAMPGROUND

Staying at Dead Horse Point State Park will cost more, but it does come with certain advantages. First of all, you can reserve the site through Reserve America. In addition, each site has a fully paved driveway or pull-through, tent pad, electrical outlets and covered picnic area at every site. Add in the fact that you are now inside one of the most photographed state parks in Utah, there is a lot going for this campground.

Entrance fees for the state park itself are $10 plus $30 per night for the campsite. The campgrounds are clean and well designed with privacy in mind. There is water and a dump station on premises.

BLM CAMPGROUNDS ON UT-128

There are several campgrounds along the Colorado River just north of Moab on Highway 128. All of these are first come, first served and each has the same basic amenities, including a picnic table and fire pit. None have water and provides only the basic vault toilet, but they all have a campground host on duty. These campgrounds are the farthest from Island in the Sky but are centrally located if you are looking for one site for the duration of your stay within Canyonlands and Arches NPs. The other great feature of these campgrounds is the Colorado River. Each campground offers a different scenic view of the river as it quietly rolls by.

There aren't any dump stations at these BLM campgrounds, though there is a dumping station at the Farm & City Feed Store located at 850 S Main St. in Moab. It will be on your right-hand side on the south side of town. The place is super nice, charges $5 for dumping and carries a limited supply of RV parts.

GOOSE ISLAND

This is the closest of the Highway 128 BLM campgrounds, located just 1.4 miles (2.3 km) from Highway 191. There are 19 sites available at $15 per night. The campground is against a high red rock wall and gets good shade in the afternoon. While many of the sites are close to the river, the high banks of the river's edge make cooling off a challenge.

GRANSTAFF, DRINKS CANYON, HAL CANYON, OAK GROVE AND UPPER BIG BEND

All of these campgrounds are designated for tent camping only and are offered on a first come, first served basis at $15 per night. Like all of the campgrounds in this area, you are setting up and sleeping next to the Colorado River. This whole section of campgrounds is situated in a wide valley of red rock carved by the river. All of them have suitable flat campsites and while you are next to a highway, traffic is practically non-existent after sunset. The biggest

Balanced Rock

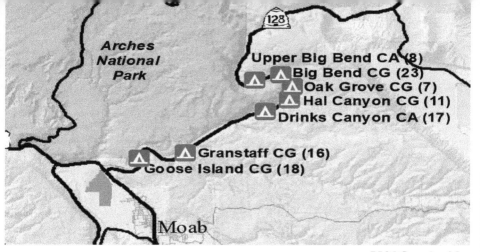

differentiation between these sites are availability and distance from the parks you are visiting. Granstaff is one of the more popular sites since it is the closest tent only campground to both Arches and Canyonlands. Granstaff is also a great starting point for the Porcupine Rim Trail, a popular mountain biking trail.

Big Bend

Big Bend is 7.4 miles (11.9 km) from Highway 191 and can accommodate large RVs. There are 23 campsites and good afternoon shade similar to Goose Island. While Big Bend is 6 miles (9.7 km) farther out, there are several advantages to this campground. It contains a sandy beach and river walkway as well as more expansive views than Goose Island. It is also close to the popular Negro Bill trailhead, which is a pleasant 2-mile (3.2 km) hike along a year-round stream to a 243-foot-span natural arch named Morning Glory Bridge.

Private Campgrounds in Moab

There are several private campgrounds in and around Moab itself. These offer full hookups and have the obvious advantage of being in town, so you are closer to restaurants and other common amenities. There are many private RV campgrounds to choose from in Moab, and not all are listed here.

Moab Valley RV Park

1773 N Hwy 191, Moab, Utah 84532, (435) 259-4469

Located right at Highway 128, this RV park has 69 sites that accommodate RVs up to 60 feet. This park is close to both Canyonlands and Arches NP. Amenities include full hookup; a large, clean swimming pool, a hot tub and free Wi-Fi. Price per night varies by site type and whether you are staying a weekday, weekend or holiday. Prices begin at $39 per night and go as high as $55 per night for two people. Each person over six is an additional $5 per night.

Moab Rim RV Park

1900 South Hwy 191, Moab, Utah 84532 (888) 599-6622

Located just as you enter Moab. 28 sites for RVs up to 60 feet. Full hookup pull-through sites for $39 plus tax for two people, includes cable TV and Wi-Fi plus 50A and 30A power. There are also power-only sites for $34 plus tax for two people. Stay a week and get the 7th night for free.

109

Okay RV Park

3310 Spanish Valley Drive, Moab, Utah 84532, (435) 259-1400

Nice and clean just outside of south Moab. 73 sites accommodating RVs up to 80 feet, ranging from $39 to $45 a night. Kids stay free from June to August for RV sites. Free Wi-Fi. Subtle rustic southwest charm.

DINING IN MOAB

The Atomic Grill & Lounge

BURGERS, meals for under $20, 1393 N Hwy 191, Moab, UT 84532, (435) 259-5201, theatomicmoab.com, open 11:30am - 10pm

The Atomic is a fancy burger joint. One can get duck bacon on their burger or a burger made from grass fed buffalo. Overall, this is a lot of fanfare for a burger and expectations are higher, but not always met.

Jailhouse Cafe

AMERICAN, meals for under $20, 101 N Main St, Moab, UT 84532, (435) 259-3900, open daily, 6:30am - 12pm

Awesome breakfasts, from the waffles or omelets to the eggs Benedict. The thick cut bacon is downright heavenly.

El Charro Loco

MEXICAN, meals for under $30, 812 S Main St, Moab, UT 84532, (435) 355-0854, open daily for lunch 11am - 10pm

If you are looking for large plates of Sonora style Mexican, smothered with melted cheese, savory sauces, and just enough spice to keep things interesting, head to El Charro Loco. Their specialty is the Charro Loco Plate, a dish big enough to split between two people and is essentially a pineapple stuffed with tender meats and vegetables. The carne asada and their tacos are delicious as well. There are two caveats with this place, its small so come early and they don't serve alcohol, so you won't find a margarita on the menu.

Sunset Grill

AMERICAN, meals for under $60, 900 N Main St, Moab, UT 84532-2178, (435) 259-7146, www.moab-utah.com/sunsetgrill, open Mon - Sat 5pm - 10pm

Sunset Grill is one of the go to destinations for causal fine dining in Moab. Situated above the town with great panoramic views of Moab and surrounding red rock cliffs, they offer everything from two kinds of prime rib, steaks, seafood, duck, trout, lemon chicken, and crowd pleasures such as french onion soup for starters and creme brule to finish things off. There is a decent selection of wine, beer, and cocktails to choose from as well. Another plus - they offer free shuttle service to and from their restaurant from pretty much anywhere in Moab. Just call (435) 259-7777 for pickup.

Arches Thai

THAI, meals for under $20, 60 N 100 W, Moab, UT 84532, (435) 355-0533, archesthai.com, open daily, 11am - 9pm, closed Tuesdays

Delicious and fresh Thai food. Creamy and robust curry's and their drunken noodles are especially amazing. Great for lunch or dinner.

Sabaku Sushi

SUSHI, meals for under $30, 90 E Center St, Moab, UT 84532, (435) 259-4455, sabakusushi.com, open daily, 5pm - 10pm, closed Mondays

If you are from California, the first thought might be to pass on "desert sushi". Fortunately, Sabaku Sushi won't be a disappointment. They offer a nice selection of rolls that are yummy and fresh. One plus is the absence of fake crab and the sparseness of spicy tuna. These ingredients have been overused in some establishments to help pad their bottom line while lessening the quality.

Quesadilla Mobilla

MEXICAN, meals for under $10, 89 N Main St, Moab, UT 84532, (435) 260-0289, quesadillamobilla.com, open daily, 11am - 5pm

Quesadilla Mobilla is a locally award winning food truck offering delightful twists on the standard Mexican cuisine. They offer dishes with fun names such as Enchanted Chicken, Dirt Bag, and Fiery Fungus, (don't get too worried, that one is really just a quesadilla with jalapenos and sautéed mushrooms). Great food, reasonable prices.

Bangkok House Too

SUSHI AND ASIAN, meals for under $30, 59 S Main St, Suite 8, Moab, UT 84532-2522, (435) 355-0168, open for lunch daily 11:30am - 10pm, Mondays from 5-10pm

Bangkok House Too was once just Bangkok House and served Thai. The new establishment serves up a great selection of sushi rolls, sashimi, nigiri, and poke along with a large selection of typical Thai curries and noodle. While it can be a bit of a red flag for a restaurant to try to be multiple things and pull it all off, Bangkok House Too does a great job offering the usual suspects found on both western Japanese and Thai menus. If you have a group that wants both, Bangkok House Too won't disappoint.

North and South Windows

Moab Diner

AMERICAN, meals for under $20, 189 S Main St, Moab, UT 84532, (435) 259-4006, www.moabdiner.com, open daily, 6am - 10pm, closed Sundays

This is a wonderful place to sit down, relax and enjoy yourself. Set in a true American diner atmosphere, they serve great breakfasts, lunches and dinners. You will pass by their selection of ice creams as you are seated, which are downright tempting, so save room and treat yourself.

Desert Bistro

AMERICAN, meals for under $60, 36 S 100 W, Moab, UT 84532, (435) 259-0756, desertbistro.com, open daily, 5:30pm - 9:30pm, closed Mondays

The ambiance of the Desert Bistro is warm and elegant. The menu will be hard to choose from because there are so many delicious sounding offerings. Their wine selection is strong and the food itself lives delightfully up to expectations from the presentation to the taste. It is hard to go wrong within this high end dining experience.

The Blu Pig

BARBECUE, meals for under $30, 811 S Main St, Moab, UT 84532, (435) 259-3333, blupigbbq.com, open daily, 11:30am - 10pm

The Blu Pig offers hearty, mouthwatering barbecue and cocktails in an upscale atmosphere. The service is great and the portions are hearty. They also have nightly live music seasonally.

El Charro Loco

MEXICAN, meals for under $20, 812 S Main St, Moab, UT 84532, (435) 355-0854, open daily, 11am - 10pm

The folks at El Charro Loco do have a way with Mexican cuisine. Gooey, rich, and savory, they won't disappoint if you have a craving for something south of the border. The ambiance of the restaurant is a bit ho hum, but the chef makes up for it in the artfully plated dishes. El Charro also has a small bakery serving Mexican deserts.

98 Center

ASIAN FUSION, meals for under $20, 98 E Center S, Moab, UT, 84532, open daily, 11:30am - 9pm, closed Tuesday

Hip, bright atmosphere combines with fresh and flavorful Asian and Vietnamese cuisine at 98 Center. The chef's take on just about every menu item is a delight to the taste buds. This is farm to table taken to a new level, from their signature cocktails to the many savory twists and turns of their dishes. Great salads too!

In Devils Garden

Susie's Branding Iron

AMERICAN/STEAKHOUSE, meals for under $20, 2971 S Hwy 191, Moab, UT 84532, (435) 259-6275, susiesbrandingiron.com, open daily, 11:30am - 9pm

Susie's Branding Iron is a cute western themed place with red and white checkered tablecloths and pictures of "The Duke" on the wall. Their menu mainly consists of burgers and steaks, but they also offer Navajo Tacos, Rueben sandwiches, and fried chicken amongst other eclectic offerings. The food quality is good throughout and the prices reasonable.

Cowboy Grill

AMERICAN, meals for under $30, Redcliffs Lodge, Mile Post 14 Hwy 128, Moab, UT 84532, (435) 259-2002, redcliffslodge.com

The Cowboy Grill is a restaurant located within the Redcliffs Lodge. The lodge itself is a ways from the main drag, about 30 minutes, but the trip is worth it for the overall experience. The drive is incredible, following up the Colorado River with high red rock cliffs on either side. As described earlier, once at the lodge, there is so much to do, including their movie museum, horseback riding and wine tasting. The grill serves up the usual suspects, such as pork chops, steak, and salmon. If you do come here for a meal, be sure to allow time to see everything Redcliffs Lodge has to offer.

☕ Coffee and Sweets! ☕

Eklecticafe

COFFEE AND SANDWICHES, 352 N Main St, Moab, UT 84532, (435) 259-6896, open daily, 7am - 2:30pm

Eklecticafe serves coffee drinks along with a breakfast and lunch menu. The coffee here is good and pairs nicely with their breakfast burrito and other egg dishes. Though they also serve lunch, Eklecticafe is definitely known for their breakfasts, which consistently hits the spot and leaves one's tank full to explore the great southwest.

MOYO - MOAB FROZEN YOGURT

YOGURT, 331 N Main St, Moab, UT 84532, (435) 355-0010, moabyogurt.com, open daily, 1pm - 9pm,

Moab Yogurt offers a wide variety of yogurt selections including gluten, fat, and dairy free options. Plus they have a full buffet of toppings to choose from. They also serve Italian ices with fresh fruit and frozen custard and sorbets. A clean and fun place to get a treat.

SWEET CRAVINGS BAKERY + BISTRO

COFFEE, 397 N Main St, Moab, UT 84532, (435) 259-8983, cravemoab.com, open daily, 8am - 3pm

Sweet Cravings Bakery offers espresso drinks alongside pastries, deserts, and a full breakfast and lunch menu. The bakery will definitely delight the sweet tooth. Their main course offerings are good and healthy, especially their salads, but the ambiance is a bit underwhelming.

LOVE MUFFIN CAFE

COFFEE, BREAKFAST, 139 N Main St, Moab, UT 84532, (435) 259-6833, lovemuffincafe.com, open daily, 6:30am - 1pm

Love Muffin Café is open earlier and offers the usual breakfast menu but with an edge towards healthier items. There are vegan options, though carnivores will also find a robust list of dishes as well. They also offer a selection of baked goods, including donuts and muffins. The atmosphere is hip and modern. This is a something for everybody establishment and good for groups wanting to hit the trail early.

YETI'S FROZEN BLAST

GELATO AND YOGURT, 125 N Main St, Moab, UT 84074, (435) 882-5087, open daily, 11am - 9pm, closed Sundays

Yeti's has a small offering of yogurt, soft serve ice cream and Italian ices. There are newer and arguably fresher places to get a frozen treat in Moab, but the staff is friendly and what they do offer will hit the spot.

MOAB COFFEE ROASTERS

COFFEE, 90 N Main St, Moab, UT 84532, (435) 259-2725, moabcoffeeroasters.com, open daily, 7am - 8pm

There are two sides of the Moab Coffee Roasters "bean". On the one hand, when it comes to the coffee, it's great. They offer a satisfying menu of espresso drinks both hot and cold that will satisfy the need for caffeine. They roast their own beans and the baristas certainly know how to pour a "god shot". But if you are in a service town that gets the crowds that Moab does, it's hard not to try to maximize the retail space to cover as many options as possible. That's the flip side of this coffee house. It's also a gelato, Italian soda and smoothie shop, plus it shares its space with a clothing shop. The purity of the perfect espresso moment gets a bit diluted, leaving a touristy aftertaste.

WAKE & BAKE CAFÉ

COFFEE, 59 S Main St, Moab, UT 84532, (435) 259-2420, wakeandbakecafe.net, open daily, 7am - 3pm

Wake & Bake offers espresso drinks alongside a full breakfast and lunch menu. They have a wide selection of offerings food wise, including a full sweet and savory crepe section. That said, this place doesn't make the top of the food chain. Lines can be slow and the service overall, from attitude to the actual service itself, could benefit from improvement. The food is good, but you'll need to look past the occasional moments of self-entitlement from the staff.

CRYSTAL'S CAKES AND CONES

CUPCAKES AND ICE CREAM, 26 W Center St, Moab, UT 84532, (435) 259-9393, crystalscakesandcones.com, open daily, 3pm - 9pm, closed Sundays

Crystal's offers fresh cupcakes baked daily and a lip smacking selection of ice cream. The real treat here is cupcake ala mode, especially on a hot Moab summer day. Yumm!

WICKED BREW ESPRESSO DRIVE THRU

COFFEE, 1146 South HWY 191, Moab, UT 84532, (435) 259-0021, wickedbrewcoffee.com, open daily, 6am - 2pm

Their title says it all, tasty espresso drinks without leaving your vehicle. They have a full menu of hot and cold drinks and even offer coffee beans to go by the pound. One distinction is their offering of flavored coffee drinks such as the "Bob Marley" (banana, coconut, and chocolate). With a flavoring or without, this is a great alternative to the over roasted cookie cutter coffee chains.

ARCHES HISTORY

The history surrounding Arches NP is similar to Canyonlands NP in that the chronicle begins with early ancestral peoples and includes a nod to Mormon influence followed by a small group of recent advocates who helped in the formation of the park. Still there are differences in the amount of inhabitation, in the hardships of the parks most famous settler, John Wesley Wolfe, and of the tenacity of one man who helped bring both Arches and Canyonlands to the attention of the United States.

Wolfe Ranch Cabin

EARLY INHABITANTS

The most interesting aspect of early inhabitation is that there isn't much evidence that much occurred. The hunter-gatherer period during the Ice Age of 10,000 years ago shows some evidence that they hunted in the Courthouse Wash and Salt Valley. There are pockets of chert and chalcedony quartz that were used for making stone tools in these areas and the honing of rock into sharp dart points. Crude knives and fur scrapers can still be found as debris piles in these areas.

While common in the Mesa Verde National Park, Arches was much farther north for the ancestral Puebloan territories. As such, there was little inhabitation by these agriculturalists and hunter people of two thousand years ago. There are a scant few dwellings in Arches, thought to be for seasonal use. While evidence of habitation during this period is scarce, there was a fair number of rock drawings created during this period.

With the prolific arches in the area, it is easy to imagine this area held a special significance for the Puebloan people. It is difficult to know whether their lifeway was better suited to the lands farther south, or if they refrained from inhabiting the area consciously because of the arches themselves.

Puebloan people began to leave the region about 700 years ago for a number of reasons, mainly because of consistent drought. Other tribes such as the Ute did make their way into the Arches region. The petroglyph panel near Wolfe Ranch depicts a hunting scene with humans on horseback. The Utes were introduced to horses by the Spanish in the late 1700s. While there is no evidence beyond the rock art, it is possible that this was a seasonal site for the Utes. It brings one to ponder; did they visit Delicate Arch with the same passion as folks do today? It is easy to imagine the hike up to Delicate Arch as a playground for young Ute children, playing hide and seek among the rocks. Perhaps a group of older boys hunted smaller game in the hopes of coming back to the tribe with a feeling of accomplishment and pride. These are likely products of imagination, something perhaps to help take your mind off the steep trails as you head to Delicate Arch.

JOHN WOLFE AND OTHER SETTLERS

Moab and the surrounding area was settled more slowly than other U.S. Southwest territories. The original inhabitants were often hostile and the terrain itself was as rugged as it was arid. Dry summers, cold winters, little water and hostile Indians kept many settlers away. It wasn't until 1877 that Moab itself was established—a good 33 years after Brigham Young started his settlement of Utah. By 1883 the Denver and Rio Grande Western Railroad was completed, and along with it came a welcome increase in stability for the early pioneers.

Park Avenue

John Wesley Wolfe was a Civil War veteran who suffered from a leg injury during the war. His injury was painful, especially during the harsh Ohio winters, so he decided to look for a warmer, dryer climate. The tamer lands and warm climes of Moab spoke to John. He settled in the Salt Valley region with his son Fred in 1888. Wolfe built a cabin on the banks of Salt Wash, which was as isolated from Moab as it is today. What the land did have was water. John and his son dammed the wash and used it to irrigate a garden. The water wasn't suitable for drinking, which came from a spring some three quarters of a mile (1.2 km) away.

Fiery Furnace

John and his son were comfortable with their "make do" lifestyle. They built a very simple one-room cabin. They grazed a few cattle under the Bar DX brand on his 100 acres and even built a corral for them. Here is an excerpt of a letter from John to his family back home:

We have started a cattle spread on a desert homestead. We call it the Bar—DX Ranch. Fred and I live in a little log house on the bank of a creek that is sometimes dry, sometimes flooded from bank to bank with roaring muddy water. We are surrounded with rocks—gigantic red rock formations, massive arches and weird figures, the like of which you've never seen. The desert is a hostile, demanding country, hot in summer, cold in winter. The Bar—DX Ranch is a day's ride from the nearest store, out of the range of schools.

John was married for the duration he lived with his son, and while he continually promised to return, he spent another eighteen years at the ranch. His wife refused to go west and never did join her husband in Utah. In 1906 Wolfe's daughter, Flora Stanley, her husband Ed and their two small children Esther and Ferol came out to live with her father and brother. John sent money from his pension check for the train ride out to Utah and met them at Thompson Springs (now Thompson, Utah).

John put the family in his wagon and rode them the 30 miles (48 km) back to his ranch by horse. The tiny log cabin with only a dirt floor brought his daughter Flora to tears. John promised to build a new cabin and a dugout cellar in the spring of 1907. This cabin was built from logs carried from the banks of the Colorado River, six miles (10 km) away and included a proper floor. In spite of these new digs, the newcomers stayed on the Wolfe Ranch for less than two years before moving to Moab.

John Wolfe sold the ranch to Tommy Larson in 1910 and returned to Ohio. There he lived out the rest of his life, dying on October 22, 1913 at the age of 84.

Tommy Larson sold the ranch to Marvin Turnbow and his partners Lester Walker and Stib Beeson. In 1927, Turnbow helped as a camp hand for the U.S. Geological Survey and for many years both USGS maps and National Park Service maps listed the cabin site as "Turnbow Cabin." The ranch was sold to Emmett Elizondo in 1947, who later sold it to the National Park Service. John Wolfe's granddaughter, Mrs. Esther Stanley Rison, and his great-granddaughter, Mrs. Hazel Wolfe Hastler, visited the cabin in 1970, providing details for the historical record. The ranch site was renamed "Wolfe Ranch" shortly thereafter.

PARK FOUNDERS AND ADVOCATES

The Salt Valley and the surrounding territory of Arches NP were mainly off the national radar until the turn of the twentieth century. It had not been part of the earliest expeditions by the hardy Jesuit priests and was not explored during John Wesley Powell's or Fremont's many ventures into the Southwest. For the most part, the land of the Arches fell into that of southwest lore, the truth known only to those in Moab and other locals. In 1911, Loren "Bish" Taylor began to describe the wonders of Moab as editor of the local Moab newspaper. Loren loved to explore the local area and had taken over the Moab newspaper at the tender age of 18. He wrote about all of Moab, including the rainbows of rock within Arches, through the 1940s.

Another early proponent of Arches was John "Doc" Williams, Moab's first doctor. John did a fair number of "house calls," going from ranch to ranch on horseback. On his rides through Salt Valley, he often climbed out of the northern end of the valley to a spot now known as Doc Williams Point. On many rides, "Doc" and "Bish" rode and explored the regions together.

By 1923 word of the unique lands and numerous arches spread to the board members of the Rio Grande Western Railroad, who were looking for additional tourist stops to attract rail passengers. They were impressed with the what they heard about the area and began a campaign to get the U.S. Park Service to include the land in its collections. Little did anyone know the magnitude

programs to reuse resources. Prior to this movement, the nation's concerns were growing regarding what was then a relatively untethered industrial condition. While there is always more that can be done to minimize water, air and soil pollution, the efforts of this movement have created an overall improvement in environmental conditions.

Sand Dune Arch

of the unique qualities park or the true number of arches. At the time, they thought there were only 90 arches within the park and not the 2000 arches by current count. On April 12, 1929, President Herbert Hoover signed 1,920 acres in the Windows and 2,600 acres in Devils Garden as Arches National Monument.

The formation of Arches as a national monument in the early 1920s helped shelter the park from the flurry of uranium exploration in the mid 1940s and 1950s. While that put some additional burden on what would become Canyonlands NP, it also helped limit the damage of that park to some extent. In 1949, Bates Wilson became the custodian of Arches and Natural Bridges National Monuments and helped bring much-needed attention to the Canyonlands area. He was an influential voice in the creation of Canyonlands NP. He also had a large hand in shoring up Arches. When he began his stewardship of Arches in 1949, the park had no paved roads, no campground, no trails, and no visitor center. By his retirement in 1972, the park had doubled in size, gained more amenities for the tourist and had gone from being a national monument to a national park.

Bates managed one park ranger from 1956 to 1957 who had a knack for describing the soul of the desert while not being shy about his feelings toward preservation over tourism. Edward Abbey lived in "a little tin government housetrailer" near Balanced Rock. He was part of a movement of environmental activism that continued into the 1970s and even today, bringing to bear the creation of the Environmental Protection Agency and national awareness toward protecting the environment. The activist movement did a lot to help reduce air and water pollution and set up recycling

Edward Abbey's work included Desert Solitaire, an eloquent and personal account of his time spent as a ranger at Arches. Edward's book saw the move toward expanding national awareness toward parks like Arches and the resulting infrastructure needed to support the increased volume of tourists. He wrote of his concerns of creating park policy that strayed from preservation, that by the simple act of increasing the number of cars and people coming to the park, we would destroy them. It is interesting to note that park policy continues to struggle with this notion today, finding a balance between making the treasures available to the nation while protecting them. It is hard to say whether Abbey's books helped his cause or accelerated the amount of traffic to the park. His books brought national awareness through descriptions that beckoned the readers to see for themselves the lonely and magnificent call of the desert.

ARCHES GEOLOGY

THE ARCHES

The first question one might ask is why are there so many arches in Arches National Park? Seriously, nowhere else on the planet are there over 2000 catalogued arches and countless remnants of previous arches in one place. Arches of sandstone rock can be found all over the Colorado Plateau, yet here, there must have been ideal conditions to help create so many of these sweeps of curvaceous wonder. The truth is there were a number of forces at play to create the ideal environment for these wonderful rock formations. Like the ingredients of Canyonlands, geological oddities, salt, stability, and just the right amount of erosion have played a part.

The area around Arches NP was at one time an inland sea, spreading from horizon to horizon. Starting 300 million years ago, these seas would come, dry up, and return, twenty-nine times in all. Each time the waters evaporated, they left behind salt beds that eventually grew to more than five thousand feet thick. This is once again the now hopefully familiar Paradox Formation. The salt was then covered by a tremendous amount of rock and sand. Just as we learned earlier, the salt, which is less dense than the rock and now under intense pressure from the rock above it, started to flow very slowly. It was forced westward, blocked by faults and eventually collected into a dome 2 miles (3.2 km) high, 3 miles (4.8 km) wide and 70 miles (113 km) long. Since the salt was less dense than the rock, it was able to float through the rock layers above it but never reached the surface. This took 75 million years.

Then the salt finally reached equilibrium with the rock above it and stopped flowing. Then, on top of all that salt and rock, over a mile deep of additional rock was deposited. When the Colorado Plateau was itself pushed upwards, water and lots of time eroded away all but a thin layer of the rock above the salt dome. This thin rock layer around the salt dome cracked, and when the rock layer was finally exposed to the surface, the salt underneath was exposed to the elements. It slowly washed away, and the dome of rock collapsed and formed what is now known as Salt Valley. At the valleys edge, this geological activity created long thin, vertical monoliths of rock called fins.

Okay, so what does this have to do with perfect arch creation? On either side of Salt Valley, the fins of rock continued to erode. With the absence of any earthquakes in the area, these narrow fins were left to the devices of water erosion and became perfect for arch creation.

The erosion of the fins is the same. Water eats away at some of the calcium carbonate cement in the rock until a hole is formed. Then erosion and gravity weighing on the now unsupported rock slowly enlarge the hole over time. Since there are no earthquakes in this area, the hole is allowed to enlarge to unbelievable spans, creating the delicate and immense arches you see before you.

As you travel deeper along the main stretch of Arches NP, you are actually traveling up the northern edge of Salt Valley. The conditions here were perfect, the deposit of a large amount of salt, years of erosion, the cracking of the rock layer into nice slabs that became vertical fins of rock perfect for arch making. This area is amazing in its perfection of arch creation. Nowhere on this earth have geologic conditions come together so well for this rather marvelous phenomenon to occur.

PETRIFIED DUNES

If you think about it, there really isn't any such thing as a petrified dune, so why is there a spot in Arches with such a namesake? Well, they do look like sand dunes frozen into place and yes, they were in fact at one time sand dunes before being covered with other sedimentary layers. In reality, they are simply rock formations eroded from the sand dune beds of 65 million years ago. Petrified sand dunes are simply sandstone, so these are simply sandstone formations that look like dunes of sand.

Still, given the connection of these current formations to their sand dune past, perhaps there is something else going on here. Perhaps these are ghost dunes forced to continually resurrect themselves in dune-like shapes, perpetually stuck as geologic echoes of happier times when sands could roam freely and openly here in Arches. On a walk among these formations, is that just the wind you hear or the cries of long dead dune souls yelling out against some ancient curse to be freed! It's probably just the wind and perhaps too much sun, but you will never know for sure.

Double O Arch

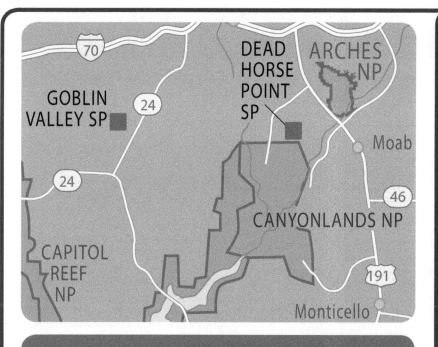

Colorado River from Dead Horse Point

Parks Near Canyonlands - Island in the Sky District & Arches

Camping in Park:

- Goblin Valley Campground: 10 T/15 RV + 2 yurts, drinking water, showers, flush toilets, 4 first come-first served, rest are reservable through Reserve America: (800) 322-3770 or at www.reserveamerica.com

Getting There:

- From Moab, UT: Take US-191 North to I-70 West to UT-24 West. Total distance is 101 mi / 162 km to park

Goblin Valley is a unique place in terms of geologic formations. Here is an area that contains thousands of hoodoos. However, this is not your typical hoodoo formation. They are short and stubby toadstool shaped things, each with a unique personality. Whether you call them hoodoos or goblins, this is a fun little place.

HIKING GOBLIN VALLEY STATE PARK

VALLEY OF GOBLINS

Easy – distance and time varies

Most visitors just walk off the rim from the overlook and wander among the goblins. If you do come to this park, at least do this. It is cool to see these formations up close and there are some unique rock formations that you can only experience by getting down among them.

CARMEL CANYON TRAIL

Easy – (1.6 mi / 2.6 km), round trip, allow 1 hour

A fun and short hike that walks past Goblin Valley and into the badlands and the very short Carmel slot canyon. The trail also includes a trip to Molly's Castle Overlook. This is another good hike for kids. The slot canyon does get narrow but is never very intimating.

CURTIS BENCH TRAIL

Easy – (2.1 mi / 3.4 km), round trip, allow 1 hour

This is an easy trail to the Curtis Bench, which gives a nice panoramic view of the Henry Mountains and the goblins in their valley below. There are also views of Molly's Castle, Three Sisters, and Wild Horse Butte.

ENTRADA CANYON TRAIL

Easy – (2.4 mi / 3.9 km), round trip, allow 30 minutes

Another easy trail suitable for small children leading into red rock badlands. Unique and somewhat unnatural looking hoodoos in a setting that seems like you are walking in a gigantic dried mud patch.

LITTLE WILD HORSE CANYON

Strenuous – (8.0 mi / 12.9 km), round trip, allow 4 – 5 hours

This is a great hike just outside of Goblin Valley State Park. Little Wild Horse Canyon is one of the most accessible slot canyons in the entire Grand Circle. In fact, it's so accessible, you cross the entrance to Little Wild Horse Canyon on the way into the park. The visitor center at Goblin Valley has a brochure on the hike that is worth picking up. Pick up the trailhead by backtracking about 0.25 miles from the visitor center to a maintained dirt road with a sign for Little Wild Horse Canyon. The trailhead with restrooms and a trail register is another 5.3 miles down this road.

The hike starts along a seasonal wash and after 0.3 mile heads into the spectacular slot canyon of Little Wild Horse Canyon and then left onto a connector road into the slightly wider Bell Canyon for the return. Little Wild Horse is 3.6 miles, 1.6 for the connector road and 1.8 for Bell Canyon. There are signposts marking the way but these can be hard to read and even find. Little Wild Horse is suitable for most hikers while Bell Canyon has some Class 3 scrambles to negotiate. If in doubt, return via Little Wild Horse Canyon.

Camping in Park:

- The Kayenta Campground: 21 T/RV + 3 yurts, hookups, drinking water (limited), restrooms, 4 sites are first come-first served, rest are reservable through Reserve America: (800) 322-3770 or online at www.reserveamerica.com

Getting There:

- From Moab, UT: Take US-191 North to I-70 West to UT-24 West. Total distance is 101 mi / 162 km to park

Dead Horse Point State Park is located adjacent to the Island in the Sky District of Canyonlands as well as the town of Moab. The state of Utah has done a great job in providing a great camping, hiking and mountain biking experience within the park's boundaries. Given the popularity of mountain biking in Moab, Dead Horse Point has become a mecca for mountain bikers, especially those that are just starting out in the sport. There is no exposure and none of the trails requires a lot of experience to enjoy them.

There are a number of trails that are designed specifically for the mountain bike, though hikers can use them too. And while this book is geared more for the hiker, there really is nothing quite like tearing through a single track, finding that satisfying center point between your bike and your body, even when the bike is outstretched to the right while your body is angled to the left.

For those hikers that aren't crazy about sharing the road at 2 - 3 miles an hour with something that can go a lot faster, there are hiking only trails too. But hopefully, with over 79 parks and hundreds of trails described, certainly dear hiker, you won't mind if the mountain biking loops are described first for this park.

MOUNTAIN BIKING IN DEAD HORSE POINT STATE PARK

All mountain bike loops in Dead Horse Point State Park can be hiked by foot as well. In some cases, the hiking and mountain biking trails parallel each other, making it easy to cross over to the hiking only trails if you are on foot.

There are three loops in the park, ranging in ease and distance traveled, from 1.4 miles to 9.0 miles round trip. Many folks do all three in one session.

BIG CHIEF LOOP

Moderate – (9.0 mi / 14.5 km), round trip, allow 2 hours for bikers, 4 hours for hikers

The longest of the three loops. The trail starts out on the Great Pyramid Loop and then continues on to Big Chief. Both loops together make up the nine-mile loop. Big Chief Loop is similar in difficulty to Great Pyramid and in fact for much of the journey is a little easier. The highlights of this trail are Big Chief Overlook, which offers great views of the distant La Sal Mountains and added remoteness. If you want to do all three loops, allow about 2 hours 30 minutes.

GREAT PYRAMID LOOP

Moderate – (4.2 mi / 6.8 km), round trip, allow 1 hour for bikers, 2 hours for hikers

Similar red rock terrain as Intrepid Loop, but with more elevation up and down as well as a slight increase in the amount of uneven terrain and one spot that is more slick rock than trail. For folks that only mountain bike a little, this is a fun bit of single track. The trail connects with the Colorado Overlook as well as Pyramid Canyon Overlook.

119

There are lots of goblins at Goblin Valley State Park

Intrepid Loop

Easy – (1.4 mi / 2.3 km), round trip, allow 20 – 30 minutes for bikers, 45 minutes for hikers

This is the most laid back of the three loops and the shortest. Mostly level, with minor bits of uneven terrain. High points include the Colorado Overlook, which is easily accessible. Good for a pleasant family bike outing.

Hiking Dead Horse Point State Park

Nature Trail

Easy – (0.3 mi / 0.5 km), round trip, allow 10 minutes

Pick up a brochure at the visitor center for this pleasant interpretive walk. The brochure will point out different aspects of the geology and flora at numbered locations.

Now, as you start out on this trail you will pass a snack shack and they have some tempting items, which can be a problem for this hike. There are two ways to manage the snack shack. Either a) realize you have no willpower whatsoever and completely give into temptation before you even hit the trail under the justification that it's still a trail and you need sustenance or b) hold off until after the hike as a reward for conquering this paved quarter-mile long monster. Either way, have a little fun and get something for yourself, you deserve it!

Colorado Overlook Trail

Easy – (1.0 mi / 1.6 km), round trip, allow 30 minutes

This trail parallels the Intrepid Loop for half its length. Hike is along the rim with great views of the Colorado River.

East Rim Trail

Easy – (4.0 mi / 6.4 km), round trip, allow 2 hours

The distance listed for this trail is round trip just for East Rim plus the spur trail out to Basin Overlook. Many visitors do both the East and West Rim, which is 5.7 miles with all the overlook spur trails. This trail gives nonstop panoramic views of the canyon and surrounding area. Basin Overlook provides a glimpse of Chimney Rock and Pyramid Butte.

West Rim Trail

Easy – (6.2 mi / 10.0 km), round trip, allow 3 hours

Similar to East Rim in commanding views, West Rim mileage noted here is if the trail was done as a there and back including the spur trails to Rim, Shafer Overlook and Meander Overlooks. Again, it is a better hike overall to combine the East and West Rim trails and make it a loop.

Big Horn Overlook Trail

Easy – (3.4 mi / 5.5 km), round trip, allow 90 minutes

This trail heads cross-country through pinyon juniper woodlands to an overlook and some large pothole formations. Similar views as West Rim Trail.

The iconic view from Dead Horse Point with the La Sal Mountains in the background

[Bryce]: *Mom?*

[Mom]: *Yes?*

[Bryce]: *That billboard over there—what is that?*

[Mom]: *It's an advertisement for a buffet. That's where you can go and eat as much as you want from all the things shown on that billboard, plus a lot more. They even have a whole section just for desserts!*

[Bryce]: *Really? They actually have these things in Vegas?*

[Mom]: *Yep.*

[Bryce]: *My mind is so messed up right now.*

Just Park it Anywhere

We were closing in on Vegas! After months of planning and several near-cancellations, we were finally almost there. Around me was the darkness of the desert, but in the distance I could begin to see the glow of Vegas lights. I looked over at my wife Angela sitting in the passenger seat. She was taking a nap, as was our youngest, Bryce. Everest was playing with some handheld video console, with the volume turned off per my set of driving rules. You could hear the drone of rapid finger play as he tried his best to get to the next level of whatever game he was playing. Ang looked so content, so peaceful. Even in sleep she somehow exuded her Southern Bell charm. She was slumped over, yet still managed to look dignified. I took in this serene scene and realized fully and for the first time, we were finally on vacation.

This would be a good trip, it would be a trip we would talk about, laugh about and reminisce about for years to come. It took a lot of convincing, a tremendous amount of planning, but here we were, doing the Grand Circle, the vacation of a lifetime. Seven national parks, all in an RV. Each park would be a new experience for the family. I couldn't wait. Even the RVing part would be a first. Ang hated camping, but she was really getting into the idea of an RV. Bryce was ecstatic; we were going to his namesake park, Bryce Canyon. So what if we picked his name because of its Celtic origins and not because of the park. To him, this was major. He met the idea of traveling in an RV like any 9-year-old would, as if what we were doing was completely magical. Bryce was our wonder, our set of eyes to see things the way they should be seen. He helped us understand the true fascination of what we were doing simply because to him, this was all completely new territory.

Even our 14-year-old Everest was unnaturally buoyant and dare I say elated, though he showed it with the usual nonchalant composure of a teenage boy. Still, since the trip began, he was behaving a lot closer to the wonderful kid we had imagined having—less sarcastic, less cynical, less moody, less like us adults. He was behaving like a kid; it was great. All of this was great. Our first stop would be Vegas. It would help ease us into all that roughing it we were about to do, plus it was more cost effective to pick up the RV in Vegas as opposed to our home state of California.

It wasn't too late, but it was fully dark, about 9 pm. I had been tracking the glow of the distant Vegas lights on the horizon for the past twenty minutes. I knew to look for it and had been watching it get pleasantly closer as I made good time. We were maybe 40 miles from the "city that never sleeps." Another half hour or so, and we would be checked in and planning what to do next.

The serenity of this fine moment was disrupted by a subtle, disconcerting noise. It wasn't a loud noise, but it wasn't a good noise either. It was the sound of something metallic lightly bouncing inside the engine.

I gave a casual glance over at my wife. Still fast asleep, she wasn't hearing it. I was relieved. She didn't like car trouble. The car's care was put directly under my attention and she had very simple but tough standards in this area. If the car worked, I received neither accolade nor praise for I was simply doing my job. If however, the car didn't work, for whatever reason, my fault or otherwise, this was an entirely different matter. She never let the gas gauge get below halfway. Monitors and meters requesting the car be examined or maintained were completed in quick order. The washer fluid was always filled, Purel was always available and country was always on the radio. These were her rules for the car. Follow them and life was good. Stray, and I faced certain peril.

That sound meant one thing: the car was no longer functioning properly. If she heard that sound, it would create a catastrophic series of events. Every missed oil change, every forgotten tire pressure check and every delayed maintenance of our 14-year marriage would come under scrutiny. Events that I couldn't possibly

121

begin to remember would be recounted by her in the most minute detail, all building to an open and shut case putting me to blame for the car's misfortune Normally Ang was a quite dignified woman, but when it came to matters of motor vehicles, she took an altogether different tone. I gritted my teeth. "Come on, car, don't screw up on me now," I thought.

I carefully reached for the radio and turned it on with the silence of a ninja; setting the volume low enough so as not to wake her, but enough to try to drown out the rattle coming from the engine.

For about twenty minutes I listened for the sound through the music, waiting for pauses in the songs and trying to figure out what the heck that engine noise was. It was as if keys were being munched by the pistons, playing rhythmically with an undertone of cringe. I was starting to wince at the sound, looking like someone who had just opened a rank garbage can, but fortunately my wife still hadn't noticed. I kept looking over oh so casually, she was now half asleep, staring out into the darkness, the glow of Vegas off in the distance, its larger-than-life array of lights denting the night's sky. The crunching sound, on the other hand, was doing the opposite of what I wanted it to. It was getting louder.

During a pause between songs, the metallic sound was unmistakable. Clankity clankity, clankity clack. Clankity clankity, clankity clack. I glanced at the speedometer, then the rearview mirror, then my wife. She was no longer looking out the passenger window. She was now looking at me, with deep concern.

"What's that sound?" she asked.

"I don't know. It's been going on for a while now. We'll have to get it checked out in Vegas."

Ang turned the music down and focused her keen senses on the crunching noise. Her eyes narrowed in reaction to the mystery, her head cocked a bit sideways to hear the sound better.

"It sounds like the engine," she declared.

"What's that sound?" Bryce chimed in.

"I don't know, Bryce. Your mother and I are trying to figure it out," I said calmly.

"It sounds like the engine," Bryce declared. "Mom, do you hear it?"

"What's that sound?" Everest added.

"It's the engine!" Bryce said with a tone of impatience.

"Shrugs," Everest replied.

At this point I'm thinking, "Crap, there is no getting around this, everyone is hearing it. I'm screwed."

I turn off the radio completely and we all listen to this horrifying sound. It invades our wonderful little world like some sentient being. It now has a life of its own, commanding our attention. Clankity clankity, clankity clack.   Clankity clankity, clankity clack. We fall under its spell. There is nothing we can do but listen to the terrifying yet peacefully rhythmic sound of the engine tearing itself apart.

I keep thinking the same three thoughts. "Should I keep driving? Should I pull over? We are so close!" Then, as if to show its displeasure at my turning off the music, the rhythmic sounds ceased and the car literally hopped, then sputtered and began making sounds that made those clankity clack sounds seem oddly pleasant and normal. The car was dying.

There was a thick air of concern as I pulled off I-15 and made a left onto an unnamed road. No one said a word. There were no streetlights, no house lights. We were out in the middle of nowhere. I could make out that we were next to a housing development under construction. I could see the vague silhouettes of half-framed houses and big construction equipment.

I figured we were somewhere near the town of Enterprise, Nevada and a mere 10 miles from our destination. The glow of Vegas was bright enough you could almost touch it, the lights an oasis of warm hospitality. I kept driving toward the light under some vain hope that driving slower would be enough to bring the car back to normal. The car was able to sputter another ten feet before the engine went into a virtual free fall of cacophony and then seized to a stop in one final gasp. In a heroic gesture, I quickly maneuvered the drive into neutral and coasted to the side of the road with our last vestiges of momentum.

For a brief moment, we sat in silence. I tried to turn over the motor, as if maybe it was just some bad gas.

But I was only able to get as far as the grind of the starter. The car was dead, very much dead. We were in the middle of a hot dry desert night, far from anything that resembled civilization save the mocking glow of Vegas and some construction equipment. It was at that point that my sweet dear loving wife lost it completely.

"What the heck did you do?" Ang yelled.

"I think the car died." I replied, as if stating the obvious would help calm the matter. It didn't.

"You killed the car? Oh for the love of all that is green and golden, you killed the car! How did you kill the car? How are we going to get to Vegas? Our entire vacation is now ruined, just simply ruined! Oh my dear lord, I knew we should never have gone on this trip. Didn't I tell you we needed to have the car thoroughly examined before we went on this trip?"

"Well, I ah…"

"This is absolutely the last thing in the entire world that we could possibly want to have happened. We have reservations at the Mandalay Bay. They take your first night you know; it's nonrefundable! We will be sleeping in this dang car all night!" And so she went on asking questions that could not be answered, spilling accusations of malcontent and crafting worst case scenarios involving our having to somehow tow the car all the way back to our mechanic in California due to the shifty distrust of any mechanic that calls Las Vegas home.

At some semblance of a pause and with my impatience showing, I blurted, "Look, can you just call triple A? My phone died a few hours ago."

Her eyes brightened and she pulled out her iPhone as if it were her salvation. She unlocked it, held it in front of her face like a tri-coder and said in her most commanding voice, "Siri, I want you to call triple A." I was always impressed that Siri could understand Southern drawl.

"Triple A. There are 15 results that match that query. Which one would you like?"

"Fifteen results! Come on", she said to no one. She looked at her phone again. "Siri, call A-A-A".

Siri came back with, "Uh oh, I can't make that phone call." Siri was not helping.

"Let me see the phone," I said. I looked at it—the signal icon went from one bar to that cross through the bars stating you are completely screwed. Great, I thought. I got out of the car and tried twisting the phone around, walking in a circle, and holding the phone in the air while shaking it, which are all proper tricks to get a smart phone to function when all you have to work with is desperation. None of these tactics were working. We were not only stuck, we had no cell phone. This was not going to be good news to tell the wife.

Everyone was standing outside of the car at this point. They were following me around, watching me perform my cell phone reception ritual, waiting to understand the verdict of this dance to the cell phone gods. I looked over. Angela, my dear sweet wife, the love of my life, looked at me with the intent of a cobra ready to strike its victim. There could be only one answer that would calm her down at this point, and I didn't have it. The only thing I could do was state the obvious. I handed the phone back to her and said, "We are out of cell range".

"What!" she exclaimed before going into an uncontrolled fury that if channeled properly, could likely have powered a small casino. I envisioned people looking up from their gaming tables all the way back in Vegas, wondering what all that yelling could be about. I envisioned taxi drivers and pedestrians, shopkeepers and club bouncers, all stopping whatever they were doing to glance out into the desert with curious looks. I hoped one of them would perhaps get in their car to see what could possibly be causing this uproar, but alas, we were not so lucky.

Now mind you, this unchecked broken dam of ferocity that is my wife is a rare event. She is typically even tempered for the most part, but from her perspective, we were stuck, miles from help, it was dark, and the car was dead. Plus, who knows what was lurking out in the darkness, so factor in that the kids were in danger. The reality of the matter was we had been driving all day and our car was so close to a nice fluffy bed we could almost feel it. That was a lot for anyone to take in. The best thing for me to do was to let her do her thing. The dam had broken, and there really wasn't anything anyone could do but watch the churning waters of her vitriol engulf me.

I decided to have a look at the engine. Nothing but the calm steaming heap of a broken engine looking back, which is to say, I had no idea what happened to it. Ang was now alternating her argument with me and the completely useless Siri. It really wasn't Siri's fault that we had no cell reception, but I was thankful she was in this with me. I started feeling sorry for Siri.

At round four of Ang's torrent I said, "Look, honey. I am sorry, so sorry about the car. I'm not sure what happened. I'm sorry about your phone. I'm sorry about my phone. This all sucks, trust me. I'm sorry about everything here. I do, however, need a few moments to figure out what to do next. So I'm going over here to think." I pointed randomly into the darkness and then headed in that direction. For a while, I walked without thinking. I kept hearing Siri toying with my wife's patience, informing her of her now low battery life, that there was no cell reception way out here, that Siri was happy to occasionally find a phone signal and give directions to AAA plumbing in nearby Enterprise. I kept walking until I met up with a bulldozer. I stopped there at this beast and stared at it. The bulldozer stared back, in a welcoming kind of way. It seemed to understand what I was going through. And then I thought, "Maybe…"

I tried the door. It was unlocked! I found keys tucked into the ashtray compartment. Could these really be "The Keys," the heavenly keys to this bulldozer? I slipped the key into the ignition and turned it to the first position. The thing made a large warning beep sound. "No way!" I thought. "No Way! Salvation!"

I began to rationalize this new find in my head. What if we just borrowed this bulldozer? The folks who own it would understand. I mean it's in the middle of the night, we are stranded, and I'm not really stealing it, just borrowing it. I've got children after all; I'm just ensuring their safety. The owner of this bulldozer must be a father. Certainly he would understand if I drove his bulldozer a few miles to get us into cell range. This idea was a good one.

The more I thought about this, the more it made sense. And why stop at getting us to within cell range? Why not just take this thing all the way to the hotel? I imagined myself for a moment tooling down Las Vegas Boulevard. There was only the one seat but Ang and the kids could somehow cram into the cab with me. I couldn't just leave them while I drove off in a bulldozer. We could put the luggage in the scooped blade. I mean why not?

The idea distilled into sheer genius in my head. This could work! This could actually work! Besides, they say anything can happen in Vegas. This is certainly anything! We could even wave at the people as if we are in some type of bulldozer parade traveling slowly down The Strip! You there in that convertible, yes we are waving at you! You might be traveling in style, buddy, but we are traveling in a bulldozer!

I'd pull into the Mandalay Bay with the other cars, and man would I love to see the look on the valet's face when I pulled up. I would, of course, lower the scoop to make it easy for him to get to the luggage. Then I would get out of the cab as if I owned it and throw him the keys with a knowing smile and a correctly timed, "Here you go, fine sir. Don't scratch it!" We would enter Mandalay Bay like we owned it, in slow motion, just like in the movies. I'd feel like Batman. Batman in a bulldozer, going to Vegas with his family, in plaid shorts and a T-shirt. That's right. Batman. It was playing out so well in my head. How could we not make this our Vegas entrance?

I had no choice at this point. We had to do this. I turned the key further and the engine started. A huge plume of black smoke came out of the exhaust in front of me. Now to figure out how to operate the thing. Just then Everest and the rest of the family ran over to where I was.

"Dad! Dad! What are you doing?"

"I'm solving the problem, son. Get this, we are going to ride this bulldozer right here into Las Vegas! That is what we are going to do. Son, get the luggage."

"Dad, while you guys were arguing I used my phone and called a taxi. I was going to tell you but you ran off and we didn't know where you went. I told them what exit we got off. They said they'd be here in about 15 minutes."

Of course! Ev had his own phone and it usually got better reception. How could I have forgotten this? I slumped in the tractor seat dejected. "You mean, no bulldozer?"

"Step out of the cab, Dad, before you hurt someone."

I turned the engine off; my dream had been killed by the pragmatic ways of my own son.

"Didn't he do good work?" Ang asked, nodding at Everest. "He called them all by himself. I'm so proud of you!" She gave Everest a tremendous hug and then looked at me inquisitively. "Were you really thinking you were going to drive that thing? Let me guess, you were thinking you could drive it to the hotel, I bet. My goodness, I'm not sure if your head is on straight sometimes." She laughed.

"Is that chuckling I hear? I'm glad to see you've come back to us," I said.

"I'm sorry for all that hollering. Thanks for letting me get it all out. I just kind of lost it for a bit I guess."

I looked back at the bulldozer as we walked to our car. "You know, guys, someday I will drive a bulldozer down Las Vegas Boulevard."

"We all have our dreams, Dad," Bryce stated matter-of-factly. "But if you do, I'm calling shotgun."

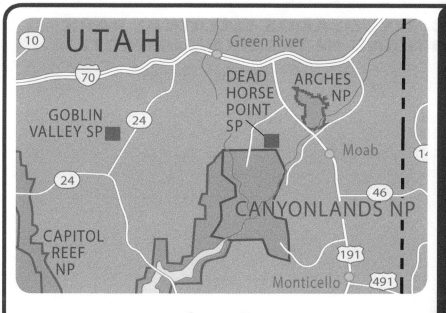

Quick Facts

Official Park Website: www.nps.gov/cany

Visitor Center:

- General Information: (435) 719-2313
- Backcountry Reservation Office: (435) 259-4351
- Island in the Sky Visitor Center: (435) 259-4712

Park Size: 337,598 acres

Established: 09/12/1964

Visitors: 0.6 million (2015)

Experience Level:

- Family Friendly to Backcountry Hiker

Park Accessibility:

- Okay for 2WD and RVs, 4WD in some areas
- Day and Overnight Use

Nearest Town with Amenities:

- Moab, UT is 30 mi / 48 km from park

Getting There:

- From Capitol Reef NP: Take UT-24 East, I-70 East, US-191 South, and UT-313 West for 156 mi / 251 km to park entrance
- From Moab, UT: Take US-191 North and UT-313 West for 30 mi / 48 km to park entrance

Canyonlands National Park – Island in the Sky District

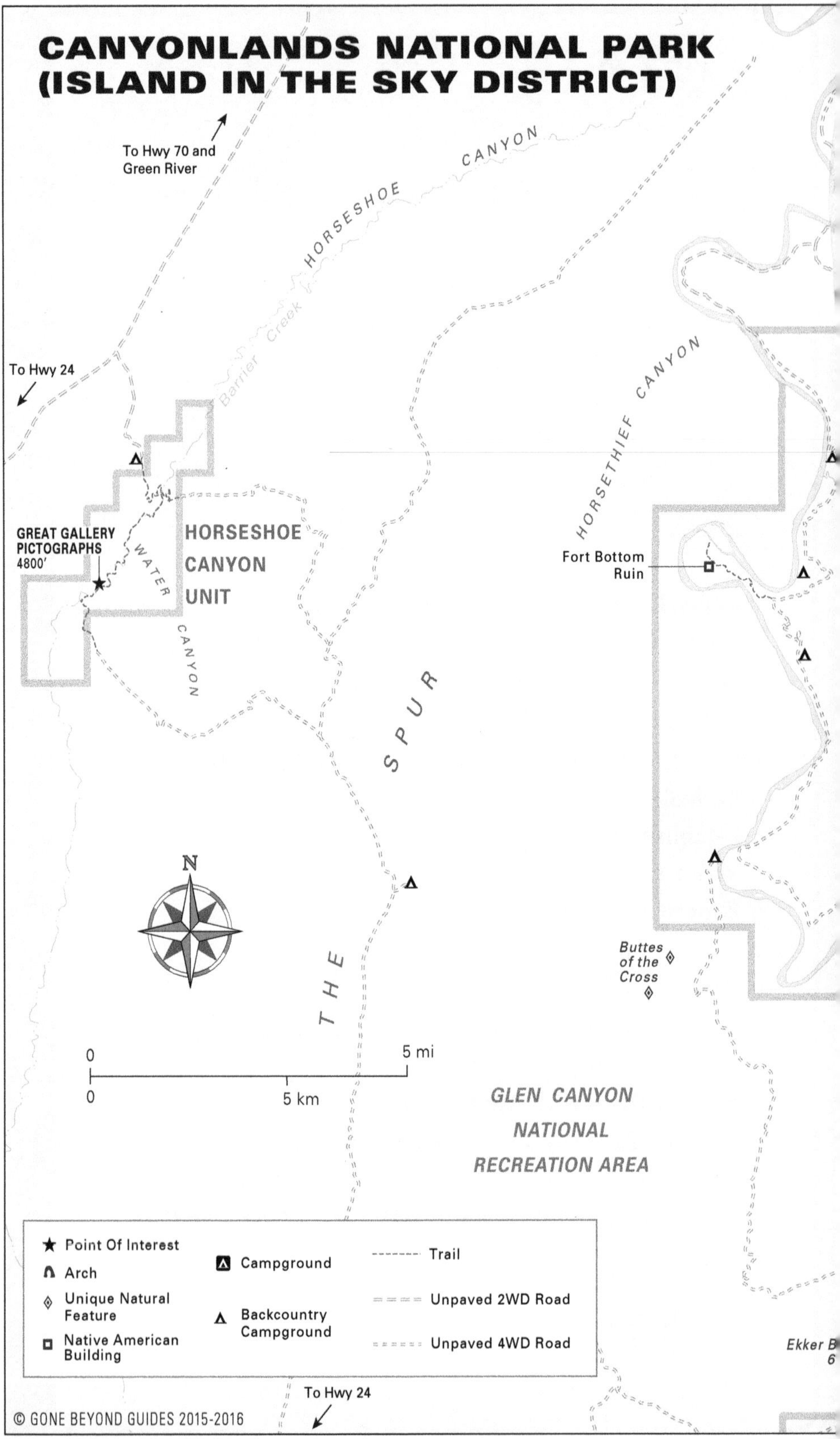

CANYONLANDS NATIONAL PARK
(ISLAND IN THE SKY DISTRICT)

To Hwy 70 and
Green River

HORSESHOE CANYON

Barrier Creek

HORSETHIEF CANYON

To Hwy 24

GREAT GALLERY
PICTOGRAPHS
4800'

HORSESHOE
CANYON
UNIT

WATER CANYON

Fort Bottom
Ruin

THE SPUR

N

Buttes
of the
Cross

0   5 mi

0   5 km

GLEN CANYON
NATIONAL
RECREATION AREA

★ Point Of Interest	▲ Campground	------ Trail
∩ Arch		==== Unpaved 2WD Road
◊ Unique Natural Feature	▲ Backcountry Campground	===== Unpaved 4WD Road
▫ Native American Building		

To Hwy 24

Ekker B
6

© GONE BEYOND GUIDES 2015-2016

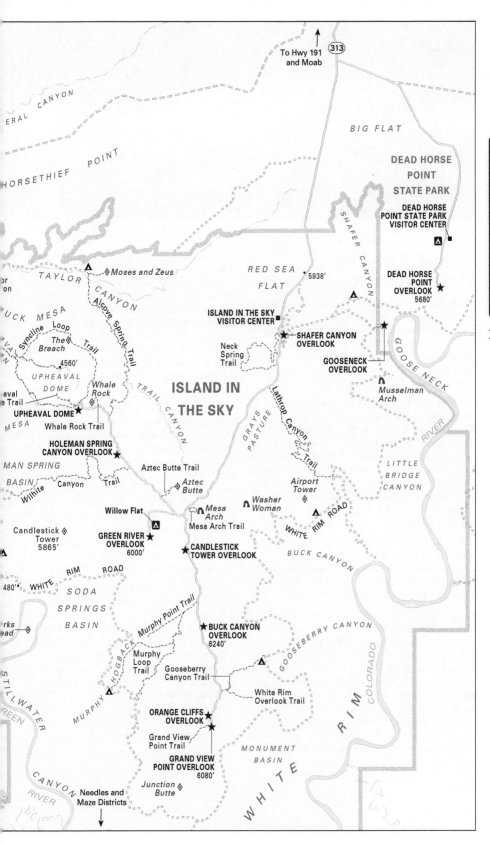

To Hwy 191
and Moab

313

BIG FLAT

DEAD HORSE
POINT
STATE PARK

DEAD HORSE
POINT STATE PARK
VISITOR CENTER

ERAL CANYON

HORSETHIEF POINT

SHAFER CANYON

DEAD HORSE
POINT
OVERLOOK
5680'

RED SEA
FLAT

5938'

GOOSE NECK

TAYLOR

◇ Moses and Zeus

Alcove Spring Trail

CANYON

ISLAND IN THE SKY
VISITOR CENTER

SHAFER CANYON
OVERLOOK

GOOSENECK
OVERLOOK

UCK MESA

Syncline Loop Trail

The
Breach

4560'

UPHEAVAL
DOME

Whale
Rock

TRAIL CANYON

ISLAND IN
THE SKY

Neck
Spring
Trail

RIVER

GOOSE NECK

Musselman
Arch

MESA

aval
e Trail

UPHEAVAL DOME ★

Whale Rock Trail

HOLEMAN SPRING
CANYON OVERLOOK ★

MAN SPRING

BASIN

Wilhite

Canyon

Trail

Aztec Butte Trail

◇ Aztec
Butte

GRAYS PASTURE

Lathrop Canyon

Canyon

Trail

Airport
Tower
◇

LITTLE
BRIDGE
CANYON

Candlestick ◇
Tower
5865'

Willow Flat

GREEN RIVER
OVERLOOK
6000'

CANDLESTICK
TOWER OVERLOOK ★

◠ Mesa
Arch
Mesa Arch Trail

◠ Washer
Woman

WHITE RIM ROAD

BUCK CANYON

480' •

WHITE RIM ROAD

SODA

SPRINGS

BASIN

rks
ead ◇

Murphy Point Trail

BUCK CANYON
OVERLOOK
6240'

MURPHY HOGBACK

Murphy
Loop
Trail

Gooseberry
Canyon Trail

GOOSEBERRY CANYON

COLORADO

STILLWATER

REEN

CANYON
RIVER

ORANGE CLIFFS
OVERLOOK ★

Grand View
Point Trail

GRAND VIEW
POINT OVERLOOK
6080'

Junction ◇
Butte

White Rim
Overlook Trail

MONUMENT

BASIN

WHITE RIM

Needles and
Maze Districts

Through Mesa Arch to Washer Woman

WHAT MAKES CANYONLANDS SPECIAL

Canyonlands NP is Utah's largest national park and yet the least visited. To the true explorer, the person who wants to see what's at the top, around the corner and on the other side, Canyonlands is certainly overwhelming. The sheer size of the park, the number of mesas, monoliths, buttes, fins and canyons encompasses several lifetimes of exploration.

The park is carved in part by two major rivers, the Colorado River and the Green River. They connect within Canyonlands NP, one an earthy green and the other a Navajo sandstone red. There are arches, such as Druid Arch, that seem as if some giant built a massive rendition of Stonehenge. Mesa Arch is amazing for a different reason—it sits precariously on the edge of sheer cliff. Mesa Arch is also known for giving visitors an unforgettable sunrise that will sit on your top ten list of best sunrises ever seen.

Canyonlands NP is divided by the rivers themselves into three major sections. With its proximity to the town of Moab, Island in the Sky is the most visited, followed by Needles to the south, while the remote section called the Maze receives the least visitation.

Island in the Sky is a large broad mesa that has grand views of 100 miles (160 km) or more on a clear day. There are roads that take the visitor to multiple observation areas, each with a unique view. From the top you can see across to the Maze, down into the twists and turns of the Green River, and you might even recognize famous monoliths, such as the 305-foot solitary sandstone pillar called Standing Rock. To really explore Island in the Sky, you may want to consider renting a jeep or a jeep guided tour. This will allow you to get down off the mesa and into some of the canyons you look down on from the overlooks. There are a several hikes on the mesa as well as others that require dropping into the canyons below.

The Needles District is less crowded and has exceptional hiking opportunities that are easily accessible. This section of the park is vastly different from the Island in the Sky District in that the visitor is immediately in the canyons, allowing close and personal views of the various pinnacles. Needles is named after the many monoliths banded in red and white Cedar Mesa sandstone. The monoliths go by funny names like Paul Bunyan's Potty and Caterpillar Arch. Druid Arch is one of the gems of this section and is one of the most popular longer hikes in Needles.

The Maze District is the third and least visited district in Canyonlands NP, receiving only 3 percent of its total visitors. This is with good reason as it is one of the most remote places in the nation. Visitors to this rugged area must have a high degree of self-sufficiency and overall desert skills. Typical visits to this region are 3–7 days simply because of the preparation and planning that goes into such a trip. The Maze holds remarkable journeys, vast silence, tests of ones abilities and purity within adventure. For most visitors, these journeys will have to remain dreams, something pragmatically unattainable. This remote location, out of reach yet only just, helps add to the siren call of Canyonlands NP.

There is a fourth element to the park, the rivers themselves. Before joining together, the Green and Colorado Rivers independently carve deeply into the sandstone layers, creating quiet channels of water with sheer walls of rock on either side. Once the Green River merges with the Colorado, the combined power of these waters creates a 46-mile (74 km) stretch of rapids through Cataract Canyon. From high above at the confluence overlook, you can hear the roar of the rapids. Down in the river visitors can experience some of the wildest rapids in North America, with some stretches as intense as anything you'll find in the Grand Canyon.

There is nothing quite like Canyonlands. Whether you simply look out at the vast southwestern vistas from the top of the Island in the Sky, hike to Druid Arch, spend a week in the Maze or shoot down either of the park's two rivers, you will have a life memory. There is, as Edward Abbey once said, nothing else like it in the world.

THINGS TO DO IN CANYONLANDS NATIONAL PARK

RIVER RAFTING

Rafting the Colorado River with a competent tour company is a safe way to have a story you can tell well into your nursing home years. There is much adrenaline-pumping and exhilaration, many brief moments of unholy terror and, simply put, a tremendous amount of overwhelming adventure. You are seeing Canyonlands up close and personal, sure, but what you are really doing is exploring some of the last untamed wilderness in the contiguous United States. Canyonlands is vast, and it is nearly impossible to see it all in a normal vacation window. If you need to focus your visit, white water rafting is certainly a top consideration.

You will benefit from a little planning. There are many tour companies, but many of them are simply affiliate travel agencies disguised as rafting companies. They will book whatever you want but without any guarantee or knowledge that the river is running in the manner you imagined. It pays to go with knowledgeable outfitters that can help you plan the trip that's right for you. This guidebook references only the highest recommended local rafting tour groups operating in Moab.

Another reason to put some planning muscle into a rafting trip is that they aren't cheap. Costs range from a couple hundred dollars per person for scenic overnighter trips to $1000-plus per person for the multiday whitewater rafting trip.

When to go is important. Between May–June and sometimes into July, Cataract Canyon is a popular destination. This is a 46-mile (74 km) section just after the confluence of the Green and Colorado rivers. The spring runoff creates intense whitewater.

The canyon is obstructed by tremendous boulders that create up to Class V rapids (Class VI is considered un-runnable, so Class V are serious rapids). Some of the rapids are notorious enough to get their own names, including Satan's Gut, The Claw and "Little Niagara." Most of Cataract Canyon is Class III to IV.

From July to October Cataract Canyon is still a great adventure, but the lowered water levels come with lowered whitewater difficulties. Many visitors find themselves disappointed since most of the rafting sites show photos of the exciting torrents of spring and not the tempered waters of summer. If you are looking for full immersion into true whitewater, go in the spring.

How long you go is important. Some tour guides offer 1-day trips, but they are long days and cut out much of the soul of a rafting trip. They get you there, you shoot some rapids, and then you come back. If you can help it, don't do a 1-day trip. The most popular durations are 2-3-day trips. These will include more hiking side canyons, eating BBQ or some other hot meal with your fellow rafters, explorations into native ruins and a chance to sleep out under the stars with the Colorado by your side. Many tour groups offer even longer tours of up to six days. In general, the longer you can get out, the more you will see and experience.

Don't feel it has to be Cataract Canyon. There are many destinations offered by the same tour groups that do Cataract Canyon. Some of these are outside of Canyonlands and include travel as part of the package. Desolation Canyon is a great destination if you are looking for Class II–III rapids and perhaps more isolation. There are still rapids up to Class IV in Westwater Canyon during the summer and is the go-to spot for summer whitewater.

For first-timers or for a more relaxed scene, Fisher Towers (aka 'The Daily') provides some mild rapids and is appropriate for children of ages five and up. Fisher Towers is considered one of the most scenic parts of the Colorado in Utah.

Recommended Rafting Outfitters:

Adrift Adventures:

378 North Main Street, Moab, Utah, Phone: (435) 259-8594 or (800) 874-4483

NAVTEC Expeditions:

321 North Main Street, Moab, Utah, Phone: (435) 259-7983 or (800) 833-1278

Sheri Griffith River Expeditions:

2231 South Highway 191, Moab, Utah, Phone: (800) 332-2439

Cataract Canyon Whitewater

EXPLORE BY 4WD

Canyonlands NP is a rough and rugged realm. The term "road" is at times a loose and relative word and is best understood under the guidance of a 4-wheel drive high clearance vehicle. The 100 miles (160 km) of White Rim Road, for example, is considered moderately difficult under favorable weather conditions. There are some sections, such as Elephant Hill and the Silver Steps, which will certainly test one's 4WD skills. I've seen younger kids drive up a slope as sort of a race and I've also seen fathers ask their families to get out during certain sections due to the very real feeling that your jeep will tip over.

The point here is if you are looking for real adventure, renting a jeep or other 4WD vehicle in Moab will certainly not disappoint. If you'd rather not do the driving but still want to see the backcountry by vehicle, you can hire someone to lead the way on your adventure. Either way, exploring Canyonlands NP by 4WD is again one of those life moments you will be talking about for, well, the rest of your life.

For tours and guides, Adrift Adventures and NAVTEC Expeditions (listed in the rafting section) are both great outfitters. They offer a wide range of tours from single- to multi-day trips.

Recommended Jeep Tours and Rentals:

Canyonlands Jeep Adventures

225 South Main Street, Moab, Utah
Phone: (866) 892-5337

Enterprise Rent-A-Car

Moab Airport, N Highway 191, Moab, Utah Phone: (435) 259-8505

Cliffhanger Jeep Rental

40 West Center Street, Moab, Utah
Phone: (435) 259-0889

DRIVING AROUND

Canyonlands NP is smack dab in the middle of a Grand Circle journey. Blistered, sunburned, sore and drained from the heat, the thought of doing nothing more than driving to an overlook and peering over the edge may seem to be the perfect thing to do. If this is your group, take heart; there are many overlooks in Canyonlands NP, each with stunning grand views that make up the definitive heart of the Southwest.

Most of the overlooks are naturally atop the Island in the Sky. These are listed in order of appearance as you enter the Island in the Sky District.

SHAFER CANYON OVERLOOK

Easy to miss as you come in, this overlook is more of a pull-out for an RV and is easily navigated as you make it back out of the park. What makes this view cool is the view of the 4WD Shafer Road, which somehow manages to twist and turn its way through tight loops down the canyon.

GREEN RIVER OVERLOOK

As you head into the park's Island in the Sky District, turn right toward Upheaval Dome and look for the spur road to Green River Overlook. There is ample parking with a short paved access trail to the edge of the mesa. The views on Green River Overlook are spectacular, and while it's hard to call any one of the overlooks here "the best," this is certainly a contender.

Shafer Canyon Overlook and Road

HOLEMAN SPRING CANYON OVERLOOK

From Green River Overlook, turn left and continue toward Upheaval Dome. Again, this one is easy to miss as it is more of a pull-out and best viewed coming back from Upheaval Dome. The overlook has northern views of the park.

BUCK CANYON OVERLOOK

This overlook is a loop for easy driving and parking and overlooks the eastern side of the mesa, offering very different views from the other more westward facing turnouts.

GRAND VIEW POINT OVERLOOK

This is the end of the road and most southern overlook in the Island in the Sky District. The overlook offers some of the most dramatic views in the park commanding a broad swath to the west and south of the park. This is definitely worth the drive.

HIKING IN THE ISLAND IN THE SKY DISTRICT OF CANYONLANDS NP

NECK SPRING

Moderate – (5.8 mi / 9.3 km), round trip, allow 4 -5 hours, elev. Δ: 300 ft / 91 m, trailhead at Shafer Canyon Overlook

Neck Spring is popular for many reasons. It's a loop and while it does have some elevation gain and loss, the trail isn't as steep as some of the other routes that take the hiker off the mesa top. It's also close to the visitor center as well as Shafer Trail Road, which is fun to watch as 4WD cars snake their way down the side of a cliff. Neck Spring Trail has thick patches of pinyon juniper and overall much plant diversity.

The trail is very well marked, giving both views of interior canyon cliff faces as well as some panoramic views. Remains of old watering troughs and a cabin remnant can be found, indicating the historic ranching days that preceded the park. A small portion of the loop parallels the road.

LATHROP CANYON

Strenuous – (21.6 mi / 34.8 km), round trip, multi day backpacking trip, elev. Δ: 2,000 ft / 610 m, trailhead is two miles into park from visitor center

With 2,000 feet in steep elevation gain/loss, this is one of the more strenuous hikes in the park. The trail heads off the mesa, steeply down to the Colorado River. The first 2.6 miles are single track across open low brush meadows and some slickrock. This portion makes for an easy hike to the rim of the mesa and incredible views.

The next jaunt is steeply down another three miles to connect with White Rim Road. Much of this portion is on open rock with markers. While the cairns are well laid out and easy to follow, the path itself is not a straight line, so be sure to have the next cairn in sight as you pass the one next to you. Backtracking your way to the marked route can be a puzzler.

The trail ultimately eases as it cuts into a sandy wash that connects with White Rim Road, your next arduous portion of the journey. Be sure to make a point to your fellow hiking companions that the "White Rim Road Segment" is about to begin and to be fully prepared for this section. After making a lot of fuss about how hard this leg will be, make a right onto this rugged and torturous 4WD drive road and walk several hundred feet and then turn left onto Lathrop Canyon Road, thus ending this leg of the journey. Before making the turn however, be sure to take a dramatic pause in gratitude to the team that this segment was completed safely, praising the group for their hard efforts. Maybe do a head count or something to make sure everyone "made it". Continue on Lathrop Canyon Road to the Colorado River. There are picnic tables and an outhouse at the river.

View from Aztec Butte Trail

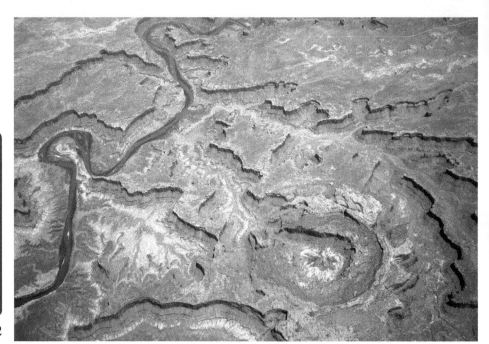

Aerial shot of Upheaval Dome and the Green River

It is worth just doing the initial portion of this trail and turning around at the rim. For those that do the full distance, there are many spur trails to archaeological sites and old mining areas, as well as the usual assortment of arches, spires, flat boulders and all around spectacular scenery. If you are looking for a full immersion hike into Canyonlands, this will satisfy that hunger.

MESA ARCH

Easy – (0.5 mi / 0.8 km), round trip, allow 30 minutes, elev. Δ: 100 ft / 30 m, trailhead just before junction to Upheaval Dome Road

Mesa Arch is easy to find, easy to hike and has incredible views. The trail ends at Mesa Arch, which spans 50 feet and sits right on the edge of a 500-foot cliff wall. Other arches, including the well-known Washer Woman Arch, are visible. This hike is great for sunrise shots and is popular with photographers due to the ability to capture the light, views and arch all in one shot.

AZTEC BUTTE

Moderate – (2.0 mi / 3.2 km), round trip, allow 60 - 90 minutes, elev. Δ: 200 ft / 61 m, trailhead 1 mi north-west on Upheaval Dome Road

This is a very rewarding and unique trail as it offers a lot of variety in a small package. The visitor will enjoy hiking through level, undisturbed grasslands toward the distant dome-shaped butte rising above. There is a short, steep climb to the rim of the butte where one can see ruins of Pueblo granaries. The trail loops around the top of Aztec Butte, providing inspiring views of Taylor Canyon.

MURPHY POINT

Moderate – (3.6 mi / 5.8 km), round trip, allow 2 hours, elev. Δ: 100 ft / 30 m, trailhead is 3 mi south on main park road from Upheaval Dome junction

See Murphy Loop for some additional elements of the trail description. The trail starts nicely across a flatland of short brush and then down a cairn marked area of slickrock to Murphy Point. Elevation gain is a modest 168 feet. Murphy Point offers an overlook to panoramic views of the many canyons that feed into the Green River. It's an immersive alternative to the drive up overlooks without having to do a steep descent off the mesa.

MURPHY LOOP

Strenuous – (10.8 mi / 17.4 km), round trip, allow 5 – 6 hours, elev. Δ: 1,100 ft / 335 m, trailhead at Murphy Point trailhead

Murphy Loop is similar to many of the hikes in Island in the Sky District. The hike begins well enough along a blissfully flat section of brushy flatlands, followed by an insane descent via a bunch of short switchbacks leading to the lower regions of Canyonlands. Going clockwise on this loop puts one into an epic wash before connecting briefly with White Rim Road. From here, the trail climbs up a hogback ridge and follows it back to the loop junction. Some areas of steep slickrock, exposed ledges and need for navigational skills are involved in completing this trail.

Highlights to be found on this trail include Murphy Point which gives commanding views of Murphy Basin and down into the Green River. (See Murphy Point for details on that spur trail).

The other highlight is Murphy Hogback, a mesa narrow enough to feel as if you are walking across an ancient land bridge but wide enough to give the full pleasure of walking on the flatlands of a mesa top. This thin plateau allows for amazing views on either side.

GRAND VIEW POINT

Easy – (2.0 mi / 3.2 km), round trip, allow 1 hour, elev. Δ: 50 ft / 15 m, trailhead at Grand View Point

If you have been driving on the park's Grand View Point Road and on getting to the end, wish you could go just a little bit further, Grand View Point Trail is the answer. Starting at the parking lot for Grand View Point Overlook, the short little trail gets the hiker away from all those pesky cars and to very edge of Island in the Sky Mesa. This is an excellent hike for those limited on time.

GOOSEBERRY CANYON

Strenuous – (5.4 mi / 8.6 km), round trip, allow 4 - 5 hours, elev. Δ: 1,400 ft / 427 m, trailhead at Grand View picnic area

This is one crazy steep trail that leads off the mesa top down to Gooseberry Canyon, which is an impressive draw draining into the Colorado River. The trail drops down some 1,200 feet in just 0.7 miles via a series of well-built switchbacks. Make sure whatever time it took to get down is doubled for the trip back up. The trail then follows a dry wash to White Rim Road near Gooseberry Canyon.

Gooseberry provides some great views, starting with a 200-foot cliff face on all sides of the canyon and then stretching to the canyon floor. Peering over the edge into the canyon allows for the realization that you started this hike by peering across an overlook and then hiked for miles to end at another equally impressive overlook. This hike really shows the magnitude of Canyonlands NP.

WILHITE CANYON

Strenuous – (12.2 mi / 19.6 km), round trip, allow 6 – 7 hours, elev. Δ: 1,600 ft / 488 m, trailhead on Upheaval Dome Road

Wilhite Canyon Trail starts amongst open brush flats and then descends at a very rapid rate (850 feet in 0.65 miles) dropping into Upper West Basin. From there, the trail winds around some impressive cliffs and then down a wash to West Rim Road. Highlights include great views of the Green River, Holeman Spring and Upper West Basins as well as a prominent monolith named Candlestick Tower to the southwest. This trail has some tough spots containing slickrock and talus rock combined with steep inclines. All in all, a typically strenuous trail, especially on the steep parts that reward the hiker with great views at each step. There is a cool slot canyon just over the road and is possible to venture into it for a bit before needing canyoneering gear. Note that this canyon is easier to get down into then it is to get out of, moderate scrambling is required here.

TAYLOR CANYON

Strenuous – (20.0 mi / 32.2 km), round trip, multi day backpacking trip, elev. Δ: 2,000 ft / 610 m, trailhead at Trail Canyon trailhead on Upheaval Dome Road

Taylor Canyon shares a few similarities to the Lathrop Canyon trek described below. Both step off of the mesa and require long steep descents, both are incredibly scenic and worth the effort and both lead to one of the major rivers of the Southwest. In Taylor Canyon's case, the water source in question is the Green River versus the Colorado River for the Lathrop Canyon trail. As described, the trail is a nice two-day loop, which includes Upheaval Dome and the gravity defying spires named Moses and Zeus.

Take Upheaval Dome Road to the Trail Canyon trailhead pullout and begin the steep descent into Trail Canyon. This trail does require a fair amount of skill, as there are several areas where minor scrambling and trail finding is needed. The trail makes its way to an obvious sandstone fin on the north side of the canyon, which can be used as a guide. The canyon bottom is reached after 2.1 miles.

From here, head north to a juncture where Trail Canyon merges with Taylor Canyon and the loop trail around Zeus and Moses. These two spires are quite impressive, shooting straight up, the tallest being 410 feet. Take the right trail to do the short loop around the spires and then left into Taylor Canyon. After a short distance is Taylor Campground, which is a dry camp with one pit toilet. This campsite has a lot to offer in views as it sits at the juncture of two canyons with the spires of Zeus and Moses framing the left of the camp. Good coffee, your favorite breakfast foods, and the campsite's view help make for a perfect morning moment.

Continuing on, the trail becomes a 4WD road. Travel on Taylor Canyon Road west for 5.2 miles passing humongous rocks the size of semi-trucks. At now 12 miles into the hike, you are at the Green River and Labyrinth Campground, a second choice for rolling the bag out for the night. Labyrinth does offer the lush, cooling Green River as a backdrop and is a great choice. Reservations are recommended if you plan to stay here and there is a fee of $30.

From the campground pick up White Rim Trail and continue for about a mile and then turn left at the junction into Upheaval Canyon. The trail now heads up a gorge of loose talus, making for a sluggish slow uphill stretch. Some navigation is needed as the trail gets a little hard to follow in some spots. Keep heading up, 1,300 feet in all until the rim is once more under your feet. Check out Upheaval Dome on your way out and back to where you started.

Mesa Arch at Sunrise

WHALE ROCK

Moderate – (1.0 mi / 1.6 km), round trip, allow 60 minutes, elev. Δ: 100 ft / 30 m, trailhead just before Upheaval Dome parking area

Whale Rock Trail gives an alternative view of Upheaval Dome. There is a short climb up a large rock that indeed does look like a whale. The trail ends with a nice "big picture" view of Upheaval Dome.

UPHEAVAL DOME

Easy – (2.0 mi / 3.2 km), round trip, allow 60 minutes, elev. Δ: 150 ft / 46 m, trailhead at Upheaval Dome parking area

Upheaval Dome as a geological feature is explained in some detail in the Canyonlands Geology section of this book. As a hike, it allows the visitor to get out and into the slick rock of the park without much fuss. It is only a mile (1.6 km) to the first overlook. It is well worth the extra effort to the second overlook, which will take you right to the dome's edge. Be sure to follow the cairns that have been laid out to mark the way, as in some portions the trail is simply walking on slick rock with the cairns as guides.

SYNCLINE LOOP

Strenuous – (8.3 mi / 13.4 km), round trip, allow 5 - 6 hours, elev. Δ: 1,300 ft / 396 m, trailhead at Upheaval Dome parking area

For a longer hike, take this loop that circles the entirety of Upheaval Dome. There is a spur trail that leads to the center of the crater as well. Allow another 3 miles (4.8 km) for the spur trail. Another spur trail along the loop (7 mi / 11.2 km) leads to the Green River. The elevation change is about 1,300 feet. Note that this is a very rugged and strenuous trail and includes a mixture of boulder fields, steep switchbacks and plenty of slickrock. This is a fine example of a challenging hike that puts you inside one of the more remote sections of Canyonlands.

Warning: nearly all rescues in Canyonlands NP come from this trail. Route finding can be very difficult and there are many false spur trails. Also, given the various ups and downs on this loop, the actual elevation change is closer to 2900 feet. This trail is for experienced hikers only.

LODGING AND DINING

Given that Canyonland's Island in the Sky District is close to Moab, most lodging, camping and dining for this section of the park are described in the Arches National Park chapter. Arches is closer to Moab by 25 miles, which may be the reason the food tastes better when coming from Canyonland's. That said, there is one campground within the Island in the Sky District and another very close by.

WILLOW FLATS CAMPGROUND

Twelve sites are available on a first come, first served basis. Each site contains a picnic table and fire grate. Vault toilets are provided but no water. The maximum length for an RV is 28 feet. Fee is $15 per night. Groups of up to 10 people and 2 vehicles are allowed. You can inquire at the entrance booth on availability; however, the most up-to-date information is at the visitor center. The campground is worth waking up early for as it is within walking distance to the Green River Overlook. Views here at sunset often dress the red rock canyon walls and mesa tops in a warm glow as the Green River snakes its way silently in the distance.

HORSETHIEF CAMPGROUND

Horsethief Campground is located 9.5 miles (15.3 km) from the Island in the Sky visitor center on Highway 313. There are 56 sites that typically never fill up completely, even during the peak seasons. There are many sites that accommodate large RVs. Campsites are offered on a first come, first served basis and have a picnic table and fire grate. Vault toilets are provided, but there is no running water. The campground has a few trails for hiking right outside its boundaries and provides incredible stargazing opportunities. There is a campground host; cost is $15 per night.

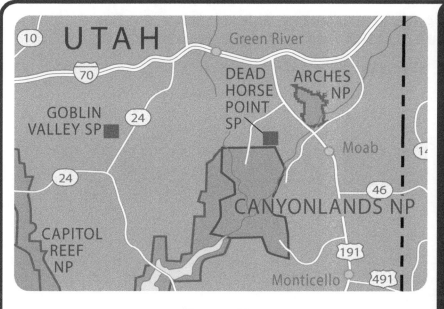

QUICK FACTS

Official Park Website: www.nps.gov/cany

Visitor Center:

- General Information: (435) 719-2313
- Backcountry Reservation Office: (435) 259-4351
- Needles Visitor Center: (435) 259-4711
- Hans Flat (Maze) Ranger Station: (435) 259-2652

Nearest Town with Amenities:

- Monticello, UT is 46 mi / 74 km from the Needles District
- Green River, UT is 82 mi / 132 km from Hans Flat (Maze) Ranger Station

Getting There:

- To Needles District: From Moab, UT: Take US-191 South and UT-211 West 30 mi / 48 km to right turn onto Lark Hart road and the park's entranceUT-313 West for 156 mi / 251 km to to park entrance
- To Maze District: From Moab, UT: Take US-191 South, I-70 West and UT-24 to Lower San Rafael Road to Hans Flat Road. Total distance to Hans Flat Ranger Station is 134 mi / 216 km.

Canyonlands National Park - Needles and Maze District

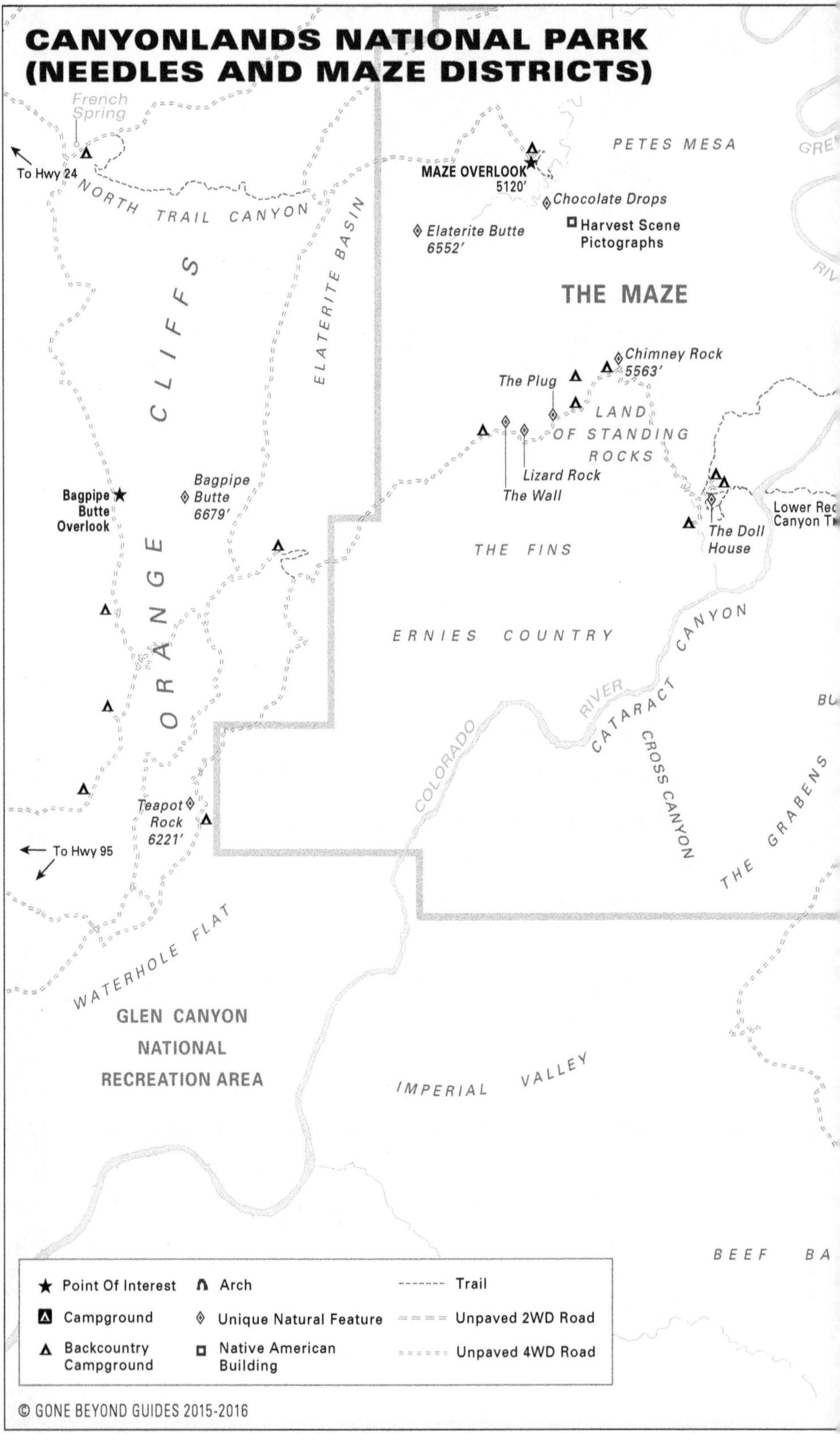

CANYONLANDS NATIONAL PARK
(NEEDLES AND MAZE DISTRICTS)

French Spring

To Hwy 24

NORTH TRAIL CANYON

PETES MESA

GRE

MAZE OVERLOOK
5120'

Chocolate Drops

Harvest Scene
Pictographs

Elaterite Butte
6552'

THE MAZE

ELATERITE BASIN

RIV

Chimney Rock
5563'

The Plug

LAND
OF STANDING
ROCKS

Lizard Rock

The Wall

Lower Red
Canyon T

Bagpipe ★
Butte
Overlook

Bagpipe
Butte
6679'

The Doll
House

THE FINS

ERNIES COUNTRY

ORANGE

CLIFFS

CANYON

CATARACT

CROSS CANYON

THE GRABENS

BU

Teapot
Rock
6221'

To Hwy 95

COLORADO

RIVER

WATERHOLE FLAT

GLEN CANYON
NATIONAL
RECREATION AREA

IMPERIAL VALLEY

BEEF BA

★ Point Of Interest	⋂ Arch	------- Trail
⚠ Campground	◈ Unique Natural Feature	= = = Unpaved 2WD Road
△ Backcountry Campground	▣ Native American Building	≡≡≡ Unpaved 4WD Road

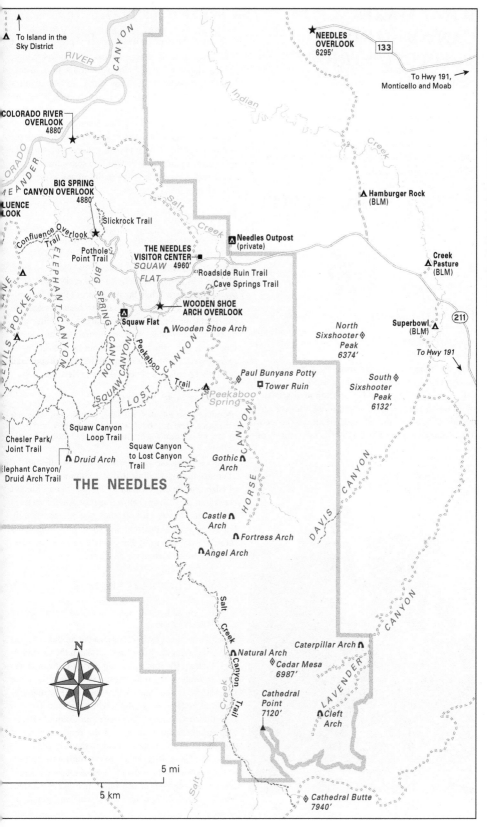

↑
To Island in the Sky District

RIVER CANYON

★ **NEEDLES OVERLOOK** 6295'

133

To Hwy 191, Monticello and Moab →

Indian

COLORADO RIVER OVERLOOK 4880'
★

MEANDER

BIG SPRING CANYON OVERLOOK 4880'

LUENCE LOOK

Confluence Overlook Trail

★ Slickrock Trail

Creek

△ **Hamburger Rock** (BLM)

Pothole Point Trail

A **Needles Outpost** (private)

■ **THE NEEDLES VISITOR CENTER**
SQUAW 4960'
FLAT

Roadside Ruin Trail

Cave Springs Trail

Creek △ **Pasture** (BLM)

△ Squaw Flat

★ **WOODEN SHOE ARCH OVERLOOK**

Superbowl △ (BLM)

211

∩ *Wooden Shoe Arch*

North Sixshooter ◇ Peak 6374'

Peekaboo

To Hwy 191 →

Trail

Paul Bunyans Potty

□ Tower Ruin

South Sixshooter ◇ Peak 6132'

∩ *Peekaboo Spring*

Chesler Park/ Joint Trail

Squaw Canyon Loop Trail

Squaw Canyon to Lost Canyon Trail

Gothic ∩ *Arch*

Elephant Canyon/ Druid Arch Trail

∩ *Druid Arch*

THE NEEDLES

Castle ∩ *Arch*

∩ *Fortress Arch*

∩ *Angel Arch*

Caterpillar Arch ∩

∩ *Natural Arch*

◇ *Cedar Mesa* 6987'

Cathedral Point 7120'

∩ *Cleft Arch*

N

5 mi

5 km

◇ *Cathedral Butte* 7940'

WHAT MAKES CANYONLANDS – NEEDLES DISTRICT SPECIAL

The Needles District is a hiker's paradise, with trails as numerous as they are varied in experience needed. Once in Needles, nearly all trailheads start from a paved road. Needles hiking is a mixture of fun and endurance, wonder and skill. It contains some of the best desert hiking in the Grand Circle.

HIKING IN THE NEEDLES DISTRICT

ROADSIDE RUIN

Easy – (0.3 mi / 0.5 km), round trip, allow 20 minutes, elev. Δ: negligible, trailhead is 0.4 mi from visitor center, left side of road

This quick loop starts right from the road and walks amongst desert brush and pinyon juniper within a wide valley, giving expansive views of sculptured sandstone off in the distance. The highlight of the trail is a small cylindrical granary tucked underneath a large alcove. The granary dates to 1270 to 1290 CE and is nicely preserved.

Along the way in Elephant Canyon

CAVE SPRINGS TRAIL

Easy – (0.6 mi / 1.0 km), round trip, allow 30 minutes, elev. Δ: 50 ft / 15 m, trailhead at Cave Spring trailhead

This tidy little loop leads to a series of small overhangs. Taking the loop counterclockwise leads to a historic and well-preserved cowboy camp complete with a corral, benches, and other items left behind. It is quite a refreshing look at a more recent chapter of history. There is a second overhang that contains a number of treasures, ranging from fern grottoes, small springs, and petroglyphs. The trail includes two ladders to help up some steep slick rock that leads to some drier alcoves as the trail winds back to the trailhead. All in all, a fun little hike.

POTHOLE POINT TRAIL

Easy – (0.6 mi / 1.0 km), round trip, allow 30 minutes, elev. Δ: negligible, trailhead is 6.2 mi from visitor center on Big Spring Canyon Overlook Scenic Drive

Another easy little hike with very little elevation gain. The trail is almost entirely on slickrock with cairns marking the way. While the namesake of the trail is important to note, the main reason to hike this one are the spectacular views. Along the way, look for little potholes that when filled with water, maintain an ecosystem for shrimp, who have figured out how to thrive out in the desert. At Pothole Point, there is a small spur trail south that heads to an overlook of the Needles.

SLICKROCK TRAIL

Moderate – (2.4 mi / 3.9 km), round trip, allow 90 minutes, elev. Δ: 150 ft / 46 m, trailhead is 6.2 mi from visitor center on Big Spring Canyon Overlook Scenic Drive

Slickrock has a bit of everything that Needles offers. There are four viewpoints that give commanding views of Island in the Sky District to the north and different views into the canyons below. The trail passes by a fragile arch and travels on both slickrock and actual trail. Each viewpoint is different and some offer long views into the canyons cut by the Colorado River. The Needles can also be seen in the distance.

CONFLUENCE OVERLOOK

Strenuous – (10.0 mi / 16.1 km), round trip, 5 - 6 hours, elev. Δ: 1,250 ft / 381 m, trailhead at Big Spring Canyon Overlook

This hike for the most part covers a fair amount of open country, leaving the hiker time to take in the surroundings. Pick up the trail at the Big Spring Canyon Overlook and follow the well-marked path along the same geologic faults that helped create the needle formations. The trail ends at an overlook where one can see and hear the confluence of the Green and Colorado rivers. Depending on the weather and the resulting color of the rivers, it is possible to see the relatively green waters of the Green River mix into the Navajo Red waters of the Colorado. The water's powerful journey is heard echoing throughout the canyon, sometimes as a distant rumble, occasionally louder as the wind changes directions.

Lower Red Lake Canyon

Strenuous – (18.8 mi / 30.3 km), round trip, long day hike or multiday backpacking trip, elev. Δ: 1,000 ft / 305 m, trailhead at Elephant Hill and Squaw Flat trailheads

This hike, which heads to the Colorado River, does have some underwhelming parts. It is quite long and while it does end up at the river, the banks are pretty heavily overgrown with tamarisks, leaving the hiker more with the thought, "Is this it?" then "We made it!!" This is primarily because the trail ends at a location along the river where it flattens out, referred to as Lower Red Lake, with a flat area on the other side called Spanish Bottom. This wetland area of the river allows for plant overgrowth and isn't the raging Colorado that most folks expect to see.

The unexpected first view of the Colorado aside, there are some great aspects to this hike. The biggest is being able to see the Grabens first hand. These long valley fingers that parallel the river are a true geologic oddity. There is (or I suppose was) a sedimentary layer formed 300 million years ago named appropriately, the Paradox Layer. This layer was composed primarily of salt, which up until 10 million years ago was compressed with such pressure from the rock layers above that the salt became more liquid than solid. When the Colorado River cut through the Paradox layer, it released the pressure and the salt moved like a slow moving paste into the river. With the salt layer gone, the upper layers collapsed into the void, forming long valleys. This makes the Lower Red Canyon Trail geologically fascinating.

The trail climbs over ridges and through grabens until the river is reached. Even if only one graben is traversed, it is worth taking the trail to see some of the unique geology that Needles has to offer.

By the way, if you do reach the river, it is possible to head to the confluence of the Green and Colorado Rivers, about 3.6 miles upstream. Along the way are picture perfect spots, devoid of the tamarisk. One can also walk downstream to check out Cataract Canyon, which holds some of the wildest rapids along the entire stretch of the Colorado.

Elephant Canyon / Druid Arch

Strenuous – (11.0 mi / 17.7 km), round trip, allow 5 - 6 hours, elev. Δ: 1,000 ft / 305 m, trailhead at Elephant Hill trailhead

This is arguably one of the best hikes in Needles, with incredible views along the entire trail ending at Druid Arch. A quick glance at a park map will show that there are many routes from which to choose. This description starts at the Chesler Park access trail and follows up Elephant Canyon.

The entire route is well marked and while the trail is long and it is not otherwise terribly strenuous except for the end. Once on the canyon floor you'll find it contains some sand and loose gravel, which makes hiking slower. This continues to the end of the canyon, where the last pitch is a steep climb of a quarter mile (0.4 km) involving a little scrambling up slick rock and even climbing a ladder.

Druid Arch itself is well worth the hike. The views along Elephant Canyon are spectacular and the arch is one of the more unique-looking arches, with much angularity and several keyhole windows within a fin-like blade of rock. The one thing any picture doesn't do is portray the enormity of the structure, which is humbling.

Joint Trail

Moderate – (11.0 mi / 17.7 km), round trip, allow 5 - 6 hours, elev. Δ: 560 ft / 171 m, trailhead at Elephant Hill trailhead

This wonderful trail holds views of red rock monoliths amongst grassland meadows. In these sections, the sky is wide and the land holds a peaceful warmth, with inviting grasses, folding into the banded colored rocks and typically deep blue skies. This area is known as Chesler Park, surrounded all around by the famous Needles spires.

Then there is the Joint Trail itself. The trail leads to a narrow slot canyon that contains a tunnel and deep narrow crevices that require some mild scrambling to travel through. Part of what makes Joint Trail special is in the way it was formed. Unlike the water carved slot canyons typical of most of the Grand Circle, this canyon is an actual fracture in the rock just wide enough to walk through. It is a very different type of canyon and when combined with Chesler Park, the Joint Trail is a contender for one of the best hikes in the Needles District.

Squaw Canyon Loop

Strenuous – (7.5 mi / 12.1 km), round trip, allow 4 hours at Squaw Flat trailhead, elev. Δ: 700 ft / 213 m, trailhead at Squaw Flat trailhead

There are some pretty steep patches and about 500 feet in elevation gain, but gives a really nice immersion into the Needles backcountry. The trail, as described here, starts in Squaw Canyon and travels to its head. From there, it's up and over into Big Spring Canyon for the return.

At the trailhead, walk within a large desert valley to a juncture. Staying left puts you into Squaw Canyon. The canyon itself starts out wide and inviting and then narrows. Stay on the trail to Squaw Canyon, avoiding the two junctures to the left to Lost Canyon. At a well-marked juncture, the trail goes up and over some slick rock, which may look challenging but is fairly easy to navigate when dry.

Take a moment at the ridge to enjoy the views and the canyon you just walked up and then come on down the other side into Big Spring Canyon. The trip down into the canyon has some steeper spots, but these are short. Note that while the slickrock offers firm holds when dry, it's a different story when wet or frozen, so use proper judgment here.

The trail ambles through Big Spring Canyon before climbing out and following closer to the Squaw Canyon side of the ridge back over and down again to the trailhead. Big Spring Canyon offers nice vegetation and great views of the Needles as you make the return.

Squaw Canyon to Lost Canyon

Strenuous – (8.7 mi / 14.0 km), round trip, allow 5 -6 hours, elev. Δ: 380 ft / 116 m, trailhead at Squaw Flat trailhead

This trail is similar to the one described above for Squaw Canyon. The hike heads up Squaw Canyon and then diverts left to Lost Canyon, traveling up that canyon and then crossing over again up and back over into Squaw. So, Squaw Canyon up, ridge climb over, Long Canyon up (if doing the canyon clockwise), ridge climb over, Squaw Canyon down and out.

There are some notable differences. This trail is a bit longer and there is reliable water to be found. The trail is marked with cairns but can be hard to follow at times, requiring a sharp eye. This hike offers a bit more challenge and skill, different views and a great hike all in all.

Peekaboo Trail

Strenuous – (10.0 mi / 16.1 km), round trip, allow 5 - 6 hours, elev. Δ: 550 ft / 112 m, trailhead at Squaw Flat trailhead

Peekaboo is an extension from Lost Canyon Trail. From the Squaw Canyon Trailhead, head up and take the first junction left towards Lost Canyon. Look for the junction again left through open country to Peekaboo Spring. The spring is situated near Salt Creek. Look for granaries hidden away in alcoves as well as some interesting pictographs and hand symbol petroglyphs.

Newspaper Rock

Some scrambling is required and there are two ladders that must be climbed to complete the journey. This is a great hike for the skilled desert hiker, offering a bit of challenge in navigation with amble rewarding views, hoodoos, large meadows, and blue sky touching red rock.

SALT CREEK CANYON

Strenuous – (22.5 mi / 36.2 km), round trip, long day hike or multiday backpacking trip, elev. Δ: 1,650 ft / 503 m, trailhead at end of 4WD road up Salt Creek or from Peekaboo Trail

This trail expands on the Peekaboo Trail listed above and continues along Salt Creek. As the creek holds water generally year long, this line of life holds plenty of archaeological sites, pictographs, petroglyphs, farming areas and numerous granaries. There is also an old log cabin built in the 1890's by a rancher named Rensselaer Lee Kirk showing some of the more recent history in Salt Creek Canyon.

OTHER THINGS TO

NEWSPAPER ROCK STATE HISTORIC MONUMENT

While not actually part of Canyonlands NP, it is right off the road en route to the Needles District. It is not only one of the most easily accessed petroglyph sites, it is one of the largest collections of rock art in North America and one of the best preserved. There are more than 650 petroglyph representations of humans, animals, abstract forms and other symbols. Some of the petroglyphs tell stories while others are seemingly random. The petroglyph panel is over 200 square feet in area and dates back some 1500 years ago to as recent as this century. Take Highway 211 toward the Needles District for 13 miles (21 km). The day use area has good parking and pit toilets.

DRIVING AROUND

WOODEN SHOE OVERLOOK

Stay to the right just after passing the visitor center to catch this first of two formal overlooks in the Needles District. There isn't much pull-through parking for this area, which can make parking an RV a bit tricky on crowded days. The pullout gives a distant view of an arch formation that looks unmistakably like a wooden shoe. While the views themselves are certainly worth a stop, the shoe is fairly well out there. If you are going for a shot of the Wooden Shoe, bring your telephoto lens.

BIG SPRING CANYON OVERLOOK

Once in Needles, follow the signs north to the end of the road at Big Spring Canyon Overlook. Easy parking for RVs. This is a great place to get out and take in the very different views compared to Island in the Sky. There are several tabletop pinnacles, which resemble tables of rock perched on a slimmer stand of rock.

LODGING IN THE NEEDLES DISTRICT OF CANYONLANDS

STAYING IN THE NEEDLES DISTRICT

SQUAW FLAT CAMPGROUND
There are 26 sites available accommodating RV lengths up to 28 feet. These sites have water, vault toilets, fire grates, picnic tables and tent pads. Cost is $20 per night and is available on a first come, first served basis.

NEEDLES OUTPOST
Needles Outpost has six campsites for $21. The sites are pretty basic, but the campground is just outside of the NP. There is a store and gas station supplying basic camping and food supplies. The prices are representative of a place literally in the middle of nowhere.

The management is brimming with character, especially one woman who gets mentioned a lot in online reviews as being rude. If you think about it, there are really only two ways to play being out in the desert and running a store, gas station, café and campground all by yourself. You are either the most radiantly enlightened person in the world or the most cantankerous. Looks like she is the latter.

During my visits, I've never met this infamous woman and have had good service. They even offered to take me around Canyonlands by plane for only the price of the gas (that was years ago; the airport has since closed). If you do meet the cantankerous woman, I highly recommend opening with either a lot of patience or the stupidest question you can possibly think of and see how things go from there.

HAMBURGER ROCK CAMPGROUND
Hamburger Rock Campground is certainly off the beaten track, but as there are few options in the Needles District, it is worth pointing out. There are some caveats to this campground. There are tent campsites total, and they are officially designed for tent camping. It is possible to drive a smaller RV into many of the sites, but you will need to navigate a 2-wheel drive unpaved road for 2.2 miles (3.5 km). The sites have fire grates, picnic tables and pit toilets, but no water. Fee is $15 per night. The adventure of taking your RV on a dirt road for a chance of finding a site large enough to park it aside, Hamburger Rock campground is one of the most enjoyable in the area. It has great views, it's quiet, it's close to Canyonlands, and it has a minor twist of adventure thrown in to keep the trip interesting.

Lodging Near Needles District

Rodeway Inn & Suites

649 North Main Street, Monticello, UT 84535, (435) 587-2489, www.choicehotels.com

While Rodeway Inn is officially in the same bucket as the other budget motels in the area, the hotel is a notch above some of the older peer offerings. The rooms have updated furnishings and overall is more refreshed. They offer an indoor pool, free breakfast, and free Wi-Fi.

Inn at the Canyons

533 North Main Street, Monticello, UT 84535, (435) 201-8648, www.monticellocanyonsinn.com

If you are looking for a little nicer place to stay in Monticello, try the Inn at the Canyons. This 3 star hotel has comfy beds and rooms that are a notch above the budget hotels in the area. Their biggest plus is the large heated indoor pool and hot tub complex, with warm wood beams and huge house plants. Free Wi-Fi, large lobby area, discounts on restaurant dining with room key, and free breakfast round out the amenities.

Blue Mountain Horsehead Inn

232 North Main Street, Monticello, UT 84535, (435) 587-2251, bluemountainhorseheadinn.com

Another in the list of budget motel offerings in Monticello. This one offers consistently good value to guests, with basic but clean rooms. Some of the rooms are quite close to the road so be sure to ask for one of the back rooms, which are quieter.

Canyonlands Motor Inn

197 N Main St, Monticello, UT 84535-8001, (435) 587-2266, magnusonhotels.com

A clean 2 star hotel offering an overall good value for folks looking to visit the Needles District of Canyonlands National Park.

The Monticello Inn

164 E Central, Monticello, UT 84535, (435) 587-2274, www.themonticelloinn.com

Newly remodeled and run with great pride, the Monticello Inn is a good value. No free breakfast here, but PJ's Restaurant is just up the street. They do offer free Wi-Fi and a small fridge. Overall, this is typically a peaceful and quiet property.

DINING NEAR THE NEEDLES DISTRICT OF CANYONLANDS

The Peace Tree Juice Cafe

AMERICAN, meals for under $20, 516 N Main, Monticello, UT 84535, (435) 587-5063, peacetreecafe.com, open daily, 7am - 10pm

Great little café, offering a robust menu of items, including a huge smoothie selection. The Peace Tree offers comfort food that leans closer to the healthier and fresher side. A great meal here.

Wagon Wheel Pizza

PIZZA, meals for under $20, 164 S Main, Monticello, UT 84535, (435) 587-2766, open daily, 11am - 9pm, closed Sundays

Typical local small town pizza joint. Wagon Wheel will satisfy the cravings in the belly.

PJ's Of Monticello

AMERICAN, meals for under $10, 216 E Center St, Monticello, UT 84535, (435) 587-2335, open daily, 8am - 9pm

PJ's offers hearty breakfasts and the standard assortment of grilled and fried sandwiches for lunch. The staff is friendly and the prices are reasonable.

Doug's Steak and BBQ

BBQ, meals for under $20, 496 N. Main street, Monticello, UT 84535, (435) 587-2255, open daily, 5pm - 10pm, closed Tuesday and Wednesday

Smoked, tender, savory, delicious BBQ and ribs. Best place for filling up after a long hike. They have a selection of beers to wash it all down with too!

The Maze District

R & F Restaurant

AMERICAN, meals for under $10, 149 East Center Street, Monticello, UT 84535, (435) 587-2440, open daily, 8am - 2pm and 5pm - 9pm

Admittedly, there is a soft spot for the small town restaurant that offers up typical home cooking. It's never fancy, often on the greasy side and always more hearty and humble than refined, but these are dying establishments and have a soul. R&F serves hot meals, served by nice people, with little fanfare, at a decent price. If turkey and mashed potatoes or burger and fries are what you are in the mood for, this is your place.

☕ Coffee and Sweets! ☕

Higher Grounds Coffee & Flash Floods Muddy Sodas

COFFEE & BAKERY, 87 S Main St. Blanding, UT 84511, (435) 678-3108, sharirene.com, open daily, 6:30am - 7pm

This is a cute non-descript place in the sleepy little town of Blanding, Utah. Blanding is on the southern end of Needles district and is likely a place you might breeze past on your way to Mesa Verde National Park. If you see signs for Hole-in-the-Rock historical site, you are close. Higher Grounds is on Main Street but isn't well marked, so use your smartphone map to pinpoint the location. Coffee? Yes. Incredible baked goods? Triple Yes! The bakery items make this a great snack stop and a welcome find in the Southwest desert.

WHAT MAKES CANYONLANDS – MAZE DISTRICT SPECIAL

The Maze District of Canyonlands is one of the most remote places in the Grand Circle. There is no food, water, gas, lodging, or other amenities other than the Hans Flat Ranger Station, which sells maps and books. To give a hint at how remote the Maze District is, getting to Hans Flat Ranger Station itself is a 2.5-hour (46 mile / 74 km) drive on a 2-wheel drive dirt road from Green River, Utah. From here, it's about 5-6 hours of driving in a high clearance 4-wheel drive vehicle just to get to the outer Maze District boundary from the ranger station. In other words, it takes a good portion of a full day just to get to the Maze from the nearest town. That's one remote national park!

This remoteness is then what really makes this area special. It is protected both by being part of a national park and also by remaining wilderness. Beyond a trek to Horseshoe Canyon, which is more accessible, a journey into the Maze takes much effort and planning, but the rewards are in equal measure. With only 3% of the Canyonland visitors heading out this way, you would be one of the lucky few.

THINGS TO DO IN THE MAZE DISTRICT

This travel guide is light on multi-day backpacking trips and since the Maze District is nothing but such trips, we will focus on the one, very amazing hike that is approachable within this otherwise remote area of Canyonlands.

Hiking in the Maze District of Canyonlands

The Maze is true desert wilderness and the trails are for the most part, more routes than actual trails. The area is remote and folks that had out this way usually plan on taking a minimum 4-5-day backpacking trip. Part of the reason is it takes nearly a full day just to get to the access points.

There is one developed trail in the Maze District and a very special one at that, Horseshoe Canyon. It is not inside the main section of the district and is an easier trip, relatively speaking. Horseshoe Canyon is definitely one of the pinnacle trails in all of the Grand Circle. To learn why, read the description below.

Horseshoe Canyon

Strenuous – (7.0 mi / 11.3 km), round trip, allow 4 -5 hours, elev. Δ: 800 ft / 244 m, trailhead described below

Horseshoe Canyon is a protected island of land separate from the main park that was added in 1971 to protect one of the most significant examples of rock art in North America. It is arguably the best example of Barrier Canyon Style rock art. It is also one of the most recognizable. The life sized anthropomorphic figures with their unique trapezoidal shapes sit as reproductions in both the Denver Natural History Museum and the Museum of Modern Art in New York.

The centerpiece of Horseshoe Canyon is the Great Gallery. Within it is a panel of rock measuring 200 feet long (61m) and 15 feet (4.6m) high. The panel contains 20 elongated floating limbless humanoid figures, all life-sized, with one measuring over seven feet (2.1m) tall. The figures seem to float as ghosts on the rock, having no feet and distinctive trapezoidal shoulders. A visit to the Great Gallery is certainly a high-water mark for any trip.

Horseshoe Canyon is a separate unit from the main section of Canyonlands NP. It is best accessed from the west near Goblin Valley State Park at Highway 24. This road is often accessible for two-wheel drive vehicles and is okay for smaller RVs.

It is graded along the 30 miles (48 km). You can also take a 47-mile (75 km) dirt road from Green River, but it has similar caveats and is longer.

Once out to the Horseshoe Canyon unit, it is an additional 7-mile (11 km) round trip hike to the Great Gallery. Allow about four hours for the hike, leaving plenty of time, water and food for the strenuous climb back out of the canyon. During the spring and fall, guided walks are held by the park's rangers. Aligning with these guided tours is an excellent way to see the petroglyphs and pictographs. The rangers do an amazing job of tying in the interesting details of what you are seeing and bringing historical context to your trip.

Go to www.discovermoab.com for a complete list of guided tours to Horseshoe Canyon and for rafting, jeep, and horseback riding tours.

Note that the roads may be closed seasonally during monsoon season. Check with the ranger station before heading out.

CANYONLANDS HISTORY

ANCESTRAL PEOPLE

Evidence indicates that the Paleo-Indians hunted in Canyonlands as far back as 10,000 years ago. They hunted large game such as the mammoth and mastodon. From 8000 BCE to 250 BCE, the lifeway of these people developed as they became more accustomed to the land. Now living in the area, they utilized stone tools and the atlatl. This period, known as the Desert Archaic Period, is represented well in art pictographs and petroglyphs. Some of the best examples of these can be found in Horseshoe Canyon, which contains twenty life-size anthropomorphic images, some seven feet tall.

The Ancestral Puebloans and the Fremont cultures inhabited the area next starting in CE 250. They are distinguished by the introduction of farming techniques. Distributions of this lifeway were centered on the few areas that had water and a proper area for farming. Salt Creek Canyon in the Needles District had a large group of ancestral Puebloans, as evidenced by storage structures and granaries. This area was believed to have been populated around CE 1200. Within a hundred years, the group abandoned this lifeway and moved south to Arizona and New Mexico for reasons that are not entirely known.

EXPLORERS AND RIVER MAPPERS

During the 1770s, the Spanish were interested in finding a route from Santa Fe, New Mexico, to their newly created missions in Monterey, California. The Spanish parties led by Escalante and Dominguez went around the difficult terrain rather than try to find a way through Canyonlands. French and American trappers looking for otter pelts did enter Canyonlands and are considered the first Europeans to have gone through the region. In 1838, a trapper named Denis Julien carved himself into history by etching his name throughout Canyonlands, along the banks of the Colorado River and even in Arches NP.

By 1859, southeast Utah was finally mapped accurately through an expedition led by Captain John N. Macomb. Macomb was sent by the U.S. Army to explore and map the Colorado Plateau with the goal of finding a wagon route from New Mexico to Utah.

In 1869, John Wesley Powell took on a bold expedition to map the Colorado River, Green River and its tributaries. Powell was a former Army major in the Civil War and had fought in the Battle of Shiloh, where he lost most of his right arm. After the Army, he became a professor of geology at Illinois Wesleyan University as well as curator of collections at the Museum of the Illinois State Natural History Society. He left a permanent position at the museum for the adventures of exploring the American West.

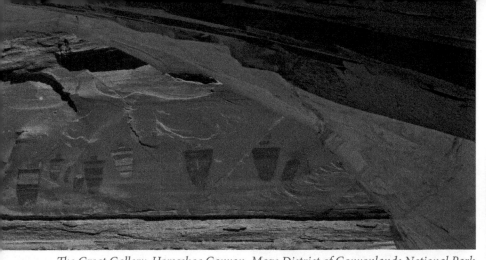

The Great Gallery, Horseshoe Canyon, Maze District of Canyonlands National Park

Powell set out with nine men, four boats and enough food for ten months. They started from the Green River in Wyoming on May 24, 1869 and finished on August 30, nearly three months later. His journey took him to the confluence of the Green and Colorado Rivers and on into the Grand Canyon and beyond to the mouth of the Virgin River.

Before his expedition, very little was known of the rivers in this area. His journey was groundbreaking on a number of accounts. He became the first European to navigate the Colorado through the Grand Canyon and was the first to give thorough accounts of the Green and Colorado rivers.

For nineteenth century America, Powell's descriptions of navigating hair-raising rapids, native encounters and dangers became instant legend. Of the ten men who started the journey, only six finished the 930-mile (1500 km) journey. Many of the features of the Colorado River, including Glen Canyon, were named by Powell and his men. Powell repeated the trip in 1871.

First Settlements and Ranching

By 1883, Mormon settlements formed near Canyonlands, including the town of Moab. The first pleasure run through Cataract Canyon wasn't done until 1907, nearly forty years after Powell's first expedition. In 1911, the first motion pictures of the canyons were filmed by Emery and Ellsworth Kolb.

The Mormon settlements took up cattle ranching primarily, and through 1975 much of Canyonlands was used for ranching. All three districts had areas that were decent for both cattle and sheep grazing. Many of the early ranchers named many of the park's features. On a mesa west of the Maze there lies a refuge called Robbers Roost, which was a hideout for cattle rustlers and outlaws, including Robert Leroy Parker, aka Butch Cassidy.

Mining Paves the Way

Up until the 1950s, Canyonlands was widely inaccessible. There were few roads, and most exploration of the area was done either on foot or by horseback. Then came the Cold War between Russia and the United States, two superpowers with drastically different opinions regarding economy and politics. The Atomic Energy Commission (AEC) was created in 1946 with a primary goal of stockpiling nuclear weapons for national defense and, ironically, to promote world peace. The AEC offered monetary incentives to anyone who had an interest in discovering and delivering uranium ore. They gave out instruction brochures explaining everything from how to prospect for uranium to how to use a Geiger counter.

The United States urgently needed uranium for national interests and put out an entire marketing campaign, including bonuses along with inflated prices, for ore. Prospectors headed into Canyonlands feeling they could earn good money mining "radioactive gold" while fulfilling a duty to their country in the interests of national security.

During this period nearly 1000 miles (1600 km) of road were built through the efforts of the AEC. Many were built through the hard hand labor of the prospectors themselves. In the end, the promise of plentiful supplies of uranium in Canyonlands didn't pan out. The prospectors left, but the roads, including White Rim Road, remained. As quickly as the miners left, casual travelers began to use these same roads to explore Canyonlands. The roads had opened up the area to the industry of tourism.

Even before the uranium mining craze, Bates Wilson had an eye on Canyonlands as a National Park. Wilson was the superintendent of the then-Arches National Monument and had tried unsuccessfully at getting Congressional attention for Canyonlands. He paused during the mining phase and fully expected it would be the end of this amazing area. With a sigh of relief that

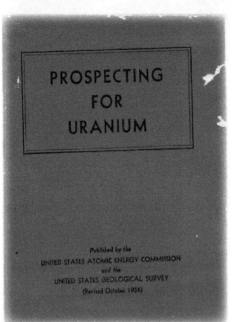

PROSPECTING
FOR
URANIUM

Published by the
UNITED STATES ATOMIC ENERGY COMMISSION
and the
UNITED STATES GEOLOGICAL SURVEY
(Revised October 1951)

What could possibly go wrong?

uranium was not all that plentiful, he was ready to take up the cause again. His early jeep tours with government officials would not be entirely in vain. They drew some early attention and awareness to the area.

In 1961, Secretary of the Interior Stewart Udall traveled by plane to the Grand Canyon. On the way, he requested the plane fly over Canyonlands and ended up circling the confluence of the Green and Colorado Rivers several times. Udall contacted Bates Wilson, and in July 1961, the two went on a much-publicized trip around the area. Wilson was keen on creating a park within the Needles District. Secretary Udall thought on more grand terms and suggested an area of one million acres. By 1962, the Canyonlands park bill was introduced, though it was trimmed back to a quarter of the initial one-million-acre plan of Udall. After some debate and posturing by locals who had pre-existing claims on the land, President Lyndon B. Johnson signed Canyonlands National Park into existence on September 12, 1964. The park was expanded on November 12, 1971, to 337,598 acres, adding the Maze and Horseshoe Canyon to the park's boundaries.

CANYONLANDS GEOLOGY

Describing the geology of a place as big as Canyonlands can be a daunting task. There is no place quite like it anywhere in the world. Describing the geologic rationale behind all those canyons, fins, grabens, pinnacles, monoliths, goblins, arches, upheaval domes, needles and horsts is a book in itself if you want to satisfy a geologist.

Fortunately, this book is for the average traveler and there is a much simpler big picture explanation, one that sums up Canyonlands geology nicely and leaves plenty of time to take in the view, which, let's face it, is the reason you came. This section will try to summarize the 10,000-foot view of the geological story behind Canyonlands NP and then highlight some of the most unique geological artifacts that are worth pointing out.

THE BIG PICTURE

If you have been reading the geology of each section in this guide, you have by now noticed a theme. All of these parks sit on the Colorado Plateau. This plateau comprises some two dozen layers of rock strata that were deposited beginning some 300 million years ago. Canyonlands itself displays eleven dominant layers (Paradox through Navajo Sandstone). On top of these eleven are another twelve that were more recently deposited.

Then, all these layers were lifted upward slowly enough to allow the rivers, winds, ices and general erosion to cut into them. Here's the magical part, which is true in general for the Colorado Plateau but especially true for Canyonlands NP: These enormous masses of rock, all eleven thick layers of strata, were lifted straight up for the most part. There is a slight tilt to the strata here and there, but nothing compared to the twisted chaos of what happened to the rock layers of, say, Death Valley National Park.

This is huge geologically. Events this perfect don't typically happen, especially given the time involved. All of these layers of rock strata were allowed to deposit slowly over hundreds of millions of years, one on top of another, like a cake. Then, as these massive layers were lifted up from underneath, they were done so without upsetting these cake layers. They all remained flat, level and essentially perfect. They became a canvas for the patient artists of nature to carve them into the majestic yet impossibly delicate towers and rock faces you see today.

Given this perspective, geologically speaking Canyonlands NP is a work of art. There are no volcanic mountains born out of an immense chaos of fire, no earthquakes to topple the sculptures you see before you, no lava to bury them, no immense pressures to pit one rock stratum against another. What you see is the gentle patience of water, the etchings of wind, and the chisels of ice, combined with, by our standards, an unimaginable amount of time on layers of rock that have stood in place for millions of years.

And what water there was and still is. Today there are two major rivers that flow through Canyonlands NP, and it is in large part their handiwork that shaped much of what you gaze out upon. Flash floods today can completely wipe a landscape clean. They can move boulders the size of VW Bugs and transport tons of sediment from upstream to down. Back during the Pleistocene Era, the effect of water was magnified.

There were several ice ages during this time and as the earth warmed and glaciers melted, water was a tremendous force, keeping up very well with the continual uplift from underneath. During the Pleistocene Era, water roughed out what you see. Then, as the climate changed, lesser amounts of water put their final touches on the land, creating chimneys, fins, and arches that defy belief. Look out before you. Canyonlands is stunning, a truly extraordinary place.

UNIQUE GEOLOGICAL NOTABLES

GRABENS

Grabens are a very cool feature that are not unique to Canyonlands NP but are certainly plentiful in the Needles District and deserve mention mainly for the magic act of how they are formed. Rock layers actually disappeared!

First off, what is a graben? The word graben is German for ditch or trench. Geologically, it's used to explain any linear down thrust in rock strata. Imagine a layer of rock where a section has been removed underneath it, leaving a valley.

Aerial View of Grabens in Needles District

Grabens in Canyonlands are extensive on the east side of Colorado River's Cataract Canyon running for about 15.5 miles (25 km). There are literally row after row of collapsed valleys that run roughly parallel to the Cataract Canyon of the Colorado River.

While grabens can be formed by faulting, the grabens of the Needles District did not experience any faulting because—as you now know—this is stable land. How these grabens formed is a puzzler. We start with knowing that a large portion of one of the rock layers disappeared in certain sections and the rock layers on top simply sank down through the mighty force of gravity.

So how does a large sedimentary layer underneath a bunch of other rock layers simply disappear? And why did all of these disappearing rock layers vanish in parallel lines to the Colorado River itself? The hint is the river itself along with a very interesting 300-million-year-old layer called the Paradox Formation.

Here's the secret of the Paradox Formation. It is the result of a shallow sea that deposited a large amount of salt along with other sediments. This layer was then buried by millions of years of sediment, which became rock layers themselves. The salts lay trapped until about 10 million years ago when the Colorado Plateau rose up and the Colorado River was allowed to cut all the way back down and into the Paradox Formation.

Another subtle but huge factor at play in the grabens of the Needles District is the Rocky Mountains, which tilted the Needles District slightly westward. This tilt allowed for gravity to act as a component in the grabens' formation.

We now have all the puzzle pieces to figure out how a rock layer can just disappear. We have the Paradox Formation that was primarily a large salt deposit. We know that lots of pressure was then applied to this layer, which in turn was cut into by the Colorado River, creating less pressure on the Paradox formation in that section. Also throw in that slight tilt of the Paradox Formation by the uplift of the Rocky Mountains 350 miles (563 km) away. Finally, let's add the final piece of the graben puzzle. Under immense pressure, salt flows plastically, like a slow-moving liquid.

Now we can piece together why grabens are formed near the Colorado River. The salt was under this enormous pressure from the layers above and for years it couldn't go anywhere. It was under so much pressure it started acting like a very thick liquid. Then the Colorado River cut into the layer and the salt was allowed to escape at a glacial pace into the Colorado River, being pushed by gravity and the pressure of all that rock above it. As the salt left, a void was created and the ground above then sunk down into this trench-like void, creating grabens.

The grabens of the Needles District are young geologically, beginning about 55,000 years ago and continuing today. They are thought to move very slowly, dropping nearly undetectably toward the Colorado River, about an inch per year.

UPHEAVAL DOME

While grabens are a complex but solvable puzzle, Upheaval Dome is an enigma that has yet to be solved. Located in the Island in the Sky District, Upheaval Dome looks like a 3-mile (5 km) circular meteor crater. The rock layers are completely deformed, which is a big contrast to the layers outside the dome, which are characteristically stable. The center of the structure contains rock layers that have been pushed up into a true dome. Some of the layers are pushed up such that they are nearly vertical and they are pushed up on all sides, forming a circle. The area surrounding the dome has been pushed downwards, again in a complete, very large and very natural circle.

Upheaval Dome

Upheaval Dome is estimated to be 60–170 million years old. It's easy to look at the dome and imagine a massive meteor blow to the rock strata, which caused the rocks to rebounded back up under the intense heat and pressure to form this true geologic dome. No one has found any pieces of a meteorite, however, so the thought is that it has long since eroded away, leaving only its impact.

While this is the obvious theory, it isn't the only one, leaving Upheaval Dome as one of the more hotly debated topics among geologists. The other prevailing theory is that of a salt dome. Again, we need to bring in the Paradox Formation, the 300-million-year-old rock layer that is mainly comprised of salt. Remember

it was then buried by the sediment above it and, under the immense pressure, the salts began to liquefy. The theory is that since the salt is less dense than the rock layers above it, it started to flow plastically upward as a big salt bubble. This bubble rose through weaker layers until it heaved the overlying strata, creating a dome. The sandstone continued to erode, the salt dissolved and there you have it, the resulting Upheaval Dome before you. This is called the Salt Dome Theory. There are smaller confirmed salt domes in in the world, but not within the Paradox Formation. If this theory is correct, the Upheaval Dome would be the most deeply eroded salt structure on the planet.

NEEDLES

The needles in the Needles District are, in themselves, interesting from a geologic standpoint. The Needles are comprised of a layer of rock called Cedar Mesa Sandstone. This sandstone layer is cut like a checkerboard, with parallel lines running from both north to south and another set of lines running from east to west. From the air, the sandstone truly looks like a checkerboard of red rock.

The two sets of parallel lines are created from very different geological functions. The east to west fractures are caused by the uplift of the rock strata itself. The north to south fractures are caused once again by the Paradox Formation, which runs thousands of feet underneath the Cedar Mesa Sandstone. The Paradox Formation, which has a large amount of salt in it, is slowly flowing toward the Colorado River, taking the surface layers with it. These north south formations are similar to the graben but on much smaller scale.

This criss-cross pattern is then slowly eroded at the rock joints by water and ice erosion, creating the beautiful spires that make up the Needles District. If you are able to hike among the Needles, think about how the land must have looked as a vast stretch of sand dunes 200 million years ago, how these dunes hardened into sandstone and have been slowly eroding, resulting in what you see before you. This view is but a snapshot in time. The Needles, like everything, are in constant flux.

Needles District

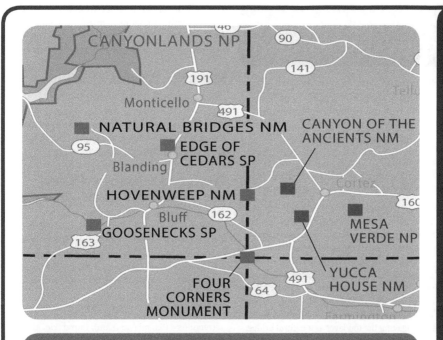

As above, so below. The Owachomo Bridge

Parks Near Canyonlands - Needles District

NATURAL BRIDGES NATIONAL MONUMENT

Camping in Park:

- Natural Bridges Campground: 13 T/RV, no water, vault restrooms, no dump station, no hookups, first come-first served
- Several backcountry campgrounds

Getting There:

- From Blanding, UT: Take UT-95 North to UT-275 North 44 mi / 71 km to park entrance

Natural Bridges National Monument is a unique place in that there are a total of three natural bridges here. From above, the overlooks peer down to the canyon below, which seems to be a confusing maze of twists and turns with huge spans of rock arching across streambeds of pale white sandstone. In reality, the area has had a number of gooseneck meanders, where the stream has created a U-shaped canyon into the strata. At three places, the water eroded through the bottom layer of the meander, leaving the top layer as a natural bridge.

Most folks take the short trips to the various overlooks and peer down to the bridges below. The scenic drive takes about an hour to see all three, not including the trip to the visitor center to get all the necessary brochures. Hiking down below is more immersive and more strenuous, as the canyon floor is about 500 feet below. All of the trails as well as the bridges themselves have awesome mythological names from the Hopi tradition, which adds to the overall ambiance of this park.

HIKING NATURAL BRIDGES NATIONAL MONUMENT

HORSECOLLAR RUIN OVERLOOK TRAIL

Easy – (0.6 mi / 1.0 m), round trip, allow 30 minutes

A fairly level trail leading to the edge of White Canyon where an Ancestral Puebloan cliff dwelling can be seen in a large alcove. This ruin is best known for its two granaries, which look like large circular barrels with doorways that look like horse collars (hence the name).

SIPAPU BRIDGE TRAIL

Easy – (1.2 mi / 1.9 km), round trip, allow 1 hour

Sipapu Bridge is the second largest natural bridge in the world, second only to Rainbow Bridge at Rainbow Bridge NM. The name Sipapu is a Hopi term for the gateway of souls into the spirit world. The trip down is steep but once on the canyon floor, the going is easier, though a bit uneven. The elevation gain/loss here is 500 feet and there is a staircase and three wooden ladders to help hikers get down safely. At the top of the stairway,

look for a set of logs reaching from the cliff wall to a large fir. Early visitors used this fir, climbing up and down it to get to the canyon floor. At the base of the tree, you can still see remnants of the earlier staircase.

KACHINA BRIDGE TRAIL

Easy – (1.4 mi / 2.3 km), round trip, allow 1 hour

Kachina Bridge is considered the youngest formed of the three bridges and is also the least dramatic from the overlook above due to the angle. Take switchbacks down 400 feet to the bridge.

OWACHOMO BRIDGE TRAIL

Easy – (0.4 mi / 0.6 km), round trip, allow 30 minutes

The easiest of the bridges to get to, Owachomo, meaning "rock mound" in the Hopi language is also the most delicate of the three bridge formation. The bridge's form suggests that it is eroding more quickly than the others. It is also considered the most pleasing to the eye, due to its thin span of rock that stretches across the sky.

LOOP TRAIL

Strenuous – (8.6 mi / 13.8 km), round trip, allow 4 -5 hours

The Loop Trail gives the complete package of all three bridges with return options along the mesa top. At the mesa, the loop has a juncture that allows for a shorter hike. Start the hike at any of the parking areas. Starting at Sipapu gives the most flexibility if you need to return early as you pass by Sipapu and Kachina before climbing back out. If you do continue to Owachomo Bridge, follow the trail up the left side of the canyon after Kachina Bridge in order to more easily navigate past the Knickpoint pour-off, a dry fall that pours water runoff into a pool below when it rains.

Sipapu Bridge

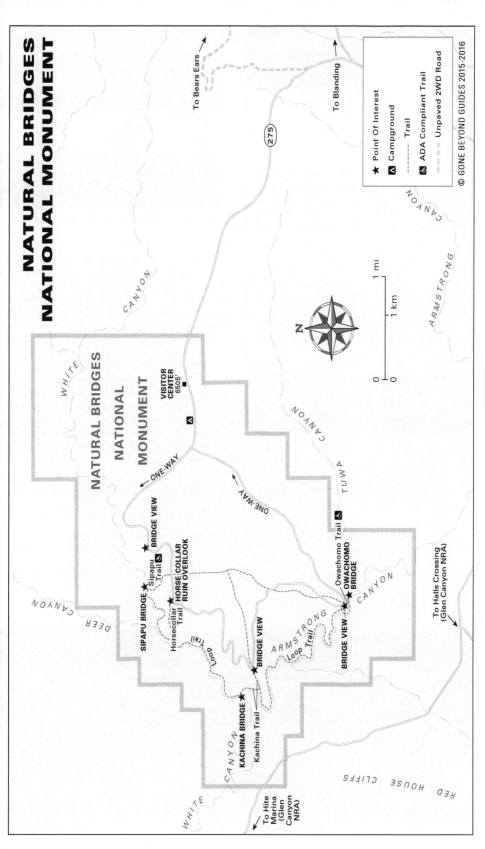

EDGE OF THE CEDARS STATE PARK

Getting There:

- From Page, AZ: Take AZ-98 East to US-160 East to US-163 North to UT-261 North to UT-316 West. Total distance is 151 mi / 243 km to park

Edge of the Cedars sits within the town of Blanding, Utah, lying south of Moab and Monticello, UT and north of the Four Corners and Mesa Verde NP. While the Ancestral Pueblo ruins are worth exploring, the highlight here is the museum, which holds a diverse selection of pottery and other artifacts. This is a great place to see the actual tools of these people and is worth seeing.

Blanding, UT is a solid little small town of about 3,500 residents. Besides being a gateway town, serving tourists on their way to the next natural park, it has economic ties within the mineral processing and agriculture industries. This is a good place to stock up on goods and grab a bite to eat.

HOVENWEEP STATE PARK

Camping in Park:

- Hovenweep Campground: 31T sites, some sites will accommodate RV's, drinking water, flush toilets, no hookups, one ADA compliant site, first come-first served

Getting There:

- From Cortez, CO: Take US-491 N/N Broadway and turn left onto Road Bb, which becomes County Road 10 in Utah. Total distance is 45 mi / 72 km to park entrance

The round ruins of Hovenweep

Hovenweep National Monument is a small park protecting several small villages of the Ancestral Puebloans on the borders of Utah and Colorado. What is unique here is the setting. Unlike the deep alcoves of Mesa Verde or the immensity of Chaco, Hovenweep was built in an arid flatland that at first glance would appear to have no surprises. Upon arrival however, it feels as if the visitor has stumbled upon something, the ruins feel unexpected and special. There is a sentiment of solitude that the land brings to one's visit which invokes thoughts that Hovenweep was more sanctuary than village. The harmony of the structures and their natural disposition against the frame of nature itself brings a sense of peace as one walks among these ruins. Hovenweep is a bit off the beaten path, but if any drive can lead to a place that inspires the spirit, then that is a road worth traveling on.

HIKING HOVENWEEP NATIONAL MONUMENT

There are six villages protected at Hovenweep. Of these, the most popular is Square Tower, which also contains the only maintained trails. The other five villages are best viewed by driving to the sites and walking amongst

the ruins via short trails that are less maintained. The other five sites are Cajon, Cutthroat Castle, Holly, Horseshoe, and Hackberry and are spread out over 20 miles. A good first step in exploring Hovenweep is picking up a visitor's guide to get an understanding of the general layout of the park.

RIM TRAIL LOOP

Easy – (1.5 mi / 2.4 km), round trip, allow 1 hour

The Rim Trail Loop is picked up just outside the visitor center and covers some of the most iconic ruin imagery in the park. Here one can see the Square Tower, Hovenweep Castle, the circular Twin Towers, and the Stronghold House, which is the first ruin found from the visitor center.

TOWER POINT LOOP

Easy – (0.5 mi / 0.8 km), round trip, allow 20 – 30 minutes

This a quick loop that travels along a peninsular section of the mesa ending at Tower Point. The canyon drops on both sides with the ruins as a backdrop, creating a nice view of the surrounding area.

HORSESHOE AND HACKBERRY TRAIL

Easy – (1.0 mi / 1.6 km), round trip, allow 1 hour

This slightly more primitive trail is a nice loop covering both the Horseshoe and Hackberry sites. Highlights include the Horseshoe Tower and Horseshoe House as well as the Hackberry group, which is one of the largest ancestral population centers in the park.

CUTTHROAT CASTLE TRAIL

Easy – (1.4 mi / 2.3 km), round trip, allow 1 hour

This site was added to the park in 1956 and showcases typical structures of the Ancestral Puebloans. It is possible to drive right up to the site, however from the trailhead junction; the road is not maintained and is suitable only for high clearance vehicles.

GOOSENECKS STATE PARK

Camping in Park:
- None

Getting There:
- From Page, AZ: Take AZ-98 East to US-160 East to US-163 North to UT-261 North to UT-316 West. Total distance is 151 mi / 243 km to park

Goosenecks State Park is an easy side trip for those traveling from the Moab area parks south towards Arizona. The park has its own state highway, UT-316, which travels 3.5 miles from its juncture with UT 261 to the Goosenecks overlook and parking area. What to do once you are there is limited. At a modest 10 acres of park, most folk's park, head to the railing and look down at the meandering San Juan River. In this section of the river, there are a number of U shaped river course ways that have been cut dramatically and deeply into the underlying strata. The view is well worth the five minutes to get there. There is also one trail that takes the more adventurous traveler down to the San Juan River shoreline.

By the way, if you are asking yourself why the river doesn't just carve a straight line, the answer has to do with the river itself. The flow of water erodes the outer banks at a faster rate, while simultaneously depositing sediment on the slower moving inner course of the river. The result of this erosional process causes a snaking pattern to form as the river cuts through the valley. Any flowing body of water can carve out a meandering course, as the principles are the same no matter the volume of the water. In the course of sandstone, this process starts very early and then essentially sets in place, eroding straight down thereafter.

View from Goosenecks State Park Overlook

Getting There:

- From Moab, UT: Take US-191 South to UT-262 East to US-160 West to NM-597. Total distance is 145 mi / 233 km to park

- From Cortez, CO: Take US-160 West/US-491 South to NM-597. Total distance is 41 mi / 66 km to park

- From Gallup, NM: Take US-491 North to US-64 West to US-160 East to NM-597. Total distance is 124 mi / 200 km to park

- From Flagstaff, AZ: Take US-89 North to US-160 East to NM-597. Total distance is 227 mi / 365 km to park

If there is an anchor to the Grand Circle, it is the Four Corners. It isn't the center of the circle, which is a shame from a perfect symmetry standpoint, but it is the symbolic center. In this one spot are captured four of the five states that make up the Grand Circle, namely Utah, Colorado, New Mexico and Arizona. Part of the overall allure of the Grand Circle is "Where does that highway lead to?" The answer to this question here is it leads to a magical place where one can stand in four states at the same time.

The park is run by the Navajo Nation and consists of a large marker indicating the location of the four corners, suitable for family photos and what not. Surrounding this marker on all four sides is a row of vendor stalls. Each stall is run by a local merchant selling the usual collection of jewelry, carved stones, arrows, feathered earrings, dream catchers, and spirit animals. While it would seem that the initial intent was to have New Mexico crafts on one side and Colorado goods on the other, at this point all of the merchants are for the most part selling Navajo crafts. Sometimes there is some Zuni and Hopi representation as well.

The flea market vibe aside, the merchants are all great folk and perhaps the best part of the monument. They come each day; they all know each other and are worth getting to know. Most are willing to share a little of their life with you if you invite them into a conversation. There is Navajo bread and other goodies for sale and basic bathroom facilities, however, true to being the center of nowhere, there is no electricity, phone service, or running water here.

Come on, you know you want to stand here!

The Photographer's Wife

There was one evening that our family walked the short distance to the edge of Mesa Arch in Canyonlands. It's a trip most people do in the morning, capturing the sunrise as it lights up the distant canyons from the edge of the horizon. For us, though, we were content to visit it at dusk. There were only a couple of cars in the parking lot, and it seemed like a quiet way to end the day.

When we arrived at the arch, an Indian gentleman, looking a little spooked, was telling his wife to watch out. He didn't realize that the arch literally sits at the edge of a cliff and tried to walk through it before catching himself at the last moment. After telling his wife, he warned us as well.

"Do be careful, it is very deceptive," he said in a dirty British accent. I smiled and thanked him. The arch was deceptive. It is a bit of a siren, drawing your attention and sloping upwards at the end so you really can't see the nothingness that follows until it is upon you.

We allowed the kids to sit on their bellies and peer over the edge while I snapped pictures. An older woman was sitting straight as an arrow on a nearby rock. I was at first drawn to her simply because I hadn't even noticed her before, though we had been there about ten minutes with her sitting fairly close to us. She had simply managed to blend with the stillness of the rocks themselves. It was only when she moved that I noticed her.

She caught me looking at her and came over. "Would you like a family photo?" she asked.

"Oh, that would be wonderful!" my wife responded.

"My name is Ella," she replied and shook my hand and then my wife's as we introduced ourselves. She had a German accent with a round face centered by a small nose. Her eyes were a clear blue that seemed to pierce through whatever walls you had in place.

Ella took a couple of pictures of us, getting us to say cheese on her commands. She took shots with the arch in frame and then suggested we get some with the Washer Woman in the background.

"That is the Washer Woman there," she said to the boys. "She is called that because she looks like a woman washing clothes. She has been here since the first time I came here in the seventies. We have some good photos of the Washer Woman."

My wife hadn't noticed the Washer Woman arch, so she corralled the boys and me once again for "a few more photos." We put on our most perfect smiles at the assigned moment and Ella pushed the camera's "easy" button. Nothing happened. We fell back to our default faces for a moment, slouched a bit, then organized back to the perfect family pose. At Ella's warm command we put our most sincere smiles and straightest of postures forward once again. We then stood in place for what seemed an eternity waiting for the depressing of what was now the camera's "take the damn photo" button. Nothing whatsoever happened again.

I ran over, with the rest of the family in place, frozen in time with smiles at the ready, the Washer Woman never once falling out of character, but the problem was not a surmountable one. The camera had run out of juice. We tried turning it off and back on several hundred times at Ang's insistence, but it was too dead for one last shot.

Ella handed the camera back to me. "Well, that is too bad, that is a great shot of your family with the Washer Woman in the background. My husband has a great shot of the two of us in that exact spot. He was a photographer."

"Where are you from?" I asked.

"Oh, originally from Germany, but that was a long time ago. Where are you folks traveling from?"

"We drove from California to Las Vegas and then rented an RV from there. We've been traveling the Grand Circle." I listed the parks we had been to.

"Oh, that sounds like an amazing journey. I did a similar trip with my husband in the early 70s. He was a photographer. I am retracing the trip in memory of him."

Everest interrupted, "Hey, Dad! Can Bryce and I walk back to the RV?"

"Sure, son. Hold on a moment, Ella. Here are the keys, no messing around and lock yourself in when you get there."

"Sure, Dad." Ev and Bryce ran back up the short trail to the motor home.

"What were the parks like back then for you?" Angela asked.

"It was a very good time… and a very hard time for us." My husband was a vice president at a company in Colorado. Then one day he came home with some results from the doctor. He had developed a form of colon cancer. It changed everything. He was forced to leave his job and we poured everything into making him well again. We lost our home and the entire time we just tried to not give up the hope he would survive it."

156

"We had to head up to Oregon to visit a doctor, a specialist. At first we were going to drive straight to Oregon. Just head up there and head straight back. But somewhere in the planning, we changed our minds and decided to make the trip something more than just driving straight to the specialist. We took what little equity we had left from selling the house and bought a motor home, more of a minivan with a stove really. It wasn't considerable but the thing didn't bother us much. We traveled to many of the same places you just described. Zion, Bryce, Arches, and here, plus Yellowstone and the Tetons."

"It was here at this arch that my husband regained himself a bit. He was strong, a very strong man, never complained. But you could see it in his expression, he wasn't himself, at least until this trip. He started taking pictures. He had a nice box camera, cherry wood frame, a special lens, he would take these 5 x 7 negatives. He had the camera since he was a boy, his father gave it to him. It was the one thing he wouldn't part with."

"He shot Mesa Arch at sunrise, standing nearly right here, where we are standing. The photo resonated with people. He opened up a photography studio and shot much of the Southwest. It was his calling. It gave him the will to live and that transferred into his photos."

"Did you ever make it to Oregon?" I asked a little puzzled.

"Oh yes, sorry! I got off track! Yes, we made it to Oregon and he went through chemo and his cancer went into remission. It was such a relief. We then set up a little studio in Boulder, Colorado and each season we would take some long outing to photograph some more of the world. Our little motor home, Tom and myself, puttering around, catching the Southwest, sometimes at its finest."

"Was he a photographer I would know?" Ang asked.

"No, he was never that famous, but we made enough money from his photography to live a good life. Even though his cancer went into remission, I think he knew his time was coming to an end. His brush with death inspired him to capture the essence of a scene. There was a soulfulness to his photography. One year we came back to this spot and he took a picture of the two of us, sitting and holding hands, here at Mesa Arch with the sunrise behind us. He made a large copy, about a meter wide and gave it to me just before he died. It was just the one shot, he usually took many, but this time he just took the one. The picture hangs in my living room over the fireplace. It is a perfect picture. The lighting is just so…I sometimes catch myself just immersed in it, the two of us together. It was the last picture he took of us."

"Soon after he gave it to me, his cancer returned and it took him. I think he knew when he took it; I can see it in his eyes when I look at the picture. It's not a sadness I see, it's a look of subtle confidence. As if he knew he would be leaving this world but was at peace with it and knew that one day I would be too."

Ang wiped a tear from her cheek and came in closer to Ella. "I'm really sorry for your loss," Angela said.

She put her arms around Ella and gave her a deep hug. I did as well. It was such a touching moment for us. Ella didn't cry but instead gazed calmly beyond to the Mesa Arch and the distant Washer Woman. As I drew away I saw a sense of knowing in her gaze, a sense of peace. She was looking at a scene that was hanging in her living room, a scene she had lost herself within on countless nights, staring at it over and over. It had become a beacon to help reconcile her loss. It was at times her entire world, that moment at the Arch with the sun's morning glow and her husband looking back at her, telling her it was okay. The scene was etched in her mind and now it was before her in real life, a memory imprinted on the canvas of reality.

We thanked Ella for her story and for taking the photos and began walking back to the RV and our kids.

"That was an amazing story," Angela remarked.

"Yeah, it was. I was a little surprised she opened up so much to us," I said.

"Oh, I don't think she cared about that. It was probably good to tell someone about her husband. I know I'd be happy to tell someone my wonderful story. It was so romantic; what a beautiful lady."

Ella had been slowly retracing the journeys she had taken with her husband for these past weeks, reliving the happiness they had shared, the moments of laughter, the near disasters, and their incredible stories, if only to them. She passed through towns that in some ways had changed and in others remained exactly the same. In the end, her pilgrimage had led her to this spot, culminating to gaze at the thing that summed up everything they were, everything they had together. In some way, I don't think she was traveling alone in her journey. The essence if not the spirit of her husband was with her.

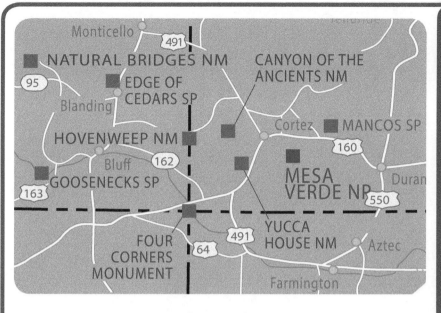

Quick Facts

Official Park Website: www.nps.gov/meve

Visitor Center: (970) 529-4465

Park Size: 52,485 acres

Established: 06/29/1906

Visitors: 0.5 million (2015)

Experience Level:

- Family Friendly to Casual Hiker

Park Accessibility:

- Okay for 2WD and RVs
- Day and Overnight Use

Nearest Town with Amenities:

- Cortez, CO is 10 mi / 16 km from park

Getting There:

- From Moab, UT: Take US-191 South, US-491 South and US-160 East 124 mi / 200 km to park entrance
- From Cortez, CO: Take US-160 E 10 mi / 16 km to park entrance

Mesa Verde National Park

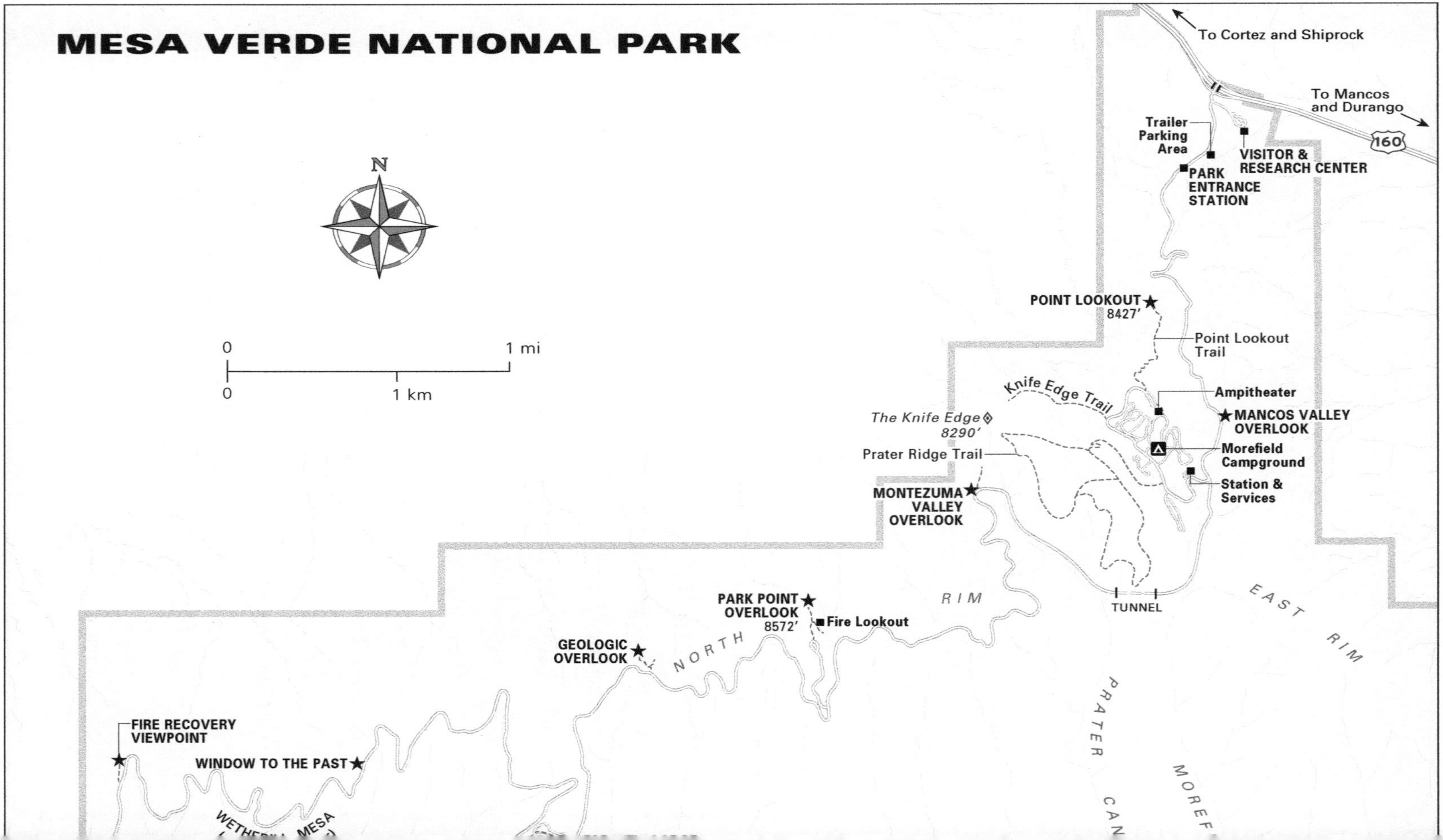

MESA VERDE NATIONAL PARK

To Mancos and Durango

To Cortez and Shiprock

160

VISITOR & RESEARCH CENTER

PARK ENTRANCE STATION

Trailer Parking Area

Point Lookout Trail

Ampitheater

MANCOS VALLEY OVERLOOK

Morefield Campground

Station & Services

POINT LOOKOUT
8427'

Knife Edge Trail

The Knife Edge
8290'

Prater Ridge Trail

TUNNEL

EAST RIM

MOREF

PRATER CAN

MONTEZUMA VALLEY OVERLOOK

RIM

Fire Lookout

PARK POINT OVERLOOK
8572'

NORTH

GEOLOGIC OVERLOOK

N

1 mi

1 km

0

0

WINDOW TO THE PAST

FIRE RECOVERY VIEWPOINT

WETHER MESA

NEW MESA

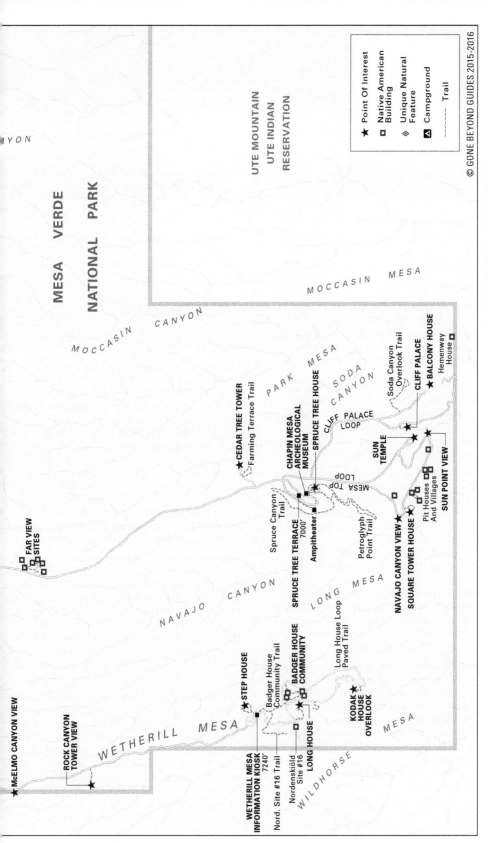

MESA VERDE NATIONAL PARK

UTE MOUNTAIN
UTE INDIAN
RESERVATION

MOCCASIN MESA

MOCCASIN CANYON

PARK MESA

SODA CANYON

CEDAR TREE TOWER
Farming Terrace Trail

CHAPIN MESA
ARCHEOLOGICAL
MUSEUM

SPRUCE TREE HOUSE

CLIFF PALACE
LOOP

BALCONY HOUSE

Hemenway
House

CLIFF PALACE

Soda Canyon
Overlook Trail

SUN
TEMPLE

Spruce Canyon
Trail

SPRUCE TREE TERRACE
7000'

Ampitheater

MESA TOP LOOP

Petroglyph
Point Trail

NAVAJO CANYON VIEW

SQUARE TOWER HOUSE

Pit Houses
And Villages

SUN POINT VIEW

FAR VIEW
SITES

NAVAJO CANYON

LONG MESA

McELMO CANYON VIEW

ROCK CANYON
TOWER VIEW

WETHERILL MESA

STEP HOUSE

Badger House
Community Trail

BADGER HOUSE
COMMUNITY

WETHERILL MESA
INFORMATION KIOSK
7240'

Nord. Site #16 Trail

Nordenskiöld
Site #16

LONG HOUSE

Long House Loop
Paved Trail

KODAK
HOUSE
OVERLOOK

WILDHORSE MESA

Point Of Interest

Native American
Building

Unique Natural
Feature

Campground

Trail

© GONE BEYOND GUIDES 2015-2016

MESA VERDE

159

Cliff Palace

WHAT MAKES MESA VERDE NATIONAL PARK SPECIAL

There is good reason to include Mesa Verde in your vacation plans. On the facts alone, it is the largest archaeological preserve in the United States and is not only a national treasure but also a globally recognized UNESCO World Heritage Site. It is the eleventh area recognized as a national park and the oldest within your tour of the Grand Circle—even older than the Grand Canyon NP. The park covers 81 square miles (210 km2) and holds more than five thousand archaeological sites and some six hundred cliff dwellings. Many of the dwellings can be seen by car, or you can do some exploration on your own through a series of trails the park has set up.

The real gem besides the cliff dwellings is the guided tours. The park offers a series of tours where the visitor can get a very personal look at the ruins. Depending on the tour, you can climb down into kivas, walk among the ruins themselves and even use cliff ladders to get out of the site. The tours are given by knowledgeable and passionate rangers, who do a fantastic job of describing what you are seeing. They bring a depth of context and details that allow you to imagine what life would have been like for the inhabitants of the cliff dwellings. There is even a 90-minute twilight tour during which the ranger takes on a character role, locked in time, giving a different contextual perspective on the Mesa Verde experience.

Another reason to make the extension to Mesa Verde is diversity. So far, the national parks you've visited are of the "Grand and Epic Southwest" variety. They are packed with amazing canyons, fins, arches, rivers, buttes and lots of red rock. Mesa Verde NP is located in a transitional zone between the desert plateau and the Rocky Mountains. The land is greener, with more trees and different flora from what you have seen so far. The weather is often milder, though don't be surprised if you get one of those famous Southwest afternoon thunderstorms. It is a welcome reprieve from the red rock simply because it's different. In addition, a drive out to Mesa puts you in the state of Colorado and makes it an easy drive to Four Corners, which is cool to visit in its own right. Mesa Verde is a welcome addition to a family vacation. It is immersive, educational and relaxing, all at the same time.

THINGS TO DO

GUIDED TOURS

As stated earlier, taking a guided tour is highly recommended. The rangers are all wonderfully passionate and well versed in what is known of the Mesa Verde inhabitants. There is no bad tour, nor is one better than another. They are all special. There are some tours that require climbing up a ladder or out onto an open rock face. The wording that the park provides causes the reader to wonder whether they will be putting themselves in danger. In reality, the wording is conservatively written to manage to the largest possible crowd. The climbing activities are easily achievable for most active visitors and are as fearful as climbing up a slide at a children's park. That said, rely on your own judgment in whether the more active tours are right for you.

There are some operating hour logistics to consider. The park runs in two seasons, each having its own operating hours. The summer/fall schedule typically runs from April/May to October/November, and the winter/spring schedule runs the rest of the year. In general, there are more tours and they are offered more frequently during the summer/fall schedule. The cost of each tour is $5 per person. You will need the ticket to take the tour and can purchase them at the visitor center. There are no refunds.

If you are going during peak season, it will help to have your preferred plan and a backup plan on which tours you want to take, as they do book up. The most popular tours are Cliff Palace and Balcony House. Given the demand, you may be asked to choose only one of these tours per day. Long House gets less traffic and can typically be combined with either the Cliff or Balcony House tours. The ticketing process can in itself take time, as there are a lot of folks there with you. Also, as stated earlier, make sure you factor in about an hour to get to the ruins and find parking.

During the summer/fall schedule, the rangers also of-fer Cliff Palace Twilight tours. These tours are limited to groups of twenty, last 90 minutes and—as the name suggests—are led in the early evening between 6:30 and 7:15 pm. This is a chance for the ranger to educate in a character that is a historical representative of the park's past. The ranger will stay in character the entire time, which is quite magical given the setting and the early evening hour. For many this is the highlight of their stay. Tickets for the Cliff Palace Twilight tours are $20 per person for all ages.

Tickets can be picked up at the following locations:

- Mesa Verde Visitor and Research Center: (main visitor center near entrance, seasonal hours, but typically 8 am to 5 pm)

- Chapin Mesa Archeological Museum (open April 15 to October 20 in 2018 with limited hours, 9 am to 4pm)

- Durango Welcome Center (in Durango at 802 Main Ave., Durango, CO, Phone: (800) 463-8726. Seasonal hours typically from 9 AM to 3 PM, check at www.durango.org)

One more tip before discussing the tours themselves: Water is the only food item that is allowed on the tours. Food, beverages, candy and gum are not permitted. Tours are an hour long, so fill up prior to your arrival.

Petroglyph Point

CLIFF PALACE TOUR

Cliff Palace is the largest cliff dwelling in the park and in the United States. It is also the most popular tour. Visitors will get a close look at what is considered the former social center of the Mesa Verde communities. The ranger-guided tour lasts one hour and does in-volve some hiking on uneven stone pathways and steps. There are small 8–10 foot (2.6 -3m) ladders that one needs to ascend a 100-foot (30m) climb. At the visitor center there are somber warnings about these ladders; however, for most people they are similar to climbing a playground slide. The total walking distance is a short quarter-mile (400m) round trip.

There are 150 rooms that make up the dwelling along with 23 kivas, round ceremonial chambers. The dwell-ing is thought to have housed 100 people. This com-munity was divided into smaller sub communities or polities. It is thought that each polity had its own kiva. The number of kivas in Cliff Palace suggests that this area was a highly social area as the ratio of rooms to kivas is much higher (nine rooms for each kiva built in Cliff Palace versus an average of 12 to 1 for the overall Mesa Verde community).

The structures are made of sandstone, mortar and wooden beams. Sandstone blocks were shaped using harder stones with mortar to seal and maintain struc-tural integrity. In some places, small "chinking" stones were placed in larger gaps. Once finished, the walls were colored with earthen pigments. A sharp eye in Cliff Palace and in the other dwellings will note that the doorways are fairly small. The average man was 5'6" while the height of the average woman was around 5'.

One of the more prominent dwellings is a large square tower known as the Square Tower House. The Square Tower House was in ruins by the 1800s and has been restored by the National Park Service. It stands 26 feet tall and has four levels.

BALCONY HOUSE TOUR

This one-hour ranger-guided tour is a little more ad-venturous than the Cliff Palace tour and explores a cliff dwelling sitting on a high ledge facing east. The eastern view meant colder winters, but the tradeoff for those liv-ing here was increased security. The ledge was only accessible via a series of small footholds carved into the cliff by the early dwellers. This is believed to be the only way into and out of the dwelling and was thus easy to defend.

Modern visitors are faced with a sim-ilar challenge, although the National Park Service has done a good job of making the journey adventurous but safe. The visitor will need to climb up a 32-foot ladder at the beginning of the tour. To get back out, one will need to bend low through a 12-foot-long tun-nel to climb two 10-foot ladders. As with all of these tours, you will need to feel comfortable that you and your party can climb the ladders.

The Balcony House is smaller than the Cliff Palace, with 45 rooms and two kivas. Don't let the smaller size fool you. Given the Balcony House was harder to get to, it was placed into the park's hands in better shape than some of the other dwellings. Many of the wooden beams can still be seen supporting roofs and sticking out of room walls. The Balcony House gives an inti-mate look at the Mesa Verde cliff dwellings. Besides the wooden beams and roofs, another favorite feature is a T- shaped doorway that can be seen during the tour.

LONG HOUSE TOUR

The Long House Tour is the longest, most in-depth and engaging tour offered. The tour is 90 minutes compared to the usual one-hour tours of Cliff Palace and Balcony House, includes a tram ride to and from the trailhead and is on the less traveled Wetherill Mesa. Unfortunately, it is also the hardest to get to for folks in an RV as vehicles over 25 feet are prohibited on the Wetherill Mesa Road. It is only open from Memorial Day to Labor Day each year. This tour is the most strenuous and requires a ¾-mile (1.2 km) hike round trip to access the dwellings.

The tour begins at the Wetherill Mesa information kiosk. Here you will board a tram that travels through a pinyon juniper forest undergoing recovery from a recent burn. Once at the Long House Trailhead, you follow a paved path downhill about 1/3 mile (0.54 km) to reach the ruins. At one point, there is a concrete staircase of 50 steps with railing.

The hike itself adds to the ambiance of discovery. The ruins are not in sight at first, only the tops of mesas and wide canyons. The hike descends through wonderful rock and pinyon juniper forests. In the summer, it is hot and dry and, while this leads to the strenuous aspects of the hike, it may give appreciation for what the early inhabitants faced. Once fully immersed in the surroundings, Long House comes into view.

After a short lecture near the ruins, the tour includes climbing two 15-foot (4.5m) ladders up into the site itself. No longer standing alongside the ruins, you are now inside them, bringing a personal aspect to experiencing the dwellings. The ruins themselves are fairly extensive, with more than 100 rooms, including multistory buildings. Long House is the second largest cliff dwelling in the park. The ranger will point out some petroglyphs along the way as well. The tour ends by taking the same trail back, this time uphill. On a hot day, the 50 concrete steps won't look as welcoming going up as they did going down. The tram will take you back to the Wetherill parking area.

SELF-GUIDED TOURS

SPRUCE TREE HOUSE (CHAPIN MESA)

Note: Spruce Tree House has been closed for the foreseeable future due to concerns relating to rock falls.

During the winter months from November to early March, the Spruce Tree House is not only a ranger-led guided tour but is free. The tours last one hour and are given three times a day. The rest of the year, it is available as a self-guided tour.

Ladder Approach at Balcony House

Spruce Tree House is the third largest cliff dwelling (Cliff Palace and Long House are larger). It is also the best preserved of the cliff dwellings. The walking distance of the tour is ½ mile (0.8 km) round trip and begins at the Chapin Mesa Archeological Museum. Visitors can meander at leisure along paths that encourage a more relaxed experience. There are around 130 rooms and 8 kivas, which were believed to have housed 60 to 80 people. There are many multistory buildings to view and a kiva that one can enter as part of the tour.

FAR VIEW SITES COMPLEX (CHAPIN MESA)

The Far View Sites are often overlooked on the drive to the more known sites at Chapin Mesa proper. The Far View Sites are unique in that these villages sit at the top of the mesa rather than in an alcove of a cliff. There were at one time 50 villages in the half square mile surrounding this area. The self-guided tour gives a nice walk among five of the villages plus a dry reservoir. The trail is unpaved but level and is ¾ mile (1.2km) long. These surface sites include Far View House, Pipe Shrine House, Coyote Village, Far View Reservoir, Megalithic House, and Far View Tower. This is a great hike if you want to round out the day's experience on your way back to the campground.

BADGER HOUSE TRAIL (WETHERILL MESA)

The Badger House Community is a series of four sites on a paved and gravel trail. The sites include Modified Basketmaker Pithouse, Developmental Pueblo village, Badger House and Two Raven House. Like Far View Sites Complex, these sites sit on top of the mesa. The trail is 2.5 mile (4km) if started at the Wetherill Mesa Kiosk or 1.5 miles (2.41 km) if you take the tram to the Badger House tram stop. The tour is both educational and peaceful.

Step House (Wetherill Mesa)

The Step House is one of the more unique self-guided tours in that one can see clear distinctions pointing to two separate occupations of the site. The first inhabitants were the Modified Basketmakers, which dated to A.D. 626. Evidence of their habitation can be found between the old stone steps on the southern edge of the site and the large boulders to the north. The area was inhabited again in BCE 1226 as evidenced by the masonry structures seen within the rest of the site. Two standouts of the ruins are a pit house and the petroglyphs.

The trail is steep and ¾ mile (1.2 km) long along a winding path. Many visitors that come to Wetherill Mesa combine the Step House self-guided tour with the ranger-led Long House tour. Allow a good half day if you decide this is the right combination for you.

HIKING MESA VERDE

POINT LOOKOUT TRAIL

Strenuous – (2.2 mi / 3.5 km), round trip, elev. Δ: 510 ft / 155 m, trailhead at Morefield Campground

This is one of the three trails that start from the Morefield Campground. The trail does pass by some Ute structures and other ruins as it makes its way to a highpoint called Point Lookout. The point stands as a natural lookout tower for the entire Mesa Verde area. It was used by the United States Calvary to signal fellow mounted forces as well as earlier by the Utes.

There is an elevation gain of about 500 feet, most of it occurring in the first half mile as the trail winds on up via a series of switchbacks. The trail continues through

Oak brush vegetation with a few more switchbacks and then more gently climbs the final half mile to the top. The trail here narrows to a knife ridge, but there is plenty of vegetation on either side. Here there are remnants of Ute structure, inscriptions, initials and other interested artifacts as you reach the top and the great views of the Mancos and Montezuma Valley.

KNIFE EDGE TRAIL

Easy – (2.0 mi / 3.2 km), round trip, elev. Δ: 59 ft / 18 m, trailhead at Morefield Campground

One of the other three hikes near the Morefield Campground, this short there and back trail gives some decent views of Montezuma Valley. The trail starts by passing between the Prater Ridge and an obvious little rock hillock called Lone Cone. There is a bit of elevation at first, but much of the trail is flat as it follows the old Knife Edge Road. The trail pretty much just ends at a sign that says, "STOP!! Trail End" indicating it's time to turn back. This short trail is nicely secluded on most days and provides a great place to take in a sunset.

PRATER RIDGE TRAIL

Strenuous – (7.8 mi / 12.6 km), round trip, elev. Δ: 710 ft / 216 m, trailhead at Morefield Campground

This loop is the longest of the three trails that start from the nearby Morefield Campground. The trail climbs until it reaches Prater Ridge and then follows along the rim of the cuesta. Like all of the trails near the campground, it is light on ruins but big on nature. Prater Ridge gives expansive views of the Montezuma Valley. This is honestly one of the best of the longer hikes in the park. It makes a complete loop, giving a variety of views of the southern Colorado countryside. If you want to make it a smaller loop, there is an obviously marked cutoff trail that trims the loop by roughly half.

Square Tower House

Farming Terrace Trail

Moderate – (0.5 mi / 0.8 km), round trip, allow 15 minutes, elev. Δ: 120 ft / 37 m, trailhead on Chapin Mesa

While the distance of this small loop trail isn't terribly long, it is fairly well exposed and can get hot. This trail gives it a nice peak into how the Ancestral Puebloans farmed the land. At first glance, it just looks like a bunch of terraces, but one learns that they made good use of water runoff, diverting it as it made its way downhill to provide much needed moisture to their crops. The whole thing is quite ingenious to see unfold before the hiker. The trail is also close to the Cedar Tree Ruins, which is worth exploring. Make a right once you retrace the loop back to the road to see a kiva and a tower remnant.

Spruce Canyon Trail

Moderate – (2.4 mi / 3.9 km), round trip, elev. Δ: 529 ft / 161 m, trailhead on Chapin Mesa

Spruce Canyon Trail begins at the Spruce Tree House trail and gives the viewer a chance to experience the ecosystem of the canyon floor. The trail heads to the bottom of Spruce Tree Canyon and then back up along the mesa top in one nice loop. Like the Petroglyph Point Trail, the loop finishes at the Chapin Mesa Archeological Museum, which is well worth exploring in its own right.

Petroglyph Point Trail

Moderate – (2.4 mi / 3.9 km), round trip, elev. Δ: 196 ft / 60 m, trailhead on Chapin Mesa

This trail begins from the Spruce Tree House trail and is one of the more pleasant hikes in Mesa Verde. The loop starts down below the mesa top, following what feels like an ancient trail used years ago. One winds through narrow rock passages among pinyon juniper forests with views of Spruce and Navajo Canyons.

The trail "ends" at the petroglyphs, which are impressive and worth the hike. From the rock art, the trailheads up to the top of the mesa for a level and easy walk back to the parking area. The hike drops you at the Chapin Mesa Archeological Museum, which is well worth a visit in its own right. Across the street is the Spruce Tree Terrace Café to finish off the hike with a well-deserved snack.

A trail guide is available and registration (at the museum) is required.

Soda Canyon Overlook Trail

Easy – (1.2 mi / 1.9 km), round trip, allow 30 minutes, elev. Δ: 72 ft / 22 m, trailhead on Chapin Mesa

This is an easy and flat hike that leads to three great overlooks from which several ruins can be viewed, including the Balcony House. There is a viewing scope installed at the canyon's edge at the middle overlook. The southernmost overlook gives the best views of Balcony House.

Nordenskiöld Site No. 16 Trail

Easy – (1.0 mi / 1.6 km), round trip, allow 30 minutes, elev. Δ: 228 ft / 69 m, trailhead on Wetherhill Mesa

This trail found in the Wetherhill Mesa section leads to an overlook of Nordenskiöld Site 16. The trail itself is flat and passes through a portion of the 2000 Pony Fire burn area. As a result, the land is a mixture of grasslands showing the wonder of recovery against a multitude of sentinel dead trees standing as silent evidence of the fire. The trail crosses a paved tram road occasionally. It is prohibited for hikers to walk the tram road, but okay to take the tram back if you want. The tram does make a stop at the Nordenskiöld site overlook, which is the end of the trail. The overlook gives a view into Site 16, a nice double alcove cliff dwelling. The site is named for Gustav Nordenskiöld, who made the first extensive excavations of the site back in 1891.

Badger House Community Trail

Moderate – (2.3 mi / 3.7 km), round trip, allow 1 hour, elev. Δ: 52 ft / 16 m, trailhead on Wetherhill Mesa

This is a rather flat but exposed trail which was hit by the 2000 Pony Fire. The trail is straightforward with a mixture of pea gravel and paved trail, offering some self-guided sections displaying various aspects of the Badger top site ruins. The top site ruins do have different qualities then the alcove ruins, so the Badger House trail helps make for a rounded experience.

Kiva in Balcony House

Coyote Village, Far View Sites

UNIQUE BACKCOUNTRY HIKES

Each year, the Mesa Verde park rangers offer up exclusive and unique backcountry hikes and tours. The offerings are different each year and are definitely worth looking into. These hikes and guided ranger tours often go to areas that are not open or even publicized. The hikes typically require advance purchase of tickets and the number of tickets available each day is limited. Each hike is very special and even unprecedented in what the open up for visitors to see and experience.

For a list of the current year's hikes, check with the park for more information by going to the following link: http://www.nps.gov/meve/planyourvisit/backcountry_hikes.htm. Some of the hikes that seem to be perennial offerings are listed below. That said, each year they change them enough to warrant going to the website for current details.

WETHERILL MESA BIKE AND HIKE ADVENTURE

Strenuous – (9.0 mi / 14.5 km), round trip, allow 4.5 hours, not including driving time

Tickets are $18.00 for adults. Tours are limited to 15 people. Bike not included (you need to bring your own). There are rental bikes available, call (970) 529-4631 for information on local bike rental places.

Kokopelli Bike and Board offers bikes for rental in Cortez (130 W Main St, Cortez, CO 81321. (970) 565-4408). Also, tour times were limited to Wednesdays and Sundays as of this writing.

This is likely one of the coolest ranger led hikes in the entire Grand Circle. You get to hike with a ranger for four miles and bike alongside for another five miles.

This isn't a tram stuffed full of people and some guy reciting into a megaphone, this is a full immersion bi-modal journey into depths of Mesa Verde accompanied by an expert.

The entire trip is filled with great views of cliff dwellings with in depth trips to Nordenskiöld #12, Double House and even includes a short hike to Long House. Allow about six hours total for the hike and driving time to the starting point from the visitor center. The trip is okay for young adults able to travel 9 miles comfortably. Also, bring plenty of water, snacks, sunscreen, and a hat. Folks must be in good overall shape for this adventure.

MESA VERDE LODGING

STAYING INSIDE THE PARK

Whether you are camping, RVing or looking for lodging, the park itself accommodates everyone. There are plenty of rooms and campsites within the park, which is good as the park involves a fair amount of driving. For folks looking for a room, Far View Lodge is your ticket. For RVers and campers, there is Morefield Campground.

Far View Lodge

Mile Marker 15, Mesa Verde National Park, CO 81330, (970) 529-4421, www.visitmesaverde.com

The Mesa Verde NP offers lodging facilities inside the park at the Far View Lodge from mid-April to mid-October. Far View is quiet, peaceful and perched high up in the park, giving views into three states. There are no TVs, no arcade rooms and no sports bars adjoining the property, just serene lodging. The downside of this place is the rooms are 50s style, basic and in need of refurbishment for the most part. The lodge offers a standard room and a kiva room. While the kiva rooms offer finer furnishings, they only come with two double or one king options only. Most of the standard rooms have two double or one queen, however there are a few standard rooms with two queens. All room come with exceptional views from your private balcony.

Morefield Campground

Likely the best part of this campground is there are plenty of spots to choose from, and they rarely fill up completely. The Morefield Campground is located just 4 miles (6.4 km) past the Mesa Verde entrance and has 267 sites, 83 of which are designated for RVs. The campground is distributed across three loops with the Ute loop being the loop designated for RV sites. There are 15 full hookup sites that are typically reserved in advance.

Montezuma Valley Overlook

166

Each site comes with the standard amenities, including a picnic table, fire pit and grill. The site is located within a scrub oak canyon filled with grasses, wild flowers, deer, wild turkeys and other fauna. On one early morning RV dumping station stop, we saw a herd of deer galloping and playing in the hill across from the station. The scene was a true spirit lifter during a typically unwanted chore.

While there are usually enough open campsites, some are only barely worthy of even a small RV. More than a few sites lean to one side, which makes cooking a challenge and sleeping uncomfortable. Keep your eye out for level sites as you drive through the loop to choose where you will stay. Please stick to the Ute Loop, which is designed for RVs. The other loops are built more for cars than RVs, plus every tent camper will look at you funny as you drive within their "tents only" loops.

There is more to Morefield than just a large campground. There are very pleasant hiking trails that start at the campground, including the Knife Edge Trail, which is a short old road that leads to great sunsets. At the entrance of the campground is a decent dumping and filling station. Just above the campground is a full service concessionaire station. There you will find many creature comforts, including free showers, which are clean and private. There is a coin-operated Laundromat, a grocery store, a gas station and a gift shop as well. This is where you will check in to reserve your campsite. Both the site and shops are run by Aramark, and they will be happy to fill you in on the details.

One other thing to keep in mind is the overall layout of Mesa Verde. There is one road into the park, which ultimately dead ends at the ruins. The campground is near the beginning of park's entrance, and it is a windy 15-mile (24 km) drive just to get to the ruins from your campsite. If you have purchased a tour, be sure to factor in the drive time.

Lodging Near Mesa Verde

Hampton Inn Mesa Verde / Cortez

2244 E Hawkins Street, Cortez, CO 81321, (970) 564-5924, hamptoninn3.hilton.com

The rooms are clean with big comfy beds, however the ambiance is a little ho hum. They offer a free breakfast, however check around before settling on this hotel. They do have a small pool that matches the underwhelming aspects of this hotel.

Retro Inn at Mesa Verde

2040 E Main St, Cortez, CO 81321-3042, (970) 670-7638, www.retroinnmesaverde.com

The owners of this hotel are just great people. They started with a classic motor inn, added some needed improvements and colorful paint, stepped back, and then decided to have some real fun. Each room number, (example: room number 1973), is decorated to the corresponding year. Outside one can play a giant game of chess, sit with Elvis or play on a tractor. Light breakfast provided. A truly fun place to stay while visiting Mesa Verde NP.

Holiday Inn Express Mesa Verde-Cortez

2121 E Main St, Cortez, CO 81321-4202, (970) 565-6000, www.ihg.com

The Holiday Inn Express in Cortez is clean and bright, with nice touches. They offer a large indoor pool and a free breakfast bar. This is a solid choice for those looking for a mid-range hotel with some amenities.

Baymont Inn & Suites Cortez

2279 Hawkins St., Cortez, CO 81321, (970) 565-3400, www.wyndhamhotels.com

This is truly a relaxing hotel and perfect for families or groups. The hotel interior's 3 stories surrounds the pool, with hanging plants that add to the overall ambiance. They offer family rooms and the rate comes with a free breakfast, free Wi-Fi, and use of their fitness center.

Best Western Turquoise Inn & Suite

535 E Main St, Cortez, CO 81321-3319, (970) 565-3778, www.bestwestern.com

Nice mid-range hotel with free breakfast and indoor pool. The hotel inside and out has a whimsical southwestern theme. The hotel will be undergoing renovations through March 2017.

American Holiday Mesa Verde Inn Cortez

640 S Broadway, Cortez, CO 81321-3430, (970) 565-3773, mesaverdeinncolorado.com

Very basic rooms that are in need of some serious upgrades. The hotel is dirty, older, and run down. There is an outdoor pool, however use this place as a last resort. This is not an "American Holiday" most people would want to take.

The White Eagle Inn & Family Lodge

2110 S Broadway, Cortez, CO 81321-9534, (970) 565-3333, whiteeagleinn.com

Family owned and operated since it was built in 1958, there is a true sense of pride in the overall management of White Eagle Inn. The hotel is low on amenities but big on clean rooms and high standards of service. The rooms are basic and a bit retro, but overall, the establishment is a good value for the money.

MESA VERDE DINING

Dining in the Park

Metate Room

AMERICAN, meals for under $60, Mile Marker 15, Mesa Verde National Park, CO 81330, (970) 529-4422, visitmesaverde.com, open April thru October, 5pm - 9:30pm

The Metate Room is the culinary crown jewel of Mesa Verde National Park. Great service, wonderfully unique entrees, and stunning views. The Metate Room is on par with some of the great dining experiences within the National Park system. They are open for breakfast, with lunch and dinner menus as well. Dinner options are far ranging, including trout and elk wellington.

Far View Terrace Cafe

AMERICAN, meals for under $20, Mile Marker 15, Mesa Verde National Park, CO 81330, (970) 529-4421, visitmesaverde.com, open seasonally, 7am - 8pm

Far View Lodge is open for breakfast, lunch, and dinner and has great views from the mesa top. The views certainly outpace the food quality, which is in line with cafeteria style quality, down to the buffet breakfasts. Expect to pay more as well. The lodge also has a bar area upstairs called the Lounge, which is open nightly and serves appetizers and other snack items.

Spruce Tree Terrace Cafe

AMERICAN, meals for under $20, 34879 Hwy 160, Mesa Verde National Park, CO 81330, (970) 529-4465, open seasonally, 9am - 6:30pm

Spruce Tree is helpful in terms of location, which is right next to many of the most popular sites. The location aside, the cafe suffers from offering average food and average service at prices that may have you reexamining your hunger.

Spruce Tree House from Bottom of Spruce Tree Canyon

Dining Near Mesa Verde

Destination Grill

AMERICAN, meals for under $20, 2121 E Main St, Cortez, CO 81321, (970) 516-1111, open daily, 4pm - 10pm

Lively atmosphere and fresh food is the theme at Destination Grill. They primarily serve burgers and beer and offer patio seating outside. Fun local Colorado scene.

Shiloh Steakhouse

STEAKHOUSE/AMERICAN, meals from under $30, 5 Veach St, Cortez, CO 81321, (970) 565-6560, www.shilohsteak.com, open daily, 11am - 9pm, closed Sunday and Monday

Steaks, ribs, and seafood are served here along with a menu of other American favorites. They deliver great meals and have a few harder to find items, such as lobster tail and country fried elk.

Thai Cortez

THAI, meals for under $20, 1430 E Main St, Cortez, CO 81321, (970) 564-3151, open daily, for lunch 11:30am - 2:30pm, dinner from 4:30pm - 9pm

Great Thai cuisine in Cortez. They serve up great curries and noodles with a variety of spice settings. If you like Thai food, this is a candidate for the best you've ever had. It's that good!

Taste of India

INDIAN, meals for under $20, 1013 E Main St, Cortez, CO 81321, (970) 564-9897, open daily, 11am - 10pm

Low on ambiance, but great Indian food, down to the home made nan. Their flavors are amazing, offering a selection of robust curries and masalas. Try the rack of lamb or the chicken tandoori, both are excellent.

La Casita De Cortez

MEXICAN, meals for under $20, 332 E Main St, Cortez, CO 81321, (970) 565-0223, open daily, 11am - 10pm, open one hour later on Fridays and Saturdays

This is really good Mexican cuisine! Everything is freshly made, comes out fast and is reasonably priced. Carne asada is a favorite.

El Burro Pancho

MEXICAN, meals for under $20, 125 E Main St, Cortez, CO 81321, (970) 565-4633, open daily, 11am - 9pm

Great Sonoran style Mexican cuisine. Big plates, big servings, hot and reasonable. Great service, reasonable prices and the décor is fun, from the hand drawn murals to the plates themselves.

Loungin' Lizard

AMERICAN, meals for under $20, 2 W Main St, Cortez, CO 81321, (970) 516-1998, lounginlizardcortez.com open daily, 9am - 9pm, closed Tuesdays

Loungin' Lizard offers a large selection of menu items that are fresh, healthy and delicious. One can get sandwiches, soups, and salads. They also offer pizza, tacos and dinner entrees such as southwest chicken marsala. Everything is plated nicely. Also, their full cocktail bar does allow one to become a true loungin' lizard.

The Farm Bistro

STEAKHOUSE/AMERICAN, meals from under $20, 34 W Main St, Cortez, CO 81321, (970) 565-3834, thefarmbistrocortez.com, Weekdays 11am - 9pm

If you're in Cortez and are looking for a treat, try The Farm Bistro. They serve up a full "farm to table" menu, offering fresh food and refreshing menu items. They offer a great selection for both lunch and dinner. The only downside? They are only open weekdays.

Stonefish Sushi & More

SUSHI, meals for under $30, 16 W Main St, Cortez, CO 81321, (970) 565-9244, open Tuesdays through Saturdays, open for lunch from 11am - 2pm, dinner from 4:30pm - 9pm. Dinner only on Mondays, closed Sundays

Really fantastic selection of rolls alongside traditional teriyaki and tempura selections. This place is a favorite of locals and tourists alike.

Pippo's Cafe

AMERICAN, meals for under $10, 100 W Main St, Cortez, CO 81321, (970) 565-6039, open daily, 6:30am - 2pm

Pippo's Café is full of local ambiance and is a go to spot with the pensioner crowd. If you like old school home cooking, this is the place for you. No fuss food and reasonable prices.

Coffee and Sweets!

The Pie Maker Bakery

COFFEE, BAKERY, 17 N Harrison St, Cortez, CO 81321, (970) 560-6039, piemakerbakery.com

A small town treat. Locally made baked goods using organic and natural ingredients. They have a selection of gluten free offerings, bagels and other breakfast items, pies, and out of this world cinnamon rolls.

Spruce Tree Espresso House

COFFEE, LIGHT FOOD, 318 E Main St, Cortez, CO 81321, (970) 565-6789, sprucetreeespresso.com, open daily, 7am - 2pm, closed Sunday

There are a lot of really cool coffee houses in Cortez and Spruce Tree Espresso House is no exception. Resembling a wizard's house with purple exterior and fairyland paintings on the outside, it is almost worth a trip inside just to see what more there could be. They offer the usual grouping of espresso drinks. Try one of their specialty drinks, such as the Mesa Verde Mocha, which is a latte with dark chocolate, peppermint and whipped cream.

MOOSE & MORE

ICE CREAM, CHOCO-
LATES, CANDIES, 12 E
Main St,Cortez, CO 81312,
(970) 560-0468, mooseand-
more.com, open daily, 12pm
- 8pm, open one hour later
Friday and Saturday

Moose & More serves up
a scoops of homemade ice
cream and chocolates along
with other items also made
lovingly by hand; including
truffles, brittles and caramel
corn. The quality is very high
here, but expect to pay a little
more for this. It's homemade,
not store bought ice cream!
Enjoy!

Step House

MESA VERDE HISTORY

The history and culture of the Mesa Verde people has
been studied in great depth. There has been so much focus and detail that it can be a bit consuming to a visitor.
If we can start with the bigger picture, perhaps it will
help to frame the context of Mesa Verde history.

About 1,400 years ago, in other parts of the world, China was printing its first books, Vikings were invading
Northern Europe and all of Europe was still recovering
from the decline of the Roman Empire. Meanwhile in
North America, there was a group of people who decided to call Mesa Verde home. They found water, food
and shelter. Over the course of 700 years they stayed in
this one place. They integrated with the land, developing such a deep tie to their surroundings that they could
listen to it and learn from it. The plants, the sky, the flow
of water, all of it became extensions of their own eyes
and ears. The land became a part of who they were
as a society. They developed laws, customs, spiritual bonds and methodologies of all sorts that helped
them get continuously better at not only living but
also thriving. During this time they continued to find
improvements in everything they did, including the
way they made their clothes, stored their food and
water, cultivated food and hunted. Their shelters im-
proved as well, becoming elaborate multi-story communities with areas set up to trade, sleep, socialize
and commune with their beliefs.

Then, they left. They didn't depart all at once; they
left over one or two generations. Mesa Verde was
no longer called home for reasons that are not truly
known. They left and went south as separate groups,
leaving their homes and most of their belongings behind. Today, there are twenty-four tribes that have a
special relationship with these Mesa Verde ancestors,
that look upon their own people and at themselves
and call the inhabitants of Mesa Verde a part of their
ancestral record.

From 1300 CE to the late 1800s, the cliff dwellings of
Mesa Verde were known only to the local tribes. In
1859, the area was named "Mesa Verde" by European
settlers. By 1874, the ruins were discovered and the first
photographs taken. As early as 1886, folks felt the place
was special enough to become a national park, and in
1906, it did, under the pen of President Theodore Roosevelt.

From its declaration as a national park through today,
the cliff dwellings and surrounding areas have been ex-
cavated and preserved to both understand and maintain this culturally significant place. In 1978, Mesa
Verde was named a Unesco World Heritage Site. Today,
the park is shared by more than 600,000 visitors each
year, allowing an up-close look at these fascinating ruins of a civilization that was called home to a society of
people for more than 700 years.

House of Many Windows

Mesa Verde's First Inhabitants

The Modified Basket Makers (550 to 750 CE)

The initial inhabitants settled in Mesa Verde some 1,400 years ago. The land was higher than surrounding land, so they could easily spot intruders from a distance. It held alcoves in cliff walls, which meant shelter with even further protection. There was water, constant water, year round, which was essential. In addition, there was enough game to hunt. It was an ideal place to live, to raise children, to grow a civilization. It is really unknown how many came to this place at first, perhaps several families, maybe even several groups that agreed to live together. They came with some crudeness, more hunting and gathering practices, but with some advancements. They could make baskets to carry things; they knew well how to use the atlatl and spear. They could hunt and bring home food for their families on a consistent basis.

The place of Mesa Verde allowed them to achieve more. They settled and learned how to make crude clay pots, which reduced the number of baskets needed, which wore out quicker. The pottery helped in so many ways, carrying water, cooking food more evenly; it was a paradigm shift. They learned to grow beans and by the end of this period replaced the spear and the atlatls with a new invention, the bow and arrow. It made hunting easier as well as provided more hides for clothing. This led to more time for social events, both for celebration and for spiritual congregation. There were items of ordinary use and items of significance, such as robes made of turkey feathers.

Developmental Pueblo (750 to 1100 CE)

By this period, the once small group was now a civilization. Buildings were architected and constructed, most facing south for warmth and with windows shaped like U, E and L shapes. The rooms were close together, wisely thought out as this provided both protection and greater warmth. The connection of the people was deeply rooted in the spirit, and religious celebration was commonplace.

During this time, the crude pottery of their forefathers was advanced upon, becoming pitchers, bowls, jars, and other implements of dishware. They began to see beyond pottery as merely utilitarian and to use it for decoration. The pottery was tastefully decorated with white clay inscribed with black patterns. Painting of interior rooms became a thing; society was alive and vibrant with artistry and color.

The scientifically minded were also busy. Their buildings became more sophisticated to meet the growing population.

1929 Photo of Navajo Boy at Balcony House

They built upward, creating towers and multi-story buildings. Their architecture was unrivaled, to be sure. The Square Tower House was the tallest building in North America until the mid-1800s. They created reservoirs for water and even dams, which allowed for better conservation of water for use during the drier months. This was born likely of need rather than forethought, as the people of Mesa Verde were to endure a 24-year drought that ultimately led to the abandonment of their home for more fertile ground. By 1300 CE, the population of Mesa Verde had gathered up and left a place they had called home for several hundred years.

EUROPEAN DISCOVERY

While the Spanish explorers of 1776 came within sight of Mesa Verde, they did not see the ruins themselves. It was the trappers and prospectors who discovered the ruins, with miner John Moss being the first one credited. Moss saw the ruins in 1873 and was impressed enough by them that he came back with friend and photographer William Henry Jackson.

Jackson was a prolific and nationally known photographer, publisher, and painter. His work has become an impressive chronicle of the early west, including the Rocky Mountains and Yellowstone. During his life of 99 years he created more than 80,000 photographs. Moss led Jackson to Two Story House, where he took the first photographs of the cliff dwellings of Mesa Verde. These photographs were subsequently published, bringing national attention to the area.

Bit by bit, more of the dwellings were found. The Wetherills settled a ranch southwest of Mancos, Colorado, and developed a relationship with the nearby Ute tribe. The Ute tribe gave the Weatherills approval to winter their cattle in the lower and warmer plateaus of what is now the surrounding Ute Mountain Tribe. Acowitz, a member of the Ute tribe, told of a place of the "old people—the Ancient Ones." He explained that the place was sacred and that the Utes never go there. However, the tale struck the imagination of the cowboys, and on December 18, 1888, Richard Wetherill and his friend Charlie Mason found and named Cliff Palace, gathering artifacts as they explored. Some of the artifacts were later sold to the Historical Society of Colorado, but much of them were kept.

The Wetherills explored and removed artifacts from several of the cliff dwellings. On one occasion, they brought along Baron Gustaf E. A. Nordenskiöld, a trained mineralogist and scientist. He was the first to bring the scientific method to the collection of artifacts in Mesa Verde, using meticulous field methods in the cataloging of the sites. In 1893, Nordenskiöld published his examinations and photographs as *The Cliff Dwellers of the Mesa Verde*. While his work drew more attention to Mesa Verde, not all of it was positive. In addition to writing the book, he shipped about 600 artifacts out of the country to Sweden, where they now reside in the National Museum in Helsinki, Finland. This initiated concerns for the need to protect Mesa Verde and the cliff dwellings.

CREATION OF A NATIONAL PARK

The area saw increasing foot traffic, artifact removal and even destruction of the ruins themselves. From Nordenskiöld's shipment in 1893 to 1906 when the area finally became a national park, Mesa Verde saw its worst treatment. Looters broke through exterior walls simply to allow more light in. Beams were used for firewood until nearly all of the roofs were lost. The Cliff Palace was damaged extensively. Some of the objects went to museums, but many were simply lost to private collections.

Fortunately, there were folks getting the right attention to the park. Virginia McClurg was tireless in her efforts to protect the history of Mesa Verde. She gave speeches worldwide and formed the Colorado Cliff Dwellers, an organization developed to reclaim the artifacts and promote preservation. Along with fellow activist Lucy Peabody, the women lobbied with members of Congress for Mesa Verde's protection.

J. Walter Fewkes, an ethnologist at the Smithsonian Institute, documented a report to the Secretary of the Interior on the horrible shape of the ruins. Their call was for the preservation and creation of a national park; however, there was a bill as late as 1904 that discussed who would have the rights to remove artifacts. At times, it seemed Mesa Verde would not receive the protection it needed. However, through years of lobbying, the efforts of these people finally paid dividends. On June 29, 1906, President Theodore Roosevelt signed legislation declaring Mesa Verde a National Park. It was the first cultural national park set aside by the National Park Service. In 1978, Mesa Verde was further recognized by the United Nations Educational, Scientific and Cultural Organization (UNESCO) as a World Heritage Cultural Site. The shipment of artifacts by Nordenskiöld remains in Helsinki at the National Museum of Finland.

MESA VERDE GEOLOGY

The main event when it comes to Mesa Verde are the cliff dwellings; however, if you think about it, the inhabitants didn't live in cliffs, they lived in alcoves that were created within the cliff walls. The alcoves are what drew the ancestral inhabitants to the Mesa Verde area and as alcoves are geologic formations, the geology of Mesa Verde suddenly becomes pretty important.

In fact, even the term mesa is a geologic term. A mesa, such as the one found in Canyonlands' Island in the Sky District, is defined as a flat-topped landform with straight cliff-like sides. The term mesa is Spanish for table and thus Mesa Verde means "Green Table." That said, even though the national park is called Mesa Verde, it isn't a mesa per se in geologic circles. Sure, it has a flat top, more or less, but it doesn't have straight cliff-like sides. No, the sides of this so-called "mesa" are sloped, which in the world of geology is known as a cuesta. What you can do with this information is anyone's guess.

Cliff Palace circa 1891

If you go around calling the place "Cuesta Verde," normal people will look at you funny and the two percent who might understand what you are saying will likely judge you as a geologic elitist. Best to just keep this information to yourself and relay it only when the there is a significant lull in the campfire discussions.

Let's get back to the main geologic feature, those alcoves. Alcoves at Mesa Verde are formed through a rather simple process. The first thing to know is that the mesas of Mesa Verde are composed of a layer of sandstone sitting on top of a layer of shale. In the rock world, sandstone is very absorbent; however, shale is not. So, you essentially have a big sponge sitting on top of a hard surface. The second thing to know is that the mesa is tilted, not much, mind you, only about 7 degrees. The third thing to know is that gravity works in Mesa Verde just like it does everywhere else.

If you put these three things together, you can understand the creation of an alcove. When it rains, the water becomes absorbed by the sponge-like sandstone. The water slowly settles downward through the sandstone until it meets the shale layer. Since all that water needs a place to go and since the land is titled 7 degrees, it naturally follows the path of least resistance by going downhill. The water continues to travel through the sandstone along the top of the shale until it finds an outlet at one of the canyon edges.

From there the water travels down the canyon as a trickling seep. The seeps of Mesa Verde remove a tiny fraction of the sandstone as the water continues

Spruce Tree House

downstream. The sandstone is chemically dissolved and physically transported away over time into the creeks and rivers below. As the alcoves become larger, they start to eat inwardly into the cliff wall. Over time, larger rocks fall, which opens the alcove up even more. The water from the seeps slowly erodes away even these larger sandstone rocks that have fallen. The end result is a large, arched alcove that is suitable for habitation.

There are a couple of other interesting tidbits about the relationship of seeps and the residents of Mesa Verde. The sponge-like property of sandstone meant the seeps could provide the inhabitants with a year-round supply of water. The seeps not only allowed folks to survive, but also allowed for agriculture. With agriculture, the residents were now sustained in one place and didn't have to roam for food like their hunter-gatherer forefathers. The alcoves also gave shelter from elements and some protection from enemies. Once again, the right conditions, a little water and an abundance of time proved to be the right ingredients to start a civilization.

Example of an alcove.

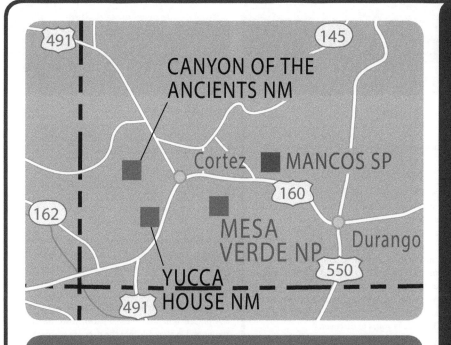

491 145

CANYON OF THE ANCIENTS NM

Cortez MANCOS SP

160

162

MESA VERDE NP Durango

550

YUCCA HOUSE NM

491

Within the Canyon of the Ancients National Monument

Parks Near Mesa Verde

YUCCA HOUSE NATIONAL MONUMENT

Camping in Park:
- None

Getting There:
- Cortez, CO is 12 mi / 19 km from the park

The park holds one of the larger Ancestral Puebloan sites, with hundreds of rooms. What makes Yucca House special however is what isn't there. There are no facilities, no visitor guides, no campsites, and no trails to be found. There is an easement access for a road to be built, but since its inception in 1919, there is no road. All that defines Yucca House is a lone-gated entrance. You walk up to it, you open the gate, and from here, you are on the same page as any other archaeologist and visitor. The place is yours to discover.

There are some paths created from use, follow these to find various mounds, some with bits of walls and other elements of ancient structures revealing themselves. The fascination is how quickly nature has taken back these lands. To walk around what is a 600 plus room complex and seeing more scrub and faint traces is a wonder in its own right.

Yucca House is a great place to stop as a side trip to Mesa Verde. It is a quick 20-minute drive from Cortez, Colorado via Highway 160E. The park is not well marked, but can be found easily with GPS navigation apps on most smartphones.

CANYON OF THE ANCIENTS NATIONAL MONUMENT

Camping in Park:
- No developed campground, backcountry camping allowed with some limitations, see park website for details.

Getting There:
- From Cortez, CO: Take US-491 South turn right onto County Road G. Continue on Road G for about 14.4 miles. Total distance is 18 mi / 29 km to park entrance

The Canyons of the Ancients National Monument is unlike any other park set aside for the preservation of Ancestral Puebloan lands. It is in a very true sense an outdoor museum meant primarily to preserve the past. To date, more than 6,000-recorded sites have been discovered over the park's 176,056 acres (roughly half the size of Canyonlands National Park). The trails are more routes and even roads into the park are scarce. Many of the ruins in this park are not publicized.

To explore this monument, it is highly encouraged that the visitor first visits the Anasazi Heritage Center for orientation and current conditions. The center is located at 27501 Highway 184, Dolores, Colorado USA 81323, Phone: (970) 882-5600. Even before going to the center, it's a good idea to watch the video created by the park's stewards from the website link below.

Canyons of the Ancients is a very special place and any visit here carries with it a sense of responsibility for the visitor. One steward of the area stated it best; the only thing you can take is that which fills your heart. Enjoy the ruins with respect and ideally from a distance. Resist the urge to take a piece of pottery or a grinding stone home with you. Even resist the urge to move them for others to see. This is a sacred and spiritual area for many.

To get a much better idea of the park, take about 10 minutes to watch the below video by the stewards of this area. These are the words of the descendants of the people who lived here and are found on the park's home page. Besides giving a good idea of the landscape of some of the ruins in the area, their message is a strong one. Visit with respect. Take nothing. Say thank you when you leave. The video can be found here. www.youtube.com/watch?v=AvAuUeJoTIQ

Yucca House NM Entrance

[Everest, giving me a big hug]: Dad, I love you.

[Me, taken back by the moment]: Hey, son! I love you too! Glad to have you on this trip.

[Everest]: Yeah, me too. (Pauses) Can I have the iPad?

Hopi Prophecy

Despite completing a worthy family hike of Delicate Arch, there was a hardened silence in the RV. I drove, equally lost within my own thoughts through Arches NP back toward our campsite. The views were spectacular and surreal, but that didn't matter, they played for no one. Our minds were on something that had happened earlier on the trail. Bryce finally broke the silence, spilling his thoughts from beginning to end, without a pause.

"I just didn't understand those kids back at the hike. Dad, did you see those kids? I mean, you know, they were climbing on the petroglyphs. They littered, they went off the trail, they were trying to catch the lizards and feed the squirrels, it was like they did everything wrong. Don't their parents know it's not right to, you know, feed the animals and dump your trash on the trail and climb on the ruins? It's not cool! It's not right for everyone else. How are people in the future going to enjoy all this stuff if they let their stupid kids climb all over these ruins?"

He was nine and while a part of me realized he was simply parroting what we had taught him, I could not have been prouder. Toward the end of our hike, we had unwittingly paired up with what looked like a single mom and her two boys. The mom was heavyset and had trouble keeping up, even though we were on a flat stretch of ground. The kids, about 7 to 9 years old, were generally hellions. We watched in complete dissatisfaction as they climbed past the barriers to touch the petroglyphs near Wolf Ranch. While I hesitated whether to say something, Bryce didn't. "Hey, you aren't supposed to be climbing up there you know!" he shouted. The boys looked at Bryce and were about to mouth back but saw their mom, who belatedly echoed Bryce's sentiment. The mom looked at me with a harsh eye as she and her tribe passed us.

An older man was standing at the petroglyphs and overheard the whole thing, watching without speaking. He had a graying mane of hair, braided in the back, a weathered face that only sun and wind could sculpt, and clear, sharp eyes. He wiped a swig of water from his mouth as he approached us.

"That's a lot of Junior Ranger badges you have on your hat son," he said to Bryce. Bryce engaged shyly at first, but the man drew him in.

"Did you get all of those yourself"? he asked.

"Yep. I got the one for Bryce Canyon in one day," Bryce said.

Our whole family was now gathering to hear the conversation. "That's great! You know we need more rangers like yourself. You seem to know not to litter and go off trail. You are a good steward of the park. Maybe one day you will want to join us rangers."

"Are you a ranger?" Everest asked, surprised. He wasn't wearing a uniform.

The man chuckled, lighting up his whole face as if it was the sun itself smiling at you. "Yes, well, I am, but I'm off duty at the moment. I just came up here to study these petroglyphs. Any idea what these Ute petroglyphs mean, Bryce?"

"Um, they look to me like a hunting party. It looks like there are Indians on horses and they are hunting some deer."

"That's a pretty good read, Bryce. Have you seen Newspaper Rock yet?"

I interjected. "No, not yet, that's a great set of petroglyphs. We plan on seeing it on our way south. We haven't been to Needles yet."

"Good good. You should absolutely see them. It's worth the drive, if only to see the petroglyphs." The man was about to close the conversation and move on but he looked at Bryce, paused for a second and then stated, "Bryce, I like how you spoke up for yourself back there. These petroglyphs have been around for almost 400 years and this park is here to help make sure that they can be enjoyed by many who come after us. There is a saying, well not so much a saying but an ancient story, that humans will be asked to decide, to choose. There will be those who respect the land

175

and those that don't. Those that don't respect the land will find themselves wishing they had, as Mother Nature has a way of self-correcting if we don't."

I looked at the ranger inquisitively. "Are you talking about the Hopi Prophecy by chance?" I had studied creation and destruction myths in school and what he said sounded familiar.

He looked back at me with equal curiosity. "Yes, actually, I was. I kind of tone it down for folks, especially our Junior Rangers". He patted Bryce on the head lightly. "I don't want to say anything that parents might find offensive."

"On the contrary, if you are familiar with the story, I'm sure the boys would be open to listening to it. Boys?" I gave a quick nod in the direction of my sons.

Bryce looked up at the ranger and said with some seriousness, "Are you a Hopi Indian? I'd like to know the Hopi story. Sure!"

"Well, my young friend. No, I am not a Hopi Indian, my name is Ralph and I'm from Flagstaff. But I did live with them for some time, teaching at a school in a place called Seba Dalkai. I learned a few things while I was living there."

"The Hopis have passed down their beliefs from one generation to the next through telling the next generation. They did not write anything down. Some of their stories are pretty remarkable. They believe that the human race has lived through four worlds. In other words, there were three other times when we grew as a race and society. However, each time the humans could not find a way to live in harmony with the earth and as a result, Nature cleansed the earth of all but a few humans who started the next world.

"Are you talking about the flood and Noah's ark?" Everest asked.

"Well, yes, that was one reset that Mother Nature did. For the Hopi, it was the end of the third world and the beginning of the fourth world. It is kind of amazing actually, all of these stories are myths, right? It's hard to say whether they happened or not. The great flood is not only in the Bible, it is a story told by many cultures and tribes spread over nearly every continent. It's pretty amazing that this "myth" is so much a part of nearly every culture. It happened so long ago that it seems hard to believe that it might have actually happened."

"The Hopi believe we are in the Fourth World. They were given predictions to indicate when that world would end and the Fifth World would begin. One of the first signs was that they would encounter white-skinned men. Of course they did, but can you imagine the telling of this story up until that time? They had never seen white-skinned men before."

The ranger continued, "The signs included that the land would be crossed by snakes of iron. Any idea what that could be?"

"Big iron snakes"? Bryce asked.

"No", he said gently. "No, these were the trains."

"Oh yeah!" Bryce and Everest both nodded.

"How about this one. They predicted that the land would be crisscrossed by a giant spider's web. What do you think that is?"

Bryce shook his head.

"Those are the power and communication lines. They cross the deserts like the fine web of a spider, right?"

"Okay, see if you can guess this one. The land shall be crisscrossed with rivers of stone that make pictures in the sun."

"Are those the roads?" Everest asked.

Ralph pointed at Everest as if he had just won something. "My goodness! That's it! Roads. The rivers of stone. Well, these signs kept coming true and part of their oral tradition was that if enough of the signs started coming true, it was time to tell outsiders, folks that weren't Hopis, about the Hopi Prophecy."

"I learned a great deal from a person I met. His name was Thomas Banyacya. He was a Hopi shaman and he was the one who told me the prophecy. He and his people felt it was time to share the story with folks outside the Hopi people. This man shared it with me in the hopes that I could one day share it with others".

"What's a shaman?" Bryce asked.

Everest looked at me. "It's a medicine man. Right, Dad?'

"Not really", Ralph answered. "The Hopi themselves are a spiritual people and live in the northern corner of Arizona. They chose where they live to help them live humbly, to help them not get too distracted. They have remained their own people because they believe they are the people of balance, the people of peace. The word Hopi means, "People of Peace". The shaman is typically the spiritual leader of the people. I guess you could say the pastor at your church is your "shaman" in a way. Each Sunday, he is the person you go to listen for guidance and to ground you in your beliefs, a person you could go to maybe if you were having trouble spiritually."

"Shamans can also heal and are typically the best connected naturalists in an area. They know the land, the plants, and the animals better than anyone does. They know the plants that will heal and the plants that can harm you. For that, they get this term of medicine man, but in my mind they are much more."

"Wow, how did you meet this guy?" Bryce asked.

"Well, I met him on the Hopi reservation. It was a long time ago, in the 80s. Mr. Banyacya was one of the four elder leaders who were appointed to tell the story of the Hopi. He even drew me a map to the prophecy rock and I've actually seen it with my own eyes."

"Meeting with Mr. Banyacya was pretty much a highlight in my life. He was considered the Gandhi of the Hopi. He worked for most of his life promoting world peace. He was able to speak before the United Nations, but I saw him before this. He was chosen shortly after the atomic bombs were dropped in Japan along with three other leaders to spread the interpretations of the prophecy. Up until that time, the prophecy was kept secret and told orally from one generation to another. In 1948, there were enough predictions that came true for them to feel it was time to tell the prophecy."

"What happened in 1948?"

"We dropped the big one," Ev said glibly.

"They dropped the bomb in 1945, I thought," Ang said.

"Exactly. We dropped the bombs on Hiroshima and Nagasaki in 1945. I guess it took the Hopis a few years to decide it was really time to bring their prophecy to the outside world."

"So going back to the Prophecy Rock, the Hopi Prophecy is drawn on a large rock near Old Orabi. It is pretty amazing, the world's destiny on one rock in the middle of the desert, at least according to the Hopi."

"Is it like a bunch of words telling a story?" Bryce asked.

"No, it's a picture carved into the rock, pretty basic really. There are lots of details and I don't remember them all but it goes something like this. There are two paths. On one path, it shows a man supporting himself by two canes. This symbolizes that he has grown to be of a very old age. On this path, corn is growing. Since corn is difficult to grow in the desert, it symbolizes that this man is in touch with his environment, he has learned to live with it. He is in balance with his surroundings. The line this man is on continues around the rock to the other side, symbolizing this path goes on for a long time.

The other path shows three men. They look like they are squatting. There is a fourth person whose head and hands are detached from his body. This symbolizes that these people think too much, they have surrounded themselves so much with material comforts that they have lost touch with themselves. They connect more with what they see, touch, and taste and have lost their connection with their hearts and with what they feel. They have stopped listening to the world around them and instead listen only to the devices they've created and the thoughts in their own heads. The prophecy tells that we as a society will become immersed with our devices, with our things and that we will in the process forget our connection with the world as a whole. The line these people are on goes straight for a bit and then abruptly becomes a jagged zigzag line of sharp angles, ending after a short time."

Everest looked agasp with his eyes open. "That totally sounds like us! Are we the headless people?"

"It is pretty amazing how the prophecy turned out. We are a society completely disconnected from the beauty of a sunrise or admiring the simple grandness of a tree. We don't take time to watch clouds drift above us or watch a bug make its way across a leaf. We've forgotten how to talk to each other, to give even a simple nod; we've forgotten that a smile is a great default face to put on. We've forgotten how to be at rest with ourselves; we must always be doing something. We've plugged into things that, for the most part, tell us nothing of real importance. I mean, really nothing. Do you kids play on the computer?"

Bryce looked at me as if looking if it was okay to answer. We were guilty of allowing our children perhaps too much screen time. "Yes," he said finally.

Ralph asked, "What do you play?"

177

Hopi Prophecy Rock

"Minecraft mainly. Other video games," said Bryce.

"And YouTube," said Everest.

"What do you watch on YouTube?" Ralph asked.

"Mostly mindless stuff, movie parodies. I have to admit, you are right. It's not high quality stuff," Ev stated.

"You aren't alone. The entire country is staring down at their devices, and we disconnect even from ourselves. We lose focus after just a few minutes. We have a great deal of difficulty simply…being. We use these devices to occupy ourselves, to distance ourselves, from ourselves. How many times a week does someone bump into you because they were paying more attention to their devices than to where they were going? How many times have you done this yourself? The Hopis saw that coming long before we did."

Ev chimed in. "So we're doomed, right? I mean obviously we have chosen to embrace the iPad over growing corn in the desert. We are all waiting for the jagged end of times, is that it?"

"The Hopi prophecy does state that there is a choice. There are a couple of other pieces to the rock that I haven't mentioned yet. There are two circles and one-half circle. The two circles represent the first two World Wars. Without getting into too much detail, the oral traditions spelled out what would mark the wars, including use of planes in WWI and the use of the bomb in WWII.

The third half circle is called the "Mystery Egg." No one knows what will happen, but something will. That something depends on us. If we continue to be destructive, to live as if there will always be resources, if we are not mindful of the planet we live on, Nature will bring balance, but it won't be pretty. The earth will be purified. If enough humans are able to live with our hearts, Nature will still test us, because of the destruction we have already caused, but this test will in the end strengthen us."

"What kind of destruction will the Mystery Egg bring?" Bryce asked.

"There's a bit of unknown here and some tellers of the prophecy differ in their interpretation. One source said the second world shaking, the Second World War, would be recognized when man used the Hopi swastika in war, which the Nazis did. The third world shaking will be recognized by a red cover or cloak. What that means though is anyone's guess."

"Do you believe in the Hopi Prophecy?" Asked Ev.

Ralph paused for a second, glanced at Ang and then looked directly at Everest and Bryce. "I'm not sure it's something you need to believe in order to understand. The message is pretty beautiful. It simply says we should live in a mindful way, guided by our hearts rather than the Internet and TV ads. For me, it says to put down the machines we've made every now and then and simply go out and look at the stars. Once in your life watch the moonrise, it's a tremendous thing

to see. Go to the ocean and just listen to the waves, become lost in them, immerse yourself in the sound they make. Try to make it through a day being genuinely nice to everyone you meet. Listen to your own heartbeat, every now and then follow the patterns of your own breath, and remind yourself that you are alive! Find some solace without an iPad in your hand; relearn how to just be comfortable in your own skin. If people are singing, sing along with them. If people are dancing, join in. Live! This is the core of what the Hopi Prophecy is saying. Get along with your fellow human beings and live with great respect for the planet that we live on."

"That is what the Hopi Prophecy is saying, and do I believe? Well, we do seem to have lost our way. There is always some disaster or war or famine somewhere. Bees are dying, there's a huge globbish mass of floating plastic in the oceans, we've overfished the seas, the polar ice caps are melting at a phenomenal rate; yes, we have certainly messed things up. The Hopis foresaw the white man coming, saw them intruding on their lands. They foresaw the trains, the wagons, the electrical lines, the World Wars. Who's to say they aren't right about what's to come? It certainly is something to think about and acknowledge. Regardless of whether it's true or not, which path would you rather live on, the one that lasts a long time or the zigzag path"?

Both of my boys looked at me and said nothing. I smiled and stated the obvious. We all want to have a happy long life. After a bit more conversation, I thanked Ralph and we completed the walk back to the RV. From there, apart from some discussion from Bryce, we drove silently back to the campground lost in our encounter with Ralph and the disrespectful boys. After dinner, both Everest and Bryce talked quietly among themselves and then came over in unison.

"Hey, Dad." Everest said. "Would you like to take a walk outside, catch some stars or something"?

Bryce was just behind his brother looking up at me with his big eyes.

"Sure, boys. Can Mom come along too?"

"Sure!" the boys exclaimed in near unison. We turned off the lights to the RV, locked up and stepped out into the warm summer night. In this river valley, the cliff walls rose darkly on either side until they met the stars. We found a little beach of sand by the Colorado River and just sat with our flashlights off. We sat and we listened. We listened to the soft currents of the river mainly, to the night critters in the distant bushes, to the wind. We watched the dry desert clouds drift lazily, darkly, under the Milky Way. There was little said and little that needed to be said. In terms of moments I return to, when the stresses of life start to consume me and I need to escape for a moment, I return to this one often. I watch the clouds go silently by and listen to the soft strength of the Colorado. The moment was simple, it was understated and it was by far one of the most content and memorable events of our trip.

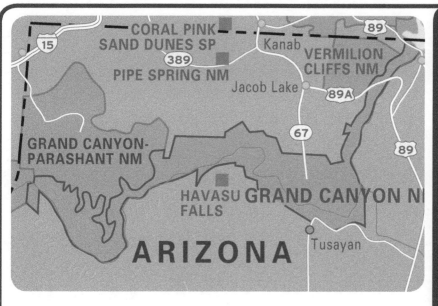

Quick Facts

Official Park Website: www.nps.gov/grca

Visitor Center: (928) 638-7888

Park Size: 1,217,262 acres

Established: 02/26/1919

Visitors: 4.8 million (2014)

Experience Level:

- Family Friendly to Backcountry Hiker

Park Accessibility:

- Okay for 2WD and RVs
- Day and Overnight Use

Nearest Town with Amenities:

- South Rim: Tusayan, AZ is less than 2 mi / 3 km from park

- North Rim: Jacob Lake, AZ is 44 mi / 71 km from park

Getting There:

- South Rim: From Mesa Verde NP, CO, take US-160 West, US-89 South, and AZ-64 West 280 mi / 451 km to south rim park entrance

- South Rim: From Zion NP, UT, take UT-9 East, US-89 South, and AZ-64 West 250 mi / 402 km to south rim park entrance

- North Rim: From Mesa Verde NP, CO, take US-160 West, AZ-98 West, US-89 South, US-89A North, and AZ-67 West 346 mi / 557 km to north rim park entrance

- North Rim: From Zion NP, UT, take UT-9 East, US-89 South, and AZ-67 West 122 mi / 196 km to north rim park entrance

Grand Canyon National Park

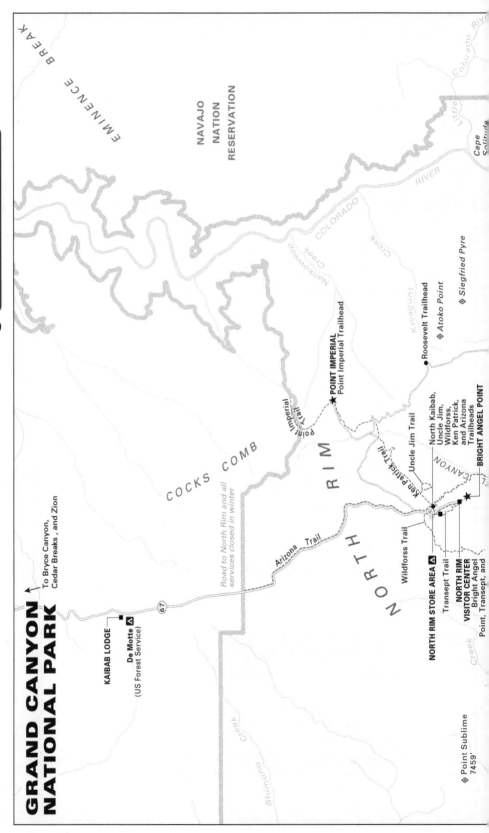

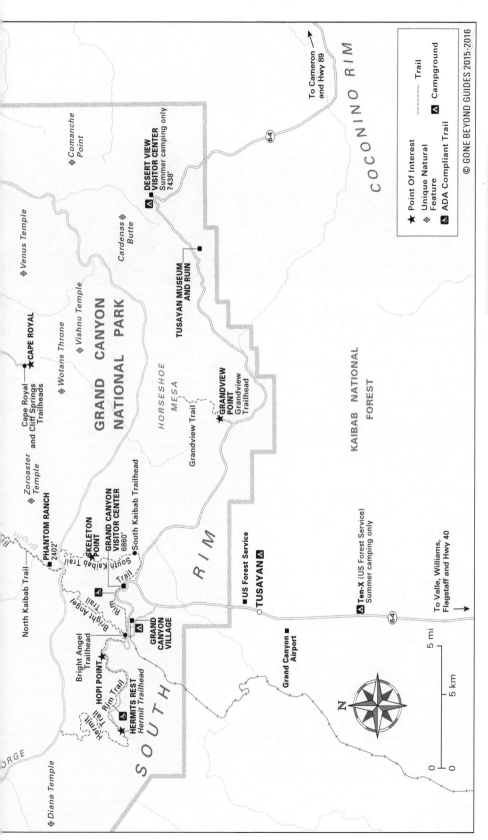

© GONE BEYOND GUIDES 2015-2016

Legend
- ★ Point Of Interest
- ◇ Unique Natural Feature
- ♿ ADA Compliant Trail
- ------- Trail
- △ Campground

To Cameron and Hwy 89

COCONINO RIM

64

△■ DESERT VIEW VISITOR CENTER
Summer camping only
7438'

■ TUSAYAN MUSEUM AND RUIN

◇ Comanche Point

◇ Venus Temple

◇ Cardenas Butte

●★ CAPE ROYAL

Cape Royal and Cliff Springs Trailheads

GRAND CANYON NATIONAL PARK

◇ Wotans Throne

◇ Vishnu Temple

HORSESHOE MESA

Grandview Trail

★ GRANDVIEW POINT
Grandview Trailhead

◇ Zoroaster Temple

■ PHANTOM RANCH
2402'

SKELETON POINT
6860'

GRAND CANYON VISITOR CENTER
● South Kaibab Trailhead

South Kaibab Trail

KAIBAB NATIONAL FOREST

North Kaibab Trail

Bright Angel Trail

Rim Trail

Bright Angel Trailhead

♿
△ GRAND CANYON VILLAGE

★ HOPI POINT

♿ HERMITS REST
Hermit Trail

Rim Trail

Hermit Trail

■ US Forest Service

△■ TUSAYAN

△ Ten-X (US Forest Service)
Summer camping only

■ Grand Canyon Airport

SOUTH RIM

◇ Diana Temple

GORGE

64

To Valle, Williams, Flagstaff and Hwy 40

N

0   5 mi
0   5 km

GRAND CANYON

Passing Storm in the Grand Canyon

WHAT MAKES GRAND CANYON SPECIAL

For many, the Grand Canyon is the pinnacle of natural beauty. It hides nothing, standing before the viewer in its humble magnificence. Each viewing brings a different experience, each play of shadow by passing cloud a different lighting. It is a masterpiece, some 17 million years in the making, one of the seven natural wonders of the world, up with the likes of Mount Everest and the Great Barrier Reef. It is one of the most recognized and most visited natural landscapes in the world.

What makes the Grand Canyon special is its non-boastful presence. It overwhelms the viewer but does not try. It amazes the eye and even soothes the soul simply by gazing at it, yet it has no mandate or imposition in approach. Each viewer can take in the Grand Canyon on his or her own terms, meet it wherever they are in their own life, and the view takes in all that baggage, weariness, and imposition and returns a warm sense of life. Considered a holy land by the original inhabitants of the area and a solemn bringer of peace by most that gaze upon it, the Grand Canyon simply is.

It is one of the few places that doesn't create an expectation to travel within it; one can gain much by simply viewing it, by scanning the horizon, peering down its canyon walls, watching the tiny thread of the Colorado and wonder as to how that little ribbon of water created all this. The Grand Canyon creates a sense of awe, an assertion of the divine, a wellness of being simply in gazing upon it. Whether during the heat of summer or the snowy accent of winter, whether from the light of sunset or the spot lit rays of sunshine pouring through the thunder clouds of a mid-day storm, each view gives comfort.

Think of the times in your life when you felt special. Those singular moments when everything went just so, that you risked the impossible and it actually worked in your favor. When you decided to do something not for yourself, but for someone else. You did that something even when it meant that only you would know of the benefit provided, an unconditional presence of selflessness. This is the Grand Canyon, providing inspiration and warm takeaways for 5 million visitors every year, giving of itself, inducing respectful wonder simply by its own manifestation. What makes the Grand Canyon special is that it gives; it gives openly, generously and without asking anything at all in return. You leave a better person having simply looked at it. There are few places in this world that can make this claim.

THINGS TO DO - SOUTH RIM

The plus for having so many visitors is the park can support a larger variety of programs. The Park Service does a very good job at catering to the broad range of visitors to the area, from casual tourists who are content to step out of their car and look over the edge to hardcore whitewater river rafters and from art enthusiasts to geocaching fans. There is something for just about everybody in the Grand Canyon. The below are a few of the highlighted activities.

RIVER RAFTING

Rafting down the Colorado is not only a popular activity, for many it is a bucket list item, something they have to do before they head on to the big national park in the sky. As a result, don't expect to show up and get on the river. Rafting is by permit only in the Grand Canyon and, depending on the activity, can take one to two years to receive a permit. The Park has made an effort to streamline the types of trips available and the permitting process for each.

That said, rafting down the Colorado through the Grand Canyon is truly a defining moment in anyone's life. It is an experience that moves beyond words, resets your definitions of awe and wonder, brings a restful peace to the soul and at times puts you in moments of unholy terror that—on getting to the other side of—help remind you just how awesome it is to be alive. It is worth the planning and the wait.

One Day Commercial River Trips:

Half day and full day smooth water river trips are available through park concessionaire Colorado River Discovery. You can purchase tickets at any of the park's lodges. The smooth water river trips are the only trips that do not require a permit and as the trip never encounters rapids, is open to all ages from four years old and up.

While these trips are gentle and without the excitement of white water, they are a great way to see the park and are highly recommended. Bring food and water, sunscreen, a hat and, of course, your camera. On a side note about the camera, yes, it's okay to bring a camera on the trip that isn't waterproof as it is unlikely you will get wet. That said, use caution. In the summer, you won't need a towel as in the heat of the day you will dry off pretty quickly. In the spring and cooler seasons, bring layers. As you will be entering at the Glen Canyon Dam, which is inside the protection of Homeland Security, you will be checked for weapons, including pepper spray and pocket knives. These will not be allowed, so don't bring them.

Transportation from the lodge to the Dam is included.

3- to 18-Day Commercial River Trips

For those who are looking for white water rapids and adventure, there are hosts of river concessioners that provide full service guided trips. Each company offers its own suite of trips and many cater to the different experiences visitors are looking for. Trips can last for as little as a few days to up to 18 days.

The upside of a guided trip is that, first and foremost, you don't need to become an expert in white water rafting. The domain of the rafter is a world unto itself. They have their own language, and while they are a friendly, tightly knitted group, it's an investment of time and money to enter their world and walk, err—paddle—among them. A guided trip comes with the security that you are riding down the Colorado with an expert at the helm.

Plus, the thoughts of where to camp, what to eat, and even where to do your business are pretty much taken care of for you. The downside is the cost and the fact that reservations need to be made one to two years in advance.

Details on what trips are offered, in what type of raft, duration and other amenities are numerous. The best place to start is the Grand Canyon NPS page, which lists all of the river concessionaires. Go to: http://www.nps.gov/grca/planyourvisit/river-concessioners.htm

2- to 5-Day Noncommercial River Trips

Permits are available to the general public starting one year in advance and are assigned on a first come, first served basis. Two noncommercial permits are authorized each day launching from Diamond Creek. Each trip is limited to a maximum of 16 people. There is no fee for the permits and they can be obtained by filling out a permit application and mailing it to the NPS permits department. While the NPS does not charge a fee for the permit, the Hualapai Tribe does charge a fee for crossing their land.

The permit can be found by going to: http://www.nps.gov/grca/planyourvisit/upload/Diamond_Creek_Application.pdf

You can also call directly: (800) 959-9164 or (928) 638-7843.

As mentioned above, you are crossing both National Park Service land and Hualapai tribal land. Hualapai means "people of the tall trees" in reference to the Ponderosa Pine. This small community of about 2,000 individuals primarily bases its economy on tourism. One way they do that is to charge a fee for each person (including drivers) and each vehicle traveling Diamond Creek Road, which they own. Cost is $64.20 for each person and vehicle, (example: 16 passengers, 2 drivers and 2 vehicles will cost $1284 total). Camping on the south side of the river (river left) above the high water mark will also require a permit from the Haulapai. More information can be had by calling the Haulapai directly at (928) 769-2219.

A Dory in Hance Rapid

The NPS permits authorize you and your group to travel for 2 to 5 days from Diamond Creek in the Lower Gorge of the Colorado River. This 52-mile (84 km) section is spectacular and includes both smooth water and some decent rapids to shoot as well as culturally significant areas. River users are asked to treat these cultural areas with respect so that future generations can enjoy them. Camping is limited but is free on the north side (river right).

One word of note: acceptance. The river has changed since the days of Powell. You will be sharing the river with many other users, especially at the launch and take-out areas. You will find motorized upstream and downstream travel from Lake Mead and even see a helicopter or two. There will be moments that are all yours, but there will also be moments that are shared with others.

Bright Angel Trail

12- to 25-Day Noncommercial River Trips

This type of self-guided river trip travels among the rugged section between Lees Ferry to Diamond Creek and is for those fully experienced in river rafting. The permits are made available through a weighted lottery. For more information, start here: http://www.nps.gov/grca/planyourvisit/overview-lees-ferry-diamond-ck.htm.

HIKING SOUTH RIM

There are many hiking trails within the South Rim of the Grand Canyon. Hikes range from pleasant to steep and all offer exceptional views. Exploring the canyon from the rim is a very nice way to enjoy the canyon's scenery if you are looking for a non-strenuous hike. Bright Angel Trail is much steeper but gets you down further into the canyon itself. Backpacking is also available via permit.

While you can go down to the river and back in one day, it is an all-day hike and is typically not recommended. The hike down and back up is often underestimated. At the rim, it is pleasantly cool and the distance perception is heavily skewed. Objects don't look that far away and look smaller than they really are. It is only when hikers get to the bottom of the river that they fully understand the enormity of the Grand Canyon. At the river's edge, it is often very hot, and while the water looks tempting, it could carry you away if you get in it, so it doesn't offer the reprieve you hoped to get. From the river's bottom, the rim is a never-ending uphill journey that you will

likely feel for a day or so afterwards. If you do go, start early and bring lots of water and pleasant little comfort foods and drinks to help you enjoy the journey.

RIM TRAIL

Easy – (13.0 mi / 21.0 km), one way, time varies on route taken, elev. Δ: 200 ft / 61m, trailhead at viewpoint at Grand Canyon Village and along Hermit Road

The Rim Trail is great for just strolling in the Grand Canyon with the view slowly changing before you. The trail starts at the South Kaibab Trailhead and extends to Hermit's Rest. It can be picked up from any overlook, and by utilizing the shuttle system one can pick up the trail and drop off it with a great deal of convenience. The trail is mostly paved and well traveled. For quieter moments, try walking it in tune to the sunrise or meander along its route in the late afternoon into dusk.

BRIGHT ANGEL TRAIL

Strenuous – (12.0 mi / 19.3 km to Plateau Point), round trip, allow 5-8 hours, elev. Δ: 3,039 ft / 926 m, trailhead west of Bright Angel Lodge

Strenuous – (17.6 mi / 28.3 km to Colorado River), round trip, allow 5-8 hours, elev. Δ: 4,888 ft / 1,490 m, trailhead west of Bright Angel Lodge

Bright Angel is a very well defined trail that ultimately leads to the Colorado River itself. While it is possible to do this in one day, as mentioned above, this is an all-day hike and not for the casual hiker. The thing to realize about Bright Angel is it is very inviting and gives wonderful views as you immerse yourself into the depths of the canyon. However, the trail is steep, which gives you the impression that you are "cooking with gas" as you travel downward. It is only on the return that you realize just how steep this trail is. Allow twice as much time for the return trip and bring twice as much water for this hot, exposed trail.

For groups with small children, going to the first switchback offers a good experience without subjecting little feet to the steeper bits just ahead. For those not looking to do a full 12-mile (19 km) hike, going to Indian Gardens offers great views and a nice stopping point before turning around. There is water to refill your canteen and even a ranger on duty most of the time. Indian Gardens is 9 miles (14.5 km) round trip. If you decide to go the 1.5 miles (2.4 km) farther to Plateau Point, you won't be disappointed. This fairly level trail takes you to a nice viewpoint of the Colorado River and surrounding canyon. This is a great spot to get a good understanding of the immensity, grandeur, and beauty of the Grand Canyon. You'll see how far you've traveled, and upon looking at the river below, you'll see how far you would still need to go, which is humbling.

SOUTH KAIBAB TRAIL

Strenuous – (6.0 mi / 9.7 km to Skeleton Point), round trip, allow 4 -5 hours, elev. Δ: 2,011 ft / 613 m, trailhead at Yaki Point off Desert View Drive

Strenuous – (12.0 mi / 19.3 km to Colorado River), round trip, allow 8 -10 hours, elev. Δ: 4,800 ft / 1,463 m,

From South Rim to Phantom Ranch: 6.9 mi / 11.1 km, to North Rim: 20.9 mi / 33.6 km

It is possible to take the South Kaibab Trail to the river and even connect over to Bright Angel, but most people do this as a multi-day trip due to the strenuous nature of the journey. Just like Bright Angel Trail, South Kaibab is steep, offers incredible views, and is very exposed. The first destination along the trail is Ooh-Aah Point, which offers an expansive view of the canyon and is less than 2 miles (3.2 km) round trip.

By the way, Ooh-Aah Point gets its name from an uncommon, nearly prehistoric language that is hotly debated by linguists as to its exact meaning. This is a rough translation, but most agree that "Ooh-Aah" means either "Wow!" or "The-Place-of-Amazing-Selfie-with-View-of-Grand-Canyon-About-One-Mile-From-Rim." You decide which translation works best for you.

There is a restroom at Cedar Ridge, but that is the extent of the facilities on the South Kaibab Trail. Cedar Ridge is about 1.5 miles (2.4 km) from the rim. Skeleton Point offers great views of the river and the surrounding area and is the recommended turnaround for day hikers.

On the question of South Kaibab versus Bright Angel, South Kaibab's fewer amenities means it is slightly less traveled than Bright Angel. That said there are very few hikers on these trails relative to the vast number of people looking over the canyon's edge at the rim. If you are looking to escape into your own personal experience of the canyon, either trail will get you there.

HERMIT TRAIL

Strenuous – (17.8 mi / 28.6 km to Colorado River), round trip, allow 8-12 hours, elev. Δ: 4,340 ft / 1,323 m, trailhead at Hermits Rest

The Hermit Trail begins at Hermit's Rest and, like all the trails described here, is accessed via shuttle. This trail is great for many reasons if you are an experienced hiker looking for something a little more rugged. It was originally built by horse thieves during the nineteenth century and is today considered a threshold trail, which means the National Park doesn't actively maintain it. There is water to be found along the trail, but it needs to be treated. Some of the trail has rutted out in areas and, in some cases, rock slides covering the trail require one to do a little scrambling to navigate around them.

South Kaibab Trail

The point here is, if you are an experienced hiker, the Hermit Trail offers just about everything, including an endpoint worthy of the journey. It is 8.9 miles (14 km) down to the river, but if you are able to make it, you are rewarded with Hermit Rapids, perhaps the strongest hydraulics and biggest waves of any set of rapids in the canyon. The Hermit Rapids help to motivate any hiker and do not disappoint. You hear them before you see them and in seeing them there is nothing but gushing awe and respect.

It cannot be overstated that this is a trail to be taken seriously. Plan—bring the right gear, including plenty of food and water, and start early if you do plan to take on this all-day hike. There is a primitive campground at the river's edge and most folks do this as an overnight trip.

GRANDVIEW TRAIL

Strenuous – (6.0 mi / 9.7 km to Horseshoe Mesa / Toilet Junction), round trip, allow 4-5 hours, elev. Δ: 2,500 ft / 762 m, trailhead at Grandview Point along Desert View Drive

Grandview is one of the quickest ways to get down into the canyon. It is very steep in some places and during the winter is dangerously icy. Crampons or some other means of traction for your footwear is required in winter. The trail offers deep views into the canyon as well as ruins of historic mining structures. Another feature of the trail is the placement of log "cribs" in some of the vertical sections of the Kaibab/Toroweap section. Many of these log supports were swept away during a landslide in the winter of 2005, but there are a few examples of these historical trail structures still around.

The Grandview Trail is not as well maintained as either Bright Angel or South Kaibab Trails. There are steep drop-offs in some areas. Use caution when hiking this trail.

MULE TRIPS

The mule rides offered by park concessionaire Xanterra are a classic way of seeing the Grand Canyon. The day trips offered change seasonally, and new offerings open up at the whim of the concessionaire. Most rides are typically 3-hour, 4-mile (6.4 km) rides. You don't need prior experience riding a mule, and your tour will include a fair amount of interesting interpretation about the geology and human history along the trail.

Overnight tours are also offered, and this ride is on par with rafting down the Colorado River in terms of generating incredible memories. You will ride your mule to Phantom Ranch located near the river. Lunch is provided and the steak dinner at the ranch is hearty and very welcome after the day's journey. As with the day trips, the overnight trips are full of interpretive narration on nearly all aspects of the park. The overnight trip to Phantom Ranch has been a high water mark for many visitors.

The downsides to the mule trips are the expense and the fact that you need to reserve the event well in advance. There is a wait list for day-before cancellations; however, the chances of people canceling are very slim. As of December 2016, it cost $551.62 for one person or $961.24 for two to ride a mule to Phantom Ranch and spend the night there.

Mule rides from the South Rim can be reserved through: Xanterra Parks & Resorts, (303) 297-2757, (888) 297-2757

VIRTUAL CACHING

For those who have never heard of this, virtual caching is the delightful marriage of treasure hunting and technology. Specifically, a "cache" is a term that denotes a bunch of stuff stowed somewhere in the wilderness. With virtual caching, a visitor uses his or her GPS system to find the cache. The reward is in part the journey and in part finding the cache, which— being virtual— means what you find is a cool location.

The National Park Service has done a wonderful job of offering an interesting way to explore the park.

You will need a GPS device (or smart phone with GPS), the park map, which is located inside the park's official newspaper, The Guide, and a copy of the instruction sheet, titled "Story of Grand Canyon." The instructions can be picked up at the Grand Canyon Visitor Center, where different coordinates are listed. Input the coordinates into your GPS device and take the shuttle or walk to the various destinations. None of the virtual caching is done off trail; everything can be found on the paved rim of the park and on the trails. Along the way, the instruction sheet acts as an educational pamphlet on different aspects of the park. Virtual caching is a cool way to discover new things about the park, and if you are navigationally challenged, perhaps a way of discovering a bit about yourself as well!

You will need to keep a record of all your coordinates, which will be necessary to solve the final clue. It takes about 4–6 hours to complete this puzzle, and the tour will take you over a good deal of the park along the way. You can, in the end, receive a certificate of completion. See the visitor center for more details.

Mule Parking

KOLB STUDIO

Art gallery, photo gallery, bookstore and place of historical interest run by the Grand Canyon Association. Near the Bright Angel Lodge

Kolb Studio

EL TOVAR HOTEL

Built in 1905, this hotel is on the National Register of Historic Places. It is noted for its Arts and Crafts as well as Mission style interior and exterior and is an incredible example of early twentieth century National Park lodge architecture.

YAVAPAI GEOLOGY MUSEUM

A great place to learn everything you wanted to know about the geology of the Grand Canyon. Many exhibits, three dimensional models and photographs along with the outdoor nature and geology "Trail of Time" where each meter traveled on the trail represents one million years of the geology of the Grand Canyon. If you think about it, the "Trail of Time" took about 2 billion years to make, so it is well worth seeing.

DESERT VIEW WATCHTOWER

Located on the East Rim of the park, the four story, 70-foot-high (21m) stone building was built in 1932 by Fred Harvey Architect Mary Colter. Mary Colter designed many of the buildings in the Grand Canyon, including Hopi House, Lookout Studio, Bright Angel Lodge, the Phantom Ranch buildings and Hermit's Rest (but not El Tovar Lodge). Patterned after the Pueblo kivas and watchtowers, the watchtower has a unique touch in its design.

SKYWALK

The Skywalk is managed by the Hualapai Tribe and is located on their tribal lands. It is a horseshoe-shaped walkway securely bolted into the canyon walls such that is juts out over the canyon itself. With the floors and sides made of glass, the structure juts out about 70 feet (21m) from the canyon rim, giving the feeling that you are suspended in air over the canyon. It is one of the most famous attractions within the western portion of the Grand Canyon. There is a separate fee for this attraction. Skywalk reservations: 1-888-868-9378 or 1-928-769-2636

DRIVING AROUND THE SOUTH RIM

Like Zion NP and Bryce NP, Grand Canyon receives too many visitors to make driving around the park practical. The NPS offers a fairly robust shuttle system to get you around, and it is not only highly recommended to use the shuttle system; it is the only method year round for some roads and during peak season for others.

In general, the shuttle system is divided into two loops, the Village Route and Kaibab Rim Route. The Village Route goes to the west and stops at Mather Campground, Trailer Village, Market Plaza, Grand Canyon Visitor Center, Shrine of the Ages, Train Depot, Bright Angel Lodge and Trailhead, and Maswik Lodge. The Village Route also stops at the Hermit's Rest Transfer, which is where you pick up the Hermit's Rest shuttle during peak season.

The Kaibab Route winds to the east and stops at the Grand Canyon Visitor Center, South Kaibab Trailhead, Yaki Point, Pipe Creek Vista, Mather Point and Yavapai Geology Museum.

You can drive on Hermit's Rest Road during the winter months and, to the east, the Desert View is a wonderful drive that ultimately takes you to the East Rim of the Grand Canyon.

THINGS TO DO - NORTH RIM

If forty is the new twenty, then the North Rim of the Grand Canyon is the new South Rim. It is harder to get to, not open year round and, as a result, it has an energy of peace, tranquility and overall slowness of pace.

Desert View Watchtower

The North Rim gets a mere 10 percent of the overall visitor traffic to the Grand Canyon, offering more chances to feel you have the park to yourself. On the South Rim, there are more amenities and it is open year-round; however, if you are going during peak season, the North Rim becomes an attractive option if you aren't prepared to share your experience with literally busloads of fellow visitors. It is the view less photographed, the road less traveled and the experience less shared, but it is still everything the Grand Canyon is known for, just from the other side of the river.

There are a couple of other things to know about the North Rim. It is at a higher elevation, ranging from 8,000 to 8,800 feet (2438 to 2682m). This is 1000 to 1800 feet higher than the South Rim. This means the weather will be cooler and the snow deeper, hence the closure of the park in winter. The other thing to note is there are fewer trails going into the canyon on the North Rim and the only one going to the river is longer and thus more strenuous because of the elevation gain.

HIKING NORTH RIM

BRIGHT ANGEL POINT TRAIL

Easy – (0.5 mi / 0.8 km), round trip, allow 30 minutes, elev. Δ: 200 ft / 61m, trailhead near visitor center

Bright Angel Point is a nice walk from Grand Canyon Lodge and nearby visitor center. There are examples of marine fossils within the rocks along the way. Be sure to pick a park brochure, which shows the location of the fossils and gives a good historical backstory of the lodge and this historic trail.

TRANSEPT TRAIL

Easy – (3.0 mi / 4.8 km), round trip, allow 1 - 2 hours, elev. Δ: 150 ft / 46 m, trailhead near North Rim Lodge

The Transept Trail starts at the Grand Canyon Lodge and follows the rim of the canyon to the North Rim Campground. Great views along the way.

KEN PATRICK TRAIL

Strenuous – (10.0 mi / 16.0 km), one way, 5 - 6 hours, elev. Δ: 600 ft / 183 m, trailhead north of visitor center at North Kaibab trailhead

The Ken Patrick Trail is named after a ranger killed in the line of duty. He is buried within the Grand Canyon, but worked at Point Reyes National Seashore and was killed by poachers in 1973.

This there and back trail is best accomplished with two cars. Starting from the North Kaibab Trailhead, the Ken Patrick Trail starts off clearly for the first 2 ½ miles but can become very difficult to find after reaching the Old Bright Angel Trail sign post. If you are an experienced hiker and this sounds appealing, simply keep north and

don't go too far from the rim. Once you pick up the Cape Royal Road, the trail becomes easier to find and maintains close to the rim all the way to Point Imperial.

UNCLE JIM TRAIL

Moderate – (5.0 mi / 8.0 km), round trip, allow 2 - 3 hours, elev. Δ: 100 ft / 30 m, trailhead north of visitor center at North Kaibab trailhead

This trail starts from the same parking lot as the North Kaibab Trailhead and meanders through the Kaibab Plateau forest to Uncle Jim's Point, which overlooks Bright Angel, Roaring Springs and an overall spectacular view of the canyon.

BRIDLE TRAIL

Easy – (1.2 mi / 2.0 km), one way, allow 1 hour, elev. Δ: 161 ft / 49m, trailheads at viewpoint at North Rim Lodge and at North Kaibab Trailhead

A gentle trail that parallels the road from the Grand Canyon Lodge to the North Kaibab Trailhead. The Bridle Trail is a great after dinner hike to take in the peace of the canyon.

NORTH KAIBAB TRAIL

Strenuous – (14.0 mi / 22.5 km), one way, allow 6-10 hours, elev. Δ: 5,780 ft / 1,762 m, trailhead north of visitor center at North Kaibab trailhead

Note that while the total distance to the river is shown, it does not include the distance back. This is because the total distance to the Colorado River and back is 28 miles and is definitely not recommended as a day hike. Folks do use the North Kaibab Trail as the starting point for a rim-to-rim hike, primarily because the trip for the longer leg of the two sides is downhill if you start on from the North Rim.

Lower Ribbon Falls

South of Point Imperial

The North Kaibab Trail is special because it is starts at a higher elevation than either South Kaibab or Bright Angel trails. The 1,000-foot increase in elevation is such that a hike down the North Kaibab Trail to the Colorado River means you will pass through every ecosystem found between Canada and Mexico. It is the least visited of the maintained trails and is also the most strenuous. It is definitely a serious day hike at 28 miles (45 km) round trip and is typically done as a backpacking trip. There are a few restroom facilities and seasonal water available, though the water will need to be treated.

The trail heads steeply down at first until it flattens out a bit as you enter into the base of Bright Angel Canyon. At 5.0 miles (8.0 km), you encounter Roaring Springs, which is a short side trip that is easily visible from the trail. Here you can see water coming directly out of the cliff, typically with a nice flow, creating a little island of moss and ferns within the desert. Roaring Springs flows into Bright Angel Creek as you continue down the trail. This is an important water source, delivering the drinking water for every visitor within Grand Canyon NP. If you make it to the Colorado River, you can see the pipe going over the river on the underside of Bright Angel Trail's Silver Bridge.

Just a little farther down at 5.4 miles (8.7 km) is a structure known as the Pumphouse Residence, or Aiken Residence. From 1973 to 2006, Bruce Aiken was an artist, NP employee, and pump master, overseeing the water supply for the park. He and his wife Mary raised three children at the canyon bottom and lucky hikers were greeted with lemonade from the children from time to time. Aiken's work reflects a fine-tuned harmony with the area of the Grand Canyon. Working mainly in oil, the light, balance, and overall portrayal of rock and water are testimonies to living within the Grand Canyon, raising a family and experiencing nearly each day of one's life for 33 years inside its walls.

Another treasure on the North Kaibab is Ribbon Falls at 8.5 miles (13.7 km). It is a little grotto in the desert cascading gently on the west side of Bright Angel Creek. It is a great place to get out of the heat of the day, which can be intense in the summer. Between the Cottonwood Campground and Bright Angel Campground, you enter the Inner Gorge, which is a narrow canyon of the 2 billion-year-old Vishnu Schist. If you make it this far, you are now walking among rock roughly half as old as the earth itself. You can connect to either the South Kaibab or Bright Angel Trail over the two bridges that cross the Colorado at the canyon bottom.

At this point you may be thinking North Kaibab is a gem of a trail, (which it is), and thus wondering if you could do a rim-to-rim adventure. The good news is you can. Trans Canyon Shuttle offers two rim-to-rim shuttles daily (go to http://www.trans-canyonshuttle.com for more info). The not-so-good news is getting reservations at one of the primitive campgrounds is a challenge. In addition, the shuttles depart early morning and early afternoon, so factor in an overnight stay at the opposing rim or hoofing it out to make the shuttle on the last day.

WIDFORSS TRAIL

Strenuous – (10.0 mi / 16.0 km), round trip allow 4 – 5 hours, elev. Δ: 400 ft / 122 m, trailhead north of visitor center west of North Kaibab trailhead

The Widforss Trail may just be the longest interpretative trail in the entire Grand Circle. Be sure to pick up a brochure at the trailhead. The trail hugs the canyon rim for the first half of the hike and then heads into a forested area to end at Widforss Point. The expansiveness of the Grand Canyon from this vista is impressive and it was a favorite of Gunnar Widforss, an early twentieth century landscape artist.

ARIZONA TRAIL

Strenuous – (12.6 mi / 20.3 km), one way, allow 5 - 6 hours, trailheads at North Kaibab trailhead and Kaibab National Forest boundary

The Arizona Trail is an 800-mile adventure that starts in Mexico and heads northward until it ends in Utah. A part of the trail leverages the existing north and south rim to rim trails of Grand Canyon NP. From the North Kaibab Trail, it continues through the park for another 10 miles before hitting the park's boundary. This portion roughly follows Highway 67, traveling through forest canopy and the Harvey Meadow.

POINT IMPERIAL TRAIL

Easy – (4.0 mi / 6.4 km), round trip, allow 1.5 - 2 hours, elev. Δ: negligible, trailhead at end of Point Imperial Road

This is an easy hike through an area recovering from a wildfire in 2000 and is great way to take in the tenacity of nature recovering from devastation. On the way, one will see young Aspens and innocent wildflowers starting anew from the aftermath of the fire. This is a great hike for a sunrise at Point Imperial.

ROOSEVELT POINT TRAIL

Easy – (0.2 mi / 0.3 km), round trip, allow 30 minutes, elev. Δ: negligible, trailhead at Cape Royal Road

More of a pleasant walk than a hike, this little ditty leads to a nice bench with great views of the canyon.

CAPE FINAL TRAIL

Easy – (4.0 mi / 6.4 km), round trip, allow 1.5 - 2 hours, elev. Δ: 150 ft / 46 m, trailhead at Cape Royal Road

An easy trail that ends at one of the higher elevation views of the Grand Canyon at Cape Final. As this trail is not often used, it provides good promise if you are looking for a secluded and peaceful hike. Cape Final is at 7,850 feet. Be careful if you decide to go onto the ledge's edge, it's a long way down.

CLIFF SPRINGS TRAIL

Easy – (1.0 mi / 1.6 km), round trip, allow 45 – 60 minutes, elev. Δ: 150 ft / 46 m, trailhead at end of Cape Royal Road

A refreshing hike through a wooded ravine to a rocky overhang containing a seeping spring. The water is not suitable for drinking directly as tempting as it may seem. The spring holds an ecosystem for ferns and moss and can provide some nice shade from the day's sun. Look for the remains of a granary from the original inhabitants of the area early into the hike.

CAPE ROYAL TRAIL

Easy – (0.6 mi / 1.0 km), round trip, allow 30 minutes, elev. Δ: 40 ft / 12 m, trailhead at end of Cape Royal Road

An easy, flat walk that allows views of Angels Window arch, the Colorado River, and if you look through the arch at the right angle, you can see both at the same time! Great photo opportunity and easy to access. There are interpretative markers along the way.

DRIVING AROUND THE NORTH RIM

There are two main drives from the visitor center and Grand Canyon Lodge that take you to canyon rim overlooks. The drives are very scenic and offer many pullouts to get out and explore the panorama of the canyon. Visiting both points can take half a day.

POINT IMPERIAL

(3 miles / 4.8 km)

Point Imperial is the highest point on the North Rim at 8,803 feet (2,683 meters). From this high vantage point you get an overview of the eastern end of the Grand Canyon, starting as the narrow walls of Marble Canyon and opening up profoundly into the Grand Canyon proper. The Painted Desert lies farther in the distance.

CAPE ROYAL

(15 miles / 24.1 km)

Cape Royal is arguably the most panoramic drive in the entire Grand Canyon. It offers views up and down the canyon as well as across, providing ample opportunities for amazing photos or simply breathtaking memories. It is a popular destination both at sunrise and at sunset for this reason. There is a natural arch known as Angels Window, where, from the right angle, one can see through the arch to the Colorado River itself. It is also possible to see the Desert View Watchtower on the South Rim.

Ewe in the canyon

El Tovar Hotel

GRAND CANYON LODGING

There are two main areas to stay within Grand Canyon National Park. The most accessible, with the most accommodations and amenities, is the South Rim, including Desert View. The South Rim is also the most popular, receiving nearly 90 percent of the park's 5 million annual visitors. The remaining 500,000 visitors head to the North Rim. Of the two, the South Rim is open year round and both offer the most lodging and camping options of any of the national parks described in this book, but is also the most visited.

SOUTH RIM LODGING

Within the South Rim of the Grand Canyon are six lodges, one ranch and three main camping destinations. If you are coming during the off-season, South Rim contains the only campgrounds and lodging that are open year round. Desert View and North Rim campgrounds close during the fall and winter months. All lodges and campgrounds book up so make sure you reserve far in advance, especially if you are vacationing during the summer months.

BRIGHT ANGEL LODGE

In terms of great views of the Grand Canyon right from your room, Bright Angel Lodge is a top pick. This is not a five star hotel, the rooms typically show wear from being constantly at capacity. However the staff are exceptional and the views are amazing. The lodge has something for every budget, from lodge rooms with a shared bathroom, private cabins and rooms and even

historic cabins. The two historic cabins, the Red Horse and Buckey O'Neill Cabin are double in price and are better suited for couples. The Bright Angel Lodge was designed by Southwest architect Mary Jane Colter in 1935 and has a warm rustic feel inside and out. Rooms are $88.51-226.45 per night with a charge of $9 per each extra person.

EL TOVAR HOTEL

This is the flagship of the entire set of lodges in the Grand Canyon and is arguably the best within the Grand Circle parks described. El Tovar opened its doors in January 1905 under the design of Charles Whittlesey, who was the Chief Architect for the Atchison, Topeka, and Santa Fe Railway. Unlike the rustic, grand, Arts and Craft designs of Stanley Gilbert Underwood, the inspirations for the El Tovar came from European decent, which gives the lodge a look reminiscent of a Swiss chalet. This was done intentionally to appeal to the vacationing elite of the era, who saw Europe and its culture as the reference for elegance. The hotel has seen all manner of the rich and famous, from President Theodore Roosevelt to Sir Paul McCartney. If you don't get a chance to stay in the El Tovar, definitely drop in to check it out. It a remarkable and historic place.

Rooms are in line with expectations with standard rooms starting at $226 for one double and $274 for one queen. For families needing two queen beds, set your sights and pocketbook on the deluxe rooms at $369. That said, if you are okay with spending three hundred dollars on a room, time to upsell you to the suite. You are staying at the El Tovar after all and if you get a suite, perhaps you will share the same room as a past famous dignitary. Many of the 78 rooms within this property are suites containing minor differences and ranging from $462 to $562. The suites offer more square footage, a sitting room and some have a private balcony. Extra persons for the standard and deluxe rooms only are $14.

191

Kachina Lodge

The Kachina Lodge has a much more contemporary feel than Bright Angel or El Tovar but also offers incredible views. The rooms are decent, basic and typically show some wear. Folks staying in this hotel need to check in at the El Tovar Hotel Front Desk. All rooms offer a king or two queens, plus your own bathroom. Street side rooms run at $235 while canyon rooms run $254 with a charge of $9 per each extra person.

Thunderbird Lodge

Similar to the Kachina Lodge in both form and function, the Thunderbird Lodge offers suitable clean basic rooms, some with spectacular views. The pricing structure is also equivalent to the Kachina Lodge. To check into the Thunderbird Lodge you need to head to the Bright Angel Lodge Front Desk.

Maswik Lodge

Maswik Lodge is a large 278 room complex set back from the canyon's edge. The overall design and architecture reflects the 1960's, which is when the facility was built. Maswik is a Hopi name for the kachina that guards all of the Grand Canyon. One thing the Maswik lodge does do is guard the family pocketbook.

South Rooms are an affordable $117 for two queens, with the North Rooms fetching $224. Extra persons are $9. Overall, the Maswik lodge gets consistently good reviews. Whether it's the price to value or the kachina Maswik helping to make for a pleasant stay, folks tend to leave satisfied.

Yavapai Lodge

The Yavapai Lodge is the largest of the lodges at 378 rooms separated into two wings of multistory structures. The best thing going for Yavapai Lodge is its proximity to the nearby Market Plaza, where a general store, deli, post office and bank can be found. It is also within walking distance of the Visitor Center and coin operated laundry. The lodge is a bit more pricey than the Maswik Lodge for this reason, with West rooms containing two queen beds coming in at $168. Extra persons are again $9 each.

Phantom Ranch

The Phantom Ranch accommodates in a manner unlike any of the other lodges or campgrounds. The ranch and the ranche's name was created from the mind of Mary Jane Colter in the 1920's. The cabins are rustic and look right out of a western movie set, built with a nice mixture of wood and native stones.

What makes the Phantom Ranch cabins special is the journey involved in getting to them. One cannot just pull up to the Phantom Ranch and roll the suitcases across the parking lot. The ranch is at the bottom of the Grand Canyon, so the only way to get to it is by mule, foot or via the Colorado River itself. For hikers there are dormitories separated by gender for $53 per night. For families, look into the complete trip combination which includes getting down to the ranch by mule, full meal options (including a steak dinner) and the cabin. Each cabin holds two people, so if you are traveling as a family, expect to reserve two cabins if you go this route. Full details on the ranch can be found here: www.grandcanyonlodges.com/lodging/phantom-ranch/

One thing to note on staying at the Phantom Ranch, you can't simply drop in and you can't announce you have extra folks out of the blue and expect them to get a place to stay. You need to reserve everything ahead of time and if you are hiking down, you need to let the ranch know you are on your way. This is one of the most popular things to do in the Grand Canyon, so plan accordingly.

Grand Canyon with clouds overhead

SOUTH RIM CAMPING

MATHER CAMPGROUND

Mather Campground is centrally located in the South Rim park area and is run by the National Park Service. There are 319 campsites available that accommodate RVs up to 30 feet. There are no hookups. If you have a larger RV or need hookups, head to Trailer Village.

Mather Campground is named for the national park's first director and is the largest campground in Grand Canyon. There is firewood for sale, there are laundry and shower facilities, and a dump and water station is available. Generators are allowed from 7 am to 9 am and again from 6 pm to 8 pm. Pine Loop is geared toward tent camping, so if you find yourself in Pine Loop, generators are not allowed. Quiet hours for the entire campground are from 10 pm to 6 am.

As in Zion NP, all sites are reservable and assigned. It is highly recommended you reserve your site prior to arriving. Reservations are taken up to six months in advance. You can stay at the campground for up to seven consecutive days and a total of 30 days per year, though if wanting to stay longer than that is a problem you are trying to solve, I'm envious! Check-in starts at noon, check-out is at 11 am. If the site is available, you can renew for another day after 9 am.

The park generally receives good marks from every aspect. It has hot showers for $2 and is close to nearby Market Plaza, which contains a cafeteria, delicatessen and grocery store. It is also close to the shuttle system, which has drop offs at every overlook in the South Rim short of Desert View. You can take the shuttle to the visitor center and Bright Angel Lodge.

TRAILER VILLAGE

Trailer Village is close to Mather Campground and about ½ mile (0.8 km) from the rim of the Grand Canyon. While it is located within the National Park, it is operated by the Xanterra concessionaire. Here you will find 80 pull-through, paved sites with full hookups. RVs up to 50 feet long can be accommodated. Each site has the usual picnic table, barbecue grill and 30 and 50-amp electrical service. You can also hook into cable TV, water and sewage if desired. The Trailer Village is open all year and starts at $49 a night. It shares the shower and laundry facility with Mather Campground at the Camper Services area, which is located farther from Trailer Village and closer to the Mather Campground. Besides this downside, the Trailer Village otherwise receives similar praise to that of Mather Campground. You are in the center of the park near the rim of the Grand Canyon. It will be difficult to not be pleased with your stay.

DESERT VIEW

The Desert View section of the park is about 25 miles (41 km) from the South Rim proper, tucked away to the east of the park. While it does get a little less traffic than the main South Rim, the Desert View Drive is typically included as part of the journey for many Grand Canyon visits. There are 50 sites available for tents and RVs up to 30 feet long. Unlike the Mather Campground, Desert View is offered on a first come, first served basis. The campground is closed by late fall and opens in the late spring, typically between October and May.

During the summer months, the campground is filled by early afternoon. The site does have a self-serve registration kiosk that accepts credit cards, though there is something kind of quaint about filling out those little campsite envelopes and having to find exact change for the $12-a-night fee.

There are bathrooms and water, but no dumping or water station, and no showers. The Desert View section has many of the same amenities as the South Rim, including its own visitor center, marketplace and Desert View Indian Watchtower, which is modeled after ancient Anasazi watchtowers and is a unique architectural feature within the park.

OTHER CAMPING

The nearby town of Tusayan has a couple of campgrounds. Ten-X Campground is open from May through September and is operated by the U.S. Forest Service. There are 70 sites available with 15 of them reservable through Recreation.gov. Fee is $10 per night. There is one group site that can be reserved for a party of 100 people.

Camper Village is commercially operated and is located about 7 miles (11 km) south of the Grand Canyon Village in Tusayan. It is open seasonally and offers hook-ups and coin-operated showers. The site offers a general store and convenient pizza; however, this should be considered as a place of last resort. It is consistently given bad reviews on the advisor sites. Call (928) 638-2887.

THE GRAND HOTEL AT THE GRAND CANYON

149 State Highway 64, PO Box 3319, Tusayan, AZ 86023, (928) 638-3333, grandcanyongrandhotel.com

The Grand Hotel has an impressive lobby that matches its names. The rooms are comfortable with big fluffy mattresses. A larger suite is also available. The indoor pool and hot tube are on the smaller side. Overall, a nice choice.

HOLIDAY INN EXPRESS GRAND CANYON

226 AZ-64, Grand Canyon Village, AZ 86023, (928) 638-3000, ihg.com

Another one of the Grand Canyon's mid-range hotels. The rooms at this Holiday Inn aren't as glamorous as some of the other similar hotels in the area, but they do have a huge indoor pool with massive panes of glass alongside a mural of the Grand Canyon. Their hot tub is also on the larger side.

GRAN CANYON PLAZA HOTEL

406 Canyon Plaza Ln, Grand Canyon Village, AZ 86023, (928) 638-2673, grandcanyonplaza.com

Recently refreshed, family operated, with a seasonal pool and Jacuzzi along with free Wi-Fi, hot tub and gift shop. This hotel accommodates large groups well.

BEST WESTERN PREMIERE GRAND CANYON SQUIRE INN

74 State Route 64, PO Box 130, Tusayan, AZ 86023, (928) 638-2681, www.bestwestern.com

Best Western offers a range of property types and their Premiere inns are a solid 3 star hotel. While there is no pool here, they do have a fitness center, hot tub, a fine dining restaurant, room service, laundry facilities, and free Wi-Fi. They also offer family rooms and suites along with standard rooms. Overall, a stay here is consistently pleasant and meets expectations.

Sunset from El Tovar

LODGING OUTSIDE THE SOUTH RIM

RED FEATHER LODGE

300 AZ-64, Grand Canyon Village, AZ 86023, (928) 638-2414, redfeatherlodge.com

Red Feather Lodge is a family owned and operated property and has been around for over 50 years. The rooms are basic but clean and they have a fairly decent sized pool with adjoining hot tub. While the rooms have been updated, a stay here is a bit nostalgic. They have kept just enough of the retro style ambiance to bring back memories of past family trips.

NORTH RIM LODGING

The North Rim receives much less traffic, is harder to get to and has limited seasons of operation. It is a mere 10 miles (16 km) from the South Rim as the raven flies but a 220-mile (354 km) journey to drive from rim to rim. Given that this side of the canyon gets closer to 500,000 visitors versus the 4.5 million on the South Rim, the pace is much more relaxed and steady. Getting to the North Rim is doable in an RV and can be a rewarding way to see the Grand Canyon. There is one main campground and one lodge on this side of the park. The North Rim of the Grand Canyon, including the campground, is not open year-round. They close for winter typically in October and reopen in mid-May.

Grand Canyon Lodge

The Grand Canyon Lodge was originally built from the design of Gilbert Stanley Underwood in 1927/28 but was severely burned in 1932 and rebuilt shortly after, though whether Underwood had a hand in the new design is under debate. It does carry a fair amount of Underwood's style. The lodge is located at Bright Angel Point and is typically an excellent alternative to the hustle and bustle happening at the South Rim.

For families, the best bet is staying in the Western Cabins, which offer two queen beds, full size bath and porch. Be sure to ask for the Rim View Cabins as opposed to the Standard Cabins. Another great option are the Pioneer Cabins, which were recently remodeled in 2009. These cabins offer two rooms with bunk beds or twin beds in one room and a queen sized bed in the other room.

North Rim Camping

North Rim Campground

There are 74 standard sites available for RVs and tents plus several more for tent only and group sites. There are no hookups, but there is a water and dump station at the campground. Firewood is available for sale at the nearby General Store.

As the campground is run by the National Park Service, many of the same rules apply as they do in the South Rim. Generators are allowed from 7 am to 9 am and again from 6 pm to 8 pm. Quiet hours for the entire campground are from 10 pm to 6 am. All sites are reservable and assigned. It is highly recommended that you reserve your site prior to arriving. Reservations are taken up to six months in advance. You can stay at the campground for up to seven consecutive days and a total of 30 days per year. Check-in starts at noon, check-out is at 11 am. If the site is available, you can renew for another day after 9 am. There are laundry and shower facilities as well as change machines nearby.

GRAND CANYON DINING

DINING INSIDE THE PARK

There are many choices within the park, including options for sit down dining, grocery markets, casual cafes, snack bars , lounges, and places to grab food to go. On the south rim, these are open year round. On the north rim, all food services (and lodging) are closed in the winter. For a full list of dining options within the park, go here: www.nps.gov/grca/planyourvisit/restaurants.htm. The options are too numerous to list in full, but a few are described that truly stand out.

SOUTH RIM DINING

El Tovar Dining Room

AMERICAN, meals for under $30, Village Loop Dr, Grand Canyon, AZ 86023, (928) 638-2631, open daily for breakfast, 6:30am–10:30am, lunch from 11am–2pm, and dinner from 4:30pm–10pm

The South Rim's El Tovar dining room and the lodge first opened in 1905 as a place to be for those traveling to the Grand Canyon. Today the dining room's timeless architecture is still just as magnificent. The service and food are consistently exceptional, making this one of the top dining destinations within the Grand Circle. This is a world class dining experience at the edge of the Grand Canyon.

Phantom Ranch Canteen

AMERICAN, meals for under $30, North Kaibab Trail, Grand Canyon National Park, AZ, (888) 297-2757, www.grandcanyonlodges.com/dining/phantom-ranch-canteen, open seasonally, specific seating times

This is one of the most unique dining experiences in the Grand Canyon. For those adventurous enough, you can dine at the bottom of the canyon. Whether you are camping overnight or doing a rim to rim hike, Phantom Ranch will be a welcome rest stop and place to fill up before moving on. They serve breakfast and dinner only and there are specific seating times for meals (so don't be late, they will close the doors during the service). Reservations are absolutely required, walk in service is not an option here.

Grand Canyon View from the North Rim

Colorado River

North Rim Dining

Grand Canyon Lodge Dining Room

AMERICAN, meals for under $30, North Rim, Grand Canyon National Park, AZ, (928) 638-2611, www.grandcanyonforever.com/dining, open seasonally, 6:30am - 9:30pm, (closed in winter)

From the dining room to the food, the dining room at the Grand Canyon Lodge is simply amazing. The architecture is big and bold, with great viewing opportunities. The service is awesome and the food is delicious as well. Dining here is a truly great experience. Hours vary and reservations recommended.

Dining Outside the Park

We Cook Pizza And Pasta

PIZZA AND PASTA, meals for under $20, 605 N State Rt 64, Tusayan, AZ 86023, (928) 638-2278 open daily, 11am - 9pm

Quick service, fresh salad bar, and the usual assortment of pizza and pasta offerings.

Yippee-ei-o! Steakhouse

AMERICAN, meals for under $30, 541 AZ-64, Grand Canyon, Tusayan, AZ 86023, (928) 638-2780, open daily, 11am - 10pm

Like many of the restaurants near the Grand Canyon Village, Yippee-ei-o! is a touristy, jam packed, get 'em in, get 'em out, order and don't complain, kinda place. I'm sure somewhere, some owner really wants to provide a better experience, but there are just so many darn tourists. All of these establishments do try their best, but the volume of people makes it hard to create a personal experience for everyone. There are exceptions though. If you go really early, especially for dinner, say 4:30 - 5:30, you get a fresh staff and not as many people. I have had some good experiences here, combined with many more where you just feel like a part of the tourist herd.

Big E Steakhouse & Saloon

AMERICAN, meals for under $30, 395 Hwy 64, Grand Canyon, AZ 86023, (928) 638-0333, bigesteakhouse.com, open daily, 11am - 9pm

The food at Big E is hearty, hot and tasty, with lots of choices. The ambiance is fun and definitely adds to the feeling you are on vacation. Big E is a good choice overall.

Plaza Bonita

MEXICAN, meals for under $20, 352 State Rd 64, Grand Canyon, AZ 86023, (928) 638-8900, open daily, 7am - 10pm

Plaza Bonita offers a good selection within the genre of Mexican cuisine. The atmosphere is done nicely in a southwest style and prices are reasonable.

The Canyon Star Restaurant and Saloon

STEAKHOUSE, meals for under $30, 149 State Rt 64, Grand Canyon, AZ 86023, (928) 638-3333, grandcanyongrandhotel.com, open daily, 2pm - 11pm

Be prepared for long wait times during the long busy season. Once seated, the food is very good. They serve up a large selection of menu items and there should be something for everyone. The ambiance is warm and bright. Overall a good place to get a late lunch or dinner.

The Coronado Room

AMERICAN, meals for under $30, 74 Hwy 64, Tusayan, AZ 86023, (928) 638-2681, grandcanyonsquire.com, open daily, 5pm - 10pm

Part of the Best Western Premier Squire Inn, The Coronado Room offers a fine dining experience. They have a wide selection of starters, soups, salads, entrees, and deserts. It's a bit pricey for the overall experience.

☕ COFFEE AND SWEETS! ☕

BRIGHT ANGEL FOUNTAIN

ICE CREAM, Rim side of Bright Angel Lodge, Grand Canyon, AZ 86023, (928) 638-2631, daily 6:30am - 10pm

The Fountain at Bright Angel is a place to get ice cream right at the edge of the Grand Canyon and the portions are generous. The downsides are long lines, poor inventory control (they keep running out of the most popular flavors) and they serve the same stuff you could buy at a store. Still, there is something very cool in being handed your own cone and getting to sit and take in the view of the Grand Canyon.

RP's STAGE STOP

COFFEE, SANDWICHES, 400 Hwy 64, Grand Canyon, AZ 86023, (928) 638-3115, rpsstagestop.com, open daily, 6:30am - 5pm

RP's offers espresso drinks along with sandwiches, salads, hot dogs and smoothies. The sandwiches are top notch and the coffee is good. They also have a solid breakfast menu.

GRAND CANYON HISTORY

From 2 billion years ago to about 11,000 years ago, the history of the Grand Canyon was almost exclusively geological in nature. First evidence of humans in the Grand Canyon dates back 10,500 years. The ancestral Pueblo people followed similar patterns described within all of the Grand Circle national parks, arriving as nomadic hunter-gatherers and shifting over to agriculturally based complex societies over the span of thousands of years. They were thought to have lived in the Grand Canyon National Park area up to 4,000 years ago.

Unique to the northern Arizona region were the Cohonina people, which is where Arizona's Coconino County gets its name. The Cohonina inhabited the areas west of the San Francisco Peaks near Flagstaff, east of the Aubrey Cliffs and south of the Grand Canyon. While they lived during the same period as the early Pueblo people (between 500 and 1200 CE), they exhibited distinctions in their society, mostly in their form of pottery. The pottery of the Cohonina was constructed using a paddle-and-anvil technique, which is a simple but very effective method for producing highly consistent and well-made pieces.

The method starts with a disk of clay and pounding on the clay with a paddle using a curved shaped piece of wood (the anvil) to provide resistance from the inside of the pot. The ceramist works her way around in a circle, paddling the clay into thin walls. The final shapes are decorated with black and gray illustrations.

The first European to see the Grand Canyon was Francisco Vásquez de Coronado. Coronado and his soldiers had set out to find the mythical Seven Cities of Gold. By the time they reached the Arizona-New Mexico state lines, their supplies were heavily depleted. They found both Zuni and Hopi villages and, after being refused entry by both tribes, forced their way in to replenish themselves. During the Zuni siege, Coronado himself was wounded. During the Hopi siege, they learned of and had Hopi scouts show them the Grand Canyon. The main purpose of visiting the canyon was the Colorado River, which they had hoped would provide a means of traveling back to the coast. The Grand Canyon proved too much for Coronado and his crew as they failed to find a route down to its shores. As a result, they were forced to turn back and head down the Rio Grande.

The Grand Canyon didn't receive another European tourist for 200 years until the two Franciscan priests who visited the Waterpocket Fold of Capitol Reef visited the canyon in 1776. Francisco Atanasio Domínguez and Silvestre Vélez de Escalante visited the canyon

Paiute Chief Tau-Gu with John Wesley Powell

along the north rim. There was one other Franciscan missionary by the name of Francisco Garcés who also visited during this time frame. Garcés was as much an explorer as he was a missionary and explored much of the Southwest region of North America, including Baja California, Arizona and Southern California. His demeanor allowed him to establish peaceful relations with many of the tribes, including the Zuni and Hopi. He not only paid a visit to the Grand Canyon but also is credited with giving the Colorado River its name.

North Kaibab Trail

Powell selected nine men and on May 24, 1869 set out from Green River Station in Wyoming down the Colorado River. Their first expedition was done on a shoestring budget but was still able to bring back much of the first scientific examination of the canyon. In the Canyon of Lodore, one of the four boats capsized, spilling most of the crew's food rations and even some of their scientific equipment, which subsequently shortened their expedition to one hundred days. The expedition was filled with much hardship and raw adventure, including constantly being cold, wet and hungry. Three men of Powell's crew finally decided to turn back and exited the canyon only to be killed by a band of Paiutes.

While the first expedition was rife with danger and lacked resources, Powell brought back enough to whet the appetites of both the scientific community and the nation. He returned two years later with redesigned boats, a chain of supply stations along the route and better funding. Hugely lacking in the first expedition, this second one had a photographer and multiple artists. Nationally acclaimed naturalist painter Thomas Moran joined the expedition in the summer of 1873, offering his artistically soothing works to the growing collection of pictorial artifacts. His "Chasm of the Colorado" hung in the lobby of the Senate in 1874 and now hangs in the Smithsonian American Art Museum.

Powell's work brought focus to the entire Canyonlands regions of the Southwest, with the Grand Canyon being the crown jewel. He gave lectures and became a national figure as Americans looked at the pictures and illustrations of the Grand Canyon in amazement. No one had ever seen anything quite like it before. After pauses of hundreds of years between scant visitations, the knowledge of the Grand Canyon was out.

Although Powell brought the Grand Canyon to the nation's attention, it was not immediately brought into the National Park's fold. There was a bill brought forth by U.S. Senator Benjamin Harrison to declare the area a national park in 1887; however, it was never passed.

There are a handful of trappers who were credited with having visited the Grand Canyon in the mid- to late 1800s, but it was the expedition of U.S. Army Major John Wesley Powell who would put the canyon on the national map as a profound place of wonder. The U.S. War Department had sent Lt. Joseph Ives to the area a decade prior to Powell's expedition to investigate the area's natural resources and find a suitable railroad route to the West Coast. Ives' group took a steamboat named the Explorer up the Colorado River from the Gulf of California. The journey took two months and, as can be imagined, was a difficult journey. They traveled some 350 miles (560km) before reaching Black Canyon, striking a rock and being forced to abandon the ship.

Ives declared the canyon "altogether valueless" and was certain that he would be among "the last party of whites to visit this profitless locality." Ives' geologist John Strong Newberry, on the other hand, was awestruck by the canyon's beauty and, after a ten year pause, convinced both the Smithsonian Institution and Powell to take a boat down the river in the Grand Canyon. Powell's expedition became the stuff of legends.

Hermit Trai

After he became president of the United States, Harrison declared the Grand Canyon to be a National Forest Preserve in 1893. There had been amplified interest in the hopes the area could be mined for lead, asbestos, copper, uranium and zinc in the 1870s and 1880s and while nearly all of the claims proved unprofitable for mining, the number of mining claims tarnished a clean ability to turn the land over to the National Park Service. While the National Forest Preserve status still allowed mining and logging, it paved the way for further protection.

This tee up by Harrison proved to be useful when President Theodore Roosevelt visited the Grand Canyon in 1903. Roosevelt was very passionate about the conservation of the natural gems of the United States and in 1906 established the Grand Canyon Game Preserve. He then added adjacent national forest lands, and on January 11, 1908 re-designated the preserve a U.S. National Monument. This move further protected the area from mining, logging, and cattle grazing in and around the Grand Canyon.

For 11 years, landholders in the area blocked the Grand Canyon from being a National Park, but the National Monument status opened the doors to tourism. Stagecoaches had been offering tours to the Grand Canyon from Flagstaff as early as 1882. By 1901, a rail line had been built to the Grand Canyon Village from Williams, Arizona. This rail line is still in use today and carries the popular Polar Express tours. Back in 1901, the 64-mile (103 km) trip cost $3.95. By 1902 the first car made it the Grand Canyon and while train was the most approachable means of travel to the canyon until the mid-1930s, the ability of travel by either train or car helped expose the merits of the Grand Canyon as a tourist destination over a mining area. On February 26, 1919, President Woodrow Wilson signed the Grand Canyon into law as the 17th national park. That year it received 44,173 visitors. Today, the Grand Canyon is one of the most popular destinations in the United States and is a required destination for travelers both home and abroad at least once in their lives. As a result, Grand Canyon NP receives nearly 5 million visitors each year.

GRAND CANYON GEOLOGY

If you've followed the route in this book, the Grand Canyon is the last in a long and hopefully worthwhile journey of seven of the best national parks in the United States. You've been on the Colorado Plateau the entire time and, geologically, the same rules apply within the Grand Canyon as they do for the other parks. Sediments were set down through various geologic events, they turned to layers of rock, the Colorado Plateau lifted up these layers just a little while back, and in a geologic blink of an eye, the Grand Canyon was formed.

There are some amazing distinctions that really set the Grand Canyon apart, however. One of the most amazing aspects is that the Colorado River is currently cutting through rocks that are 2 billion years old and are thus among the oldest visible rocks in the world. Let's put this into perspective. The earth was formed 4.5 billion years ago and this strata layer, the so-called Vishnu Basement Rocks, are the oldest rocks in the Grand Canyon and yet are less than half the age of the planet itself. If you average that out among the Grand Canyon's

199

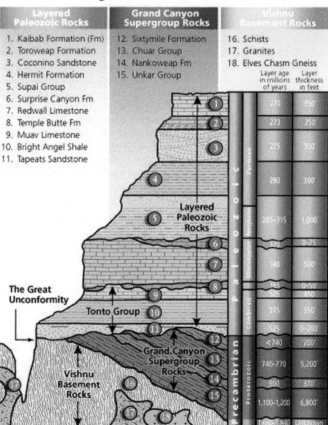

Grand Canyon's Three Sets of Rocks

Layered Paleozoic Rocks	Grand Canyon Supergroup Rocks	Vishnu Basement Rocks
1. Kaibab Formation (Fm)	12. Sixtymile Formation	16. Schists
2. Toroweap Formation	13. Chuar Group	17. Granites
3. Coconino Sandstone	14. Nankoweap Fm	18. Elves Chasm Gneiss
4. Hermit Formation	15. Unkar Group	
5. Supai Group		
6. Surprise Canyon Fm		
7. Redwall Limestone		
8. Temple Butte Fm		
9. Muav Limestone		
10. Bright Angel Shale		
11. Tapeats Sandstone		

Stratigraphy of the Grand Canyon

depth of 6,000 feet, every inch down is like stepping back 27,000 years in time. While this is a bit misleading since the rocks don't literally get older in a straight-line fashion, it is still a mind-boggling way to ponder just how old these rocks are.

What is perhaps more amazing is the short amount of time it took to form the Grand Canyon relative to the earth's overall presence. Again, the earth is about 4.5 billion years old. Most theories put the start of the Colorado Plateau uplift at a mere 17 million years ago and the formation of the Grand Canyon itself around 6 million years ago. If we compare this to a human life span of 70 years, the Grand Canyon would have formed during the last month of that person's life.

So why the Grand Canyon? Why did the river cut so deeply that it is over a mile in depth and yet so passionately that the younger rock layers found in Zion and Bryce are all washed away? Theories on all of this differ, and as the Grand Canyon is a geologist's dream come true, each theory is hotly debated. The theory most generally agreed upon is that the rock layers encourage erosion, and when it rains here, it really rains. Since the rocks don't absorb water well, when they were hit with the torrential downpours that hit the area, water was left to do what water does, erode solid rock. In the winters, ice would do its erosional duties as well, freezing and expanding in between rock crevices, breaking apart rock layers with tremendous forces.

The final piece of this theory is the Colorado River itself. While it is considered the principal river for the American Southwest even today, during the late Pleistocene era, when all that locked-up glacier water melted, the river flowed like nothing you can begin to imagine. It provided a conveyer for all that sediment getting washed down from above, pushing the entire canyon full of rock and soil downstream. Without the help of the Colorado River, none of this would have happened. It is, in fact, what makes the Grand Canyon so amazing. It isn't what is there that gives the full picture of tremendous grandeur, it is what isn't there. The Canyon was once solid layers of rock,

unencumbered and silent, untouched and buried. The Colorado River helped remove all that space between those layers to create the canyons before you by removing all those unimaginable square feet of rock and taking it somewhere else.

As to the real geology of the Grand Canyon, the geologist's geology, it is well written in many books, online references and the park's several visitor centers. As the center story of the Grand Canyon, the different layers can become quite complex. That said, it is helpful to look at the three main rock groups.

We've already described the Vishnu Basement Rocks, which are also known as the Vishnu Complex. This rock layer is 2 billion years old and is at the bottom of the Grand Canyon. Jumping up to the rim of the canyon, the Kaibab Limestone layer is a mere 230 million years old and is the youngest of the rock layers and the first of the top layer known as the Layered Paleozoic Rocks. This section stratifies down to layers that are around 500 million years old. The layer in the middle is referred to as the Grand Canyon Supergroup rocks and ranges in age from 740 million years to about 1.2 billion years old. There is a gap here between the oldest and lowest section and the one above it of about a billion years. This is referred to as the Great Unconformity and indicates a period of erosion between two periods of deposition.

The great depth of the Grand Canyon was aided not only by the rather rapid uplift of the Colorado Plateau, which allowed for a steeper cut of the Colorado River and its tributaries, but also by the Gulf of California. It is thought that the Gulf of California opened about 5.3 million years ago, which lowered the river's base level, or lowest point. This in turn increased the rate of erosion and cut most of the Grand Canyon to its current depth within a short 4 million years. Similar to digging down at the end of a little stream to allow the water to run out faster, the water picks up speed and takes more debris with it. This was apparently done on the grand scale of a major river. All of this is hotly debated, of course.

View of Ancestral Granary from Nankoweap Creek

Sunrise at Cottonwood Cove in the Vermilion Cliffs

Parks Near the Grand Canyon

MONUMENT VALLEY NAVAJO TRIBAL PARK

Camping in Park:

- The View Campground: 90 T/RV, no water, no hookups, restrooms, shower, reservations: (435) 727-5802

Lodging in Park:

- The View Lodge, reservations: (435) 727-5555

Getting There:

- From Moab, UT: take US-191 South to Olja-to-Monument Valley

- From Cortez, CO: take UT-162 West and US-163 South to Oljato-Monument Valley

If you have ever watched the classic movie Stagecoach, one of the top westerns of all time, you will notice one thing. No matter where that stagecoach is heading, they are always passing through Monument Valley. The movie was John Wayne's breakthrough role and arguably put Monument Valley on the map for America. From 1939, when the movie was made, to present, Monument Valley has become THE definitive icon of the Southwest.

The problem with any icon is it tends to become larger than reality itself and we are let down when we finally meet it. The good news with Monument Valley is it will not disappoint in this way. It is as sweeping and epic in real life as it is on film. It is a place where time seems to slow down and watching the late afternoon sun slowly slip off the monuments is a memory that will stick with you for life.

Monument Valley is easy to drive through, but to capture the impact of this area it is recommended to stay overnight. The campground set up by the Navajo Tribal Park offers some of the best viewing real estate in the park. The campsites sit on a sandy hill overlooking many of the most recognized monuments, including the Mittens. The View Hotel nearby is also recommended. The famed Goulding's Lodge is another favorite place to stay and was home for the cast and crew of the movie Stagecoach and other westerns.

In terms of hiking, the land is privately owned and actively used by the Navajo. The Wildcat Trail is the only hike that a visitor can take without a Navajo escort in the park. The trail is a 3.2-mile loop that goes completely around the West Mitten. The trail starts at The View Hotel and once down in the valley is fairly flat. Allow 2 – 3 hours to complete this hike and bring water.

There is also a 17-mile scenic drive on a maintained unpaved road, which is highly recommended. The drive is suitable for most cars and is open for day use only. If you are looking for more immersion, you can take a guided tour. These tours are really the only way to see some of the places within the park. All of the official tour operators are listed here: www.navajonationparks.org/htm/monumentvalleytours.htm

West Mitten Butte, Monument Valley

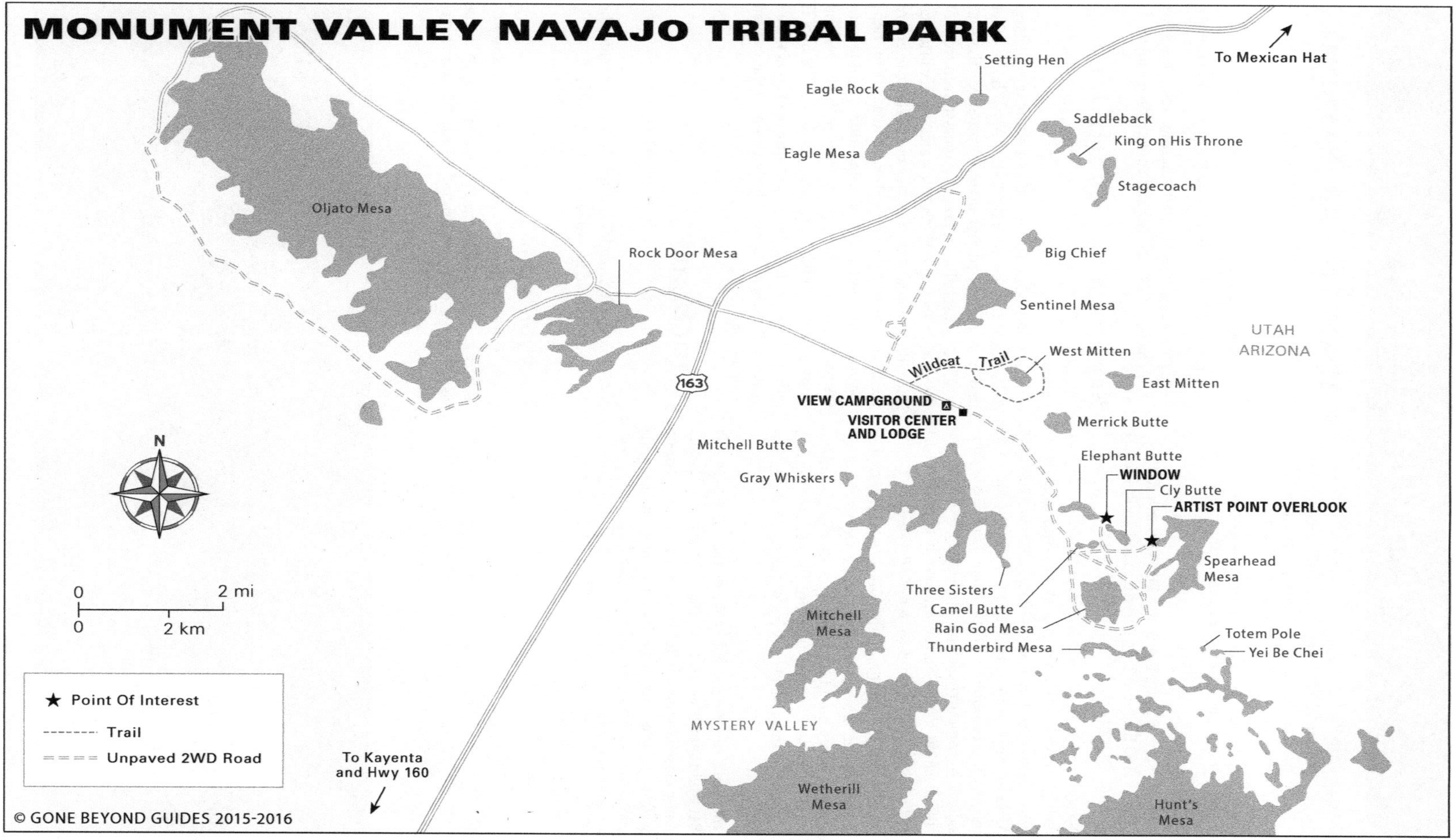

MONUMENT VALLEY NAVAJO TRIBAL PARK

To Mexican Hat

UTAH
ARIZONA

Setting Hen

Saddleback

King on His Throne

Stagecoach

Big Chief

Sentinel Mesa

West Mitten

East Mitten

Merrick Butte

Elephant Butte

Cly Butte

WINDOW

ARTIST POINT OVERLOOK

Spearhead Mesa

Totem Pole

Yei Be Chei

Hunt's Mesa

Camel Butte

Three Sisters

Rain God Mesa

Thunderbird Mesa

Eagle Rock

Eagle Mesa

Wildcat Trail

VIEW CAMPGROUND

VISITOR CENTER AND LODGE

Gray Whiskers

Mitchell Butte

Mitchell Mesa

Wetherill Mesa

MYSTERY VALLEY

Rock Door Mesa

163

Oljato Mesa

To Kayenta
and Hwy 160

N

0   2 mi
0   2 km

★ Point Of Interest

-------- Trail

= = = Unpaved 2WD Road

© GONE BEYOND GUIDES 2015-2016

203

Parks Near Grand Canyon

Camping in Park:

- Sunset View Campground: 33 T/RV, drinking water, restrooms, no hookups, some pull thru sites, no fee site, first come-first served

- Canyon View Campground: 14T, compost toilets, no water, first come-first served

Getting There:

- From Flagstaff, AZ: take US-89 North to US-160 East to AZ-564 North to Indian Route 221 for 140 mi / 225 km to the park

Navajo National Monument is comprised of three well-preserved cliff dwellings of the Ancestral Puebloans. While there had been a fair amount of plunder at Mesa Verde prior to its protection, this set of ruins was put under protection in a better state. Keet Seel is considered by some archaeologists to be the best-preserved cliff dwelling in the Southwest and Betatakin wasn't even found until after the park was created.

Besides the cliff dwellings, the redrock canyon setting and even the alcoves themselves are worth the visit. These alcoves are giant grand arcs of rock, with the centerpiece within being the ruins themselves. The first glimpse of these alcoves is breathtaking in their own right.

There are free ranger led tours of the Keet Seel and Betatakin sites. The third site, Inscription House, is currently closed to the public. There is also a short 1-mile walk to an overlook of Betatakin ruins. Amenities include two small campgrounds, picnic area, visitor center, and museum.

HIKING NAVAJO NATIONAL MONUMENT

SANDAL TRAIL

Easy – (1.0 mi / 1.6 km), round trip, allow 30 minutes

A paved and accessible trail that leads to an overlook of Betatakin cliff dwelling and surrounding canyon.

BETATAKIN GUIDED SITE TOUR

Strenuous – (5.0 mi / 8.0 km), round trip, allow 3 – 5hours

This free tour takes a different path, using the old Tsegi Point Road to the Betatakin Ruins. As with the other tour, it is ranger led and quite informative. The tour is offered seasonally. To take this tour, start in front of the visitor center at 8:15 AM for a preliminary briefing. Then, the group will need to take their vehicle to end of the navigable portion of Tsegi Point Road. From here, the road becomes trail, following along a wide peninsular portion of the canyon's rim, with alcoves and canyon floor on both sides. This portion of the hike is quite spectacular in its own right. The road ends at Tsegi Point and then climbs steeply down to the canyon floor and the ruins.

ASPEN TRAIL

Moderate – (0.8 mi / 1.3 km), round trip, allow 30 minutes

A spur trail off Sandal Trail that heads lower into the canyon and an old growth grove of Aspen trees.

CANYON VIEW TRAIL

Easy – (0.4 mi / 0.6 km), round trip, allow 30 minutes

This is an easy walk along the rim, leading from the visitor center and campground to the historic ranger station

204

Parks Near Grand Canyon

Betatakin ruins

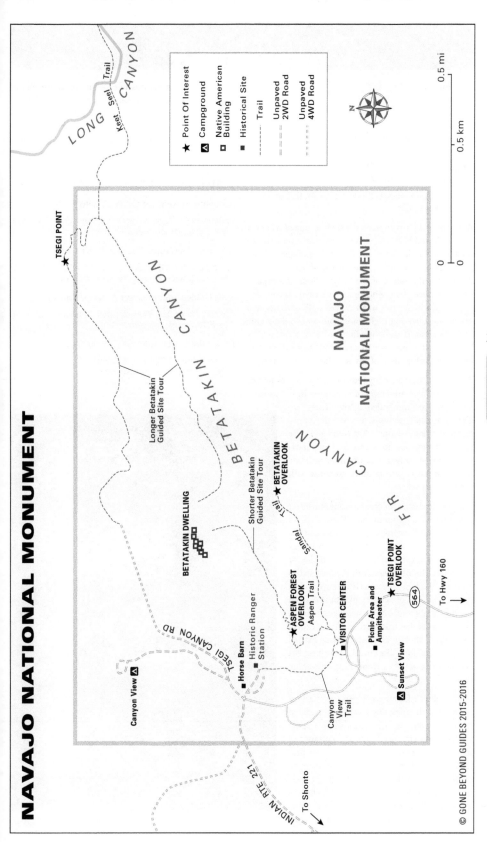

NAVAJO NATIONAL MONUMENT

LONG CANYON

Keet Seel Trail

TSEGI POINT ★

BETATAKIN CANYON

Longer Betatakin Guided Site Tour

Shorter Betatakin Guided Site Tour

BETATAKIN DWELLING

★ BETATAKIN OVERLOOK

FIR CANYON

Sandal Trail

ASPEN FOREST OVERLOOK ★

Aspen Trail

VISITOR CENTER

Picnic Area and Ampitheater ■

TSEGI POINT OVERLOOK ★

NAVAJO NATIONAL MONUMENT

564

To Hwy 160

TSEGI CANYON RD

Horse Barn ■

Historic Ranger Station ■

Canyon View Trail

Canyon View ▲

INDIAN RTE 221

To Shonto

Sunset View ▲

Legend:
★ Point Of Interest
▲ Campground
□ Native American Building
■ Historical Site
----- Trail
----- Unpaved 2WD Road
----- Unpaved 4WD Road

N

0   0.5 mi
0   0.5 km

© GONE BEYOND GUIDES 2015-2016

205

Parks Near Grand Canyon

Camping in Park:
- None

Getting There:
- From Flagstaff, AZ: take US 89 North to Page, AZ
- From Cortez, CO: take US 160 West to AZ 98 West to Page, AZ
- From Kanab, UT: take US 89 South/East to Page, AZ

Antelope Slot Canyon is, on the surface, one of the most incredible and beautiful sights one can see on a trip to the Grand Circle. If you are fortunate enough to book a high noon tour, when the beams of sunlight shine down onto the sands of the canyon floor, the experience is transcendent. Antelope Slot Canyon is a delight to the eye, with narrow water carved walls of multihued sandstone, towering high above into an infinitely blue sky. The contrast of light combined with shadow play brings out an experience that is certainly worth the trip and is often a highlight of any vacation to the southwest.

There are almost as many tour groups going to the slot canyon as there are layers of sandstone in the canyon. Some are recommended below. There are also two major sections to visit, the upper and lower slot canyons. Most tours go to the upper canyon due to access and popularity. The lower canyon can be more intimate though it too is getting more crowded with each passing year.

The best time to go for photography and effect is during the high noon tour. There is direct sunlight into the canyon at this time and the guides will toss sand high up which brings out filtered streams of light, which make for incredible photos. (Wait until the dust settles a bit for the best photos). The canyon is so narrow the sun penetrates like beams from heaven, bright and with crisply defined lines. Keep in mind that this is peak time, so expect to take your shot quickly before being herded along. If you don't like crowds, your best bet is to take one of the early morning or evening tours.

Logistically, each tour group gets into the back of an open-air truck that has been retrofitted to carry people. The driver heads into a sandy wash at a decent speed until the entrance of the canyon is reached. One tour driver pretended to be stuck in the sand, presumably to invoke the thrill of adventure. Keep your hats in your lap or tightly on your head, there is no stopping. Once out of the vehicle, the tour guide does his or her genuine best to make

the trip as intimate as possible for his group. The biggest advice is stay with your tour lead. Getting left behind has happened, but more typically, your late return to the vehicle will be met with glib looks from the fellow tour group members. Some tours feature a hoop dance back at the tour guide headquarters.

Antelope Slot Canyon Tours

Adventurous Antelope Canyon Photo Tours

Highway 98, Page, AZ 86040, Phone: (928) 380-1874, www.navajoantelopecanyon.com

Antelope Slot Canyon Tours by Chief Tsosie

55 S Lake Powell Blvd, Page AZ 86040, Phone: (928) 645-5594, www.antelopeslotcanyon.com

Ken's Guided Tour of Lower Antelope Canyon

Indian Route 222, Page, AZ 86040, Phone: (928) 606-2168, lowerantelope.com

Dixie Ellis' Lower Antelope Canyon Tours

Indian Route 222, Page, AZ 86040, Phone: (928) 640-1761, antelopelowercanyon.com

High noon sunbeams

Parks Near Grand Canyon

Camping in Park:

- Contact Havasupai Tourism at: P.O. Box 160 Supai, AZ, 86435, Phone: (928) 448-2121 or (928) 448-2141, (928) 448-2174, or (928) 448-2180

- Havasu Falls Campground: Reservations required, call Havasupai Tourism numbers listed above, (keep trying if no answer), 250T, drinking water, restrooms, no campfires, day ranger on duty in season

Getting There:

- From Flagstaff: take US I-40 west to Historic Route 66 west at Seligman and turn right onto Indian Road 18 for 65 miles to trailhead at Hualapai Hilltop.

Within the entirety of the Grand Circle, Havasu and Mooney Falls are arguably the pinnacle of destinations. It is the soul of the Southwest, willing to accept all those that travel to it and yet the area continues to retain a serene simplicity and purity. If ever there should be an item at the top of your bucket list of places to go within the Grand Circle, this is that place.

HIKING HAVASU AND MOONEY FALLS

HAVASU AND MOONEY FALLS

Strenuous – (24.0 mi / 38.6 km), round trip, 2-day backpacking trip

First things first, get reservations and pay the fees. One will need to pay a $35 entrance fee plus an environment fee of $5, (each fee is per person). Camping is an additional $17 per person per night. Your entire party will be billed double this amount if you come without reservations, assuming there is availability. There is also a 10% tax on all purchases and a $5 Environmental Care Fee. Total for one night camping is $62.71 per person and $81.41 for two nights. The season opens on February 1st each year and 300 permits are given each day.

Now that you know the particulars on permits and camping, the next thing you will need is luck. The word is out on Havasu Falls and it is very difficult to get a permit. The best approach is to mark your calendar for February 1st and then start dialing every number listed repeatedly until you get through. It is not unheard of for multiple folks trying from different phones to take several days to finally get through. As rough as this sounds, many do get through on the first day. The only good news here is this is the same process whether you are hiking alone or are booking for a professional tour company.

The sublime waters of Havasu Falls

If you do have a group helping you to get the permits, have a plan A, B and C for dates and make sure you have a communication system for when you finally do get through. The season usually books out within weeks, but there is always hope that there will be a cancellation if you don't want to wait until next February to get in line.

Located within the Havasupai Reservation, the trip does get a lot of visitors during peak season. Start by finding a parking spot near the trailhead, which is situated about 1,000 feet off the canyon bottom. Right from the trailhead, you will see you are in a special place. The views down and around are amazing.

The hike heads steeply down to the valley floor via a series of switchbacks. There are plenty of mules along this trail and one needs to be especially diligent on this part. If you see mules coming, stick to the canyon wall side and not the cliff side. The mules often travel at a decent clip giving the backpacker little time to react. Hugging a wall in these instances tends to fair better than clinging to the edge of a cliff. This is especially true in a narrow section later on. The mules have the right of way on this trail.

Most of the hike travels along the wash, with great views of towering orange-red walls on either side. At about mile 7 into the journey, the trail narrows. Be especially aware of mules here. The hiking here is shadier and thus cooler unless you are doing this stretch at high noon.

The slot canyon opens into Havasu Creek and shortly thereafter to the peaceful village of the Supai People. The town holds 208 residents, give or take and is officially the most remote inhabited community in the lower 48. Besides flying in by helicopter (or as the locals call it, "cheating"), the only way in is via the Havasupai Trail. It is the last community in the United States to have its mail delivered by mule.

Havasu Falls are 2 miles from the town of Supai. These two miles deeper into the canyon are utterly sublime. The water is a light blue green turquoise. The distinctive hue comes from the strong reflection of the underlying limestone creek bed. It's not just the falls that are this color, the entire creek from Supai on are a gem like color of paradise found.

Havasu Falls and Mooney Falls further on are tall, roaring sheets of water and simply beyond words. Both are amazing and both must be seen. Getting to Mooney Falls requires a Class 3 descent to the bottom, some 210 feet below. Aids include a tunnel, ladders, handholds, railings, and footholds. This section is quite steep and exposed in areas and not for those that have a fear of heights. In addition, these areas become bottlenecks and one may have to stand in place as they wait for folks to come up or down. Finally, it should not be attempted when the conditions are wet or otherwise unfavorable, as sections can get very slippery. There is a campground in between the Havasu and Mooney Falls.

If you do want to send a post card home from Supai, note that the post office is closed on weekends. If you do go on a weekend, some locals are willing to mail it for you for a nominal fee. The novelty of mailing anything from the community is knowing that the first leg (pun intended) is by mule, the last community in the United States to move mail in this manner.

VERMILION CLIFFS NATIONAL MONUMENT

Camping in Park:
- Stateline: 4 T, no water, no trash, restrooms, first come/first served, open year round
- White House: 5 T, no water, no trash, restrooms, first come/first served, open year round

Getting There:
- Southern Section: From Flagstaff: head north on US 89 to 89A at the Bitter Springs off ramp. From US I-15: take AZ 389 East to US 89A South
- Northern Section: From Kanab, Utah: take US 89 to the east or US 89A to the south. From US I-15: take UT 9 East to US 89 South

Vermilion Cliffs National Monument is certainly a candidate for one of the top park destinations within the Grand Circle. Nearly as large as all of the three sections of the Canyonlands and yet relatively new and unheard of, this is one of the most unspoiled parks to be found. It is also one of the most remote. The park is located north of Grand Canyon and east of the Navajo lands, touching the border of Utah, referred to as the Arizona Strip. There is no visitor center, few roads, little previous development, and only a scattered handful of trails. Vermilion Cliffs is true desert wilderness. It is untouched, insufferable, rugged, and pure. There are places within it where it feels as if no person has ever stepped foot. For the most part, Vermilion Cliffs is pure virgin sandstone, quietly being shaped over millions of years.

It was only made into a national monument in 2000, though the land had been protected under other measures prior. Much of the 280,000 acres protects the Paria Plateau, a significant mesa that spans over 20 miles and is roughly square in shape. The plateau itself is a vast desert island oasis, invoking freedom and being on top of the world. However, it is the areas along the edges of the plateau that offers some of the most amazing sections in the park, such as The Wave, a striated section of carved sandstone that has to be seen to be believed. Then there is Buckskin Gulch, a tributary of the Paria River and at a length of 20 miles is a contender for the longest slot canyon in the world.

It must be stated that not all of this wonder and remote beauty comes without some caution and regulations. Much of the land is accessed by permit only. While day use permits are more available, overnight permits are limited and can be obtained by going to the URL below and following the online instructions: www.blm. gov/az/st/en/arolrsmain.html. The caution is that this land can be extremely challenging. Flash floods, venomous reptiles and insects, sun exposure, and remoteness make this park much different than say, taking the shuttle from the Zion Lodge and taking a hike. This area is ideally suited for experienced hikers and desert backpackers.

A quick note on the permitting system. One consistent theme within all of these parks is finding a balance between preservation of the land and the ability to share it for the enjoyment and recreation of others. Vermilion Cliffs NM pushes this balance more on the preservation side. There is a capacity to the number of visitors allowed to use the park each day and while it may be frustrating if you are the unfortunate soul that didn't get a permit, you have to respect the process. The desert is fragile and takes a very long time to recover. Some parks, especially the national parks, are pushing the balance more towards recreation and the wear on them does show. Having explored all of these parks since the 1980's, the impact over just 35 years is quite evident and not in a good way. Vermilion Cliffs NM continues to retain that pristine hallowed ground of desert experience

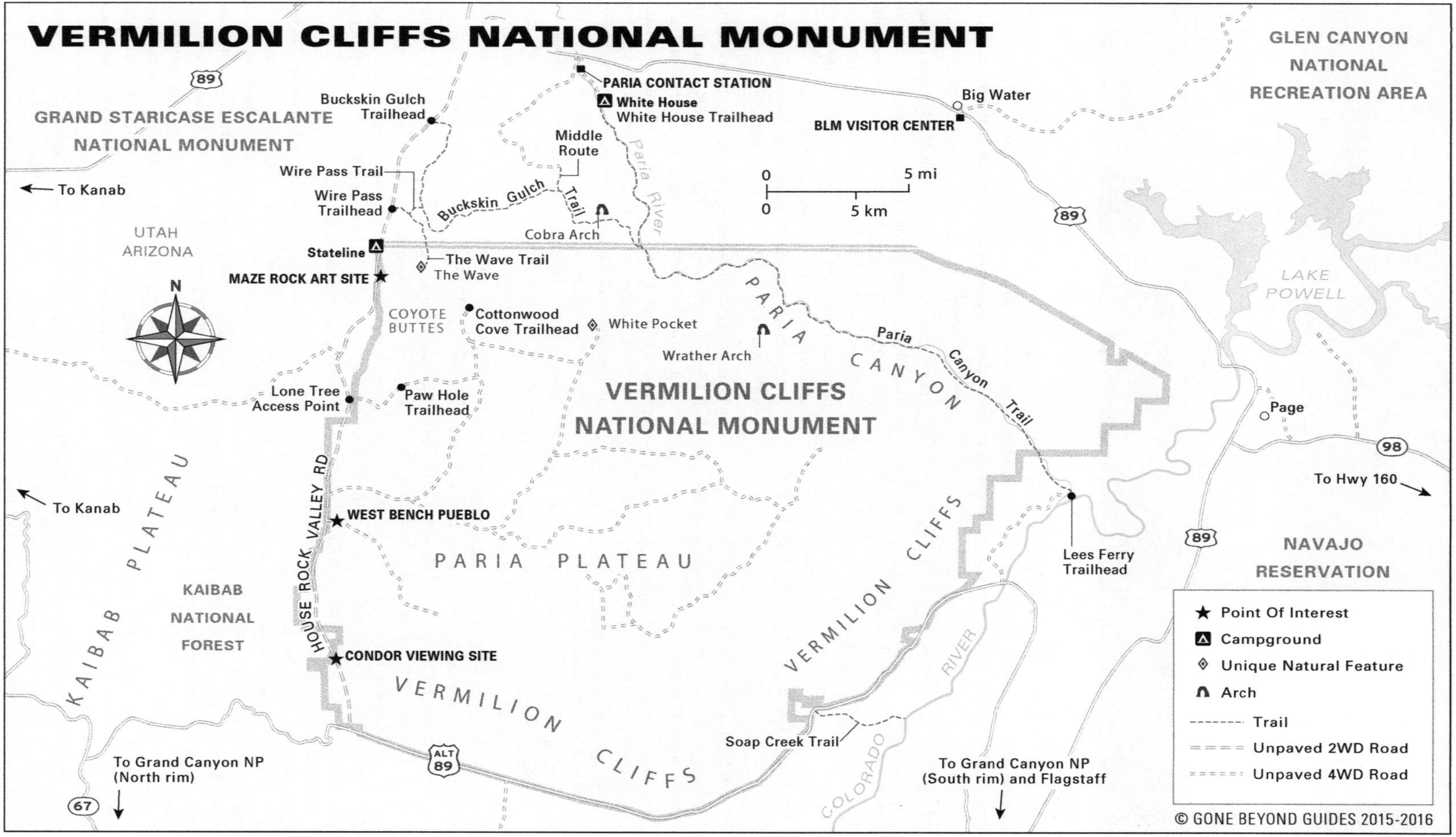

VERMILION CLIFFS NATIONAL MONUMENT

GLEN CANYON NATIONAL RECREATION AREA

GRAND STAIRCASE ESCALANTE NATIONAL MONUMENT

LAKE POWELL

← To Kanab

89

Big Water

■ BLM VISITOR CENTER

Page

98

To Hwy 160 →

NAVAJO RESERVATION

Legend:
- ★ Point Of Interest
- ▲ Campground
- ◈ Unique Natural Feature
- ∩ Arch
- ········· Trail
- ═ ═ ═ Unpaved 2WD Road
- ═════ Unpaved 4WD Road

© GONE BEYOND GUIDES 2015-2016

89

Paria River

PARIA CONTACT STATION
▲ White House
White House Trailhead

Middle Route

Cobra Arch

Trail

Buckskin Gulch

Paria Canyon Trail

PARIA CANYON

VERMILION CLIFFS NATIONAL MONUMENT

Wrather Arch ∩

◈ White Pocket

Cottonwood Cove Trailhead

VERMILION CLIFFS

Lees Ferry Trailhead

COLORADO RIVER

To Grand Canyon NP (South rim) and Flagstaff →

Soap Creek Trail

VERMILION CLIFFS

Buckskin Gulch Trailhead

Wire Pass Trail
Wire Pass Trailhead

▲ Stateline
★ MAZE ROCK ART SITE

The Wave Trail
◈ The Wave

COYOTE BUTTES

Paw Hole Trailhead

Lone Tree Access Point

PARIA PLATEAU

★ WEST BENCH PUEBLO

HOUSE ROCK VALLEY RD

CONDOR VIEWING SITE ★

VERMILION CLIFFS

ALT 89

0   5 mi
0   5 km

UTAH
ARIZONA

← To Kanab

N

KAIBAB NATIONAL FOREST

KAIBAB PLATEAU

To Grand Canyon NP (North rim) →

67

209

Parks Near Grand Canyon

because of the permit process. Not everyone will get to go, especially for those permitted areas only available by lottery, but those that do will experience the difference.

HIKING VERMILION CLIFFS NATIONAL MONUMENT

Paria Canyon Trails

Buckskin Gulch Trail

Moderate – (5.7 mi / 9.2 km), one way to Wire Pass Trailhead, allow 3 hours

Strenuous – (23 mi / 37 km), one way, to White House Trailhead, full day hike or 2-day backpacking trip

Strenuous – (47 mi / 76 km), one way, to Lee's Ferry Trailhead, 3-5-day backpacking trip

Buckskin Gulch is the longest and deepest slot canyon in the Grand Circle. The narrows extend nearly 15 miles, with some sections being but 10 feet in width. The terrain and views are as inspiring as they are varied, making this a popular hike. The slot canyon leaves for very few exits during a flash flood and rain as far as Bryce Canyon 50 miles away can drain into Buckskin. The gulch is also known for muck pools, where in the middle of summer you may find yourself with no other choice but to wade through residual pools that become foul smelling mud pots. They are normally no more than 3 feet deep, but some folks have noted being chest deep in one pool. Additionally, expect to do a fair amount of scrambling and even rappelling. In many spots, there is a rope left behind as a gesture of courtesy to rappel down the 15 foot drops, but you'll want to bring rope just in case.

There are many entry points into Buckskin Gulch. There is the Buckskin Gulch Trailhead or Wire Pass Trailhead to the east, heading downstream to a juncture where you can either head north to White House Trailhead or southeast through Paria Canyon down to Lee's Ferry. The most popular hike is from Wire Pass Trail-

head to White House Trailhead. This section describes the route starting from Buckskin Gulch Trailhead. Use this route if you want to say you hiked the full extent of Buckskin Gulch.

Take Highway 89 east from Kanab, UT 38 miles or west from Page, AZ for 34 miles and turn onto House Valley Road. This will be a right if coming from Kanab. The Buckskin Trailhead is 4.5 miles down a dirt road and is suitable for 2WD vehicles. That said, the clay-based soils are super sticky in some areas and like driving on ice in others when wet. It is not recommended, even in a 4WD vehicle, to drive this road when wet.

There is no established campground here, but camping is allowed at the trailhead. The trail is obvious and dry for most of the year to the junction to Wire Pass Trailhead, starting off fairly wide relative to the narrows later on. From the junction to Wire Pass, the canyon begins its journey as the longest narrows in the Southwest. The next big milestone is Buckskin Gulch Junction (1.8 miles, 1 hour). Here, (and beyond), the narrows are quite spectacular. Every turn is a different "wow!" moment. Along this section are The Cesspools, a stretch of murky, muddy, god-awful water that you have to wade through to continue.

The trek through this section of the narrows is 6.5 miles long, with the next milestone being Middle Route. Allow 4 hours for this part. Middle Route is yet another passage into Buckskin over a 4WD drive road and is described later in the book.

From Middle Route to Rock Fall (aka Rock Jam) is another 3 miles (allow 2 hours). This area has some rock problem areas that require scrambling. In spots, it can get quite dark, though not enough for a flashlight. Rock Fall presents the toughest of the areas where scrambling is needed. The scramble is easy enough, with some footholds into the rock for the down climb or hikers can opt for the Rabbit Hole, which is the easiest of methods to get through this scramble of rock (look for a way down through the rocks rather than up). From Rock Fall the campground and Paria River Confluence is in sight and is the spot for an overnight rest for most folks. The distance here is 1.3 miles to the campground and an-

Coyote Buttes South

other quarter mile to the confluence. Allow 1 hour. It is not recommended to camp at the confluence due to potential risk of "going to Lee's Ferry prematurely" due to flooding. The campground sits higher up providing some protection from rising waters.

The hike to the confluence is dry for the most part, aside from the mud pots and stronger seeps and springs providing some run off. While it may be tempting to get the water from these sources, it is not recommended. You will need 1.5 to 2 gallons of water for this leg in the summer, more depending on distance traveled and time spent.

If you are continuing upstream to White House Trailhead, you have another 4 hours and 7.5 miles ahead of you. This route is possible to do as a day trip, but it is a full day.

Heading downstream will take you Lee's Ferry. The total distance to Lee's Ferry from Buckskin Gulch Trailhead is 47 miles. Plan on a 3 - 5-day backpacking trip and definitely use a shuttle. Along with Paria Outpost listed above, Circle Tours, (888) 854-7862 and End of the Trail Shuttles, (928) 355-2252 offer shuttle services.

WIRE PASS TRAIL

Moderate – (5.7 mi / 9.2 km), one way to Buckskin Gulch Trailhead, allow 3 hours

Strenuous – (21 mi / 34 km), one way, to White House Trailhead, full day hike or 2-day backpacking trip

Wire Pass Trail offers an alternate entrance into Buckskin Gulch through Wire Pass Gulch. Wire Pass Trailhead is often chosen over entering directly from the Buckskin Gulch Trailhead because it is shorter and the gulch is itself a very nice set of narrows. It only cuts off 2 miles from any destination but does offer help satisfy the "slot canyon" fix a little faster than starting from Buckskin Gulch Trailhead. This trailhead is also used as the starting destination for a popular sandstone formation known as The Wave, described later on.

To get here, just follow the directions above to Buckskin Gulch Trailhead and continue on House Rock Valley Road another 3.8 miles (8.3 miles from Highway 89). Again, permits are needed as is reading all the tips provided in the Buckskin Gulch Trail description. Stateline Campground is one-mile south of the Wire Pass Trailhead and camping is allowed at the trailhead if campground is full. There are restrooms here, but no water.

Before Heading Out:

Here are some tips to ensure a safe and successful trip:

- First, get a permit. Overnight access to Buckskin Gulch is limited to 20 folks per day. The online process is listed in the web URL above.

- Speak to the BLM rangers. The rangers are the best versed in current conditions, what to expect and general guidance on how to prepare and execute this hike. Kanab Field Office – 318 North 100 East, Kanab, UT 84741 – Phone: (435) 644-4600 Fax: (435) 644-4620 or by email: utknmail@blm.gov

- Use a shuttle or two cars. These are long distances, so if you are short on time, this is best way to do this hike. Try Paria Outfitters

(www.paria.com) for shuttle services. At the very least, check out their site for the cool pics of the areas they serve.

- Check the weather forecast. Backpacker Magazine puts this as one of the 10 most dangerous hikes, primarily due to flash flood risks. As they put it, "Should thunderstorm-bloated flood waters come charging down the tunnel, you're no better than a bug in a firehose."

- Bring water shoes, plenty of drinking water, and multiple layers of clothing. There are points where the watercourse is the trail so bring some decent water shoes. While there are seeps, pools and water, it can be downright murky, so best to bring in what you need. Finally, fires are not permitted in the area, so make sure you have layer coverage for the temperature range of the trip.

Parks Near Grand Canyon

MIDDLE ROUTE

Strenuous – (1.4 mi / 2.3 km), one way to Buckskin Gulch, allow 1 - 2 hours

The Middle Route is a good alternative if you are looking to bypass many of the cold stagnant pools of water as you wind through the narrows of Buckskin Gulch. It also saves a day of hiking. It is a short easy route to navigate into the gulch via a long, sandy, unsigned, and at times impassable 4WD road with multiple forks to consider.

About midway through Buckskin Gulch, the walls of the canyon lower down to about 100 feet. Here there is a very steep crack that is possible to scramble up if one needs an early exit out of the gulch or as a means to down climb into the slot canyon. This is Middle Route. This crack is definitely for the experienced canyoneer and bringing a 50-foot rope is highly recommended for lowering packs. The crack contains steep drop offs and climbing down slickrock. Exposure aside, this is a Class 3 - 4 scramble and doesn't require any technical climbing per se.

Getting to Middle Route is not straightforward as hinted at above. It's best to consult with the Paria Contact Station for directions, road conditions and even a video of Middle Route.

212

COYOTE BUTTES NORTH

THE WAVE

Strenuous – (5.6 mi / 9.0 km), round trip, from Wire Pass Trailhead, allow 3 – 4 hours

If ever there was a destination that could compete with Buckskin Gulch, the longest slot canyon in the Southwest and perhaps even the world, it a little place called The Wave. In the Grand Circle there is a lot of red rock, so much in fact, that after a few weeks within it, one starts dreaming of fantastic mashups of slickrock canyons and formations that don't actually exist. The Wave is a place that is so fantastic; it is as if it came from one of these dreams. Seeing an image of The Wave is to reset the art of the possible within the realm of red rock. To see it in person can be surreal, as if it shouldn't exist, yet it does. As an added bonus, the whole terrain getting to it and around it is cool to explore. This area is part of the Coyote Buttes North. This is a day use only area and requires a permit. Permits are limited to 20 people a day with 10 folks chosen through a walk in lottery process the day before and 10 folks obtaining the permit via an online process via (www.blm.gov/az/paria/obtainpermits.cfm?usearea=CB).

For the online process, the lottery opens up 4 months prior to the use date. Generally, online permits for the Coyote Buttes North are hard to obtain. The cost to apply is $5 per group and you can select up to three dates. See the lottery schedule below for exact dates, but in general, the process works like this. For a permit in say the month of May, one would apply at any time four months earlier, from January 1-31, in this case. On February 1, at 1:05 PM MST, the permits holders are chosen. If you are successful, you will be notified via email and will then need to pay $7 per individual.

There is no established trail to The Wave. There are two routes, however. The most readily accessible method is to start from Wire Pass Trailhead. The drive is easy enough and more straightforward of a hike then the other method known as The Notch. The route from Wire Pass Trailhead will be described here.

Start by following the instructions to Wire Pass Trailhead listed above. Enter into Wire Pass Gulch across the road and travel down the wash for about half a mile. Take the juncture to the right, marked Coyote Buttes, where you will find an obvious trail. The trail climbs up a hill and across a desert field ending at a wash. Total distance of the trail is approximately 0.65 miles.

From here on out the trail becomes route and the area is by permit only. On the other side of the wash is a slickrock incline that is typically marked with cairns. Climb this saddle and head towards the BLM marker ahead of you. This saddle is a great point to mark if you have a GPS, as it will greatly aid in finding the trail on the return.

The Wave

A land of soulfulness and escape

Continue to follow the BLM markers south, heading towards and staying to the left of a landmark known as Twin Buttes. Once you pass by this landmark, you are about 0.6 miles from the Utah – Arizona border and 1.0 mile from the Wave. The next landmark to aim for is a narrow crack like gully in the cliffs as you continue south. As you get closer to the gully look for a small sand dune left of the gully. Climb the sand dune, then the slickrock to arrive at The Wave. There are many other features to check out in the area, including The Second Wave, The Alcove, and some petroglyphs and dinosaur tracks. See the below website for a list of all of them.

One exceptional site dedicated to The Wave feature is a site called "thewave". It covers everything outlined here and has a virtual tour of the hike itself, sunset/sunrise calculator, weather, and other details. Go here: www. thewave.info/CoyoteButtesNorthCode/Map.html

Maze Rock Art Site

Just beyond Wire Pass Trailhead and State Line Campground is a trailhead to a rich petroglyph site. There are numerous examples of Ancestral Puebloan art, including the namesake, a petroglyph that looks like a maze. Head south from State Line Campground on House Valley Road for about a mile to find the trailhead.

Coyote Buttes South

The Coyote Buttes South region of Vermilion Cliffs NM is, like its northern counterpart, accessed by permit only. The good news is the permits are much easier to obtain for this region. Just go online and follow the instructions.

https://www.blm.gov/az/paria/obtainpermits.cfm?u-searea=CB

All of the hiking here is for the experienced. Beyond needing a permit, you'll need a 4WD vehicle and topo maps. Per the BLM, these are both mandatory. As the BLM site indicates these aren't really trailheads, they are access points. After driving through deep sands and rough terrain, after figuring out on numerous occasions

which junction you should take at the many spur roads on the way, you find yourself parking at the beginning of your own adventure.

For all of the below access points listed below, there are no trails, no markers, direction signs, or navigational information once you leave the road that got you there. In places like these, there is this advice. You will find at least one piece of trash, typically a Budweiser can and you will wonder how it got there. You will have the opportunity to step where no human has stepped, and see things that no one has seen in quite the same way. You will hopefully take solace in knowing that the closest Starbucks to your tent is a good 3 hours away and that when the sun sets, you will likely see one of the darkest skies you have ever seen. This is the middle of nowhere. It is desert nirvana, BFE, God's country. Whatever you call it, the place will leave its mark on the soul as days remembered for the rest of your life.

Cottonwood Cove Trailhead

This access point leads to the Cottonwood Teepees, a series of cone shaped sandstone formations. In general, the red rock is twisted and deformed, resembling something more reminiscent to a Salvador Dali landscape.

The rocks at times look like huge spine fossils of some large monster, eroded away by time until only the backbone remains curved out on a pedestal of rock. There is also one teepee formation called the Queen, looking like a typical cone shaped formation but with the smallest of capstones on top.

Getting to Cottonwood Cove Trailhead starts by taking House Rock Road, the same road taken for Buckskin Gulch and Wire Pass Trailheads. Head south past Wire Pass for 20.2 miles and turn left on BLM 1017, (Pine Tree Road). If coming from the south, the distance on House Rock Road will be 9.4 miles to this intersection.

Mark the trip meter and take Pine Tree Road for 3.1 miles and then turn left on Red Pockets Road and begin heading in a northwest bearing. At 6.0 miles, you should see a cattle gate (leave as you found it, whether open or closed). At 8.3 miles, bear to the right and at 8.7 miles turn left onto Upper Pawhole Road. This area, called Poverty Flat has several out buildings worth checking out. At 9.0 miles keep to the right until you reach a closed gate with a sign that says Coyote Buttes Fee Area. End of the road worth driving on is at 11.4 miles. Park on your left, the Cottonwood Teepees are to the west.

PAW HOLE TRAILHEAD

Paw Hole is close to Cottonwood Cove, offering slightly different topography. It is possible to do both in one trip. Paw Hole has some interesting, often delicate striations in the sandstone. Paw Hole is a small water hole that looks like, (wait for it), a paw. One recommended route is to stay at Cottonwood Cove the first night and then Paw Hole the next. This method allows for a loop back to House Valley Road.

Coming from Cottonwood Cove, double back to BLM 1079 and take it to the signs indicating Paw Hole. To head out, continue on BLM 1079 to connect back to House Valley Road. It is not recommended to take this road to Paw Hole directly from House Valley as it is uphill and is too steep for many vehicles.

PIPE SPRINGS NATIONAL MONUMENT

Camping in Park:
- None

Getting There:
- From St. George, UT: take UT-59 South and AZ-389 East for 60 mi / 97 km to the park

Pipe Spring was first discovered in 1858 by Jacob Hamblin, a Mormon missionary on an expedition to the Hopi mesas. Two years later, James M. Whitmore and a group of fellow pioneers created a homestead and cattle operation. Building a group of homes in Navajo territory was one thing, keeping it was another. Once the Apache, Navajo, Utes, and Paiutes joined forces to start the Black Hawk War in 1866, primarily aimed at the Mormons, things came to a boiling point. After a raid of the Pipe Springs homesteads, it was decided to build a fort over the main spring.

This fortified ranch house was purchased by Brigham Young in 1872 for the Church of the Latter Day Saints (LDS). Brigham sent Mormon Bishop Anson Perry Winsor to run the ranch and he renamed it Winsor Castle. The ranch became a safe haven for travelers passing through and even acted as a refuge for polygamist wives during the late 1800's. In the end, the ranch's ties to polygamy would be its downfall and the LDS lost ownership of the property in 1887.

Today the monument is a cultural preserve, offering a 30-minute ranger led tour of the ranch house and an extensive museum and visitor center. It is also possible to take a self-guided walk amongst the out buildings, corral, and garden areas. Pipe Spring National Monument offers an informative and interesting step back in time; especially if the ranger led tour is taken. Definitely worth the drive.

The historic Winsor Castle

[Everest]: *Dad, I believe Super Mario is a communist.*

[Me]: *I've heard this theory. How did you find out about it?*

[Everest]: *YouTube and the fact he wears red overalls.*

[Me]: *I'm pretty sure he was just an opportunistic pizza guy or something.*

[Everest]: *Maybe, but I think the whole pizza thing was just to cover up his communistic tendencies.*

[Me]: *Son, are you even sure you know what a communist is?*

[Everest]: *I know red is their color.*

[Me]: *Ah. Well, this is very useful stuff; thanks for clearing it all up for me. I for one am really glad we had this conversation.*

[Everest]: *Yeah, me too. Can I watch more YouTube?*

[Me]: *Absolutely not.*

Welcome to the Colorado

While we had arrived in the wake of a thunderstorm, the Grand Canyon was no less outstanding. Absent was the normalcy of dreary wetness. Here it was replaced with spectacular awe. Threads of lightning hit the mesa tops in a chorus of visual glory combined with the rolling rumble of deep thunder. Large drops hit the windshield of our RV. The lightning struck the air sideways in almost musical patterns from left to right, randomly and without reason. We pulled the motor home over and just watched this headliner show. After a time the rain finally stopped, lifting the purest and most colorful of rainbows across the

With the sun back out, so too came the hordes of people. There were so many tourists here, unlike at any of the other parks. It was easy to reconcile that this was the most popular destination of all the parks we had visited. Some five million tourists a year come to gaze out over the edge. We passed a McDonald's seemingly in the park. It was clear we were too close to civilization. The natural beauty of the Grand Canyon was not mixing well with the darkness of capitalism.

215

My first thoughts were how to escape the masses of people. So many of them were just looking out over the edge of this vast and amazing place and going no further. Each time I saw the river poke through over a mile underneath us, I felt compelled to head to the banks and greet it. I needed to go up to this natural artist in residence of the past 17 million years and simply throw a nod, a humble little bow of respect to say "Bravo! Well done, river. Well done indeed."

Everest

The hike to the Colorado River is not an easy one. It is highly recommended that you get a permit, backpack your way to the banks, and back up. It is highly

canyon. It followed us or perhaps we followed it into the campground. We stepped out with souls refreshed and washed clean from the desert storm. The Colorado far down below changed from green to muddy brownish red. It looked at home and at peace within its rushing torrents and true colors.

NOT recommended that you go to the Colorado as a day hike. There are signs at the trailhead, as big as billboards, that state essentially that you are nuts if you try this as a day hike and downright silly stupid if you think you can attempt it without water.

The hike is a little more than 8 miles downhill, each step down taking the traveler 60,000 years back in geologic time. Then the same 8 miles back up. At the top of the mesa, you are almost 7,000 feet above sea level. The air is refreshingly cool and, as a result, misleading. Down at the river you have dropped to 2,480 feet and the temperatures are oven hot with all that baking rock surrounding you and little relief given by the river itself.

Here is what was going through my head at this point.

Okay, so the park service guides suggest that it would be nuts to do the South Rim to the river and back as a day hike, but completely insane to do it without water. Got it, they are saying brings lots of water…check. The hike is over 16 miles long, so I might want to bring some food. Yep, definitely going to need some food, a few granola bars maybe, well, wait, perhaps I should bring meals. I remember the last time I didn't pack enough food (I thought briefly back to a hike in Death Valley that almost didn't end well).

I should pack in some "just in case" clothing (as in just in case something goes wrong and I have to stay the night). Under the same loosely bound safety-first section of my thought process, I also threw in a lighter, a flashlight, a compass and a pocketknife. Finally, the map was added to the daypack.

"Okay, now only one thing to do," I said out loud to no one, "is convince my wife." I had no real strategy there. The hike would take all day, certainly. It would rob a day's vacation of family time and devote it instead to an incredibly selfish endeavor. I looked down at the Colorado River again. "Bring it" was all it seemed to say. "I'm not going anywhere." The river was calling me, so against all that marriage had taught me over those past 14 years, I approached Angela, daypack and hat in hand.

There is really no need to describe the gentle influence and suave nature in which I handled the situation, mainly because I utterly lack these characteristics. No, I usually go with some variant of dense male approach. I fall on my sword, make an argument loosely based on the wonderful attributes of pity and somehow manage to convince my wife that while yes, she probably could have done better in marriage, she did pick me knowing full well my preponderance for hiking and thus should save us the trouble and just let me go. Perhaps the only argument that had any merit involved the question, "When will I ever be back this way again?" The rest of my rationale for going was completely indefensible and could have been stopped in its tracks with ease on her part.

In the end, despite myself, she did let me go on the condition that I went as soon as I could in the morning, not dawdle on the trail, didn't wake her in leaving, and took Everest with me. (Everest had lobbied to be included as part of the negotiation early in the talks). Given I would have bought her a nice dinner and some jewelry just to go on this hike; I think I got off pretty easy.

I woke Ev up at 6 a.m. and while we made every attempt to be quiet, the reality of our packing up was loud enough to garner a few mumblings and resettling of the sleeping occupants. It was a quick hike from the campground to Kolb Studio and the beginning of Bright Angel Trailhead. We met a few likeminded hikers and exchanged the usual banter about the length and strenuousness of the hike. Some folks pointed out the young age of Everest.

After we were alone I asked him, "Do you think you are too young to go on this long of a hike, Ev?"

"Mm…I don't know" followed by the word "shrugs" while shrugging his shoulder. "I think I'll be fine, but this will be the longest hike I've ever done."

"I think you'll make it, but you will certainly feel it toward the end of the hike, guaranteed."

"Shrugs," Ev grinned. "I'm sure you will feel it too, Old Hinges."

"Old Hinges? Does that mean I can call you Young Hinges?"

"No, sorry. That just doesn't sound right. Everest works, though!" he beamed.

The first part of the hike descends steeply, and we made good time, eating granola bars while we walked. The trail started to lighten a bit in its severity and we settled into a cadence that took us to Indian Gardens, the main resting spot, primitive campground and watering hole for the weary traveler. We were hardly weary just yet and decided we should continue the final three miles to the river without further hesitation.

The second leg didn't go quite as fast as the first. The sun no longer hidden by the canyon walls, it now beat down upon us. I looked at the time and realized it was already well into midmorning. It was hot but not completely unbearable, and the downhill trend helped immensely. We heard the river long before we reached it, but reach it we did. Everest detoured to the nearby pit toilet while I walked toward the banks of the Colorado. It was a raging young vibrant thing, all red and muddy from the recent rains. As I approached the water's edge, I saw two rafts coming down. One rafter oared close to shore, waved and yelled out with exuberance, "Welcome to the Colorado!" He then threw out two cans of Budweiser, held together by their plastic ring. The beers landed on the sand right at my feet. I grinned ear to ear at this wondrous synchronicity and waved back a big, "Thanks!" The river continued to roar as the oarsman sat back into place to navigate further onward as they traveled out of site.

"What are those, Dad?"

"Beers!" I exclaimed.

"Seriously? Where did you get them"?

I pointed at the nearly vanished rafters and said, "Those guys."

"Wow," Ev said, looking at the rafters. "That's really cool." He paused for a moment, looking at the beers. "You know, we made it. We're here, Dad! This would be a great time to have that iconic father-son first beer moment, right?"

"I'll tell you what. Let's do this hike again when you are 21 and if someone throws a couple of beers at my feet, I'll be happy to share them with you.   Until then, that's a big fat no on the beer moment."

Ev remained ever nonplussed as he released a drab felt, "Lolz."

After the two beers landing at my feet in the middle of the desert, at the shores of the Colorado River no less, I felt pretty good. I couldn't help but draw a correlation that I had come down to pay tribute to the river and it had in its own way paid tribute back. That made these beers special and I wanted to have one, but I knew if I did, I'd be in for a head pounding in that heat. I put them in my pack to save for when I got back up.

As I put away the beers, I noticed that a couple was eyeing us with some insistence. I pretended to not notice that they were watching us, but after the sixth glance over and meeting with eye contact, the woman decided to come over.

It was clear from her accent she was from Germany. "Pardon us. We came down the trail and did not bring enough water. We were thinking maybe you could sell us some water or a can of soda or something."

I thought about the huge billboard-like sign that warned against doing this hike without water—that serious illness can occur, even death. The warning is printed in several languages and shows a man holding his head in a near death posture. It is impossible to miss, which led me to one singular conclusion: my own stubborn obstinacy toward such warning signs obviously comes from the Germanic side of my heritage.

The husband didn't look like he was doing well at all. There was a hot sun baking down on us at this point, and it was definitely having an effect on the man. I opened up my daypack and handed them my second water bottle, which was untouched at this point as we had refilled at Indian Gardens.

"Here, drink as much as you want. How much water did you bring with you?"

"How much? None."

"You didn't bring any?" I asked in disbelief and then caught myself. I was shocked. It was then I noticed they didn't even carry a daypack. For whatever reason, they thought this hike was a casual stroll. It was clear the park service needed a bigger warning billboard.

They both drank a little and then tried to hand the water bottle back. I pushed it back toward them, shaking my head.

"Feel free to drink the whole bottle. We can get more in 3 miles at Indian Gardens. Did you get water there on the way down?" Everest handed them his spare water bottle. The couple would now have two quarts of water in them.

"No", the woman said. "We didn't see any water coming down."

"Which way did you come down?" I asked.

"We came down South Kaibab Trail."

The husband said something. "Fragen Sie ihn, ob er uns zu einem der Biere geben. "

"Sorry, my husband doesn't speak English. He was wondering if you have more water that you can sell or have a container we can buy."

I thought about the beers and handed one can to them. The man looked a little better but it was obvious he would need more water to get to the top.

217

"Here, take this can. Now it's beer, so don't drink it! It will dehydrate you more if you do. The best thing is to carry this with you to Indian Gardens and then pour out the beer and use the container to fill it with water. Indian Gardens is 3.2 miles up from here on the Bright Angel Trail. I highly recommend you take that trail out as it has good water whereas South Kaibab has no water."

I debated giving them my spare water bottle but decided against it. My son and I needed a good deal of water to get back. The beer can would have to get them back up. I knew there was typically a ranger at Indian Gardens and told them that, explaining that the ranger could help them further.

The woman nodded and took the can and then handed it to her husband. He looked at the can and went to open it. I warned her again about not drinking the beer, that drinking it wouldn't help, that it would only dehydrate them more. She nodded vaguely at me while the husband continued to look drained and gruff.

We parted ways after showing them where Bright Angel Trail was and repeating my advice several times as if repetition would help. Everest and I sat at the river's edge and ate lunch, pondering how many people come down this way completely unprepared, despite the rather obvious signs the park service put up warning people not to do stupid things. We stopped giving stupid people a hard time for being stupid when we came full circle to the fact that we ourselves were ignoring the park's warnings. A sixteen-mile hike was not for the beginner, to be sure. Above all things, water is the single most important item one should bring. Common sense, planning for shade optimization and plenty of food were up there at the top as well.

The hike back was as expected, a thoroughly strenuous and exhausting trek. The first jaunt back to Indian Gardens, however, was easy enough. We refilled our water bottles and asked fellow resting hikers about the Germans we had met. I told them about the can of beer we gave them.

"Yeah, we heard about these guys. I heard the husband drank the beer shortly after they got the can. They found the ranger and he helped them out I think."

I laughed. I guess it was too much to ask. Of course, they drank the beer! What was I thinking?

From Indian Gardens, I was reminded of another sign posted on Bright Angel Trail. It said, "Caution! Down is Optional. UP IS MANDATORY." The remainder of the trail was grueling. It started uphill and didn't

let up, with the final 1.6 miles being the steepest. You climb a full 1300 vertical feet in that last mile and a half. Still, what choice was there? Up was mandatory. The sign made perfect sense. We couldn't stay where we are, we couldn't stay down at the river; we needed to go up. The sun fell low enough to provide shade for the remaining few miles. A train of pack mules shared the journey with us for a short while, looking as excited as we were to be climbing the steep incline. Finally, as with all hikes, we made it back to the top and paused to look back at what we had accomplished. It was late afternoon and the Grand Canyon was lit with magnificent sunshine contrasting with darkness of shadow. Families and couples, young and old, were at the canyon's edge, just taking in the grandeur. The Grand Canyon, no matter how one enjoys it, has a way of settling any restlessness of soul, removing if only for a moment the dark buildup on one's spirit. It is the magnum opus for the Colorado River in a gallery of natural masterpieces strung along its banks.

I sat at the rim and gazed out at this wonder immersed in thoughts, lost in quiet wonder of the river's long journey.

At its birth in the quiet green valley of the Southern Rocky Mountains, just below the La Poudre Pass, the Colorado River trickles like a cooing infant. The water is clear and crisp, reflecting sunlight in prisms of clean light. It gathers in abundance as it travels, and by the time it leaves its namesake state, it is still just as pure but now gushing with abundance of whitewater, rushing as a boy sprinting in play. There are moments of stillness intertwined here and there, at times the river slows down to take note of its surroundings before rushing further downstream.

By the time it meets the confluence of the Green River, the largest tributary of the Colorado, it has reached a manner not unlike a young adult. It bucks and bubbles, flowing through the Cataract Canyon in the Canyonlands with a sense of immortality, roiling with energy and at times with bullheaded stubbornness. Here the river is met with a true adversary, solid rock. It cuts through in a tormented agreement between the centuries of stone, determined and with a sense that nothing can stand in its way.

Then the river enters the Grand Canyon. The Colorado continues to cut through stone unabated, carving its way over a mile deep into the bedrock of Earth. If we were to continue with the analogy of the Colorado as an anthropomorphism, then here as a fully formed adult the river created its legacy. The Grand Canyon stands as no other. More than merely grand, more than just a canyon, it is a work of natural art, a dedication of the life's work of one river given tremendous blocks of stone to mold.

The Colorado then leaves its Grand Canyon of a legacy and continues downstream, winding downwards in energy, becoming stiller, ending as a quiet tinkering, a river delta spread wide as fingers of soft dying water into the Gulf of Mexico. Here it is but a shadow of its sturdier self, gasping a presence more like its origin than its heyday. It silently returns into the grander oceans, its individuality lost and absorbed in the union. The Colorado River is much like life itself, starting out so pure, finding wonder in its innocence and with a small amount of wisdom, performing feats that amaze and at times strike fear. Then in adulthood it finds its way, makes a lasting impression, a contribution to mankind before whiling its last days as only a shadow of what it once was. The Colorado's 1,450-mile journey alone is a lesson.

Then, however, there is another lesson within the river, that in place, it is timeless. When you gaze out on the flowing waters, you are seeing something that has never been seen before, maybe similar but not exactly the same. The water flowing upstream toward you is in the future. The water that has passed and is no longer in view is the past. The river that lies inside your field of vision is therefore the constant present. It is always now at the banks of the Colorado, no matter what bank you happen to be on. Never before has this scene before you been witnessed. Perhaps scenes similar, sure, but not this one, not the very one that passes before you. The sight before you has been building up, building for centuries just waiting to display itself at this moment. With that in mind, each viewing of the Colorado is special. The mighty Colorado, always changing, yet seemingly eternal. We take this grand design of nature for granted all too often, but the fact remains that you can never step twice on the same piece of water. Each moment is evidence of renewal.

I gazed out at the river below us with those thoughts in the back of my mind. Ev and I took one last look and then headed back toward our home. The shuttle bus arrived, and we boarded it as outsiders. We were dirty, tired and sun baked specters in a bus full of clean and eager tourists. In the RV, we showered, we ate, we satiated our thirst, and at night I dreamt of the hike we had lived out during the day.

In my dream, the rafter who had thrown me the keepsake cans of beer pulled over to allow Everest and me to get in. We floated downstream as a team, hungry for wonder. We joined in their madcap adventures of white water rafting, side canyon explorations and sleeping under the dark canopy of touchable stars. In this dream, new stories are told, new books are written, lives are lived—a world within a world existing eternally along the banks of the Colorado.

Then, without pause or notice, the dream flowed around a bend into the unknowable realm of deep unconsciousness. Untethered to our wants and struggles, we floated into the currents of shared emptiness. The Milky Way passed above us in silence once again. The moon, too, rose high and over. Nocturnal animals patrolled while other animals slept in cuddled burrows. And inside the RV, we slept as well, the canvas of our thoughts wiped clean for the next day to draw upon.

CONCLUSION

For me, both the visitation of these parks and the writing of this book has been a mixture of adventure and reflection, a personal journey that has at times been both spiritual and fulfilling. The Colorado Plateau offers a lifetime of exploration and the national parks that have been set aside for all of us to enjoy are without a doubt some of the most amazing places in the world to visit. It is a bit of a conflict to say you could spend decades here when most of us get only 2–3 weeks, but even if that is all the time you are able to carve out to explore these great lands, it will be time that imprints upon your soul and sticks with you as one of the fonder memories in your life.

Zion with its massively tall red rock walls, Bryce and its fruit loop charms, the peaceful magic of Capitol Reef, the immensity of Canyonlands and the overwhelming number of rings and windows of Arches. All are unique, amazing and quite honestly beyond any language to fully describe. They aid us in defining majesty and grandeur, challenge our limits of wonder, help us to understand and find a deeper connection with ourselves. I continue to be amazed by the fact that each of these gems was created by nothing more than the humble drops of water, the gentle caress of air and simple tenacity.

The trip to Mesa Verde is different, it is cultural, it takes you back historically and it leaves you with a respect that you have journeyed not through the caves of savages but through the hewn walls of an advanced civilization. If you remove the electronics and the improvements of technology, you come to realize these people loved, suffered, held hands, nurtured their young and lived together with a sophistication that is equal to our lifestyles today.

Then there is the Grand Canyon. Your vacation has come to an end and you look out at this wonder with a sense of peace. You are somehow a different person— at peace with yourself, at peace with your loved ones, at peace with the gift of light, rock and color before you. It is okay, it is enough, to just gaze, to do nothing more, for what lays before you is that magnificent. The Grand Canyon crowns and encapsulates everything that you have seen on this trip. It is, therefore, quite possible that you will come to realize that the canyon is as much at peace with you as you are with it. You realize that it wants nothing from you, that it is exactly where it should be. If you are lucky, that thought will extend to everything in your life. In that moment, it's all good; there is nothing more that life can give you that will make you any more content and perfect than you are right now. This is the secret of the Grand Circle, and it gives of its secret easily and freely. You need do nothing to obtain it. It will find you at one point or another along your travels.

220

View from Yavapai Point on the South Rim

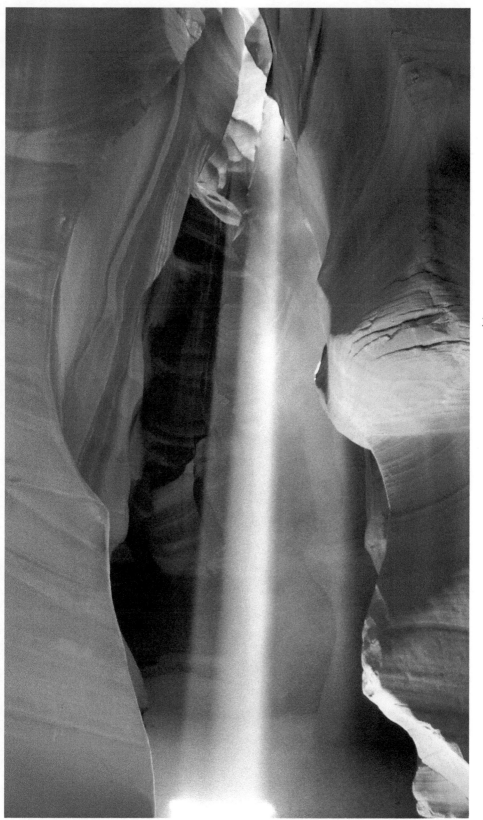

PHOTO ATTRIBUTES

Attributions and permissions given where indicated.

Just Park it Anywhere

- North and South Windows, by Eric Henze

Canyonlands National Park

- Mesa Arch, by Michael Rissi, CC-BY-SA-3.0-migrated
- Raft in Big Drop 1, Cataract Canyon, by NPS, PD US NPS
- Shafer Canyon Overlook, Axcordion, CC-BY-SA-3.0
- Aztec Butte Trail, by Ronnie Macdonald, CC-BY-2.0
- Upheaval Dome, by Doc Searls, CC-BY-2.0
- Canyonlands with view of Green River, by Nikater, PD-self
- Sunrise on the Mesa Arch, Canyonlands National Park, by Alwynloh, CC-BY-SA-3.0,2.5,2.0,1.0
- Druid Arch Trail, by RichieB_pics, CC-BY-2.0
- Druid Arch, RichieB_pics, CC-BY-2.0
- Newspaper Rock, Cacophony, CC-BY-SA-3.0
- The Maze, by (WT-shared) ThatShawGuy, CC-BY-SA-3.0
- Canyonlands Sentinels, by John Fowler, CC-BY-2.0
- Prospecting for Uranium instruction book, by Eric Henze
- Arial View of Grabens, NPS Photo by Neal Herbert, CC-BY-2.0, PD US NPS
- Upheaval Dome, by USDA, PD US Government
- Needles, by Jesse Varner, CC-BY-SA-2.5

Parks Near Canyonlands

- Owachomo Bridge, by NPS, PD US NPS
- Sipapu Arch, by (NPS photo by Jacob W. Frank), CC-BY-2.0
- Cutthroat Unit, by (NPS photo by Andrew Kuhn), CC-BY-2.0
- Goosenecks State Park, by Gernot Keller, CC-By-3.0
- Four Corners, by Rich Torres, CC-By-SA-3.0

The Photographer's Wife

- The photo taken by "Ella", Eric Henze

Mesa Verde National Park

- Cliff Palace, Mesa Verde, Ben FrantzDale, CC-BY-SA-3.0,2.5,2.0,1.0
- Petroglyph Point, Adam Baker, CC-BY-2.0
- Balcony House ladder, Ken Lund, CC-BY-SA-2.0
- Square Tower House, Ben FrantzDale, CC-BY-SA-3.0,2.5,2.0,1.0
- Kiva, by Ken Lund, CC-BY-2.0
- Far View Site, Don Graham, CC-BY-SA-2.0
- Wetherill Mesa Road, Ken Lund, CC-BY-SA-2.0
- First Glimpse of Spruce Tree House from the Bottow of Spruce Tree Canyon, Ken Lund, CC-BY-SA-2.0
- House of Many Windows, Axcordion, CC-BY-SA-3.0,2.5,2.0,1.0
- Step House, Ken Lund, CC-BY-SA-2.0
- Weatherhill Mesa, Ken Lund, CC-BY-SA-2.0
- Emmett Harryson, a Navajo, in doorway. 1929, George A. Grant (1929-1954), PD-USGOV-INTERIOR-NPS
- Cliff Palance circa 1891, NPS, US-PD
- Spruce Tree House, CC-BY-SA-3.0,2.5
- Oak Tree House, Ken Lund, CC-BY-SA-2.0

Parks Near Mesa Verde

- Canyon of the Ancients, by BLM, CC-BY-2.0
- Entrance, by Nationalparks, CC-BY-SA-2.5

Hopi Prophecy

- Hopi Prophecy Rock sketch, by Eric Henze

Grand Canyon National Park

- Grand Canyon, by NPS Digital Image Archives, PD US NPS
- A Grand Canyon Dory maneuvers through Hance Rapid, NPS Photo by Kristen M. Caldon, PD US NPS
- Bright Angel Trail, by NPS, PD US NPS
- Grand Canyon switchbacks, by NPS Digital Image Archives, PD US NPS
- The Grand Canyon South Rim, by Sebastian Toncu, CC-BY-SA-3.0-migrated, CC-BY-SA-2.5,2.0,1.0
- Kolb Studio, by NPS, PD US NPS
- Desert View Watchtower, by Kevin A. Trostle, CC-BY-3.0
- Ribbon Falls, North Kaibab trail, PD-self
- South of Point Imperial, by NPS, PD US Government
- Ewe in Canyon, by Ronthemon2, PD-self
- El Tovar, by Wolfgang Moroder, CC-BY-SA-3.0
- Grand Canyon panorama, by chensiyuan, CC-BY-SA-3.0,2.5,2.0,1.0
- Sunset from El Tovar Hotel, by NPS, PD US NPS
- Canyon View from the North Rim, by Khlnmusa, CC-BY-SA-3.0
- Colorado River, by Tenji, CC-BY-SA-3.0-migrated
- Portrait of J. W. Powell with Indian," black-and-white photograph, presumably by explorer Frederick Samuel Dellenbaugh, a member of John Wesley Powell's second Colorado River expedition. PD-US
- North Kaibab Trail, by NPS, PD US NPS
- This sunrise view is looking north as the Hermit Trail begins to climb the west side of Cope Butte, NPS Photo by Michael Quinn, PD US NPS
- Grand Canyon Geology, by NPS, PD-USGov

Parks Near Grand Canyon

- Vermilion Cliffs, by Bob Wick, BLM California, CC-BY-2.0
- Monument Valley, by Luca Galuzzi (Lucag), CC-BY-SA-2.5
- Betakin Ruins, by John Fowler, CC-BY-2.0
- Antelope Canyon, by Moyan Brenn, CC-BY-2.0
- Havasu Falls, by Moondigger, CC-By-SA-2.5
- Coyote Buttes South, by John Fowler, CC-BY-2.0
- The Wave, by Lobineau, CC-BY-SA-3.0-migrated-with-disclaimers
- Vermilion Cliffs, by Bob Wick, BLM California, CC-BY-2.0
- Pipe Springs, by John Fowler, CC-BY-2.0

Welcome to the Colorado

- Everest in Antelope Canyon, by Eric Henze
- Colorado River, by NPS, PD US NPS
- Bright Angel Canyon, by Tenji, CC-BY-SA-3.0-migrated

Conclusion

- View from Yavapai Point on the South Rim, NPS photo by M. Quinn, PD US NPS
- Near Buckskin Gulch, PD
- Antelope Canyon, by Moyan Brenn, CC-BY-2.0
- Accidental Self Portrait, Tea Kettle Junction, Death Valley, by Eric Henze

Special thanks to John Fowler. I choose by eye alone and look who took the picture afterwards. I am always pleasantly surprised to find that it was you John that took the photo. You have a great eye, thanks for putting some of your pictures into public domain so that all can share in your gift. ~ Eric

ACKNOWLEDGMENTS

First off, I want to thank MRoy Cartography for their wonderful map making, headed by Molly Roy. I came in with a request to make these the best maps out there and she fully delivered.

I am extremely thankful for the constant ebb and flow of feedback from my growing focus group, whom I used day in and day out as a sounding board for ideas, research, and pretty much for every aspect of this book. This is never a one-man shop; I couldn't do what I do without them. These include Ernie, Chris, Frank, Joel, George, Geoff, Jeff, Peggy, John, and Angela.

A special thanks to the National Park Service and its employees. There has never been a time when you weren't able to support this effort, which is remarkable given how much you all do. I truly appreciate all that you do for us as a nation and for all the help and assistance you have given me. To NPS - - Happy 100th birthday!

I also want to thank the states of Utah, Arizona, New Mexico, Colorado, and Nevada. Each of you protects some of the best and most remote lands in the United States. Each state, I commend you for your efforts here.

To every inn and restaurant owner that I spoke to and helped me with the dining and lodging research, thank you. Thank you too to all the bookstores that have supported me through the years and an equally big thanks to my distributors. Plus, a huge shout out to the Grand Circle Association!

A special thanks to my readers and small bookstores. This book is for you! Thank you for reading this book! May it help give you the best vacation you ever had.

To Maggie, John, Jeff, Terry, Judge, Cliff and everyone that was a part of my life at Verde Valley School. You are the catalysts for this and all of my books. I take to heart the best advice ever on writing, by author and VVS teacher John Griffiths. "Work on your book an hour every single day and eventually, you will complete it." This advice is why you are reading this book. VVS, thank you for the gift of tenacity.

And finally and most importantly, to my wife Angela and two boys, Everest and Bryce, thank you. The time you have given me to create these books is a true blessing, both in the adventures we have taken and in the many hours writing and editing away you have given me. You bring laughter, joy, and contentment to every moment of my life!

224

You can reach the author through our FaceBook page:

www.facebook.com/GBG.GoneBeyondGuides

ISBN-10: 0-9971370-8-8

ISBN-13: 978-0-9971370-8-8

Eric Henze began his writing career at the age of twelve with a sci fi short titled "5:15", tackling a plot around a timepiece that could end the world. His passion for hiking started in Sedona, Arizona where he lived in his youth. It expanded to peak bagging in the Sierra Nevada Mountains and then the Andes of South America, where he lived as a Peace Corp volunteer for two years, climbing many of the peaks of Ecuador and Peru. A highlight was climbing Sangay, an active volcano that often shoots VW size rocks at climbers to maintain their attention. In his own words, "It was a delight".

His passions for writing, hiking, and adventure have led to a series of guidebooks for both the National Park Service and the California State Parks. A portion of the proceeds of all of his books will go towards directly supporting these parks.

By day, the intrepid author works for "a little startup in Redmond" known as Microsoft, working as a consultant, helping transform the healthcare industry through reinvention of the customer experience, like using machine learning to predict death for CHF patients or developing a mobile social app to connect parents whose children are working through similar illnesses. He is lives with his wife, two awesome boys, and a "blue-eyed merle " Australian Shepard named Sedona.

His children have noted that his last words will be while driving through the Southwest and seeing some point of interest. As he pulls over the car yet again and starts heading towards some far distant rock, canyon, or sparkly entangled mylar birthday balloon, these last words will be, "I'll be right back, I'm going go check that out".

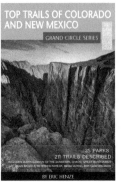

Lightning Source UK Ltd.
Milton Keynes UK
UKHW020834181219
355602UK00005B/46/P